TRANSFORMING
Your Temperament

TRANSFORMING
Your Temperament

BY TIM LAHAYE

INSPIRATIONAL PRESS
NEW YORK

Previously published in three volumes:

SPIRIT-CONTROLLED TEMPERAMENT, copyright © 1966 by
Post, Inc., LaMesa, California.

TRANSFORMED TEMPERAMENTS, copyright © 1971 by
Tyndale House Publishers.

WHY YOU ACT THE WAY YOU DO, copyright © 1984 by
Tim LaHaye.

Published in 1991 by

Inspirational Press
A division of LDAP, Inc.
386 Park Avenue South
Suite 1913
New York, NY 10016

Inspirational Press is a registered trademark of LDAP, Inc.

Published by arrangement with Tyndale House Publishers.

Library of Congress Catalog Card Number: 90-86014

ISBN: 0-88486-040-X

Printed in the United States of America.

CONTENTS

PREFACE

There is nothing more fascinating about man than his temperament! It is temperament that provides each human being with the distinguishing qualities of uniqueness that make him as individually different from his fellowmen as the differing designs God has given to snowflakes. It is the unseen force underlying human action, a force that can destroy a normal and productive human being unless it is disciplined and directed.

Temperament provides man with both strengths and weaknesses. Although we like to think only of our strengths, everyone has weaknesses!

God has given the Christian the Holy Spirit, who is able to improve man's natural strengths and overcome his weaknesses. The author's intent in this book, with the help of John Medina's drawings, is to help you understand how the Holy Spirit will help you overcome your weaknesses.

I
Spirit-Controlled
TEMPERAMENT

1

YOU'RE BORN WITH IT!

"Why is it that I can't control myself? I know what's right and wrong—I just don't seem to be able to do it!" This frustrated plea came from a fine young businessman who had come to me for counseling. It wasn't the first time I had heard that plaint in one form or another; in fact, it is a very common experience.

The Apostle Paul no doubt felt that same way when he said, ". . . for to will is present with me; but how to perform that which is good I find not. For the good that I would I do not: but the evil which I would not, that I do. Now if I do that I would not, it is no more I that do it, but sin that dwelleth in me." (Romans 7:18-20)

Paul differentiated between himself and that uncontrollable force within by saying, "It is no more I that do it, but sin that dwelleth in me." The "I" is Paul's person, the soul, will, and mind of man. The "sin" that dwelled in him was the natural weaknesses that he, like all human beings, inherited from his parents.

We have all inherited a basic temperament from our parents that contains both strengths and weaknesses. This temperament is called several things in the Bible, "the natural man," "the flesh," "the old man," and "corruptible flesh," to name a few. It is the basic impulse of our being that seeks to satisfy our wants. To properly understand its control of our actions and reactions we should distinguish carefully between temperament, character, and personality by defining them.

Temperament

Temperament is the combination of inborn traits that subconsciously affects man's behavior. These traits are arranged genetically on the basis of nationality, race, sex and other hereditary factors. These traits are passed on by the genes. Some psychologists suggest that we get more genes from our grandparents than our parents. That could account for the greater resemblance of some children to their grandparents than to their parents. The alignment of temperament traits is just as unpredictable as the color of eyes, hair, or size of body.

Character

Character is the real you. The Bible refers to it as "the hidden man of the heart." It is the result of your natural temperament modified by childhood training, education, and basic attitudes, beliefs, principles, and motivations. It is sometimes referred to as "the soul" of man, which is made up of the mind, emotions, and will.

Personality

Personality is the outward expression of ourselves, which may or may not be the same as our character, depending on how genuine we are. Often personality is a pleasing facade for an unpleasant or weak character. Many are acting a part today on the basis of what they think a person should be, rather than what they really are. This is a formula for mental and spiritual chaos. It is caused by following the human formula for acceptable conduct. The Bible tells us, "Man looketh on the outward appearance, and God looketh on the heart," and "Out of the heart proceed the issues of life." The place to change behavior is inside man, not outside.

In summary, temperament is the combination of traits we were born with; character is our "civilized" temperament; and personality is the "face" we show to others.

Since temperament traits are received genetically from our parents and hence are unpredictable, one should keep in mind some of the character factors that influence temperament. Nationality and race certainly play a part in one's inherited temperament. We use such expressions as, "an excitable nationality," "an industrious nationality," "a cold nationality," to describe what seems to be apparent.

While on a missionary tour to Mexico, I noticed the vast differences in the tribes that I observed. The Sapotaco Indians impressed me greatly. Many tribes had been shiftless, indifferent, and careless in their mode of life. The Sapotacos, however, were a very industrious and often ingeniously capable tribe. In one city we visited, they were actively pursuing the technical trade of weaving, and their sense of responsibility was in sharp contrast to anything we had observed in other tribesmen. The skills were learned, but the adaptability and desire to learn them were so universal throughout the tribe that it could only be an inherited trait.

A person's sex will also affect his temperament, particularly in the realm of the emotions. Women are usually considered to be more emotionally expressive than men. Even the hardest of women will weep at times, whereas some men never weep.

Temperament traits, whether controlled or uncontrolled, last throughout life. The older we get, however, the softer and more mellow our harsh and hard traits tend to become. Man learns that if he is to live at peace with his fellow man, it is best to emphasize his natural strengths and subdue his weaknesses. Many are successful in developing their character and improving their personality, but comparatively few are able to change their temperament. Yet—it is possible, as we shall see in the next chapter.

2

TEMPERAMENT CAN BE CHANGED!

The Apostle Paul put into words the heart-cry of despair felt by every sincere individual who laments his weaknesses of temperament: "Oh, wretched man that I am! Who shall deliver me from the body of this death!" (Romans 7:24) His answer is electrifying, "I thank God through Jesus Christ our Lord!"

Yes, temperament can be changed! This is clearly seen from II Corinthians 5:17 where Paul wrote: "Therefore if any man be in Christ, he is a new creature: old things are passed away; behold, all things are become new."

Since temperament is our "old nature," what man needs is a "new nature." That "new nature" is imparted to man when he receives Jesus Christ into his life. The Apostle Peter could speak on this subject from personal experience, for his temperament was vastly changed by receiving the "new nature." In II Peter 1:4 he refers to those who have been "born again" by faith in Jesus Christ as having become ". . . partakers of the divine nature, having escaped the corruption that is in the world through lust." The "divine nature" which comes through Jesus Christ is the only escape from the control of our natural temperament, for only through Him are we made "new creatures."

There have been unusually self-controlled individuals who have changed part of their temperament and most of their conduct, but they have not cured all of their weaknesses. Even they have had their besetting sins. Satan knows our major temperament weaknesses, and you can be sure he will use his power to defeat us. His greatest delight in regard to Christians is to see them defeated by their own weaknesses. The victory, however, is available through Jesus Christ whose Spirit can make all things new in the believer's life.

Dr. Henry Brandt, one of the leading Christian psychologists in America, once stated to a group of ministers that if his patients would not accept Jesus Christ, he could not help them. He knew of no cure in the realm of psychology for all of man's behavior problems, but in Jesus Christ he had found the answer.

To further illustrate his absolute confidence in the power of Jesus Christ, Dr. Brandt once stated: "You can use your background as an excuse for present behavior only until you receive Jesus Christ as your personal Lord and Savior. After that you have a new power within you that is able to change your conduct."

As a pastor, I have been thrilled to see the Spirit of God take a weak, depraved temperament and transform it into a living example of the power of Jesus Christ.

Admittedly, all Christians do not experience this transforming power. Just ask a convert's husband or wife, or in some cases, children! In fact, I'm sorry to have to admit that the majority of Christians do not see a *complete* transformation of their temperament. The reason is abundantly clear: the Christian has not remained in an "abiding" relationship with Jesus Christ. (See John 15:1-14) But that does not change the fact that the moment the individual received Jesus Christ, he received the "new nature" which is able to cause "old things to pass away and all things to become new." We shall see that the filling of the Holy Spirit is not only commanded by God for every Christian (Ephesians 5:18), but this filling results in the Holy Spirit so controlling a man's nature that he actually lives the life of Christ. Before we come to that subject, however, it would be good for us to examine the basic types of temperament so we know what to expect the Holy Spirit to do with us.

3

MEET THE FOUR BASIC TEMPERAMENTS

More than 400 years before Christ, Hippocrates, the brilliant Greek physician and philosopher, propounded the theory that there are basically four types of temperament. He erroneously thought that these four temperament types were the result of the four body liquids that predominated in the human body: "blood"; "choler" or "yellow bile"; "melancholy" or "black bile"; and "phlegm." Hippocrates gave names to the temperaments that were suggested by the liquids he thought were the cause; the Sanguine—blood, Choleric—yellow bile, Melancholy—black bile, and Phlegmatic—phlegm. To him, these suggested the lively, active, black, and slow temperaments.

The idea that temperament is determined by body liquid has long been discarded, but strangely enough, the four-fold classification of temperaments is still widely used. Modern psychology has given many new suggestions for classification of temperaments, but none has found more acceptance than those of ancient Hippocrates. Perhaps the best known of the new classifications is the two-fold separation of "extrovert" and "introvert." These two do not provide sufficient separation for our purposes. We, therefore, shall present the four-fold temperament descriptions of Hippocrates.

The reader should bear in mind that the four-fold temperaments are basic temperaments. *No person is a single-temperament type.* We have four grandparents, all of whom make some contribution through the genes to our temperament. They may all have been of different temperaments, therefore all men are a mixture of temperaments, although usually one predominates above the rest. There are varying degrees of temperament. For example, some may be 60 percent sanguine and 40 percent melancholy. Some are a blend of more than two, possibly all four, such as 50 percent sanguine, 30 percent choleric, 15 percent melancholy and 5 percent phlegmatic. It is impossible to determine ratios and blends, but that is not important. What is important for our purposes is to determine your basic temperament type. Then we can study your potential strengths and weaknesses, and offer a program for overcoming your weaknesses through the power of God in you.

There is a danger in presenting these four types of temperaments; some will be tempted to analyze their friends and think of them in the framework of, "What type is he?" This is a demoralizing and precarious practice. Our study of temperaments should be for *self-analysis only*, except to make us more understanding of the natural weaknesses or shortcomings of others.

Now I would like to have you turn the page and meet . . .

Sparky Sanguine

Sparky Sanguine is the warm, buoyant, lively and "enjoying" temperament. He is receptive by nature, and external impressions easily find their way to his heart, where they readily cause an outburst of response. Feelings predominate to form his decisions rather than reflective thoughts.

Mr. Sanguine has an unusual capacity to enjoy himself and usually passes on his hearty nature. When he comes into a room of people, he has a tendency to lift the spirits of everyone present by his exuberant flow of conversation. He is a thrilling story teller because his warm, emotional nature almost makes him relive the experience in the very retelling of it.

Mr. Sanguine never lacks for friends. Dr. Hallesby said, "His naive, spontaneous, genial nature opens doors and hearts to him." He can genuinely feel the joys and sorrows of the person he meets and has the capacity to make him feel important, as though he were a very special friend, and he is—as is the next person he meets who then receives the same attention.

He enjoys people, does not like solitude, but is at his best surrounded by friends where he is the life of the party. He has an endless repertoire of interesting stories which he tells dramatically, making him a favorite with children as well as adults, and usually gaining him admission at the best parties or social gatherings.

Mr. Sanguine is never at a loss for words. He often speaks before thinking, but his open sincerity has a disarming effect on many of his listeners, causing them to respond to his mood. His free-wheeling, seemingly exciting, extrovertish way of life often makes him the envy of the more timid temperament types.

His noisy, blustering, friendly ways make him appear more confident than he really is, but his energy and lovable disposition gets him by the rough spots of life. People have a way of excusing his weaknesses by saying, "That's just the way Sparky is."

The world is enriched by these cheerful, sanguine people. They make good salesmen, hospital workers, teachers, conversationalists, actors, public speakers, and occasionally they are good leaders.

Now meet the second temperament type . . .

Rocky Choleric

Rocky Choleric is the hot, quick, active, practical, and strong-willed temperament. He is often self-sufficient, and very independent. He tends to be decisive and opinionated, finding it easy to make decisions for himself as well as for other people.

Mr. Choleric thrives on activity. In fact, to him, "life is activity." He does not need to be stimulated by his environment, but rather stimulates his environment with his endless ideas, plans and ambitions. His is not an aimless activity, for he has a practical, keen mind, capable of making sound, instant decisions or planning worthwhile, long-range projects. He does not vacillate under pressure of what others think. He takes a definite stand on issues and can often be found crusading against social injustice or unhealthy situations.

He is not frightened by adversities; in fact, they tend to encourage him. He has dogged determination and often succeeds where others fail, not because his plans are better than theirs, but because he is still "pushing ahead" after others have become discouraged and quit. If there is any truth in the adage, "Leaders are born, not made," then he is a born leader. Mr. Choleric's emotional nature is the least developed part of his temperament. He does not sympathize easily with others, nor does he naturally show or express compassion. He is often embarrassed or disgusted by the tears of others. He has little appreciation for the fine arts; his primary interest is in the utilitarian values of life.

He is quick to recognize opportunities and equally as quick at diagnosing the best way to make use of them. He has a well organized mind, though details usually bore him. He is not given to analysis, but rather to quick, almost intuitive appraisal; therefore, he tends to look at the goal for which he is working without seeing the potential pitfalls and obstacles in the path. Once he has started toward his goal he may run roughshod over individuals that stand in his way. He tends to be domineering and bossy and does not hesitate to use people to accomplish his ends. He is often considered an opportunist.

Mr. Choleric's attitude of self-sufficiency and strong will makes him difficult to reach for Christ in adulthood. Even after he becomes a Christian, this spirit makes it difficult for him to actively trust Christ for daily living. Choleric Christians probably find it hardest to realize what Christ meant when he said, "Without me, you can do nothing." There is no limit to what he can do when he learns to "walk in the Spirit" and to "abide in Christ."

Many of the world's great generals and leaders have been Cholerics. He makes a good executive, idea man, producer, dictator, or criminal, depending upon his moral standards.

Like Mr. Sanguine, Mr. Choleric is usually an extrovert, although somewhat less in intensity.

Now I would like to have you meet the third temperament type . . .

Maestro Melancholy

Maestro Melancholy is often referred to as the "black, or dark temperament." Actually he is the richest of all the temperaments, for he is an analytical, self-sacrificing, gifted, perfectionist type, with a very sensitive emotional nature. No one gets more enjoyment from the fine arts than the melancholy.

By nature he is prone to be an introvert, but since his feelings predominate he is given over to a variety of moods. Sometimes his moods will lift him to heights of ecstasy that cause him to act more extroverted. However, at other times he will be gloomy and depressed, and during these periods he is definitely withdrawn and can be quite antagonistic.

Mr. Melancholy is a very faithful friend, but unlike the Sanguine, he does not make friends easily. He will not push himself forward to meet people, but rather lets people come to him. He is perhaps the most dependable of all the temperaments, for his perfectionist tendencies do not permit him to be a shirker or let others down when they are depending on him. His natural reticence to put himself forward is not an indication that he doesn't like people. Like the rest of us, he not only likes others but has a strong desire to be loved by them. Disappointing experiences make him reluctant to take people at their face value, thus he is prone to be suspicious when others seek him out or shower him with attention.

His exceptional analytical ability causes him to diagnose accurately the obstacles and dangers of any project he has a part in planning. This is in sharp contrast to the Choleric, who rarely anticipates problems or difficulties, but is confident he is able to cope with whatever problems arise. This characteristic often finds the Melancholy reticent to initiate some new project or in conflict with those who wish to. Occasionally when he is in one of his great moods of emotional ecstasy or inspiration he may produce some great work of art or genius. These accomplishments are often followed by periods of great depression.

Mr. Melancholy usually finds his greatest meaning in life through personal sacrifice. He seems to have a desire to make himself suffer and will often choose a difficult life vocation involving great personal sacrifice. Once chosen, he is prone to be very thorough and persistent in his pursuit of it and is more than likely to accomplish great good.

No temperament has so much natural potential when energized by the Holy Spirit as the Melancholy. Many of the world's great geniuses—artists, musicians, inventors, philosophers, educators, and theoreticians, were of the melancholy temperament. It is interesting to note that many outstanding Bible characters were either predominantly melancholy in temperament or had strong melancholy tendencies, such as Moses, Elijah, Solomon, the Apostle John and many others.

Now I would have you examine the fourth temperament type . . .

Flip Phlegmatic

Flip Phlegmatic gets his name from what Hippocrates thought was the body fluid that produced that "calm, cool, slow, easy-going, well-balanced temperament." Life for him is a happy, unexcited, pleasant experience in which he avoids as much involvement as possible.

Mr. Phlegmatic is so calm and easy-going that he never seems to get ruffled, no matter what the circumstances. He has a very high boiling point and seldom explodes in anger or laughter, but keeps his emotions in control. He is the one temperament type that is consistent every time you see him. Beneath the cool, reticent, almost timid personality of Mr. Phlegmatic is a very capable combination of abilities. He feels much more emotion than appears on the surface and has a good capacity to appreciate the fine arts and the better things of life.

Mr. Phlegmatic does not lack for friends because he enjoys people and has a natural dry sense of humor. He is the type of individual that can have a crowd of people "in stitches" and never crack a smile. He has the unique capability of seeing something humorous in others and the things they do. He has a good, retentive mind and is often quite capable of being a good imitator. One of his great sources of delight is "needling" or poking fun at the other temperament types. He is annoyed by the aimless, restless enthusiasm of the Sanguine and often confronts him with his futility. He is disgusted by the gloomy moods of the Melancholy and is prone to ridicule him. He takes great delight in throwing ice water on the bubbling plans and ambitions of the Choleric.

He tends to be a spectator in life and tries not to get too involved with the activities of others. In fact, it is usually with great reluctance that he is ever motivated to any form of activity beyond his daily routine. This does not mean that he cannot appreciate the need for action and the difficulties of others. He and Mr. Choleric may see the same social injustice but their response will be entirely different. The crusading spirit of the Choleric will cause him to say, "Let's get a committee organized and campaign to do something about this!" Mr. Phlegmatic would be more likely to respond by saying, "These conditions are terrible! Why doesn't someone do something about this?" Mr. Phlegmatic is usually kindhearted and sympathetic but seldom conveys his true feelings. When once aroused to action, however, he proves to be a most capable and efficient person. He will not take leadership on his own, but when it is put on him he proves a capable leader. He has a conciliating effect on others and is a natural peace-maker.

The world has greatly benefited by the gracious nature of the efficient Phlegmatic. He makes a good diplomat, accountant, teacher, leader, scientist, or other meticulous-type worker.

Now that you have met the four temperaments, you no doubt realize why "people are individuals." Not only are there four distinct types of temperaments that produce these differences, but the combinations, mixtures and degrees of temperament multiply the possible differences. In spite of that, however, most people reveal a pattern of behavior that indicates they lean toward one basic temperament.

Recently I had an experience that graphically portrayed the difference of temperament. It was necessary for me to find a Thermofax machine while speaking at a summer high school camp. In the small town nearby, the only one available was in the Education Center. When I arrived by appointment, I found nine people hard at work. The calm, orderly and efficient surroundings made me realize that I was in the presence of individuals of a predominately Melancholy or Phlegmatic temperament.

This was later confirmed as the superintendent carefully computed my bill and refused to take my money because it was against the rules. Instead, he took me to the meticulous treasurer, who took us to the bookkeeper, who in turn relayed us to the cashier, who finally arranged for me to give my $1.44 to the switchboard operator, who kept the petty cash, lest some of their bookkeeping records would have to be altered. The clincher was the petty cash box, which clearly revealed the touch of the perfectionist. Her change had been carefully stacked in neat piles of quarters, dimes and nickels.

As I surveyed the placid environment and noted their calm but definite concern for this minor problem, my mind flitted hilariously to the scene of the sales office where they had sold the overhead projector. There the sales staff, chief executive, and all the employees were predominately of the extrovertish, Choleric or Sanguine temperaments. The place was a disorganized mess! Papers were strewn everywhere, telephones and desks unattended, the office was a hubbub of noisy activity. Finally, above the din of voices I heard the sales manager say to the staff, with a look of desperation, "One of these days we are going to get organized around here!"

These two scenes show the natural contrast of the inherited traits that produce human temperament. They also point out the fact that all four of the basic temperaments which we have described are needed to give variety and purposefulness in this world. No one temperament can be said to be better than another. *Each one contains strengths and richness, yet each one is fraught with its own weaknesses and dangers.*

Now that you have been introduced to the four temperament types, let us examine more carefully their natural strengths.

4

TEMPERAMENT STRENGTHS

The Sanguine

No one enjoys life more than Sparky Sanguine! He never seems to lose his childlike curiosity for the things that surround him. Since

ENJOYING

OPTIMISTIC

his emotions are so receptive to his environment, even the unpleasant things of life can be forgotten by a change of environment. It is a rare occasion when he does not awaken in a lively mood, and he will often be found whistling or singing his way through life, if his circumstances are reasonably conducive to happy thoughts. Boredom is not a part of his make-up, for he can easily turn to something that fascinates him.

The natural trait of Mr. Sanguine that produces both his hearty and optimistic disposition is defined by Dr. Hallesby: "The Sanguine person has a God-given ability to live in the present." He easily forgets the past so his mind is never befogged by the memory of heartaches or disappointments. Neither is he frustrated and fearful by the apprehension of future difficulties, for he does not give the future that much thought. The Sanguine person lives for the present, consequently he is prone to be very optimistic. He has the capacity to be fascinated by little things as well as big, consequently life is enjoyable today. He is always optimistic that tomorrow, whatever tomorrow holds, will be as good as today, or even better. A little thought and planning on his part today might insure that tomorrow will be even better, but that does not seem to be a part of his natural thought pattern.

He is easily inspired to engage in new plans and projects and his boundless enthusiasm often carries others along with him. If yesterday's project has failed, he is optimistic that the project he is working on today will definitely succeed.

FRIENDLY

The outgoing, handshaking, backslapping customs of the cheerful Sanguine stem basically from his genuine love for people. He enjoys being around others, sharing in their joys and sorrows, and he likes to make new friends. It distresses him to see someone who does not enjoy himself at a party and will frequently go out of his way to include this type of person in a group. His love for people is almost invariably returned.

COMPASSIONATE

One of the greatest assets of Mr. Sanguine is that he has a tender, compassionate heart. No one responds more genuinely to the needs of others than the Sanguine. He literally is able to share the emotional experiences, both good and bad, of others. He, by nature, finds it easiest to obey the Scriptural injunction, "Rejoice with those that do rejoice, and weep with those that weep." As a medical doctor, Mr. Sanguine's outstanding characteristic is his "good bedside manner."

The sincerity of Mr. Sanguine is often misunderstood by others. They are deceived by his sudden changes of emotion. They fail to understand that he is genuinely responding to the emotions of others. No one can love you more nor forget you faster than Mr. Sanguine. He has the pleasant capacity to live in the present; consequently, he enjoys life. The world is enriched by these cheerful, responsive people. When motivated and disciplined by God, they can be great servants of Jesus Christ.

The Choleric

Mr. Choleric is usually a self-disciplined individual with a strong tendency towards self-determination. He is very confident in his own

ability and very aggressive. He is a man of "continual motion," but unlike the Sanguine, this activity is well planned and meaningful.

Once having embarked upon a project he has a tenacious ability that keeps him doggedly driving in one direction. Of him it could rightly be said, "This one thing I do." His singleness of purpose often results in accomplishment. He may think his methods or plans are better than others but in reality his success is the result of determination, and stick-to-it-tiveness rather than superiority of planning.

The Choleric temperament is given over almost exclusively to the practical aspects of life. Everything to him is considered in the light

of its utilitarian purpose and he is happiest when engaged in some worthwhile project He has a keen mind for organization, but finds detail work distressing. He can quickly appraise a situation and diagnose the most practical solution. As a doctor, he is ideal to serve on an ambulance squad where time is at a premium in cases of emergency treatment. Many of his decisions are reached by intuition more than analytical reasoning.

Mr. Choleric has strong leadership tendencies. His forceful will tends to dominate a group, he is a good judge of people, and is quick and bold in emergencies. He not only will readily accept leadership when it is placed on him, but will often be the first to volunteer for it. He is typically known as the "take-over guy." If he does not become too arrogant or bossy others respond well to his practical direction.

Mr. Choleric's outlook on life, based on his natural feeling of self-confidence, is almost always one of optimism. He is adventuresome to the point of even leaving a secure position for the challenge of the unknown. He has a pioneering spirit.

When he appraises a situation, he does not see the pitfalls or potential problems, but merely keeps his eye on the goal. He has the unshakeable confidence that no matter what difficulties arise, he will be able to solve them. Adversity does not discourage him, instead it whets his appetite and makes him even more determined to achieve his objective.

The Melancholy

Mr. Melancholy has by far the richest and most sensitive nature of all the temperaments. He is genius-prone, that is, a higher percentage of geniuses are Melancholy than any other type. He particularly excels in the fine arts with a vast appreciation for life's true values. He is emotionally responsive but, unlike the Sanguine, is motivated to reflective thinking through his emotions.

Mr. Melancholy is particularly adept at creative thinking and at high emotional peaks will often launch into an invention or creative production that is worthwhile and wholesome.

Mr. Melancholy has strong perfectionist tendencies. His standard of excellence exceeds others' and his requirements of acceptability in any field are often higher than either he or anyone else can maintain. This tendency leads him to much introspection, and he often relives events and decisions made in the past, thinking how much better he would do it if given another opportunity.

The analytical abilities of the Melancholy, combined with his perfectionist tendencies, make him a "hound for detail." Whenever a project is suggested by a Choleric or Sanguine temperament,

Mr. Melancholy can analyze it in a few moments and pick out every potential problem they will encounter. He often appears to be against things by his constant reference to potential problems. But they are real to him.

This analytical ability well qualifies him for such fields as mathematics, theoretical science, diagnostic medicine, architecture, philosophy, writing and other exacting vocations.

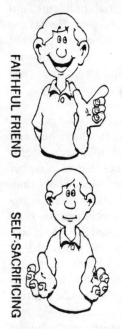

FAITHFUL FRIEND

SELF-SACRIFICING

Those blessed with the Melancholy temperament do not have to strive to be faithful; with them it is natural. A Melancholy person usually does not attract a large number of friends as does the Sanguine, but he will keep those he attracts and would literally "lay down his life for his friends."

A Melancholy person can always be depended upon to finish his job in the prescribed time or to carry his end of the load.

Mr. Melancholy rarely seeks to be in the limelight, but prefers to do the behind-the-scenes task. He often chooses a very sacrificial vocation for life, for he has an unusual desire to give himself to the betterment of his fellow men.

Mr. Melancholy has the wonderful capacity of knowing his limitations and so rarely takes on more than he can do.

He is prone to be reserved and rarely volunteers his opinion or ideas. When asked, however, he almost always has an opinion and when it is offered, his answer indicates that he has analyzed the situation quite deeply and offers an opinion well worth hearing. He does not waste words like the Sanguine, but is usually very precise in stating exactly what he means.

The Phlegmatic

The unexcited good humor of the Phlegmatic keeps him from being intensely involved with life and things so that he can often see humor in the most mundane experiences. His dry sense of humor evokes peals of laughter from others. He seems to have a superb inborn sense of timing in the art of humor and a stimulating imagination.

He is highly qualified by nature to be a counselor. His slow, easy-going manner makes it easy for him to listen, whereas the Sanguine and Choleric temperaments find it difficult to sit still long enough to hear the heartaches of others. He also has the ability to keep from identifying himself with the person, therefore he can be objective. He does not blurt out his advice, but gives thoughtful counsel well worth hearing.

Mr. Phlegmatic is dependability itself. Not only can he be depended upon to always be his cheerful, good-natured self, but he can be depended upon to fulfill his obligations and time schedules. Like the Melancholy, he is a very faithful friend and although he does not get too involved with others, he rarely proves disloyal.

Mr. Phlegmatic is also practical and efficient. He conserves his own energy by thinking, thus he early develops his capabilities to analyze a situation. Since he is not emotionally stimulated to make sudden decisions, he has a tendency to find the practical way to accomplish an objective with the least amount of effort. He works well under pressure. In fact, he often does his best work under circumstances that would cause other temperaments to "crack."

His work always bears the hallmark of neatness and efficiency. Although he is not a perfectionist, he does have exceptionally high standards of accuracy and precision. The neatness of his desk top in the midst of a great project is always a source of amazement to the more active temperaments. But he has just found that putting everything in its exact spot is much easier and less time consuming in the long run, therefore, he is a man of orderly habits.

Summary

The variety of strengths provided by the four temperament types keeps the world functioning properly. No one temperament is more desirable than another. Each one has its vital strengths and makes its worthwhile contribution to life.

Someone facetiously pointed out this sequence of events involving the four temperaments: "The hard-driving Choleric produces the inventions of the genius-prone Melancholy, which are sold by the personable Sanguine and enjoyed by the easy-going Phlegmatic."

The strengths of the four temperaments make each of them attractive, and we can be grateful that we all possess some of these strengths. But there is more to the story! As important as are the temperament strengths, even more important, for our purposes, are their weaknesses. It is our intent in the next chapter to contrast the strengths of the temperaments with their weaknesses. Our purpose in so doing is that you diagnose your own weaknesses and develop a planned program for overcoming them.

Don't be afraid to be objective about yourself and face your weaknesses. Many people have decided what basic temperament they are at this point in the study then changed their mind when confronted with their unpleasant weaknesses. Strengths carry corresponding weaknesses, so face them realistically, then let God do something to change them.

5

WEAKNESSES OF TEMPERAMENTS

The Sanguine

When studied carefully, the boundless activity of the Sanguine temperament proves to be little more than restless movement. He is

often impractical and disorganized. His emotional nature can get him instantly excited and, before really analyzing the entire picture, will have him running off "half-cocked" in the wrong direction. He does not often make a good student because of this spirit of restlessness. This carries over into his spiritual life, where he finds it difficult to concentrate on reading the Word of God. His lifelong pattern of restless activity in the long run usually proves unproductive. The Sanguine person seldom lives up to his potential. Frequently his life is spent running from one

tangent to another, and unless disciplined, is not lastingly productive.

Mr. Sanguine usually gets by on the power of his dynamic personality. But that dynamic personality is often a facade that covers a weak character. His greatest basic problem is that he is weak-willed and undisciplined. If Mr. Sanguine would discipline himself, there would be no limit to his potential in life.

He is a great one to start things and never finish them. If approached to take a Sunday School class or position in the church, his instant response is "yes." Thinking the matter through in the light of his time, abilities, and other responsibilities is not a part of his make-up. He loves to please. He does not know his limitations, and although he functions well as a "front man" for a group, without the stimulus of the group he finds it very difficult to methodically do the necessary preparatory work.

Without meaning to do so, he easily forgets his resolutions, appointments, and obligations. He cannot be depended upon to keep a time schedule or meet deadlines.

Perhaps the most dangerous result of his weak will is seen in the fact that he is prone to modify his moral principles to his surroundings and contemporaries. He is not a man of resolution or loyalty.

EGOTISTICAL

Mr. Sanguine's pleasing personality, which often makes him appear more mature in his youth than his contemporaries, gives him a prominent position early in life that can magnify his natural egotism. He can go overboard and become obnoxious by dominating, not just the major part of the conversation, but all of it. He also, through the years, has a tendency to talk more and more about himself and be occupied with things of interest to himself and think others are equally interested in them.

The emotional instability of Mr. Sanguine can be seen in Dr. Hallesby's statement, "He is never far from tears." This is true, in spite of the fact that he is the "enjoying temperament." He discourages easily and can drift into a pattern of excusing his weaknesses or feeling sorry for himself.

EMOTIONALLY UNSTABLE

His warm nature can produce spontaneous anger, and in a sudden outburst he can "fly off the handle." However, after he has exploded he will forget all about it. He is the type of person that fits the cliché often heard, "He never gets ulcers, he just gives them to everyone else." This emotional instability makes him feel genuinely sorry for his explosive outburst, and he will readily apologize. In the spiritual realm Mr. Sanguine is often found repenting for the same thing over and over again.

No one type of temperament has a greater problem with lust than does that of Mr. Sanguine. Since he is emotionally receptive, he can be tempted more easily than other types, but he is also equipped with a weak will that finds him frequently giving in to this temptation. His ability to live in the present is a danger in this regard, since he has a tendency to think more of the immediate temptation than of the wife and children at home. One of the things he should seek by the Spirit's guidance is the gift of "temperance" or "self-control." He should obey the Scriptural injunction to "flee youthful lust" and "make no provision for the flesh to fulfill the lust thereof."

Like the other three temperaments, Mr. Sanguine's greatest need is the filling of the Holy Spirit. The basic spiritual needs of the Sanguine temperament are "temperance or self-control, long-suffering, faith, peace and goodness."

The Choleric

The admirable characteristics of Mr. Choleric carry with them some serious weaknesses. The most prominent are his hard, angry, impetuous, self-sufficient traits.

Mr. Choleric has a serious emotional deficiency. Christian compassion is foreign to his nature, and he tends to be thick-skinned and unsympathetic toward other people, their dreams, accomplishments, and needs. He has a tendency to look on the sympathetic response of the Sanguine as "sentimental drivel."

Much of the energy that propels the Choleric toward the attainment of his goal is generated from his hot-tempered disposition. He can become violently angry, and even after exploding his wrath upon those objects of his displeasure will continue carrying a grudge. He has been known to be very revengeful, going to almost any lengths to repay someone for an injustice done him. This angry disposition causes him much discomfort in life and can make him an undesirable person to be around. Physically he is prone to nurse an ulcer before he is forty years of age, and spiritually he grieves the Holy Spirit through bitterness, wrath and anger.

HOT-TEMPERED

CRUEL

There is a strange streak of sheer cruelty in Mr. Choleric that causes him to run roughshod over the feelings and rights of others in his effort to achieve his purpose. Unless he is given a strong moral standard, he will not hesitate to break the law or resort to any crafty means necessary to succeed. Many of the world's most depraved criminals and dictators have been Cholerics.

Mr. Choleric's ability to be decisive also produces an impetuous tendency that causes him to get into trouble and launch programs that he is later sorry for. However, because he is so proud, he stubbornly and tenaciously sees them through. It is very difficult for him to apologize,

IMPETUOUS

and many times he will blurt out cruel, blunt, and sarcastic statements that are very cutting. It is difficult for him to show approval, and in marriage this is often one of the causes of heartache on the part of his companion. He may have so much self-control that even in his hottest fits of anger he will not strike his wife but instead use the more devastating club of disapproval. There is nothing more devastating to a person's self-respect than being disapproved of by the person he loves most.

SELF-SUFFICIENT

Mr. Choleric's strong tendency toward independence and self-confidence makes him a very self-sufficient individual. A few stages of success can make him very proud, haughty, and domineering to the point where he becomes obnoxious. In spite of his capabilities, these tendencies become boring to other people and, by contrast, gives them the frustrating feeling that they can never please him.

Unless he surrenders his life to Christ while a child, it is probably more difficult to reach a Choleric person spiritually than any other in adulthood. His spirit of self-sufficiency carries over into the spiritual realm, and he does not feel that he needs man nor God. He has a tendency to look at his accomplishments as good deeds that will more than outweigh his bad deeds performed on the way to accomplishing his goals. Even after conversion to Christ, he has a difficult time realizing that he must depend upon the Lord. When he tries to read the Bible and pray, his active mind easily leaps to planning his day's activity, and somehow, unless he is deeply impressed by the Spirit of God and sees the power of the supernatural, he looks on a regular devotional life as being somewhat impractical and a waste of his time. Of all the temperaments, he probably has the greatest number of spiritual needs, which are love, peace, gentleness, long suffering, meekness and goodness.

The Melancholy

The self-centered traits of the Melancholy temperament are superbly described by Dr. Hallesby, and for that reason I quote his entire description. "He is surely more self-centered than any of the other temperaments. He is inclined to that kind of self-examination, that kind of self-contemplation which paralyzes his will and energy. He is always dissecting himself and his own mental condi-

tions, taking off layer after layer as an onion is peeled, until there is nothing direct and artless left in his life; there is only his everlasting self-examination. This self-examination is not only unfortunate, it is harmful. Melancholies usually drift into morbid mental conditions. They are concerned not only about their spiritual state; they are also unduly concerned about their physical condition. Everything that touches a melancholic is of prime importance to him, hence no other type can so easily become a hypochondriac."*

This self-centered trait in the Melancholy, if not corrected, can actually ruin his entire life. Combined with his sensitive nature, his self-centeredness makes it very easy for him to be offended or insulted. He literally "carries his feelings on his sleeve." He is prone to be suspicious, given over to "evil surmisings." If two people are talking in hushed tones, he is almost certain to jump to the conclu-

*Temperament and the Christian Faith. O. H. Hallesby, 1962, Augsburg, Pub. Hse.

sion that they are talking about him. This type of thinking can lead, in severe cases, to a persecution complex.

Because of his perfectionist and analytical traits, Mr. Melancholy is prone to be pessimistic. He not only can see the ultimate end of a project, but what is more real to him, all of the problems that will be encountered. Many times these problems, in his mind, far outweigh the good accomplished in the whole endeavor. Not only that, he is sure that the end result will not be nearly as good as promised, and since he has been disappointed in the past, he is sure to be disappointed again.

This pessimistic outlook makes him indecisive and fearful of making decisions because he doesn't want to be wrong and fall short of his own perfectionist standards.

No one can be more critical than the Melancholy. He has the tendency to be unyielding in his expectations of other human beings and cannot happily take less than their very best. Many a perfectionist has ruined a normally good marriage because his partner measured up to only 90 percent of what was expected of her. The small part of error is looked at through his magnifying glass of perfectionism, and instead of seeing all the good, he sees an amplification of the bad. This criticism, if not spoken, is often conveyed through a proud, haughty, sometimes arrogant attitude because he looks upon people who do not share his perfectionist standards as being inferior. It should be borne in mind that he is just as critical of himself as he is of other people.

When it comes to marriage, the Melancholy often has a most difficult time making the decision to take the "fatal plunge." He is prone to "idealize" a woman from a distance, and then when he gets to know her, as lovely as she may be, he finds that she is only a human being and has her weaknesses. Many times a Melancholy will actually love the woman in spite of her weaknesses but hesitate to marry her because of them. Dr. Hallesby states, "A great many men are unmarried simply because they are Melancholic. They themselves may think that they are Melancholy because they are bachelors." The truth of the matter is they are probably bachelors because they are Melancholy.

No one manifests a greater mood change than does the Melancholy. On occasions he will be found at high emotional peaks of exuberance, but these are usually the exception and not the rule. More frequently, Mr. Melancholy will be found (when not energized by the Holy Spirit) to be very gloomy, depressed or going through a period of great despair. It is this common tendency that caused Hippocrates to think of him as the "black" fluid type.

MOODY

This moodiness causes a vicious circle. Even those who like him when he is "acting like himself" will become annoyed or disgusted with him when, for seemingly no reason, he is going through a gloomy period. They will consequently avoid him, and his sensitive nature will immediately pick this up and plunge him into greater depths of gloom. This one trait alone can wreck the entire life of a Melancholy person unless he turns to Jesus Christ for the joy and peace that He alone can give. This moodiness is often the result of his self-centered thinking pattern, which must be changed to produce a healthy mind and make it possible for his rich and capable nature to produce its maximum potential. The gloomy moods of Mr. Melancholy often lead him into a habit of escaping present reality through the practice of daydreaming. Because he is so dissatisfied with the imperfect present, he has a tendency to look back on the past, which becomes more pleasant the farther it gets from him. When he tires of thinking of the past, he dreams of the wonderful future. This type of thinking that lets him escape from reality is most dangerous indeed! It not only paralyzes his will and energy, but can lead to schizophrenia.

A Melancholy person should earnestly seek the Holy Spirit's help in getting his eyes up off himself and onto the "whitened harvest field" of needy people around him. One of the most dynamic illustrations of the power of the Gospel of the Lord Jesus Christ is to see a gloomy, moody, Melancholy person transformed by God's grace and armed with the Great Commission so that he has a lofty purpose for living that directs his conscious thinking toward others rather than himself.

Another characteristic of the Melancholy temperament is that he is prone to be revengeful. In himself he finds it very difficult to forgive an affront or an insult.

REVENGEFUL

Although he appears on the surface to be calm or quiet, many times there is turbulent hatred and animosity burning within. He may never put it into action, as would a Choleric, but he may harbor this animosity and desire for revenge for many years.

This unforgiving spirit and seeking for revenge sometimes outweighs his brilliant deductive ability and causes him to make decisions on the basis of prejudice. He may seek to destroy a very worthwhile project with which he is basically in agreement, merely because the person leading the project has at some time in the past offended him. Although he does not generally erupt into violent anger, if animosity is harbored long enough, it may cause him to lose complete control of himself in a fit of rage.

Now that we have seen both the strengths and weaknesses of the Melancholy temperament, our attention is drawn to an interesting fact. The temperament with the greatest strengths and potential is also accompanied by what seems to be the largest of potential weaknesses. This may account for a personal observation that there are very few "average" Melancholies. That is, a Melancholy person will utilize his strengths to the point that he stands above his fellows or he will be dominated by his weaknesses and sink beneath the level of his fellows, giving himself over to becoming a neurotic, disconsolate, or hypochondriac-type individual that neither enjoys himself nor is enjoyed by others.

Melancholy people should take great consolation in the fact that many of the most outstanding men in the Bible were predominantly Melancholy. The success, however, of all these men was that they "believed God." Faith in Christ lifts a person beyond his own temperament to the point that he lives the "new life in Christ Jesus." The primary needs of the Melancholy are love, joy, peace, goodness, faith, and self-control.

The Phlegmatic

The outstanding weakness of Mr. Phlegmatic is that he is prone to be slow and lazy. He often appears to be "dragging his feet," because he resents having been stimulated to action against his will, so he goes along just as slowly as he can.

SLOW & LAZY

His lack of motivation tends to make him a spectator in life and produces the inclination to do as little as necessary. This characteristic keeps him from initiating many of the projects that he is thinking about and very capable of executing, but to him, they just seem "too much work." The restlessness of the Sanguine and the activity of the Choleric often annoy him because he is afraid they may motivate him to work.

Because of his keen sense of humor and his ability to be a detached observer, he finds it easy to use his witty ability to tease

TEASE

others that annoy him or threaten to motivate him.

Dr. Hallesby has said in this regard: "If a Sanguine person enters warm and enthusiastic, the Phlegmatic person becomes cold as ice. If the Melancholic comes pessimistic and lamenting the miseries of the world, the Phlegmatic becomes more optimistic than ever and teases him beyond endurance. If a Choleric enters, brimful of his plans and projects, it is an exquisite pleasure for the Phlegmatic to throw cold water on his enthusiasm and with his level-headedness and keen understanding it is an easy matter for him to point out the weaknesses of the Choleric's proposition."

If he chooses he can even use his humor and wit as a decisive tool to get others all stirred up and angry while he himself never loses his composure or becomes excited.

STUBBORN

Mr. Phlegmatic often exhibits the weakness of selfishness. This trait often becomes more apparent through the years, for he learns to protect himself.

He frequently finds himself in stubborn opposition to change of any kind. His reason is that it will get him too involved. He wants to be conservative, particularly in conserving of his own energies.

As he matures, he can often learn to

disguise his stubborness through his easy-going good humor, while becoming even more stubborn. Each time he is forced by the activity of others into projects and activities that turn out poorly, he becomes even more resistive to future suggestions. This stubborness has a tendency also to make him stingy and selfish, for his first thought usually is, "What is this going to cost me?" or "What will this take out of me?" Although selfishness is a basic weakness of all four temperaments, Mr. Phlegmatic is probably cursed with the heaviest dose.

INDECISIVE

Mr. Phlegmatic often becomes more indecisive through the years, caused basically by his reticence to become "involved." His practical insight and calm, analytical ability can usually find a better method for doing something, but by the time he comes up with it, one of the activists already has the group moving on their program. Therefore, he only half-heartedly enters in, in proportion to what he feels is required of him, because down in his heart he feels his plan is better.

Another thing that makes him indecisive is that even though he can analyze a situation and come to a practical method for achieving it, he will often weigh the method against whether or not he wants to get that "involved." Thus he is prone to vacillate between wanting to do something and not wanting to pay the price. This indecisive practice can soon become a deep-rooted habit that outweighs his naturally practical turn of mind.

The primary needs of the Phlegmatic are love, goodness, meekness, temperance and faith.

Summary

This completes our quick glance at the basic weaknesses of the temperaments. I hope it wasn't too discouraging. Dr. Hallesby expressed the shortcomings of the four temperaments in their relationships to other people in the following statement: "The Sanguine type enjoys people and then forgets them. The Melancholic is annoyed with people but lets them go their own crooked ways. The Choleric makes use of people for his own benefit; afterwards, he ignores them. The Phlegmatic studies people with supercilious indifference." This makes all the temperaments appear hopeless, but temperament is not character or personality or—more importantly—Spirit-controlled temperament.

Recently my wife had an experience that graphically illustrates the contrast between two of these natural temperaments. It happened while she was seated in the back of a San Diego Rapid Transit Bus. The bus stopped to pick up a passenger and was delayed an unusually long time. Several of the passengers became irritated and craned their necks to see what was holding them up. Finally, at about the point that some tempers were ready to erupt, an elderly, crippled woman came into view, paid her fare, then slowly and laboriously took her seat. When she was seated, she turned around and, with the most disarming Sanguine smile on her lovely face, said with a loud, cheery voice, "Thank you so much for waiting for me. I'm sorry I delayed you." My wife was absolutely amazed at the transformation of attitude on the part of even the most grumpy passengers as they were forced to respond with a smile to Mrs. Sanguine's cheery greeting. This dear lady had that pleasant Sanguine capacity of being able to forget the unpleasant past, not fear the unpleasant future, but to enjoy the beautiful sunshine of the present, and she made others respond to her mood.

The bus had scarcely gone two more miles when again there was a long delay. Believe it or not, another crippled woman got on the bus and took the seat directly opposite Mrs. Sanguine. My wife couldn't determine from that distance whether the second lady was a Mrs. Choleric or Mrs. Melancholy, but there was no radiance, no smile, no joy, nothing but the marks of bitterness, resentment and misery etched deeply on her face. The moment she was seated, Mrs. Sanguine got to work! Greeting her with her cheery smile, she began laughing and joking with her unhappy neighbor, and within a matter of minutes had her companion giving forth with a smile that other passengers had not believed she was capable of.

This story illustrates many things, but I would like to use it to show that circumstances do not have to determine our reactions. Our strengths or weaknesses of temperament prevail by our choice. To be sure, not all Sanguine crippled people are cheerful and not all Melancholy crippled folk are morose. But Christians can overcome natural weaknesses and enhance natural strengths through the supernatural filling of the Holy Spirit.

The Spirit-Filled Man

6

THE SPIRIT-FILLED TEMPERAMENT

"The fruit of the Spirit is love, joy, peace, long-suffering, gentleness, goodness, faith, meekness, temperance. . . ."
Galatians 5:22-23

The Holy Spirit-filled temperament does not have weaknesses; instead it has nine all-encompassing strengths. This is man as God intends him to be. It does not matter what one's natural temperament is; any man filled with the Holy Spirit whether Sanguine, Choleric, Melancholy or Phlegmatic, is going to manifest these nine spiritual characteristics. He will have his own natural strengths, maintaining his individuality, but he will not be dominated by his weaknesses. The nine characteristics of the Spirit will transform his weaknesses.

All of these characteristics are found illustrated in the life of Jesus Christ. He is the supreme example of the Spirit-controlled man. A fascinating study of the life of Christ would be to catalog the illustrations of these nine characteristics as they appear in the Gospels. We shall mention some as we study each characteristic.

These nine characteristics represent what God wants each one of His children to be. We shall examine each in detail that you might compare them with your present behavior. Now that you have a better and more objective look at both your strengths and weaknesses, you should be able to look to the Holy Spirit for His filling that you may become the kind of person God wants you to be. Needless to say, any individual manifesting these characteristics is going to be a happy, well-adjusted, mature and very fruitful human being. It is my conviction that there is a longing in the heart of every child of God to live this kind of life. This life is not the result of man's effort, but the supernatural result of the Holy Spirit controlling every area of a Christian.

The first characteristic in God's catalog of Spirit-filled temperament traits is *love*. It is revealed as love both for God and for our fellowmen. The Lord Jesus said, "Thou shalt love the Lord thy God with all thy heart, and with all thy soul, and with all thy mind," and ". . . thou shalt love thy neighbor as thyself."

LOVE

Very honestly, this kind of love is supernatural! A love for God that causes a man to be more interested in the Kingdom of God than in the material kingdom in which he lives is supernatural, for man by nature is a greedy creature. Love for his fellowman, which has always been a hallmark of the devout Christian, is not limited by temperament. True, Mr. Choleric as a Christian may need to go to the Holy Spirit for love more frequently than does Mr. Sanguine, but if the Spirit controls his life, he too will be a compassionate, tenderhearted, loving individual.

There are some people with strong humanitarian tendencies by nature who have expressed love in exemplary acts. But the love described here is not just for those who stir admiration or compassion in us, but for all men. The Lord Jesus said, "Love your enemies . . . and do good to them that despitefully use you." This kind of love is never generated by man but can only be effected by God. In fact, one of the thrilling evidences of the supernatural in the Christian experience is to see two people who have "personality conflicts," which is another expression for temperament conflicts, grow to genuinely and easily love one another. The twelve apostles represented all four of the temperament types previously studied, and yet the Lord Jesus said to them, "By this shall all men know that ye are My disciples, if ye have love one for another." Many a church heartache could have been avoided had the filling of the Holy Spirit been sought for this first characteristic of the Spirit-filled temperament.

If you would like to test your love for God, try this simple method given by the Lord Jesus. He said, "If ye love Me, keep My commandments." Just ask yourself, "Am I obedient to His commandments as revealed in His Word?" If not, you are not filled with the Holy Spirit.

The second temperament characteristic of the Spirit-filled man is *joy*. R. C. H. Lenski, a great Lutheran theologian, gave this comment concerning the gracious emotion of joy. "Yes, joy is one of the cardinal Christian virtues; it deserves a place next to love. Pessimism is a grave fault. This is not fatuous joy such as the world accepts; it is the enduring joy that bubbles up from all the grace of God in our possession, from the blessedness that is ours, that is undimmed by tribulation. . . ."

The joy provided by the Holy Spirit is not limited by circumstances. Many have the mistaken idea that they can be happy if their circumstances work out properly. Really, they are confused about the difference between happiness and joy. As John Hunter of Capernwray, England, said, "Happiness is something that just happens because of the arrangement of circumstances, but joy endures in spite of circumstances." No Christian can have joy if he depends upon the circumstances of life. The Spirit-filled life is characterized by a "looking unto Jesus, the Author and Finisher of our faith," which causes us to know that "All things work together for good to them that love God, to them that are the called according to His purpose." (Romans 8:28)

In the Scripture "joy" and "rejoicing" are frequently presented as expected forms of Christian behavior. They are not the result of self-effort but are the work of the Holy Spirit in your life, which causes you to "commit your way unto the Lord, and trust also in Him." The Psalmist said in referring to the spiritual man's experience, "Thou hast put gladness in my heart more than they have when their grain and their new wine is increased." (Psalm 4:7)

The Apostle Paul, writing from a prison dungeon, said, "Rejoice in the Lord alway: and again I say rejoice." (Philippians 4:4) The reason he could say that is because he had learned to experience the Spirit-filled life. For it was from the same prison cell the Apostle had said, "I have learned in whatsoever state I am therewith to be content." Any man that can rejoice and be content while in prison has to have a supernatural power! The Philippian jailer saw the genuine but supernatural joy reflected in the lives of Paul and Silas when thrown into jail for preaching the Gospel. He heard their singing and praising the Lord and must have been deeply impressed.

This "fruit" of the Spirit is woefully lacking in many Christians today, which keeps them from being fruitful in the matter of winning people to Christ, because the world must see some evidence of what Jesus Christ can do in the life of the believer today in order to be attracted to Him. This supernatural joy is available for any Christian regardless of his basic or natural temperament. Jesus said, "These things have I spoken unto you, that My joy might remain in you, and that your joy might be full." (John 15:11) He also stated in John 10:10b, "I am come that they might have life, and that they might have it more abundantly." That abundant life will reveal itself in the Christian through joy, but it is only possible as he is filled with the Holy Spirit.

Martin Luther said, "God does not like doubt and dejection. He hates dreary doctrine, gloomy and melancholy thought. God likes cheerful hearts. He did not send His Son to fill us with sadness, but to gladden our hearts. Christ says: 'Rejoice, for your names are written in heaven.'"

PEACE

The third temperament trait of the Spirit-filled man is *peace*. Since the Bible should always be interpreted in the light of its context, it behooves us to examine the context. The verses just preceding this in Galatians 5 describe not only the works of the natural man without the Spirit, but also his emotions. His emotional turbulence is described by ". . . hatred, variance (strivings), jealousies, wrath, divisions and envyings." We readily see that the further man gets from God, the less he knows of peace.

The "peace" spoken here is really two-fold. Someone has described it as "peace with God" and the "peace of God." The Lord Jesus said, "Peace I leave with you, My peace I give unto you. . . ." (John 14:27) The peace He leaves us is likened to "the peace of

God," for in the same verse He defines it as the peace of an untroubled heart: "Let not your heart be troubled, neither let it be afraid." The preceding verse, John 14:26, describes the coming of the Holy Spirit to believers as "the Comforter, which is the Holy Spirit." Thus we see that our Lord predicted the Holy Spirit would be the source of the "peace of God."

Peace *with* God, which is the "peace I leave with you," is the result of our salvation experience by faith. Man outside of Jesus Christ knows nothing of peace in relationship with God because his sin is ever before him and he knows he is accountable before God at the Judgment. This nagging fear robs man of peace with God all through his life. However, when this individual takes Jesus Christ at His word and invites Him into his life as Lord and Savior, Jesus Christ not only comes in as He promised to do (Revelation 3:20), but He immediately cleanses all his sin (I John 1:7,9). When the realization of God's forgiveness of his sin really grips his heart, man has peace with God. Romans 5:1 states it, "Therefore, being justified by faith, we have peace with God through our Lord Jesus Christ."

The peace of God, which is the antidote to worry, is not so automatically possessed by Christians as the peace *with* God. The "peace of God," which is untroubled in the face of difficult circumstances, is illustrated by the Lord Jesus who was sound asleep in the lower part of the ship while the twelve disciples were frightened beyond rationality. That ratio of twelve to one is very clearly evident among Christians today. It seems that when life's sea becomes turbulent through the raging winds of circumstance, twelve Christians will fret and fume and worry, while only one will have enough peace in his heart to trust God to take care of him in those circumstances. The twelve will be prone to worry all night, which further complicates their emotional, physical and spiritual life, while the one who "believes God" will get a good night's sleep, awaken refreshed and be available for God's use the next day. Circumstances should never produce our peace. We should look to God for peace; only He is consistent.

Just becoming a Christian does not spare us from the difficult circumstances of life. However, the Holy Spirit's presence in our lives can supply us with one of life's greatest treasures: "the peace of God," in spite of any circumstances. The Apostle Paul had this in mind when he wrote the words, "Be careful (worried or anxious) for nothing; but in everything by prayer and supplication with thanksgiving let your requests be made known unto God. And the peace of God, which passeth all understanding, shall keep your hearts and minds through Christ Jesus." (Philippians 4:6-7) An untroubled, unworried, peaceful individual facing the circumstances of life possesses a peace "which passeth all understanding." That is the "peace of God" which the Holy Spirit longs to give every believer.

These first three characteristics, *love*, *joy* and *peace* are emotions which very definitely counteract the most common weaknesses of temperament such as cruelty, anger, indifference, pessimism, gloom and criticism. They stand as adequate reasons for living the Spirit-filled life, but this is only the beginning.

LONGSUFFERING

The fourth temperament trait of the Spirit-filled man is *longsuffering*. Patience and endurance are the most prominent synonyms which have been suggested by Bible commentators for this spiritual characteristic. A very simple suggestion is, "Longsuffering means suffering long." It would be characterized by an ability to bear injuries or suffer reproof or affliction without answering in kind—as the Apostle Peter said about the Lord Jesus: ". . . who, when reviled, reviles not again." This is the kind of dependability that Dr. Bob Jones must often have had in mind when using his classic statement, "The greatest ability is dependability." A longsuffering person is one who can do the menial, forgotten and difficult tasks of life without complaining or seething, but graciously, as unto the Lord. He finishes his task or suffers affronts while manifesting the loving Spirit of Christ.

GENTLENESS

The fifth characteristic of the Spirit-filled temperament is described in the King James Version as gentleness. Most of the modern translators of the Greek New Testament seem to change this to kindness or goodness, which make it almost synonymous with the next characteristic of the Spirit. In so doing, they tend to lessen the importance of this almost-forgotten form of behavior. It is a thoughtful, polite, gracious, considerate, understanding act of kindness which stems from a very tender heart. The world in which we live knows little of such tender-heartedness. It is the result of the compassion of the Holy Spirit for a lost and dying humanity.

The hurrying, bustling and pressurized life we live tends to make even some of the finest of Christians annoyed at the interruptions of "the little people." The Lord Jesus' gentle spirit serves as an illustration when contrasted with the disciples' cruel attitude toward the children who had been brought by their parents to be blessed by Him. The Scripture tells us that the disciples rebuked those who brought them, but Jesus said, "Suffer the little children to come unto Me and forbid them not." (Mark 10:13-14)

This gentle characteristic of the Holy Spirit never asks such questions as, "How often must I forgive my brother when he sins against me?" or, "Should I forgive a brother who does not ask for forgiveness?" or, "Isn't there a limit to how much a person can stand?" The Holy Spirit is able to give gentleness in the face of all kinds of pressures.

Jesus, who possessed the Holy Spirit "without measure," pictured Himself as a shepherd gently caring for easily injured sheep, and He, through His followers, tenderly cares today.

The sixth characteristic of the Spirit-filled man is called goodness, which is defined as "generous of self and possessions." It is benevolence in its purest sense. It includes hospitality and all acts of goodness that flow from the unselfish heart that is more interested in giving than receiving. Paul told Titus, the young preacher, that he should so preach that "they which have believed in God might be careful to maintain good works." (Titus 3:8) Man is so selfish by

GOODNESS

nature that he needs to be reminded by the Word of God and the indwelling Holy Spirit to occupy himself with goodness. It is obviously, then, a person who is more interested in doing for others than for himself.

All four of the natural temperaments are prone to be selfish and inconsiderate; thus all need this trait of goodness. It is particularly needed by those with melancholy tendencies as a cure for depression and gloom, caused by an over-indulgence in self-centered thought patterns. There is something therapeutic about doing for others that lifts a man out of the rut of self-thought. As the Lord Jesus said, "It is better to give than to receive."

Many a Christian has cheated himself out of the blessing of the Holy Spirit's inspired impulse to do something good or kind for someone else by not obeying that urge. Instead of bringing joy to someone else's life by that act of kindness, the self-centered person stifles the impulse and sinks deeper and deeper in the slough of despondency and gloom. It is one thing to get good impulses; it is quite another to transmit them into acts of goodness. D. L. Moody once stated that it was his custom, after presenting himself to the Holy Spirit and asking to be led of the Spirit, to act upon those impulses which came to his mind, provided they did not violate any known truth of Scripture. Generally speaking, that is a very good rule to follow, for it pays rich dividends in mental health in the life of the giver.

The seventh trait of the Holy Spirit-filled man is faith. It involves a complete abandonment to God and an absolute dependence upon Him. It is a perfect antidote to fear, which causes worry, anxiety and pessimism.

Some commentators suggest more than faith's being involved— namely faithfulness or dependability. But actually, a man who has Spirit-inspired faith will be faithful and dependable. The late Dr. William G. Coltman, former pastor of the Highland Park Baptist Church of Highland Park, Michigan, used to say, "When the Spirit is in control, life goes forward under the full conviction of God's ability and power."

In a vital way faith is the key to many other Christian graces. If we really believe God is able to supply all our needs, it is going to

cause us to have peace and joy and will eliminate doubt, fear, striving and many other works of the flesh. Many of God's people, like the nation of Israel, waste 40 years out in the desert of life because they do not believe God. Far too many Christians have "grasshopper vision." They are like the ten faithless spies who saw the giants in the land of Canaan and came home to cry, "We are as grasshoppers in their sight." How could they possibly know what the giants thought of them? You can be sure they did not get close enough to ask! They did just what we often do—jumped to a faithless conclusion. Unbelief, which is fear, will be considered later.

The Bible teaches that there are two sources of faith. The first source is the Word of God in the life of the believer. Romans 10:17 states, "Faith cometh by hearing and hearing by the Word of God." The second is the Holy Spirit. Our text, Galatians 5:22-23, lists faith as a fruit of the Spirit. If you find that you have a temperament that is conducive to doubts, indecision and fear, then as a believer you can look to the filling of the Holy Spirit to give you a heart of faith which will dispel the emotions and actions of your natural nature, including fear, doubt, anxiety, etc. It will take time, however; habits are binding chains, but God gives us the victory in Christ Jesus. "Wait on the Lord: be of good courage, and He shall strengthen thine heart: wait, I say, on the Lord." (Psalm 27:14)

The eighth temperament trait of the Holy Spirit-filled man is meekness. The natural man is proud, haughty, arrogant, egotistical and self-centered, but when the Holy Spirit fills the life of an individual he will be humble, mild, submissive and easily entreated.

The greatest example in the world of meekness is the Lord Jesus Christ Himself. He was the Creator of the universe, and yet was willing to humble Himself, take on the form of a servant and become subject to the whims of humanity, even to the point of death, that He might purchase our redemption by His blood. Here

we see the Creator of man buffeted, ridiculed, abused and spat upon by His own creation. Yet he left us an example of not reviling again.

This is particularly fortified when we recognize that all power and authority were given unto Him, even in the hours of His suffering. As he stated to Peter when He told him to put up his sword. "Thinkest thou that I cannot now pray to My Father, and He shall presently give Me more than twelve legions of angels? But how then shall the Scriptures be fulfilled, that thus it must be?" (Matthew 26:53-54) For our sakes He was meek that we might have everlasting life. He said of Himself, "I am meek and lowly in heart."

Such meekness is not natural! Only the supernatural indwelling Spirit of God could cause any of us to react to physical or emotional persecution in meekness. It is a natural tendency to assert one's self, but even the most angry temperament can be controlled by the filling of the Holy Spirit and made to manifest this admirable trait of meekness.

The final temperament trait characteristic of the Spirit-filled believer is self-control. The King James Version translates it "temperance," but really it is self-control or self-discipline. Someone has defined it as "self-controlled by the Holy Spirit."

Man's natural inclination is to follow the path of least resistance. Mr. Sanguine probably has more temptation along this line than any of the other temperament types, though who of us can say he has not given in to this very common temptation? "Self-control" will solve the Christian's problem of emotional outbursts such as rage, anger, fear, jealousy, etc., and cause him to avoid emotional excesses of any kind. The Spirit-controlled temperament will be one that is consistent, dependable and well ordered.

It has occurred to me that all four of the basic temperament types have a common difficulty that will be overcome by the Spirit-filled trait of self-control. That weakness is an inconsistent or ineffective devotional life. No Christian can be mature in Christ, steadily filled with the Holy Spirit and usable in the hand of God, who does not regularly feed on the Word of God. Evangelical Christians would

overwhelmingly confirm this fact, even though a very small percentage of Christians have a quiet time with any degree of regularity.

Mr. Sanguine is too restless and weak-willed by nature to be consistent in anything, much less in getting up a few minutes early to have a regular time of Bible reading and prayer.

Mr. Choleric has the strong will power to be consistent in anything he sets his mind to, but his problem is in seeing the need for such a practice. He is by nature such a self-confident individual that even after he is converted it takes some time for him to realize personally what the Lord Jesus meant when He said, "Without Me, ye can do nothing." Even when he sees the need and begins to have a regular devotional life, he has to fight the temptation to keep his practical, active mind from flitting off into many other directions or planning his day's activities when he is supposed to be reading the Word, praying or listening to the Sunday sermon.

Mr. Melancholy is perhaps most likely of the four to be regular in his devotional life, except that his analytical ability often sends him off in the quest of some abstract, theologically hairsplitting truth rather than letting God speak to him concerning his personal needs from the mirror of His truth. His regular prayer life can become a time of complaining and mourning to God about what he considers his unhappy state of affairs as he nurses his grudges and reviews his difficulties. Thus his devotional life can conceivably thrust him into greater periods of despair than he was in before. However, when controlled by the Holy Spirit, his prayer life will be characterized by "giving thanks" (I Thessalonians 5:18) and compliance with "Rejoice in the Lord always, and again I say rejoice." (Philippians 4:4)

Mr. Phlegmatic is prone to recommend a regular quiet time as a necessary part of the Christian life, but if his slow, indolent and often indifferent inclination is not disciplined by the Holy Spirit, he will never quite get around to a regular feeding on God's Word.

As you look at these nine admirable traits of the Spirit-filled man, you not only get a picture of what God wants you to be, but what He is willing to make you in spite of your natural temperament. It should, however, be borne in mind that no amount of self-improvement or self-effort can bring any of these traits into our lives without the power of the Holy Spirit. From this we conclude that the most important single thing in the life of any Christian is to be filled with the Holy Spirit. The supreme question, then, comes to mind: How can I be filled with the Holy Spirit? The answer to that question will be seen in our next chapter.

7

HOW TO BE FILLED WITH THE HOLY SPIRIT

The most important thing in the life of any Christian is to be filled with the Holy Spirit! The Lord Jesus said, "Without Me ye can do nothing." Christ is in believers in the person of His Holy Spirit. Therefore, if we are filled with His Spirit, He works fruitfully through us. If we are not filled with the Holy Spirit, we are unproductive.

It is almost impossible to exaggerate how dependent we are on the Holy Spirit. We are dependent on Him for convicting us of sin before and after our salvation, for giving us understanding of the Gospel, causing us to be born again, empowering us to witness, guiding us in our prayer life—in fact, for everything. It is no wonder that evil spirits have tried to counterfeit the work of the Holy Spirit and confuse His work.

There is probably no subject in the Bible upon which there is more confusion today than that of being filled with the Holy Spirit. There are many fine Christian people who seem to equate the filling of the Holy Spirit with speaking in tongues or some emotionally ecstatic experience. There are other Christians who because of excesses observed or heard of in this direction have all but eliminated the teaching of the filling of the Holy Spirit. They just do not recognize His importance in their lives.

Satan places two obstacles before men: (1) he tries to keep them from receiving Christ as Savior, and (2) if he fails in this, he then tries to keep men from understanding the importance and work of the Holy Spirit. Once a man is converted, Satan seems to have two different approaches. He tries to get men to associate the filling of the Holy Spirit with emotional excesses, or, the opposite swing of the pendulum, to ignore the Holy Spirit altogether.

One of the false impressions gained from people and not from the Word of God is that there is some special "feeling" when one is filled with the Holy Spirit. Before we examine how to be filled with the Holy Spirit, let us find what the Bible teaches we can expect when we are filled with the Holy Spirit.

What to expect when filled with the Holy Spirit

1. The nine temperament traits of the Spirit-filled life. (Galatians 5:22-23)

We have already examined these traits in detail in Chapter 6, but their presence in the believer's life bears further emphasis. Any individual who is filled with the Holy Spirit is going to manifest these characteristics! He does not have to try to, or play a part, or act out a role; he will just be this way when the Spirit has control of his nature.

Many who claim to have had the "filling," or as some call it, "the anointing," know nothing of love, joy, peace, longsuffering, gentleness, goodness, meekness, faith, or self-control. These are, however, the hallmark of the person filled with the Holy Spirit!

2. A joyful, thanks-giving heart and a submissive spirit. (Ephesians 5:18-21)

When the Holy Spirit fills the life of a believer, the Bible tells us He will cause him to have a singing, thanks-giving heart and a submissive spirit.

> *"And be not drunk with wine, wherein is excess; but be filled with the Spirit;*
> *"Speaking to yourselves in psalms and hymns and spiritual songs, singing and making melody in your heart to the Lord;*
> *"Giving thanks always for all things unto God and the Father in the name of our Lord, Jesus Christ;*
> *"Submitting yourselves one to another in the fear of God."*

A singing, thanks-giving heart and a submissive spirit, independent of circumstances, are so unnatural that they can only be ours through the filling of the Holy Spirit. The Spirit of God is able to change the gloomy or griping heart into a song-filled, thankful heart. He is also able to solve man's natural rebellion problem by increasing his faith to the point that he really believes the best way to live is in submission to the will of God.

The same three results of the Spirit-filled life are also the results of the Word-filled life, as found in Colossians 3:16-18.

> *"Let the word of Christ dwell in you richly in all wisdom; teaching and admonishing one another in psalms and hymns and spiritual songs, singing with grace in your hearts to the Lord.*
> *"And whatsoever ye do in word or deed, do all in the name of the Lord Jesus, giving thanks to God and the Father by Him.*
> *"Wives, submit yourselves unto your own husbands, as it is fit in the Lord."*

It is no accident that we find the results of the Spirit-filled life (Ephesians 5:18-21) and those of the Word-filled life to be one and the same. The Lord Jesus said that the Holy Spirit is "the Spirit of Truth," and He also said of the Word of God, "Thy Word is Truth." It is easily understood why the Word-filled life causes the same results as the Spirit-filled life, for the Holy Spirit is the author of the Word of God. This highlights the error of those who try to receive the Holy Spirit through a once-for-all experience rather than an intimate relationship with God which Jesus described as "abiding in Me." This relationship is possible in the Christian's life as God communes with him and fills his life through the "Word of Truth" and he communes with God in prayer guided by the "Spirit of Truth." The conclusion that we can clearly draw here is that the Christian who is Spirit-filled will be Word-filled, and the Word-filled Christian who obeys the Spirit will be Spirit-filled.

3. The Holy Spirit gives us power to witness. (Acts 1:8)

> *"But ye shall receive power, after that the Holy Ghost is come upon you: and ye shall be witnesses unto Me both in Jerusalem, and in all Judaea, and in Samaria, and unto the uttermost part of the earth."*

The Lord Jesus told His disciples that "It is expedient (necessary) for you that I go away; for if I go not away, the Comforter (Holy

Spirit) will not come unto you." (John 16:7) That explains why the last thing Jesus did before He ascended into heaven was to tell His disciples, "But ye shall receive power, after that the Holy Spirit is come upon you: and ye shall be witnesses unto Me. . . ."

Even though the disciples had spent three years with Jesus personally, had heard His messages several times, and were the best trained witnesses He had, He still instructed them "not to depart from Jerusalem, but wait for the promise of the Father." (Acts 1:4) All of their training obviously was incapable of producing fruit of itself without the power of the Holy Spirit. It is well known that when the Holy Spirit came on the day of Pentecost, they witnessed in His power, and three thousand persons were saved.

We too can expect to have power to witness when filled with the Holy Spirit. Would to God that there was as much desire on the part of God's people to be empowered to witness in the Spirit as there is to have some ecstatic or emotional experience with the Holy Spirit.

The power to witness in the Holy Spirit is not always discernable, but must be accepted by faith. When we have met the conditions for the filling of the Holy Spirit, we should be careful to believe we have witnessed in the power of the Spirit whether or not we see the results. Because the Holy Spirit demonstrated His presence on the day of Pentecost so dramatically and because occasionally we see the evidence of the Holy Spirit in our lives, we come to think that it should always be obvious, but that is not true. It is possible to witness in the power of the Holy Spirit and still not see an individual come to a saving knowledge of Christ. For in the sovereign plan of God He has chosen never to violate the right of man's free choice. Therefore, a man can be witnessed to in the power of the Holy Spirit and still reject the Savior. The witness may then go away with the erroneous idea of having been powerless merely because he was unsuccessful. We cannot always equate success in witnessing with the power to witness!

Recently it was my privilege to witness to an 80-year-old man. Because of his age and a particular problem, I made a special effort to meet the conditions of being filled with the Holy Spirit before I went to his home. He paid very close attention as I presented the Gospel by using the "four spiritual laws." When I finished and asked if he would like to receive Christ right then, he said, "No, I'm not ready yet." I went away amazed that a man 80 years of age could say he was "not ready yet" and concluded that I did not witness in the power of the Holy Spirit.

A short time later I went back to see the man and found that he had passed his 81st birthday. Once again I started to present the Gospel to him, but he informed me that he had received Christ. He had restudied the four spiritual laws which I had written out on a sheet of paper, and alone in his room he got down on his knees and invited Christ Jesus into his life as Savior and Lord. Afterward, I wondered how many other times in my life, because I had not seen an immediate response to the Gospel, I had wrongly concluded that the Spirit had not filled me with His power to witness.

To be sure, a Christian life, when filled with the Holy Spirit, will produce fruit. For if you examine what Jesus referred to as "abide in Me" (John 15) and what the Bible teaches in relationship to being "filled with the Spirit," you will find they are one and the same experience. Jesus said, "He that abideth in Me and I in him, the same bringeth forth much fruit. . . ." Therefore, we can conclude that the abiding life or the Spirit-filled life will produce fruit. But it is wrong to require every witnessing opportunity to demonstrate whether or not we are empowered by the Spirit to witness. Instead, we must meet the conditions for the filling of the Holy Spirit and then believe, not by results or sight or feeling, but by faith, that we are filled.

4. The Holy Spirit will glorify Jesus Christ. (John 16:13-14)

> *"Howbeit when He, the Spirit of truth, is come, He will guide you into all truth; for He shall not speak of Himself; but whatsoever He shall hear, that shall He speak: and He will shew you things to come.*
> *"He shall glorify Me: for He shall receive of Mine, and shall shew it unto you."*

A fundamental principle should always be kept in mind regarding the work of the Holy Spirit: He does not glorify Himself, but the Lord Jesus Christ. Any time anyone but the Lord Jesus receives the glory, you can be sure that what is done is not done in the power of or under the direction of the Holy Spirit, for His express work is to glorify Jesus. This test should always be given to any work that claims to be the work of God's Holy Spirit.

The late F. B. Meyer told the story of a woman missionary who came to him at a Bible conference after he had spoken on the subject of how to be filled with the Holy Spirit. She confessed that she was never consciously filled with the Holy Spirit and was going to go up to the prayer chapel and spend the day in soul-searching to see if she could receive His filling.

Late that evening she came back just as Meyer was leaving the auditorium. He asked "How was it, sister?" and she said, "I'm not quite sure." He then asked what she did, and she explained her day's activities of reading the Word, praying, confessing her sins and asking for the filling of the Holy Spirit. She then stated, "I do not feel filled with the Holy Spirit." Meyer asked her, "Tell me, sister, how is it between you and the Lord Jesus?" Her face lit up and with a smile she said, "Oh, Dr. Meyer, I have never had a more blessed time of fellowship with the Lord Jesus in all of my life." To which he replied, "Sister, that is the Holy Spirit!" The Holy Spirit will always make the believer more conscious of the Lord Jesus than Himself.

Now, in review, let us summarize what we can expect when filled with the Holy Spirit. Very simply, it is the nine temperament characteristics of the Spirit, a singing, thanks-giving heart that gives us a submissive attitude, and the power to witness. These characteristics will glorify the Lord Jesus Christ. What about "feeling" or "ecstatic experiences"? The Bible does not tell us to expect these things when we are filled with the Holy Spirit; therefore, we should not expect that which the Bible does not promise.

How to be filled with the Holy Spirit

The filling of the Holy Spirit is not optional equipment in the Christian life, but a command of God! Ephesians 5:18 tells us, "And be not drunk with wine, wherein is excess, but be filled with the Spirit." This statement is in the imperative mood; thus we should accept it as a command.

God never makes it impossible for us to keep His commandments. So, obviously, if He commands us to be filled with the Holy Spirit, and He does, then it must be possible for us to be filled with the Holy Spirit:

1. Self-examination (Acts 20:28 and I Corinthians 11:28)

The Christian interested in the filling of the Holy Spirit must regularly "take heed" to "examine himself." He should examine himself, not to see if he measures up to the standards of other people or the traditions and requirements of his church, but to the previously mentioned results of being filled with the Holy Spirit. If he does not find he is glorifying Jesus, if he does not have power to witness, or if he lacks a joyful, submissive spirit or the nine temperament traits of the Holy Spirit, then his self-examination will reveal those areas in which he is deficient and will uncover the sin that causes them.

2. Confession of all known sin (I John 1:9)

> *"If we confess our sins, He is faithful and just to forgive us our sins, and to cleanse us from all unrighteousness."*

The Bible does not put an evaluation on one sin or another, but seems to judge all sin alike. After examining ourselves in the light of the Word of God, we should confess all sin brought to mind by the Holy Spirit, including those characteristics of the Spirit-filled life that we lack. Until we start calling our lack of compassion, our lack of self-control, our lack of humility, our anger instead of gentleness, our bitterness instead of kindness, and our unbelief instead of faith, as sin, we will never have the filling of the Holy Spirit. However, the moment we recognize these deficiencies as sin and confess them to God, He will "cleanse us from all unrighteousness." Until we have done this we cannot have the filling of the Holy Spirit, for He fills only clean vessels. (II Timothy 2:21)

3. Submit yourself completely to God (Romans 6:11-13)

> *"Likewise reckon ye also yourselves to be dead indeed unto sin, but alive unto God through Jesus Christ our Lord.*
> *"Let not sin therefore reign in your mortal body, that ye should obey it in the lusts thereof.*
> *"Neither yield ye your members as instruments of unrighteousness unto sin: but yield yourselves unto God, as those that are alive from the dead, and your members as instruments of righteousness unto God."*

To be filled with the Holy Spirit, one must make himself completely available to God to do anything the Holy Spirit directs him to do. If there is anything in your life that you are unwilling to do or to be, then you are resisting God, and this always limits God's Spirit! Do not make the mistake of being afraid to give yourself to God! Romans 8:32 tells us, "He that spared not His own Son, but delivered Him up for us all, how shall He not with Him also freely give us all things?" It is clear from this verse that if God loved us so much as to give His Son to die for us, certainly He is interested in nothing but our good; therefore, we can trust Him with our lives. You will never find a miserable Christian in the center of the will of God, for He will always accompany His directions with an appetite and desire to do His will.

Resisting the Lord through rebellion obviously stifles the filling of the Spirit. Israel limited the Lord, not only through unbelief, but, as Psalm 78:8 tells us, by becoming a "stubborn and rebellious generation; a generation that set not their heart aright and whose spirit was not steadfast with God." All resistance to the will of God will keep us from being filled with the Holy Spirit. To be filled with His Spirit, we must yield ourselves to His Spirit just as a man yields himself to wine for its filling.

Ephesians 5:18 says, "Be not drunk with wine . . . but be filled with the Spirit." When a man is drunk, he is dominated by alcohol; he lives and acts, and is dominated by its influence. So with the filling of the Holy Spirit, man's actions must be dominated by and dictated by the Holy Spirit. For consecrated Christians this is often the most difficult thing to do, for we can always find some worthy purpose for our lives, not realizing that we are often filled with ourselves rather than with the Holy Spirit, as we seek to serve the Lord.

This summer, while speaking at a high school and college camp, we had a thrilling testimony from a ministerial student who said that for the first time he realized what it meant to be filled with the Holy Spirit. As far as he knew, he had not been guilty of the usual sins of the carnal Christian. Actually, he had only one area of resistance in his life. He loved to preach, and the possibilities of being a pastor or evangelist appealed to him very much, but he did not want the Lord to make a missionary out of him. During that week the Holy Spirit spoke to the lad about that very vocation, and when he submitted everything to the Lord and said, "Yes, I'll go to the ends of the earth," for the first time he experienced the true filling of the Holy Spirit. He then went on to say, "I don't believe the Lord wants me to be a missionary after all; He just wanted me to be willing to be a missionary."

When you give your life to God, do not attach any strings or conditions to it. He is such a God of love that you can safely give yourself without reservation, knowing that His plan and use of your life is far better than yours. And, remember, the attitude of yieldedness is absolutely necessary for the filling of God's Spirit. Your will is the will of the flesh, and the Bible says that "the flesh profiteth nothing."

Yieldedness is sometimes difficult to determine when once we have solved the five big questions of life: (1) Where shall I attend college? (2) What vocation shall I pursue? (3) Whom shall I marry? (4) Where shall I live? (5) Where shall I attend church? A Spirit-filled Christian will be sensitive to the Spirit's leading in small decisions as well as the big ones. But it has been my observation that many Christians who have made the right decisions on life's five big questions are still not filled with the Spirit.

Someone has suggested that being yielded to the Spirit is being available to the Spirit. Peter and John in Acts 3 make a good example of that. They were on their way to the temple to pray when they saw the lame man begging alms. Because they were sensitive to the Holy Spirit, they healed him "in the name of Jesus Christ of Nazareth." The man began leaping about and praising God until a crowd gathered. Peter, still sensitive to the Holy Spirit, began preaching; "many of them which heard the Word believed; and the number of the men was about five thousand." (Acts 4:4)

Many times I fear we are so engrossed in some good Christian activity that we are not "available" when the Spirit leads. In my own life, I have found that when someone asks me to do some good thing and I give a negative response, it is the flesh rather than the Spirit. Many a Christian has said "no" to the Holy Spirit when He offered an opportunity to teach Sunday School. It may have been the Sunday school superintendent that asked, but he too had been seeking the leading of the Holy Spirit. Many a Christian says, "Lord, here am I, use me!" but when asked to go calling or witnessing is too busy painting, bowling or pursuing some other activity that interferes. What is the problem? He just isn't available. When a Christian yields himself unto God, "as those that are alive from the dead," he takes time to do what the Spirit directs him to do.

4. Ask to be filled with the Holy Spirit (Luke 11:13)

> *"If ye, then, being evil, know how to give good gifts unto your children: how much more shall your heavenly Father give the Holy Spirit to them that ask Him?"*

When a Christian has examined himself, confessed all known sin and yielded himself without reservation to God, he is then ready to do the one thing he must do to receive the Spirit of God. Very simply, it is to ask to be filled with the Spirit. Any suggestion to present-day believers of waiting or tarrying or laboring or suffering is man's suggestion. Only the disciples were told to wait, and that was because the day of Pentecost had not yet come. Since that day, God's children have only to ask for His filling to experience it.

The Lord Jesus compares this to our treatment of our earthly children. Certainly a good father would not make his children beg for something he commanded them to have. How much less does God make us beg to be filled with the Holy Spirit which He has commanded. It is just as simple as that! But don't forget Step 5.

5. Believe you are filled with the Holy Spirit! And thank Him for His filling.

> *"And he that doubteth is damned if he eat, because he eateth not of faith: for whatsoever is not of faith is sin."* (Romans 14:23)
> *"In everything give thanks: for this is the will of God in Christ Jesus concerning you."* (I Thessalonians 5:18)

For many Christians the battle is won or lost right here. After examining themselves, confessing all known sin, yielding themselves to God and asking for His filling, they are faced with a decision: to believe they are filled, or to go away in unbelief, in which case they have sinned, for "whatsoever is not of faith is sin."

The same Christian, who when doing personal work tells the new convert to "take God at His Word concerning salvation," finds it difficult to heed his own advice concerning the filling of the Holy Spirit. He will tell a new babe in Christ, who lacks assurance of salvation, that he can know that Christ is in his life because He promised to come in if He were invited, and "God always keeps His Word." Oh, that the same sincere personal worker would believe

God when He says: "How much more shall your heavenly Father give the Holy Spirit to them that ask Him?" If you have fulfilled the first four steps, then thank God for His filling by faith. Don't wait for feelings, don't wait for any physical signs, but fasten your faith to the Word of God that is independent of feeling. Feelings of assurance of the Spirit's filling often follow our taking God at His Word and believing He has filled us, but they neither cause the filling nor determine whether or not we are filled. Believing we are filled with the Spirit is merely taking God at His Word, and that is the only absolute this world has. (Matthew 24:35)

Walking in the Spirit

"This I say then, Walk in the Spirit, and ye shall not fulfill the lust of the flesh." (Galatians 5:16)
"If we live in the Spirit, let us also walk in the Spirit." (Galatians 5:25)

"Walking in the Spirit" and being filled by the Holy Spirit are not one and the same thing, though they are very closely related. Having followed the five simple rules for the filling of the Holy Spirit, one may walk in the Spirit by guarding against quenching or grieving the Spirit (as we will describe in the next two chapters) and by following the above five steps each time he is aware that sin has crept into his life. Being filled with the Holy Spirit is not a single experience that lasts for life. On the contrary, it must be repeated many times. In fact, at first it should be repeated many times daily. This can be done while kneeling at your place of devotion, at the breakfast table, in the car en route to work, while sweeping the kitchen floor, while listening to a telephone conversation—in fact, anywhere. In effect, walking in the Spirit puts one in continual communion with God, which is the same as abiding in Christ. To "walk in the Spirit" is to be freed of your weaknesses. Yes, even your greatest weaknesses can be overcome by the Holy Spirit (Chapter 10). Instead of being dominated by your weaknesses, you can be dominated by the Holy Spirit. That is God's will for all believers!

8

GRIEVING THE HOLY SPIRIT THROUGH ANGER

> *"Let no corrupt communication proceed out of your mouth, but that which is good to the use of edifying, that it may minister grace unto the hearers.*
> *"And grieve not the holy Spirit of God, whereby ye are sealed unto the day of redemption.*
> *"Let all bitterness, and wrath, and anger, and clamor, and evil speaking, be put away from you, with all malice:*
> *"And be ye kind one to another, tenderhearted, forgiving one another, even as God for Christ's sake hath forgiven you." (Ephesians 4:29-32)*

Grieving the Holy Spirit through anger, bitterness, wrath or other forms of human cussedness probably ruins more Christian testimonies than any other kind of sin.

This text makes it very clear that we "grieve" the Holy Spirit of God through bitterness, wrath, anger, clamor, evil speaking and malice, which is enmity of heart. For some reason, otherwise consecrated Christians seem reluctant to face as sin these emotions that stem from anger. Instead, it is common to stop advancement in the Christian life with victory over such external habits as drinking, gambling, profanity, etc., without coming to grips with the emotions that churn within. Although unseen, anger is every bit as much a sin as these overt practices. Galatians 5:20 lists hatred, strife and wrath in the same category as murders, drunkenness and revelings, saying, ". . . of the which I tell you before as I have also told you in time past, that they which do such things shall not inherit the Kingdom of God."

Anger—a universal sin

Anger is one of two universal sins of mankind. After counseling several hundred people, I have concluded that all emotional tension can be traced to one of two things: anger or fear. I cannot think of a single case involving individuals or couples who were upset but that the basic problem stemmed from an attitude that was angry, bitter and vitriolic, or fearful, anxious, worried and depressed. I have dealt with some people who were both angry and fearful. Dr. Henry Brandt, in his book *The Struggle for Peace*, points out that anger can cause a person to become fearful. Dr. Raymond L. Cramer, another Christian psychologist, says in his book *The Psychology of Jesus and Mental Health*: "At times anxiety expresses itself in anger. A tense, anxious person is much more likely to become irritable and angry."[1] Anxiety is a form of fear; therefore, from these two Christian psychologists we can conclude that an angry person can also become a fearful person, and a fearful person can become an angry person. Anger grieves the Holy Spirit, and fear quenches the Holy Spirit, as we will point out in the next chapter.

In our study of the temperaments we found that the extrovertish sanguine and choleric temperaments are angry-prone, while the melancholy and phlegmatic are fear-prone. Since most people are a combination of temperaments, they could well have a natural predisposition to both fear and anger—if, for example, they are predominantly sanguine with possibly 30 percent melancholy tendencies. Then, too, from the statements cited from Dr. Brandt and Dr. Cramer, it would seem that the angry-prone temperament's expression of anger could cause fear, and the indulgence of the fear-prone habit of the melancholy and phlegmatic temperaments could cause the emotional problems of anger and hostility. It is my personal opinion that these two emotions bring more Christians into bondage to the law of sin than any other emotions or desires. Thank God there is a cure for these weaknesses through the Holy Spirit!

The high cost of anger

If man really understood the high price paid for pent-up wrath or bitterness and anger, he would seek some remedy for it. We shall consider the high cost of anger emotionally, socially, physically, financially, and most important of all, spiritually.

A. Emotionally

Suppressed anger and bitterness can make a person emotionally upset until he is "not himself." In this state he often makes decisions that are harmful, wasteful or embarrassing. We are intensely emotional creatures, designed so by God, but if we permit anger to dominate us, it will squelch the richer emotion of love. Many a man takes his office grudges and irritations home and unconsciously lets this anger curtail what could be a free-flowing expression of love for his wife and children. Instead of enjoying his family and being enjoyed by them, he allows his mind and emotions to mull over the vexations of the day. Life is too short and our moments at home too brief to pay such a price for anger.

Dr. S. I. McMillen, a Christian medical doctor, has written a very interesting book entitled *None of These Diseases*. There he makes these interesting statements:

"The moment I start hating a man, I become his slave. I can't enjoy my work any more because he even controls my thoughts. My resentments produce too many stress hormones in my body and I become fatigued after only a few hours' work. The work I formerly enjoyed is now drudgery. Even vacations cease to give me pleasure . . . the man I hate hounds me wherever I go. I can't escape his tyrannical grasp on my mind. When the waiter serves me porterhouse steak with french fries, asparagus, crisp salad, and strawberry shortcake smothered with ice cream, it might as well be stale bread and water. My teeth chew the food and I swallow it, but the man I hate will not permit me to enjoy it . . . the man I hate may be many miles from my bedroom, but more cruel than any slavedriver, he whips my thoughts into such a frenzy that my innerspring mattress becomes a rack of torture."[2]

Anger takes many forms. Many people do not regard themselves as angry individuals because they don't understand the many disguises anger takes. Consult the following chart for a description of the 16 variations of anger.

Bitterness	Wrath
Malice	Hatred
Clamor	Seditions
Envy	Jealousy
Resentment	Attack
Intolerance	Gossip
Criticism	Sarcasm
Revenge	Unforgiveness

B. Socially

Very simply, an angry person is not pleasant to be around; consequently, those who are angry, grumpy or disgruntled are gradually weeded out of the social lists or excluded from the fun times of life. This is a price that a partner is often asked to pay for the anger of his mate, which in turn may increase their anger toward each other and limit what otherwise could be an enjoyable relationship.

The social price paid for inner anger and bitterness is seen more clearly in detail as a person progresses in age. We have often heard someone ask the question, "Have you noticed how ornery and cranky Granddad is getting in his old age?" What seems to be a change is not a change at all. Granddad just loses some of his inhibitions and the desire to please others as he grows older and reverts more to the candid reactions of childhood. Children do not try to hide their feelings, but express them, and elderly people return again to this same custom. Granddad begins to act the way he has felt all his life. This bitter, resentful and often self-pitying spirit makes him unbearable to have around, which in turn makes life more difficult for him in his old age. What a tragedy if Grand-dad is a Christian and did not let God's Holy Spirit "mortify the deeds of the flesh" many years before.

C. Physically

It is difficult to separate the physical price paid for anger from the financial, because anger and bitterness produce so much stress which in turn causes physical disorder so that thousands of dollars are spent needlessly by Christian people for doctors and drugs. Doctors and medical associations today have released various statistics showing that from 60 to as high as 90 percent of man's bodily illness is emotionally induced, and anger and fear are the main culprits! (Just think of the missionaries that could be sent to the foreign fields and the churches that could be built with 60 percent of the money Christians pay for medical expenses.)

If doctors are correct in their estimates, and we have no reason to believe they are not, this is money and talent wasted. How can our emotions actually cause physical illness? Very simply, for our entire physical body is intricately tied up with our nervous system. Whenever the nervous system becomes tense through anger or fear, it adversely affects one or more parts of the body. Both Dr. McMillen and Dr. Brandt refer in their books to an illustrated example drawn by Dr. O. Spurgeon English in his book *The Automatic Nervous System*. The following example based upon the works of the flesh described in Galatians 5 and Ephesians 4 was inspired somewhat by Dr. English's illustration.

Proverbs 4:23 says, "Keep thy heart with all diligence; for out of it are the issues of life." Therefore, the heart to which the writer of Proverbs referred was not the blood-pumping station we recognize as keeping our body in motion, but the emotional center located between our temples. In order for any body movement to take place, a message must be conveyed from the emotional center to the member to be moved. This message is given with lightning-like speed, and we are not conscious of the source from which it originates. For example, when a shortstop sees the flash of a ball to his left, his body, arms and legs seem to move in one coordinated movement spontaneously, but it has not been spontaneous at all; before he ever moved a muscle, his emotional center sent its impulses of action through the nervous system, notifying his members precisely what to do in that given situation.

If the emotional center is normal, then the functions of the body will be normal. If, however, the emotional center is "upset" or behaves in an abnormal manner, a reaction will be generated through the nervous system to almost every part of the body.

A man without Christ

This drawing of a man without Christ shows the three most important parts of man's being: the will, the mind and the heart (or emotional center). Man is affected emotionally by what is placed in his mind. What he places in his mind is determined by his will; therefore, if man wills to disobey God and records things on the files of his mind that cause emotions contrary to the will of God, these emotions trigger actions that displease God.

All sin begins in the mind! Man never commits sin spontaneously. Long before man commits murder he has harbored hatred, anger and bitterness in his mind. Before he commits adultery he has harbored lust in his mind. Filthy pornographic literature stimulates the mind to evil, whereas the Word of God calms the emotions of man and leads him in the ways of righteousness. Someone has said, "You are what you read." Man chooses through his will whether to read pornographic literature or something wholesome such as the Bible. His mind receives whatever his will chooses to read or hear, and his emotions will be affected by whatever he puts in his mind. That is why Jesus Christ gave the challenge to man, "Thou shalt love the Lord thy God with all thy heart, with all thy soul (will) and with all thy mind."

Dr. McMillen states, "The emotional center produces these widespread changes by means of three principal mechanisms: by changing the amount of blood flowing to an organ; by affecting the secretions of certain glands; and by changing the tension of muscles."[3] He then points out that the emotions of anger or hatred can cause the blood vessels to dilate, permitting an abnormal supply of blood to the head. The cranium is a rigid structure without room for expansion; consequently, anger and wrath can very easily give a person severe headaches.

A doctor friend illustrated the way in which our emotions can cause ulcers and many other stomach diseases by restricting the flow of blood to the stomach and other vital organs. He doubled up

A Man Without Christ

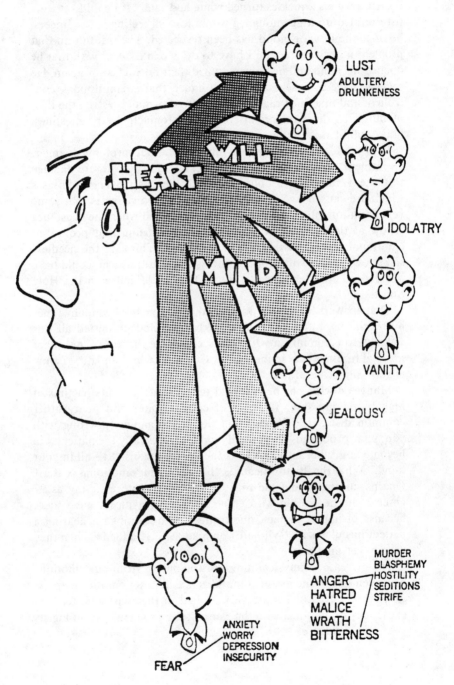

his fist until his knuckles turned white and said, "If I could keep my fist doubled up long enough, I would lose all feeling in my fingers, because the flow of blood has been restricted. The solution to that problem is very simple; all I have to do is relax." And with that he opened his hand and his fingers turned their normal color again. He said we have a muscle over our stomach that is emotionally controlled, and in a fit of rage it will tighten down and restrict the flow of blood to the vital organs of heart, stomach, liver, intestines, lungs, gallbladder, etc.

It is easy to see from this illustration that prolonged anger, resentment, hatred, wrath or bitterness could cause severe damage to these organs of the body. Dr. McMillen lists over 51 diseases which are caused by emotional stress. He even suggests that some very common infectious diseases are contracted when the resistance is low at the time of exposure, the reason being that prolonged emotional stress can reduce our resistance. Think of the needless sicknesses because of emotional stress of Christians who could have avoided all that heartache if they had been "filled with the Holy Spirit."

That answers for me the question that has been asked many times by rebellious, bitter Christians: "Why has God permitted all this sickness to come into my life?" It seems from the above and other medical findings that in most cases God didn't "permit" it; personal anger—sin—caused it.

Many a doctor has been forced to tell heart patients, victims of high blood pressure, sufferers of colitis, goiter and many other common diseases: "We can find nothing organically wrong with you; your problem is emotionally induced." Usually the patient will become angry because he thinks the doctor means, "It's all in your mind." What the doctor means is "It's all in your emotional center." One psychologist told me that he would estimate as many as 97 percent of the people who come to him with ulcers have them because of anger. In fact, one of his first questions on hearing a patient has ulcers is, "Who are you mad at?" He added, "Then they usually get mad at me."

The increase in physical illnesses originating from our emotions has given rise to the use of tranquilizers and other emotion-depressants. These treatments are very limited in their lasting effect because they do not deal with the cause of the problem. Psychologists tell us that man is not able to fully control his emotions even by his will. I agree, for I have found that nothing short of the power of Jesus Christ is able to make an angry, bitter, vitriolic individual loving, compassionate, gentle and kind. The cure for this problem through Jesus Christ will be given in chapter 10.

D. Spiritually

The highest price of all paid for an angry, bitter disposition is in the spiritual realm. Jesus Christ came to give us not only eternal life when we die, but abundant life here and now. That life can only be experienced by "abiding in Him" or "being filled with the Spirit." No man can abide in Christ or be filled with the Spirit who grieves the Holy Spirit, and "anger, bitterness, wrath, clamor and enmity of heart" grieve the Holy Spirit of God.

Grieving the Holy Spirit limits the work of God in an individual's life, keeps him from becoming mature in Christ Jesus, and hinders him from being the glowing, effective, fruitful Christian that he wants to be. Churches are filled today with evangelical Christians just like the children of Israel, who never fully possessed their possessions. Continual grieving of the Spirit of God through anger keeps the child of God from enjoying all that Jesus Christ has for him today. This affects the believer not only in this life but in the life to come, for we should be occupying ourselves with laying up treasures in heaven, which can be done only as we walk in the Spirit. Again we say, the most important single thing to any Christian is that he walk in the Spirit, but to do so he must let God cure his natural weakness of inner anger and turmoil.

The basic cause of anger

What causes a perfectly normal, likeable, congenial human being to suddenly react with heat and anger? The full realization and acceptance of the answer to that question provides the Christian with his first giant step toward its cure. Stripped of all the facade and fancy excuses for condoning anger, of calling it "old nick" or "my natural Irish disposition," we are confronted with an ugly word—*selfishness*. Although we love to excuse our weaknesses and justify them to ourselves as we nurse our grudges and indulge in angry, vengeful, bitter feelings, they are all motivated by selfishness. When I am angry, it is because someone has violated my rights and I am interested in myself. When I am bitter against someone, it is because they have done something against me, and again I come back to selfishness. Vengeance is always inspired by selfishness.

A lovely Christian lady came to my study to tell me her side of the problems in her home. When I confronted her with the fact of her angry, bitter spirit, she blurted out in her defense, "Well, you'd be angry too if you lived with a man who constantly ran roughshod over you and treated you like dirt!" Admittedly, he was not treating her the way a Christian man should, but her reaction could not possibly be caused by generosity; instead, it was plain old selfishness. The more she indulged in her selfishness and let anger predominate, the worse her husband treated her.

I confronted her with the fact that she had two problems. She looked at me rather startled and asked, "Did I hear you correctly— I have two problems? I only have one, my husband." "No," I said, "you have two problems. Your husband is one problem, but your attitude toward your husband is another. Until you as a Christian recognize your own sin of selfishness and look to God for a proper attitude, even in the face of these circumstances, you will continue to grieve the Holy Spirit of God." The change in that woman in almost one month's time was almost unbelievable. Instead of using her husband as an excuse to indulge in anger, she began to treasure her relationship to Jesus Christ more than the indulgence of her own selfishness. She went to Him who has promised to "supply all your needs according to His riches in glory by Christ Jesus" and began to experience victory over bitterness, wrath, anger, and all those emotional attitudes that grieved the Holy Spirit. Instead of waiting for a change in her husband's behavior, she literally changed her husband's behavior by hers. She told me that when God gave her victory over her own reaction to his miserable disposition, she began being kind to the one who was "despitefully using her," just as our Lord had instructed. Since love begets love and we reap what we sow, it was not long before the husband began to respond with kindness.

As fantastic as it may seem, I have observed this in the lives of those individuals who are willing to recognize inner anger and turmoil as the sin of selfishness and look to God for the grace, love, and self-control which He promises to them who ask Him. If you are reaping a crop of anger, bitterness and hatred, a little investigation will indicate to you that you have been sowing a crop of anger, bitterness and hatred. The Bible tells us, "Whatsoever a man soweth, that shall he also reap." If you had been sowing love, you would be reaping love. If you are not reaping love, may I suggest that you change the seeds you are sowing.

REFERENCES

1. Raymond L. Cramer, *The Psychology of Jesus and Mental Health*, © 1959. Cowman Publications, Inc. page 27, used by permission.
2. S. I. McMillen, *None of These Diseases*, © Fleming H. Revell Company, page 73, used by permission.
3. Ibid., page 60.

9

QUENCHING THE HOLY SPIRIT THROUGH FEAR

"Rejoice evermore.
"Pray without ceasing.
"In everything give thanks: for this is the will of God in
Christ Jesus concerning you.
"Quench not the Spirit." (I Thessalonians 5:16-19)

Quenching and grieving the Holy Spirit are the two sins one must guard against in order to maintain the Spirit-filled life. We have already seen that one grieves the Holy Spirit through anger. We shall now see that we quench the Holy Spirit through fear. Quenching the Holy Spirit is stifling or limiting Him. Neither grieving nor quenching the Holy Spirit eliminates Him from our life, but they do seriously restrict His control of our body which God would otherwise strengthen and use.

Our text indicates that the Spirit-filled Christian should be one who is able to "rejoice . . . always" (Philippians 4:4) and "in everything give thanks." (I Thessalonians 5:18) Anytime the Christian does not rejoice or give thanks in *everything*, he is out of the will of God. That docs not mean only in good circumstances, for ever the natural man rejoices in enjoyable circumstances. But when the Scripture tells us "rejoice evermore" and "in everything give thanks," it means in any circumstance. Therefore, in order for man to give thanks for everything, he must live by faith. It is faith in God's love, God's power and God's plan for our lives that keeps us rejoicing through the Spirit in whatever circumstances we may find ourselves. An unhappy, unthankful attitude that quenches the Holy Spirit is caused by unbelief in the faithfulness of our God, which produces fear as we face the uncertain circumstances of life. Thus I would have you examine the subject of quenching the Holy Spirit through fear.

Fear is universal

The first reaction to the sin of disobedience on the part of Adam and Eve was one of fear. When Adam and Eve "heard the voice of the Lord God walking in the garden in the cool of the day . . . Adam and his wife hid themselves from the presence of the Lord God amongst the trees in the garden. And the Lord God called unto Adam and said unto him, where art thou? And he said, I heard Thy voice in the garden and I was afraid because I was naked and I hid myself." (Genesis 3:8-10)

From that day to this the further man goes in disobedience to God, the more he experiences fear. The converse is also true. The more man obeys God, learns about God and leans upon Him for every need, the less he experiences fear. The universal nature of fear is easily seen in the fact that the Lord Jesus Himself so frequently admonished His disciples with such phrases as "fear not, little flock," "be not faithless, but believing," "O ye of little faith," and "Let not your heart be troubled, neither let it be afraid." Never in the history of the world has the universal problem of fear gripped so many and caused such devastation in the minds and bodies of men as the day in which we live. World conditions are not conducive to peace and faith today, for they cause many to lose their moorings and be afraid. The news media in our country constantly remind us of brutalities, wars, fightings, riotings, rapings and all kinds of frightful behavior. There is very little in the average daily newspaper that calms the emotions, but much that will turn man's natural fears into terror. In addition, there is what former President Kennedy referred to as the "Damocles sword" constantly hanging over our heads in the form of a nuclear holocaust.

It is comforting for the child of God, in the face of such fear reaction to world conditions, to heed the words of the Lord Jesus Christ who said, "Ye shall hear of wars and rumors of wars: *see that ye be not troubled.*" (Matthew 24:6) Even though fear is universal, God's children do not have to be dominated by this vicious emotional destroyer.

Reader's Digest for October, 1964, carried a popular reprint by Joseph Fort Newton, former pastor of St. James Church, Philadelphia, entitled "A Minister's Mail." He stated: "For some years I conducted a newspaper feature, 'Everyday Living,' which reached millions of people. Out of the mountains of letters not more than half a dozen ever brought up any question of theology, such as the differences which divide the religious communions. The first thing that these letters show is that Private Enemy No. 1 in human life is neither sin nor sorrow; it is fear. The one most rife is fear of ourselves, and that is not healthy. Men today fear failure, breakdown, poverty, fear lest they be unequal to the demands made upon them. So few have any material security; and we have set so much store by such security that the lack of it assumes hideous forms and gigantic dimensions in the night, robbing us of the rest needed to do our work aright. It is this self-fear which makes life an agony. Next to fear—if not a form of it—is the nagging, gnawing worry which wears us out and unfits us for living. Worry is a tiny rivulet seeping into the mind like slow poison, until it paralyzes us. Unless it is checked, it cuts a channel into which all other thoughts are drained."[1]

Fear, like anger, takes many forms. The accompanying chart describes the main variations.

An entire book could be devoted to this subject alone, but we shall limit ourselves to four categories.

The emotional cost of fear

Every year countless thousands of individuals fall into mental and emotional collapse because of fear. Electric shock treatments and insulin shock treatments are becoming more and more common as forms of treatment to patients suffering from the tyrannical force of fear. Many a fearful person draws into a shell and lets life pass him by, never experiencing the rich things that God has in store for him, simply because he is afraid. The tragedy of it all is that most of the things he fears never happen. A young businessman addressing a sales company somehow came up with the figure that 92 percent of the things people fear will occur never take place. I cannot attest to the accuracy of his figure, but it is obvious in looking at anyone's life that the overwhelming majority of the things that cause our fear do not take place or are not nearly as severe as we thought they would be.

Expressions of Fear

Anxiety	Worry
Doubts	Inferiority
Timidity	Cowardice
Indecision	Suspicion
Superstition	Hesitancy
Withdrawal	Depression
Loneliness	Haughtiness
Overaggression	Social Shyness

I counseled a woman who ten years before drove her husband from her because she was so emotionally upset due to fear. She became obsessed with the idea that another woman was going to take her husband away from her, and her emotionally upset mind caused such erratic and abnormal behavior in the home that she drove her husband away from her, though the "other woman" never existed.

The emotional cost of fear is very clearly seen in the statement by Dr. S. I. McMillen. "About nine million Americans suffer from emotional and mental illness. As many hospital beds are filled by the mentally deranged as are occupied by all the medical and surgical patients combined. In fact, one out of every 20 Americans will have a psychotic disturbance severe enough to confine him in a hospital for the insane. Mental disease is indeed the nation's No. 1 health problem. What does it cost to take care of the patients in our mental hospitals? The annual cost is about one billion dollars. Besides, outside the asylums there are a vast number who do not need confinement but who are incapable of supporting themselves.

They work little or not at all and constitute a great burden on the taxpayer."[2] This cost does not include the heartache and confusion in the families from which these patients are admitted to sanitariums and asylums. Mothers or fathers are left to raise children singlehandedly, and children often go untrained or uncared for as a result of emotional illness of one parent or the other.

The social cost of fear

The social cost of fear is perhaps the easiest to bear, but it is expensive nonetheless. Fear-dominated individuals do not make enjoyable company. Their pessimistic and complaining spirit causes them to be shunned and avoided, thus further deepening their emotional disturbances. Many otherwise likeable and happy people are scratched off social lists and cause their companions to be equally limited simply because of ungrounded fears.

The physical cost of fear

Fear, like anger, produces emotional stress, and we have already seen that medically speaking this accounts for two-thirds or more of all physical illness today.

Some of the diseases mentioned by Dr. McMillen are high blood pressure, heart trouble, kidney disease, goiter, arthritis, headaches, strokes and most of the same 51 illnesses which he listed as caused by anger. In illustrating the effect of fear upon the human heart, he quotes Dr. Roy R. Grinker, one of the medical directors of Michael Reese Hospital in Chicago. "This doctor states that anxiety places more stress on the heart than any other stimulus, including physical exercise and fatigue."[3] Dr. McMillen points out that fear causes a chemical reaction to take place in the human body, as illustrated when the saliva seems to be drained from our mouth as we stand up in a speech class to speak. Such a reaction does not harm a person, because it is shortlived, but that type of experience indulged in hour after hour because of fear can cause physical damage to the body.

A doctor friend explained it to me in this way. We have an automatic alarm bell system that rings whenever we are confronted with an emergency. If the door bell rings at 2 a.m., you are awakened suddenly and in complete control of your faculties, no matter how sound a sleeper you happen to be. This is God's natural gift to the human being. What has happened is that your adrenal gland has been triggered by the fright of the emergency and has secreted adrenalin into your bloodstream, causing you to be immediately in control of all your faculties; in fact, you will probably be stronger and more mentally alert than normally so that you might adequately cope with the problem.

When I pastored a country church in South Carolina, one of the men of the congregation was speeding his expectant wife to the hospital to be delivered of her child As they came down the muddy mountain road, the front of the car slipped into the ditch. In the face of the emergency his adrenal gland pumped adrenalin into his system; he leaped around in front of the car and literally slid it back up onto the road, got back into the car and drove his wife to the hospital. The next day in the parking lot of the hospital he tried to prove to incredulous friends that he had lifted the front of his Model A Ford, but to his amazement he could not budge it one inch. He used every ounce of energy and strength at his command, but the car would not move. What he didn't understand was that he had possessed super-normal strength because of his God-given emergency alarm system the night before that was not available for the parking lot demonstration.

My doctor friend explained that this does not cause any damage to the human body because after the emergency is over the adrenal gland settles down to its normal function and the bloodstream throws off the excessive adrenalin chemical with no ill effects. That is not the case, however, of the man who sits down at one o'clock in the afternoon to pay his bills and suddenly is overcome with fear because he does not have enough money in his checking account to pay for everything he owes. Hour after hour, as long as he worries, his adrenal gland is pumping adrenalin into his bloodstream, a process which can ultimately create much physical damage. This is sometimes the cause of excessive calcium deposits, and it sometimes produces the pain-racked bodies of arthritis sufferers.

I know a lovely Christian lady who has been afflicted with arthritis and was finally restricted by the disease to a wheelchair. She had every medical treatment known to science and was finally told by her third arthritis specialist, "I'm sorry, Mrs. _____, but we can find nothing organically wrong with you. The cause of your arthritis is emotional." When I heard that analysis, my mind went back to my childhood when she was in perfect health. Even though we enjoyed going to her house for the delicious cookies that she baked, we referred to her as "the professional worrier." She worried about everything. She fretted over her husband's employment, and he worked 30 years for the same company and never knew a day without pay. She was apprehensive about the future of a daughter who today has a lovely home and five children. She was anxious about her weak, sickly son who grew up to be a 6 foot-4 inch, 225-pound tackle for a Big Ten football team. I can hardly think of anything she didn't worry about, and all to no avail.

No wonder the Lord Jesus said in His Sermon on the Mount, "Take no thought for your life, what ye shall eat, or what ye shall drink; nor yet for your body, what ye shall put on. . . ." (Matthew 6:25) Literally, that is "take no anxious thought." Again the Holy Spirit tells us, "Be anxious for nothing." (Philippians 4:6) Anxiety and worry which stem from fear cause untold physical suffering, limitations and premature death not only to non-Christians, but also to Christians who disobey the admonition to: "commit thy way unto the Lord and trust also in Him." (Psalms 37:5)

One day I called upon what I thought was an older woman who was bedridden. I was amazed to find that she was 15-20 years younger than I had estimated. She made herself old before her time by being a professional worrier. As gently and yet as truthfully as I could, I tried to show her that she should learn to trust the Lord and not worry about everything. Her reaction was so typical it bears repeating. With fire in her eye and a flash of anger in her voice she asked, "Well, someone has to worry about things, don't they?" "Not if you have a heavenly father who loves you and is interested in every detail of your life," I replied. But that dear sister didn't get the point. I hope you do!

Thank God we are not orphans! We live in a society that accepts the concept that we are the products of a biological accident and a long unguided process of evolution. That popular theory, which is rapidly falling into scientific disrepute, is not only incorrect but is enslaving mankind in a prison house of physical torture due to fear. If you are a Christian, memorize Philippians 4:6, 7, and every time you find yourself worrying or becoming anxious, pray. Thank God that you have a heavenly father who is interested in your problems, and turn them over to Him. Your little shoulders are not broad enough to carry the weight of the world or even your own family problems, but the Lord Jesus "is able to do exceeding abundantly above all that we ask or think." (Ephesians 3:20)

How thrilled I was recently when a little girl in our Beginners

Department quoted her memory verse for me. She said, "I learned in Sunday school today what God wants me to do with my problems. For He said, 'Casting all your care upon Him; for He careth for you,' I Peter 5:7." Much of the physical suffering and consequent heartache, including financial difficulties, that occur in the average Christian home would be avoided if believers really acted upon that verse.

The spiritual cost of fear

The spiritual cost of fear is very similar to the spiritual cost of anger. It quenches or stifles the Holy Spirit, which keeps us from being effective in this life and steals many of our rewards in the life to come. Fear keeps us from being joyful, happy, radiant Christians and instead makes us thankless, complaining, defeated Christians who are unfaithful. A fearful person is not going to manifest the kind of life that encourages a sinner to come to him and say, "Sir, what must I do to be saved?" If Paul and Silas had let their fears predominate, the Philippian jailer would never have been converted and we would not have the great salvation verse, Acts 16:31.

Fear keeps the Christian from pleasing God. The Bible tells us, "Without faith it is impossible to please God." (Hebrews 11:6) The eleventh chapter of Hebrews, which is called the "Faith Chapter," names men whose biography is given in sufficient detail throughout the Scriptures to establish that they represent all four of the basic temperament types. The thing that made these men acceptable in the sight of God is that they were not overcome by their natural weakness of either fear or anger, but walked with God by faith. Consider these four men representative of the four temperament types: Peter the Sanguine, Paul the Choleric, Moses the Melancholy and Abraham the Phlegmatic. It is difficult to find more dynamic illustrations of the power of God working in the lives of men than these four. "God is no respecter of persons." What He did to strengthen their weaknesses He will do through His Holy Spirit for you!

What causes fear?

Because fear is such a universal experience of man and because most of the readers of this book will be parents who can help their children avoid this tendency, I would like to answer this question simply in layman's terms. There are at least eight causes of fear.

1. Temperament traits

We have already seen that the melancholy and phlegmatic temperaments are indecisive and fear-prone. Although Mr. Sanguine is not nearly as self-confident as his blustering way would have us believe, he too can become fearful. Very few cholerics would not have some melancholy or phlegmatic tendencies, so that conceivably all people will have a temperament tendency toward fear, though some more than others.

2. Childhood experiences

Psychologists and psychiatrists agree that the basic needs of man are love, understanding and acceptance. The most significant human thing that parents can do for their children—short of leading one's children to a saving knowledge of Jesus Christ—is to give them the warmth and security of parental love. This does not exclude discipline or the teaching you diligently avoid:

Over-protection. An over-protective parent makes a child self-centered and fearful of the very things happening to him that his parent is afraid will happen. Children quickly learn to read our emotions. Their bodies can far more easily absorb the falls, burns and shocks of life than their emotions can absorb our becoming tense, upset or hysterical over these minor experiences. The fearful mother that forbids her son to play football probably does far more harm to his emotional development by her repeated suggestions of fear than the damage done to Junior if his front teeth were knocked out or his leg broken. Legs heal and teeth can be replaced, but it takes a miracle of God to remove the scar tissues of fear from our emotions.

Dominating children. Angry, explosive parents who dominate the lives of their children or who critically pounce upon every failure in their lives often create hesitancy, insecurity and fear in them. Children need correction, but they need it done in the proper spirit. Whenever we have to point out our children's mistakes, we should also make it a practice to note their strengths and good points, or at least criticize them in such a way as to let them know that they are still every bit as much the object of our love as they were before.

The more I counsel with people, the more convinced I am that the most devastating blow one human being can inflict upon another is disapproval. The more a person loves us, the more important it is for us to seek some area in his life where we can show our approval. A 6-foot-2 inch husband in the midst of marriage counseling said rather proudly, "Pastor, I have never laid a hand on my wife in anger!" As I looked at his timid, cowering, 110 pound wife, I knew by the look in her eye what she was thinking: "Well, I would a thousand times rather that you beat me physically than constantly run me down and club me with disapproval."

The Spirit-filled parent is inspired through his loving, compassionate nature to build others up and to show approval whenever possible. Even in the times of correction he will convey his love. To do otherwise with our children is to leave lasting fear-scars on their emotions.

3. A traumatic experience

Child assault or molesting leaves a lasting emotional scar that often carries over into adulthood, causing fear concerning the act of marriage. Other tragic experiences in childhood frequently set fear-patterns into motion that last throughout life.

During the past few years our family has enjoyed some wonderful occasions water skiing. The only member of the family that has not tried it is my wife, and she is deathly afraid of the water. I have begged her, encouraged her and done everything I could to entice her to get over this fear of the water, but to no avail. Finally last summer I gave up. She made one Herculean attempt to overcome this fear by donning a wetsuit that could easily sustain her body in water. She then put on a life jacket, which also by itself could sustain her in water, and very hesitantly lowered herself over the side of the boat. The moment her hand left the security of the boat and she was floating freely in the water, I noted a look of terror in her eyes. For the first time I really understood how frightened she was of the water. Upon questioning her, I found that it all went back to a childhood experience in Missouri when she came within an eyelash of drowning. These experiences leave hidden marks on a person's emotions that often follow them through life.

4. A negative thinking pattern

A negative thinking pattern or defeatist complex will cause a person to be fearful of attempting any new thing. The moment we start suggesting to ourselves "I can't, I can't, I can't" we are almost certain of failure. Our mental attitude makes even ordinary tasks difficult to perform when we approach them with a negative thought. Repeated failures or refusal to do what our contemporaries are able to accomplish often causes further breakdown in self-confidence and increases fear. A Christian need never be dominated by this negative habit. By memorizing Philippians 4:13 and seeking the Spirit's power in applying it, one can gain a positive attitude toward life.

5. Anger

Anger, as pointed out in the previous chapter, can produce fear. I have counseled individuals who had indulged bitterness and anger until they erupted in such explosive tirades that they afterward admitted, "I'm afraid of what I might do to my own child."

6. Sin produces fear

"If our heart condemn us not, then have we confidence toward God" (I John 3:21) is a principle that cannot be violated without producing fear. Every time we sin, our conscience reminds us of our relationship to God. This has often been misconstrued by psychiatrists who blame religion for creating guilt complexes in people which, they said, in turn produced fear. A few years ago our family doctor, who at that time was not a Christian, made the following statement to me: "You ministers, including my saintly old father, do irreparable damage to the emotional life of men by preaching the gospel." I questioned his reason for such a statement and he said, "I took my internship in a mental institution, and the overwhelming majority of those people had a religious background and were there because of fear induced by guilt complexes."

The next day I attended a ministers' meeting where Dr. Clyde Narramore, a Christian psychologist from Los Angeles, gave a lecture on pastoral counseling. During the question period I told him of the previous day's conversation and asked his opinion. Dr. Narramore instantly replied: "That is not true. People have guilt complexes because they are guilty!" The result of sin is a consciousness of guilt, and guilt causes fear in modern man just as it did to Adam and Eve in the Garden of Eden. A simple remedy for this is: "Walk in the way of the Lord."

7. Lack of faith

Lack of faith, even in a Christian's life, can produce fear. I have noticed in counseling that fear caused by lack of faith is basically confined to two common areas.

The first is fear concerning the sins of the past. Because the

Christian does not know what the Bible teaches in relationship to confessed sin, he has not come to really believe that God has cleansed him from all sin. (I John 1:9) Sometime ago I counseled with a lady who was in such a protracted period of fear that she had sunk into deep depression. We found that one of her basic problems was that she was still haunted by a sin committed 11 years before. All during this time she had been a Christian but had gone through a complete emotional collapse, haunted by the fear of that past sin.

When I asked if she had confessed that sin in the name of Jesus Christ, she replied, "Oh, yes, many times." I then gave her a spiritual prescription to make a Bible study of all Scripture verses that deal with the forgiveness of sins. When she came back into my office two weeks later, she was not the same woman. For the first time in her life she really understood how God regarded her past sin, and when she began to agree with Him that it was "remembered against her no more," she got over that fear.

A man I counseled who had a similar problem gave me a slightly different answer when I asked, "Have you confessed that sin to Christ?" "Over a thousand times," was his interesting reply. I told him that was 999 times too many. He should have confessed it once and thanked God 999 times that He had forgiven him for that awful sin. The Word of God is the cure for this problem, because "Faith cometh by hearing, and hearing by the Word of God." (Romans 10:17)

The second area in which men are prone to be fearful because of lack of faith concerns the future. If the devil can't get them to worry about their past sins, he will seek to get them to worry about God's provision in the future, and thus they are not able to enjoy the riches of God's blessing today. The Psalmist has said, "This is the day which the Lord hath made; we will rejoice and be glad in it." (Psalm 118:24) People who enjoy life are not "living tomorrow" nor worrying about the past; they are living today.

Anyone who thinks about the potential problems and difficulties he might encounter tomorrow will naturally become fearful unless he has a deep, abiding faith in God's ability to supply all his need. My wife shared with me a very beautiful saying she heard which bears repeating: "Satan tries to crush our spirit by getting us to bear tomorrow's problems with only today's grace."

If you are worrying about tomorrow, you can't possibly enjoy today. The interesting thing is that you can't give God tomorrow;

you can only give Him what you have, and you have today. Dr. Cramer quoted a comment by Mr. John Watson in the Houston Times which read:

"What does your anxiety do? It does not empty tomorrow of its sorrow, but it empties today of its strength. It does not make you escape the evil; it makes you unfit to cope with it if it comes."[4]

Now I think you are about ready to face the primary cause of fear. The above seven causes of fear are only contributing factors. The basic cause for fear is . . .

8. Selfishness—the basic cause of fear

As much as we don't like to face this ugly word, it is a fact nonetheless. We are fearful because we are selfish. Why am I afraid? Because I am interested in self. Why am I embarrassed when I stand before an audience? Because I don't wish to make a fool of myself. Why am I afraid I will lose my job? Because I am afraid of being a failure in the eyes of my family or not being able to provide my family and myself with the necessities of life. Excuse it if you will, but all fear can be traced basically to the sin of selfishness.

Don't be a turtle

A Christian woman went to a Christian psychologist and asked, "Why am I so fearful?" He asked several questions. "When you enter a room, do you feel that everyone is looking at you?" "Yes," she said. "Do you often have the feeling your slip is showing?" "Yes." When he discovered she played the piano he asked, "Do you hesitate to volunteer to play the piano at church for fear someone else can do so much better?" "How did you know?" was her reply. "Do you hesitate to entertain others in your home?" Again she said, "Yes." Then he proceeded to tell her kindly that she was a very selfish young woman. "You are like a turtle," he said. "You pull into your shell and peek out only as far as necessary. If anyone gets too close, you pop your head back inside your shell for protection. That shell is selfishness. Throw it away and start thinking more about others and less about yourself."

The young lady went back to her room in tears. She never thought of herself as selfish, and it crushed her when she was confronted with the awful truth. Fortunately, she went to God, and He has gradually cured her of that vicious sin. Today she is truly a "new creature." She entertains with abandon, has completely thrown off the old "shell," and consequently enjoys a rich and abundant life.

Who wants to be an oyster?

A similar statement is made by Dr. Maltz in his book, *Psycho-Cybernetics*: "One final word about preventing and removing emotional hurts. To live creatively, we must be willing to be a little vulnerable. We must be willing to be hurt a little, if necessary, in creative living. A lot of people need a thicker and tougher emotional skin than they have. But they need only a tough emotional hide or epidermis—not a shell. To trust, to love, to open ourselves to emotional communication with other people is to run the risk of being hurt. If we are hurt once, we can do one of two things. We can build a thick protective shell, or scar tissue, to prevent being hurt again, live like an oyster, and not be hurt. Or we can 'turn the other cheek,' remain vulnerable and go on living creatively.

"An oyster is never 'hurt.' He has a thick shell which protects him from everything. He is isolated. An oyster is secure, but not creative. He cannot 'go after' what he wants—he must wait for it to come to him. An oyster knows none of the 'hurts' of emotional communication with his environment—but neither can an oyster know the joys."[5]

Once fear has been faced as a sin rather than excused as a behavior pattern, the patient is well on the road to recovery provided he knows Jesus Christ and is willing to submit himself to the filling of the Holy Spirit. A more detailed cure for fear will be given in the chapter, "How to Overcome Your Weaknesses Through the Filling of the Holy Spirit."

REFERENCES
1. Joseph Fort Newton, "A Minister's Mail" *Reader's Digest* Reprint (October, 1964).
2. McMillen, op. cit. page 116.
3. Ibid., page 62.
4. Cramer, op. cit., page 28.
5. Maxwell Maltz, *Psycho-Cybernetics*, © Wilshire Book Co., pages 151–152, used by permission.

10

DEPRESSION, ITS CAUSE AND CURE

A study of emotionally-induced illness would not be complete without a look at depression. Almost every one has known what it is to be depressed. During the last two years it has been my privilege to be in several churches speaking on family-life subjects in which I spend a night each on anger, fear and depression. I have made it a point the night before speaking on depression to ask the audience, "How many of you will honestly admit that at some time in your life you have been depressed?" To my knowledge every hand has been raised, attesting to the universal experience of depression.

Dr. Cramer, in his treatment of this subject, states: "Emotional depression is widespread if not almost universal. Severe depressed states have characterized human history ever since Adam's dejection following his expulsion from the Garden of Eden. Depression is an emotional illness to which many of our socially most useful and productive people are subject. Depressive traits cover a wide range of professional groups—the sophisticated and highly intelligent are not exempt!"[1]

Just being depressed does not mean that there is anything wrong with your intelligence . . . I have known people who had no education and those with Ph.D.'s alike depressed. I am acquainted with a man and his wife who are getting their Ph.D.'s in psychology at the same time, and they are both seriously depressed. Perhaps the fact that each has to live with a psychologist and be subject to perpetual analysis is enough to depress them!

Depression is defined by Webster's dictionary as "the state of being depressed . . . dejection, as of mind . . . a lowering of vitality of functional activity . . . an abnormal state of inactivity and unpleasant emotion." God never intended man to live like that! It has always been God's intent that man enjoy a peaceful, contented, and happy life, referred to in Scripture as the "abundant" life. No Christian filled with the Holy Spirit is going to be depressed. Before a Spirit-filled believer can become depressed, he must first grieve the Spirit through anger or quench the Spirit through fear. Before we examine the specific causes of depression, let us examine the heavy costs.

The high cost of being depressed

Every negative human emotion indulged in over a period of time takes a heavy toll on a person. Depression is not just an emotional state, but the result of a particular thinking pattern which we shall discuss near the end of this chapter. But it too takes a heavy toll. Consider the following five costs as only part of the price one pays for depression, depending on how serious and prolonged it is.

1. Gloom and pessimism

When a person is depressed, he is gloomy and pessimistic. Everything looks black, and even the most simple things become difficult. It seems a common practice for a depressed person to "make a mountain out of a molehill." That does not make for good fellowship; consequently a depressed person is not sought out by his friends, and thus he tends to become more depressed. People do not seek the companionship of the depressed in spirit, but the lighthearted. Selfish motive? Yes, but true nevertheless. The gloomy, pessimistic spirit of the depressed person usually makes him a very lonely individual.

2. Apathy and fatigue

Another price paid by the depressed person is apathy and fatigue. These conditions, like anger and fear, involve very fatiguing emotions. It takes considerable energy to be angry all day or to lie awake worrying all night, and this expenditure of energy does not leave an angry or fear-dominated person with much pep to enjoy the pleasurable blessings of life. But depression is often worse than fear and anger in that it tends to neutralize man's natural ambitions. Since molehills look like mountains, his attitude usually is,

"What's the use?" and he pessimistically sits on his stool of gloom and does nothing.

Man needs the sense of accomplishment that comes with a task well done. This feeling of well-being so needed by the depressed person is repelled by his apathy, which is the enemy of all achievement; it certainly is not the soil from which the seeds of "goals," "projects" and "visions" grow. The Bible tells us that "without a vision the people perish." That is true not only in the spiritual realm, but also in the mental realm. If people do not have a vision or goal to which they are working, mentally they are living in a vacuum of apathy that saps the vitality of their energy.

This lack of vision accounts for much of the apathetic behavior of young people today. Our society has overprotected them to the point that it has failed to challenge them. Now we have a growing generation on our hands that may not be willing to defend their country against an evil enemy like Communism. This attitude will carry over into many other areas of life, and with the increase in specialization it is going to be increasingly difficult to succeed in business and professional life. The younger generation needs greater motivation today than any preceding generation, but instead has less.

This indicates that we can expect an increase in depressed people. But thanks to God, there is victory from this depression through Jesus Christ our Lord. The rise in depressed individuals will increase the number of souls who will recognize their need of outside stimulus in seeking a cure. This fact should quicken the consciousness of Spirit-filled believers with the fact that all about them are apathetic, depressed, empty-hearted, no-vision souls that desperately need Christ. This is the most thrilling day the world has seen in several generations to live the Spirit-filled life as a demonstration of what Jesus Christ is able to do for an individual.

3. Hypochondria

Another problem occasioned by depression is hypochondria. A depressed person has aching pains, a sore stomach, and numerous difficulties without any known cause. He can learn the art of being sick to excuse his apathy. Some people use this "tool" to avoid what they think are unpleasant tasks by pretending to be sick. They don't call it pretending, or even think of it so, of course; it is very real to them, but usually unnecessary.

The ability of the human mind to cause physical pain is seen in the case a doctor friend of mine had recently. He has used hypnosis in his practice to deliver babies, calm the nervous, assist weight control, relieve tension caused by traumatic experiences and cure many other maladies. A golfer came in "to be hypnotized and have my trick elbow cured." It seems he had the "traumatic experience" of losing a championship golf match by seriously overputting the ninth cup. When he came to the 18th hole, he thought about it again, and his elbow seemed to hurt. Again he was overputting the cup. Ever since then his elbow ached whenever he picked up his putter, particularly when he came to the ninth or eighteenth green. Through hypnotic suggestion this "terrible pain" was eliminated.

In this same way aches and pains can enslave a depressed person any time he thinks of some unpleasant task or experience. Millions of dollars and untold human suffering are the price being paid for this hypochondria-type sickness induced by depression.

A healthy mental attitude toward things can hardly be overemphasized. I remember counseling with a housewife who "hated housework." She loved her home, children and husband but by her own testimony "hated to do dishes, and it irks me because my husband won't buy me a dishwasher." She had made a martyr of herself every time she stood at the kitchen sink. What was the problem? It was her attitude toward the doing of the dishes that made her sick. It was her attitude that made it an unpleasant, boring, exhausting task that almost destroyed the many other blessings which surrounded her but which she was overlooking. She was forgetting the lovely home, furniture, faithful husband and healthy children. Instead, she was focusing upon a pet peeve through the magnifying glass of self-interest. This is always a formula for depression.

Actually, a degree of stress created by tackling a difficult task, or one we think difficult, is good for a person, presupposing a positive mental attitude toward it. Dr. McMillen has said, "I can recall many times having to make house calls on patients when I wasn't feeling well myself. I found out that the stress of making the trip often cured me of my minor aches and pains. However, if I had made the trip in the spirit of antagonism, my faulty reaction might have put me in the hospital for a week. Is it not a remarkable fact that our reactions to stress determine whether stress is going to cure us or make us sick? Here is an important key to longer and happier living. We hold the key and can decide whether stress is going to work for us or against us. Our attitude decides whether stress makes us better or bitter."[2]

4. Loss of Productivity

It is only natural that if depression leads to apathy, then it also leads to loss of productivity. Many a genius or gifted individual never realizes his potential because of his depression-induced apathy. The loss is not only in this life, but also in the life to come. (See I Corinthians 3:10-15) The Lord Jesus' parable in Matthew 25:14-30 pointed out this very thing. He pictured his return as a time for his servants' accounting, and He seriously rebuked one for being "a wicked and slothful servant." He had not murdered anyone nor committed adultery; he had merely done nothing with the talent our Lord gave him. Some Christians are going to lose rewards in this life and the life to come because they are doing nothing with the talents the Lord has given them.

Apathy produces apathy just as depression produces depression. Christians tend to become depressed and apathetic if their lives do not count for Christ. Repeatedly taking in the Word of God without expressing it to other souls has a tendency to make one depressively apathetic. Recently a young Christian that has had a problem with depression most of his life said, "Last Friday I felt wonderful! I had a great opportunity to witness my faith to a fellow employee." There is tremendous therapy in witnessing our faith to other people.

5. Irritability

A person suffering from depression is prone to be irritable. It irritates him that others are in a good, energetic mood when he is in a pensive, gloomy mood. He is also irritated by petty things that would otherwise completely escape his attention.

6. Withdrawal

Severe cases of depression lead to withdrawal. The individual tends to escape from the unpleasant realities of life, daydreaming about his pleasant childhood (which may at this point be a figment of his imagination) or building air castles about the future. This is very natural since contemplation of the present is depressing. Daydreaming, however, is a serious deterrent to an effective thinking process and not at all beneficial to mental health. It also makes a person uncommunicative and isolated.

The cause of depression

Since depression is a universal experience, it is worth our time to examine its basic causes. I will give the standard suggested causes and then turn to the most common cause.

Temperament tendencies

Although depression is common to all temperament types, there is none that is so vulnerable to this problem as the melancholy temperament. Mr. Melancholy can go into longer and deeper periods of depression than any of his fellows. Mr. Sanguine can be depressed for a brief period of time, but since he is so susceptible to his immediate environment, he experiences a change of mood as soon as he has a change of environment. Thus a cheerful companion coming on the scene can transform his mood of depression into one of joy.

Mr. Choleric is a perennial optimist, and he looks with such disdain upon depression because of its impractical resultant apathy that he does not ordinarily become a slave to it. He is not overly occupied with himself, but has long-range goals and plans which more than occupy his mind in the field of productivity, which is not conducive to depression. Mr. Phlegmatic would probably rate second in depressive tendencies among the four temperament types, though his periods of depression would not be as frequent nor as deep as the melancholy because of his basically cheerful nature and his sense of humor. It should be borne in mind, however, that we are not one solid temperament type, therefore, if a person is predominantly phlegmatic with some melancholy tendencies, he is going to be vulnerable to depression. Or if he is a combination of choleric with some melancholy, again he will experience depression. Thus we see why it is imperative to understand the universal aspect of depression.

There are three reasons why Mr. Melancholy has the problem of depression more than others.

1. His greatest weakness is self-centeredness. Everything in his life is related to self. He spends a great deal of his time in self-examination. Dr. D. Martyn Lloyd-Jones states the following: "The fundamental trouble with these people is that they are not always careful to draw the line of demarcation between self-examination and introspection. We all agree that we should examine

ourselves, but we also agree that introspection and morbidity are bad. But what is the difference between examining oneself and becoming introspective? I suggest that we cross the line from self-examination to introspection when, in a sense, we do nothing but examine ourselves, and when such self-examination becomes the main and chief end in our life."[3] Essentially, then, the difference is that self-examination is commendable when it results in doing something about that which has been discovered. Self-examination for its own sake is introspection, which produces depression.

2. Mr. Melancholy is a perfectionist; therefore, he finds it easy to criticize not only others, but himself. No person can become so distressed with his own work as Mr. Melancholy. The fact that it is far better than that of the other temperament types means nothing to him. That it does not measure up to his supreme standard of perfection bothers him and causes him to become depressed at what he considers his own failure.

Psychologists tell us that a melancholy person is often prone to be over-conscientious. Dr. Cramer expresses it this way: "The depressive takes life too seriously. He has a narrow range of interests, develops a meticulous devotion to duty, and is preoccupied with the smallest, most insignificant details. Combined with these traits there is often a compelling drive for the highest possible degree of success and excellence. The depressed person can put out a surprising amount of constructive work and assume a great deal of responsibility. He accomplishes this by driving himself ruthlessly. He is a slavedriver for getting results; he brags of his accomplishments, prides himself that his work cannot be duplicated, that no one else could possibly take his place, that his efforts are indispensable; his drive for power and control, his lack of appreciation for the feelings of others make him almost impossible to get along with."[4] Thus we see that even when he reaches his standard of perfection, he can become disagreeable, unlovable, and unappreciated which throws him into a fit of depression.

3. A perfectionist has a tendency to be unrealistic, both toward himself and others. He seems incapable of adjusting to the demands made upon him by changes in the course of life. For instance, a very active person at church—one who teaches a Sunday school class, directs youth groups, and is active in the calling program—may not recognize that duties at home also demand his attention. Certainly

the standard of Christian service at church is higher for the single person or young married couple without children than for a young mother with three small children. Home responsibilities, of course, should not be offered as an excuse for lack of church attendance, but the curtailment of *some* Christian activities should not cause Mrs. Melancholy to feel that she is forsaking her spiritual service, or that she is a success as a mother but a failure as a Christian. The truth of the matter is, she is not a success as a Christian until she is a success as a mother.

The person who already has an overloaded schedule must either neglect his family or shirk some responsibility (which makes the perfectionists guilt-stricken) when taking on additional duties. Happy is the man who knows his limitations and refuses to accept another responsibility unless he can complete the one for which he is presently accountable. It is far better to do a good job of a few things than a poor job of many things. This is particularly true of a conscientious person with perfectionist tendencies, for unless he does his best, he will never be satisfied with his accomplishments. Dissatisfaction with one's accomplishments often leads to depression.

Hypocrisy leads to depression

The average Christian who attends a Bible-teaching church soon learns the standards of the Christian life. If he attacks his weaknesses externally rather than by the control of the Holy Spirit working from within, he may become depressed. Suppose a man has a problem with resentment, bitterness and hostility. He soon learns that this is not the standard of spirituality for the Christian. Unless he handles this matter on a personal basis with God, he will try to solve it by the power of self-control. To control anger by the force of one's will is not only futile, but it will lead to an explosion somewhere in the body—high blood pressure, heart trouble, ulcers, colitis, or a myriad of other maladies, or it may result in a belated explosion. The frustration that follows an angry reaction to a given situation leads to depression. A true cure for these problems will be dealt with in detail in the next chapter. Suffice it to say here that it must come from within through the power of the Holy Spirit.

Physical problems

Physical problems can lead to depression. Whenever a person is weak, even simple difficulties are magnified. This can be avoided in

physical weakness when one bears in mind the principle given by
the Apostle Paul in II Corinthians 12:9-10, "When I am weak, then
am I strong." Paul knew that the grace of God is sufficient for a
Christian after a severe illness or at any other time in his Christian
experience.

I have observed that individuals can become depressed when
there is a mineral or vitamin deficiency. I am told that Vitamin B is
the nerve vitamin, the complete absence of which can make a
person nervous, which in turn may lead to frustration and depression. It is also apparent that some women suffer a hormone deficiency when going through the change of life, and this deficiency
often produces depression. Before a person attributes all of his
depression to spiritual reasons, physical causes should be investi-
gated by his physician; however, most people are inclined to attribute their depression to physical problems rather than consider that
it is spiritually and emotionally induced.

The devil

Most Bible teachers remind us that the devil can oppress a
Christian even if he does not indwell or possess him. It is true that
some Christians have seemingly been depressed by the devil. Personally, I am not overly impressed with this reason because the
Bible tells us "He that is in you is greater than he that is in the
world." Therefore, if a Christian is depressed by the devil, it is
because he is not "abiding in Christ" or is not "filled with the Holy
Spirit." We have already seen the nine characteristics of the Spirit-
filled life. I do not find any place for depression as caused by the
devil in the life of the Spirit-filled Christian. But it should be borne
in mind that all Christians are not Spirit-filled. We must meet the
conditions as outlined in that chapter and walk in the Spirit to
avoid being depressed by the devil.

Rebellion and unbelief

The 79th Psalm shows the way in which Israel seriously limited
God by their rebellious unbelief. God's limitation, because they
refused to trust Him in their rebellion, caused them to be depressed
with their circumstances. The terms "unbelief" and "rebellion" are
used interchangeably in this instance, for unbelief leads to rebellion
and rebellion leads to unbelief. If man really knew God as He is, he
would believe Him implicitly. But because his faith is so weak, he

has a tendency to rebel against the testings or the leading of the Lord, and rebellion and unbelief lead to depression.

Some years ago a very fine Christian worker came to me for counseling. She was already in the deep throes of apathy caused by depression. As I counseled with her, I found she was hostile toward many people, very bitter, and rebellious toward God. It seems that some well-meaning but ill-guided friend convinced her that they should have a special healing service for her that she might be "healed" of a lifelong illness. Such a meeting was held and she was declared "healed." She immediately discarded her medication and went around telling everyone of the marvelous work of God.

For some time she had no ill effects from the cessation of her medication, and then suddenly, without warning, she was gripped in the titanic vise of that lifelong disease. She returned to her doctor and resumed her medication, which arrested that problem. Nothing, however, has been invented to arrest the problem of rebellion (except acknowledging it as an awful sin and asking God to take it away). In the course of our counseling, she acknowledged that she was angry at God because He had not healed her the way she wanted Him to. She had not prayed in the will of God; instead, she had prayed in her own will, demanding that God answer her prayer exactly as she prescribed. Because He did not, she turned in unbelieving rebellion against Him, and in her frustration grew progressively depressed and apathetic. She refused to acknowledge her sin of rebellion and continued to prescribe her own cure for "healing this lifelong disease." She obviously was not aware that she had a far greater problem than her lifelong illness—namely, rebellion—and that God was using her sickness to help her realize her sin.

Instead of repenting of her sin by the simple method I prescribed and seeking God's grace to live with her illness (II Corinthians 12:9), she persisted in her rebellion. Today she is confined to a mental institution because her depression has become so severe she has lost touch with reality. This is a rare case, but it nevertheless illustrates that fact that rebellion leads to depression.

Psychological letdown

There is a natural psychological letdown whenever a great project has been completed. A very energetic and creative individual can be happy and contented while working toward a long-range goal. But when the goal is reached, it is often followed by a period of depression because the individual has not been able to mount another project to succeed the one he has concluded. This could well explain why many ministers leave their churches within six months after completing a building program. As I look back at my own life, I find that the only times I have had "itchy feet" and thought my ministry in a church finished was right after a long building program. Little did I realize that this was the natural reaction to the termination of a long-range project. The feeling of depression was eliminated when new projects and higher goals were set to replace those completed.

Elijah, the great prophet, had a similar experience after calling down fire from heaven and slaying 450 prophets of Baal. He sat down under a Juniper tree ". . . and he requested for himself that he might die; and said, it is enough; now, O Lord, take away my life; for I am not better than my fathers." (I Kings 19:4) This gifted prophet, unusually faithful to God, had strong melancholy tendencies, but because of the faithfulness of God he went on to greater heights of service for the Lord because he kept his eye on the goal of serving his Master.

Self-pity—the basic cause of depression

As important as they are, the above-mentioned elements are not the primary cause for depression. Too often they are the excuse one uses to condone depression rather than going to Almighty God for His marvelous cure. The truth of the matter is, a person becomes depressed only after a period of indulging in the sin of self-pity. I have questioned hundreds of individuals who were depressed and have yet to find an exception to this rule. I have had a number of people deny at the outset that self-pity was the cause, but upon thorough questioning they finally admitted that their thought-process prior to the period of depression was one of self-pity.

Dr. McMillen points out the many physical illnesses produced by the emotions of jealousy, envy, self-centeredness, ambition, frustration, rage, resentment, and hatred. He then observes: "These disease-producing emotions are concerned with protecting and coddling the self, and they could he summarized under one title—*self-centeredness.*"[4] He further states, "Chronic brooding over sorrows and insults indicates faulty adaptation, which can cause any condition from itching feet to insanity. The most common form of faulty reaction is *self-pity.*"[5]

The sin of self-pity is so subtle that we do not often recognize it for what it is. While I was holding meetings in a church some years ago, a very lovely Christian woman about 70 years of age came to me about her problem of "depression." This woman was a seemingly mature Christian lady with a gifted mind and many years of experience teaching an adult Bible class. She had been told by pastors of former churches, "You are the best woman Bible teacher I have ever known on a local church level," and it was apparent to me that she truly had a grasp of the Word of God.

At first I was at a loss to know how to reveal her self-pity to her, and I asked God secretly for special insight as she talked. It was not long until I found myself asking how she enjoyed her church, and her response immediately proved that I had "struck a nerve," for she said, "Nobody appreciates me around here! In fact, these people aren't very friendly. Most of the people in this church are young married couples, and they don't pay any attention to a widow like me. As far as they are concerned, I could quit coming to this church right now and they'd never miss me. They don't need me around here; in fact, I can come to this church on some Sundays and go away without anyone ever speaking to me."

There you have it! Depression caused by self-pity. Only when I wrote down those words that came from her own lips was I able to convince that dear woman that she had been indulging in the sin of self-pity, which caused her depression. I would be the first to acknowledge that self-pity is natural. But the Bible clearly teaches that we do not have to be dominated by the natural man, for we are to "walk in the Spirit." (Galatians 5:16)

One day I dropped in to see a minister friend of mine and his wife. While we were having a cup of coffee, the phone rang and the pastor went to answer it. As soon as he was out of earshot, his wife said, "I'd like to ask you something. Why is it that I have greater periods of depression today than when we were young in the ministry? Our work is going well, God is blessing, we have enough to live on, and yet I find that I go through more periods of depression now than when we had far greater problems."

Not wanting to ruin a good friendship, I reluctantly asked, "Are you sure you really want to know?" "Yes," she replied. "It isn't very pretty; in fact, it's rather ugly," I said. She insisted, "I don't care what it is, I'd like to know what causes it." As gently as I could, I informed her that she had been indulging in the sin of self-pity.

I shall never forget the look of startled amazement on her face. I don't think I would have gotten a more spontaneous response had I reached across the table and slapped her face. Fortunately, I recalled enough of our previous conversation to give her an illustration.

She had just told me how disgusted she was with the chairman of the Christian Education Committee. It seems she had formulated a project which she had been burdened about that would greatly help the young people's ministry in the church. She took it to the Missionary Committee because it had to do with future missionary volunteers. They passed it on to the Trustees because it involved finances. The Trustees passed it on to the Deacon Board because it involved the spiritual life of the church. Then it was discussed by the entire Advisory Board, composed of every elected officer in the congregation, and finally it received the unanimous vote of the church. Everyone was in a joyous mood; they had a good time of prayer anticipating God's use of this program in the future to salvage many of their youthful volunteers for the mission field.

Then it happened! The Chairman of the Board of Christian Education came to her and critically asserted, "I'd like to know why you and your husband always bypass the Board of Christian Education! It's obvious you don't feel that our Board is a necessary part of this church. I think I'll resign." For the first time the pastor's wife realized that she had inadvertently bypassed this particular board. From this point I took a chance and began to surmise her thought-pattern by saying, "You no doubt came home from prayer meeting that night and indulged in such thoughts as, 'Who does he think he is, criticizing me for a project that received the unanimous vote of the church? I'm the one who is going to do most of the work. It's adding a lot of burdens to my already heavy schedule, and what thanks do I get for it? This man is more concerned about his own petty approval than he is in the ongoing of the Lord's work.' The next day you indulged in similar self-pitying thoughts so that today you are reaping the harvest of self-pity; just as sunshine follows rain, depression follows self-pity." Dr. Maxwell Maltz made the statement, "No one can deny that there is also a perverse sense of satisfaction in feeling sorry for yourself."[6] The Bible tells us, "Whatsoever a man soweth, that shall he also reap." Whenever a person sows the seeds of self-pity, he reaps the results of self-pity in depression.

One of the best cases of self-diagnosis on this matter appeared in the sports page of the *San Diego Union*. One of the best-known football coaches in the National Football League, a former all-pro quarterback of tremendous ability, electrified the sports world by resigning suddenly. He had a good team and a brilliant quarterback, and he expected to win the National Football League championship. Somehow things seemed to go against him, and although the team won the hard games, they seemed to lose some of the easy ones. Immediately after his resignation he went into seclusion, and only after entreaties by the owners of the team, plus the other players and coaches, was he induced to reconsider, which he finally did. Later, when interviewed by sympathetic reporters, he said of the matter, "The thing that I thought of last—not quitting—was the thing I should have thought of first. I have lived a life of not being a quitter, but that's exactly what I was doing—quitting. I wasn't being rational. I don't know what happened. I just wasn't thinking right." When asked when he made the decision to return to the football team, he replied, "*When I quit feeling sorry for myself and came to my senses.* That's why I'm called the Dutchman; I guess I have to learn the hard way."

Happy is the man who, like this great football coach, can face the weakness of self-pity and diagnose it as the cause for depression. That is half the battle. For once we understand that self-pity produces depression, and that it is a sin, all we have to do is go to God for His cure. The cure for self-pity is identically the same as the cure for fear and anger, or any other human weakness, and will be dealt with in detail in the next chapter.

REFERENCES

1. Cramer, op. cit. page 35.
2. McMillen, op. cit., page 111.
3. D. Martyn Lloyd-Jones, *Spiritual Depression—Its Causes and Cure.* © Pickering and Inglis Ltd., page 17.
4. McMillen, op. cit., page 65.
5. Ibid., page 110.
6. Maltz, op. cit., page 148.

11

HOW TO OVERCOME YOUR WEAKNESSES

Using the temperaments to good advantage

The basic purpose in giving this temperament study is that we might examine both our strengths and weaknesses and go to the Holy Spirit for His filling and have His strength for our weaknesses. Dr. Henry Brandt has defined a mature person as one who "is sufficiently objective about himself to have examined both his strengths and his weaknesses and has a planned program for overcoming his weaknesses." With the aid of this temperament study you can examine both your strengths and weaknesses and, we trust, be able to construct a planned program for overcoming your weaknesses.

By closely examining the four temperament classifications, and by objectively looking at yourself, you should readily be able to determine which type you are. Keep in mind that no one is a single temperament type. Most people are predominantly one type with tendencies of at least one of the others. Once you have determined your basic temperament, pay close attention to your strengths and weaknesses. It is not God's will that your natural traits be destroyed. It is His will that Christ be glorified in every area of your life within the framework of your own personality. You may find that some of the natural strengths are being neglected in your life, or that others are being over-used until your actions are "the work of the flesh."

An honest examination of your weaknesses can be most helpful in pointing out the areas of your life that need the anointing of the Holy Spirit. Remember one important fact: If you are a Christian, you do not have to be a slave to your natural weaknesses! "Now thanks be unto God, which always causeth us to triumph in Christ . . ." (II Corinthians 2:14).

God in His wise providence has created each of us for "His pleasure" (Revelation 4:11); therefore, no man should despise his temperament, but recognize that we are "fearfully and wonderfully made" and that God utilizes man's natural temperament when it is filled with His Spirit. God has made each of us for a specific purpose; by God's power we will become the finished vessels God wants to use.

Using the temperament studies, determine which temperament you are, make a list of your natural weaknesses, and then seek the filling of the Holy Spirit to overcome them.

X-RAY OF MY TEMPERAMENT

	SANGUINE	CHOLERIC	MELANCHOLY	PHLEGMATIC
Strong Tendencies	Enjoying Optimistic Friendly	Not discouraged easily Optimistic Leader Team player Decisive Adventurous	Faithful friend Self-sacrificing	Good under pressure Witty Dependable Enjoys humor
Weaknesses	Restless Weak-willed Great starter Slow finisher Actions based upon feelings	Impetuous Lack of compassion Hard Impatient	Critical Moody	Tease Indifferent Lazy
Spiritual Weaknesses	Lust Lack of direction	Impatience	Critical	

Negative Results of the Above Tendencies	Financial problems
	Easy to over-extend time
	Unable to stay at one
	  task for a period of
	  time
	Wastes time in talking
	Starts many programs
	Procrastination
	Easily distracted
	Impatient with melan-
	  cholies
	Place time emphasis in
	  wrong areas
	Poor study habits
	Nervous as to sounds, etc.
	Instant reaction to imme-
	  diate circumstances
		Rash decisions
		Overly strict with
		  children
		Set too high standards
		Easy to take credit for
		  what God has done
		Lack of kindness
		Always prompt
		Argumentative
			Will take time from
			  business to run
			  errands
			Take dislike to people
			  who get in my way
			  or have different views
			Expect too much from the
			  children
			Meddler
				Hurt people with
				  unkind jest
				Do not put out full
				  effort at a con-
				  sistent pace

After hearing a series of messages on Spirit-controlled temperament, a Christian salesman gave himself some careful scrutiny and came up with the preceding chart showing his conclusions. I am not endorsing his method of analysis, but feel that it showed such thorough self-examination that it bears reproducing. He may not have diagnosed correctly the degrees of his temperament, for he considered himself about 45 percent sanguine, 35 percent choleric, 10 percent melancholy and 10 percent phlegmatic. Actually, he was probably a pleasant combination of sanguine-choleric. If you plan to use this form of analysis, I would suggest an additional category—that of "needed strengths."

Selfishness—the cause of man's weaknesses

The following chart more simply identifies the natural weaknesses of each temperament.

As already pointed out, the sanguine-choleric temperaments are

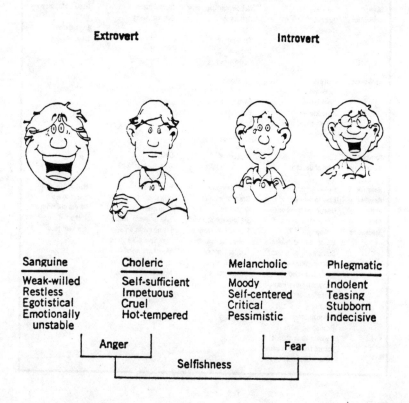

extrovertish and have a predominant anger problem, while the melancholy and phlegmatic temperaments tend to be introvertish and have a predominant fear problem. The chart clearly shows how these two, and for that matter all of man's basic weaknesses, stem from selfishness. Man's self-interest is what causes him to be restless, weak-willed, hot-tempered, impetuous, self-centered, lazy, critical, fearful or depressed. Selfishness was the original sin of Satan (Isaiah 14), Adam and Eve (Genesis 3), and Cain. A study of human history will reveal man's inhumanity to man caused by selfishness. It is man's selfishness which is the basic cause of all the heartache and misery from the beginning of time to the twentieth century. Egotism, self-centeredness, self-contemplation, self-consciousness and many other words are used to describe it, but they do not limit the fact that man's basic weakness is selfishness. This is not only true of man in his relationship to God, but in his relationship to his fellowman.

When the Ten Commandments are the standard, you will find that the unselfish man will keep them whereas the selfish man will break them. For example, the man who is unselfish toward God will humbly obey God and worship Him only; he will not take His name in vain nor will he take unto himself any graven images; and he will keep the Lord's Day rather than desecrate it for selfish purposes. In relationship to his fellowmen, the unselfish man will honor his father and mother; he will not steal, nor will he be so inconsiderate of his neighbor as to bear false witness against him, commit adultery with his wife, or covet that which is his neighbor's. From this it can easily be seen that the selfish heart is the root of all sin. It may take a variety of forms, but evil can still be traced to selfishness.

One of the hardest things for man to learn is the Lord Jesus' principle, "He that findeth his life shall lose it: and he that loseth his life for My sake shall find it" (Matthew 10:39). When man's faith and consecration have reached the point that he is willing to give his life completely to Jesus Christ, the Spirit of God will cure his problem of selfishness. This cure is basic, but through force of habit there will be occasional reversals to previous patterned behavior; when he does not continue to "abide in Christ" or "walk in the Spirit," he will revert to former behavior.

The Holy Spirit—God's cure for temperament weaknesses

As pointed out in chapter 6, the nine characteristics of the Spirit-filled man supply a strength for every one of your natural weaknesses. It is not God's will that you be dominated by your inherited weaknesses, but that you be filled with the Holy Spirit and thus freed from them.

The Holy Spirit does not automatically indwell every human being. On the contrary, He indwells only those who have received Jesus Christ by faith as Savior from sin. The Bible tells us, "If any man have not the Spirit of Christ, he is none of His" (Romans 8:9). That is, he is not a child of God if he does not have the Holy Spirit. But if he trusts in Christ, then God has sent the Holy Spirit into his heart. If you have never received Jesus Christ as your Lord and Savior, then your primary need is to right now humble yourself and invite Him into your life. The Bible tells us, "Whosoever shall call upon the name of the Lord shall be saved" (Romans 10:13). If you are willing to acknowledge Jesus Christ as Lord of your life, then invite Him in or, as the Bible says, "Call upon the name of the Lord." Salvation is not a long, tedious process—it is an instantaneous experience. Jesus called it being "born again" and likened it to physical birth. Your physical birth was an instantaneous experience, and by the same token so should be your spiritual birth. It is true that the Spirit of God speaks to our hearts through the Word of God over a long period of time, and many people go through a long process of considering their acceptance of Christ, but in order to receive Him one must have a distinct experience of calling upon the name of the Lord.

Jesus Christ Himself said to individuals, "Behold, I stand at the door, and knock: if any man hear My voice, and open the door, I will come in to him, and will sup with him, and he with Me" (Revelation 3:20). The word "sup" means to fellowship; if you desire the fellowship of Christ through His Spirit, then you must invite Him into your life. Only by this means can you have your past sins forgiven, your soul saved, and your life indwelt by the Holy Spirit. The Holy Spirit fills the lives only of believers, and believers are those who have invited Jesus Christ to come in and dwell within them as Lord and Savior. If you are seeking any other way of overcoming your weaknesses, or for fellowshiping with God, you will seek in vain. Jesus Christ said, "I am the way, the truth, and the life: no man cometh unto the Father, but by Me" (John 14:6). If you have never called upon the name of the Lord Jesus, may I urge you right now to do so. He is the only way to the Father, the only source of power to overcome your weaknesses.

Overcoming your weaknesses

If you are a Christian, you already possess the power to overcome your weaknesses! That power is the Holy Spirit. If you are filled with the Holy Spirit as defined in chapters 6 and 7, He will overcome your weaknesses. If, however, you find that you grieve or quench the Holy Spirit by indulging in anger, fear, or any of the other weaknesses on the preceding weakness chart, there is a cure for you. In spite of its general nature, you will find the following planned program for overcoming your weaknesses to be very effective.

1. Face your weaknesses as sin!

Don't offer excuses for your weaknesses such as "that's my nature" or "I can't help it, that's the way I am." Too many Christians are mental escape artists and refuse to face their shortcomings and weaknesses as sin. Just because escapism is a common practice of our day, there is no excuse for Christians to indulge in it. Be a realist. If you know Christ, you can face anything. The Bible tells us, "I can do all things through Christ which strengtheneth me" (Philippians 4:13). Either that statement is true or false. If it is false, then God is a liar, the Bible is untrustworthy, and we can forget the entire Christian message! This position is unthinkable and, frankly, would leave man with no possible cure. If a man does not know Jesus Christ, he may refuse to face the facts of his own weaknesses, for he does not have access to the power of God's Spirit to cure them. But that is not your problem if you are a Christian. Therefore, face your weaknesses as sin.

Alcoholics Anonymous makes it very clear that the first step toward curing alcoholism is for an alcoholic to face the fact that he is an alcoholic. By the same token, if you do not face the fact that you are an angry, bitter, resentful Christian or a fearful, anxious, worried Christian, you will go to your grave dominated by anger or fear. If you are a depressive individual as a result of indulging in the sin of self-pity, you will go to your grave marred by the effects of long periods of depression. No matter what your weakness, take the first giant step toward the cure by facing the fact that it is a sin and then go to God for His marvelous cure.

2. Confess your sin every time!

I John 1:9 tells us, "If we confess our sins, He is faithful and just to forgive us our sins, and to cleanse us from all unrighteousness."

Every Christian should memorize that verse and use it every time he sins. That verse, although used appropriately for sinners needing salvation, is really written to Christians. John addresses "my little children," for he is speaking to those who are children of God by faith. Someone has called this verse "the Christian's bar of soap." It is intended to be used regularly to keep us from going through long periods of time with sin in our lives.

The Bible tells us: "If I regard iniquity in my heart, the Lord will not hear me" (Psalm 66:18). A Christian's prayer life is short-circuited as long as there is unconfessed sin in his life. If he does not face his anger and fear as sin, his prayer effectiveness will be curtailed. However, that prayer life can be reestablished the moment confession is sought.

"How often should I use I John 1:9?" is a question that has often been directed to me. My answer is always the same: "Every time you sin and as soon as you are conscious of the sin." Don't let time elapse between the sin and the confession. Every time you "blow your top" or become fearful or depressed, you grieve or quench the Holy Spirit. The instant you are conscious of that sin, confess it and thank God for His faithful forgiveness and restoration.

3. Ask your loving heavenly Father to take away this habit

> *"And this is the confidence that we have in Him, that if we ask anything according to His will, He heareth us: And if we know that He hear us, whatsoever we ask, we know that we have the petitions that we desired of Him." (I John 5:14-15)*

Victory over fear and anger is the will of God. These verses make it crystal clear that we can be confident in having the answer to our prayers when we ask according to His will. Therefore, when we ask God to cure our habitual weaknesses, we can be confident He will. Jesus said, "All power is given unto Me in heaven and in earth. Go ye therefore and teach all nations . . ." (Matthew 28:18-19). Since the Lord Jesus has all power and has demonstrated that power by creating the heavens and the earth, which includes man, certainly He has the power to overcome our natural weaknesses.

4. Believe God has given the victory

Romans 14:23 tells us that "whatsoever is not of faith is sin." Many Christians are hindered right here because they do not "feel cured" after they have asked for the cure. Our feeling has nothing to do with it. Instead, we need to rely upon the promises of God and expect victory. You can do all things through Christ which strengthens you. That includes being gracious instead of angry, trusting instead of fearful. Commit your way unto the Lord instead of worrying about things.

The best way I know to accept victory—after you meet the conditions—is to thank Him by faith for that victory. I Thessalonians 5:18 tells us, "In everything give thanks: for this is the will of God in Christ Jesus concerning you." Since the will of God is that we give thanks in everything, then by faith we can give thanks for the cure for our weaknesses when we have obediently asked Him for victory.

5. Ask for the filling of the Holy Spirit (Luke 11:13)

To further help you to overcome your weaknesses, I would remind you to ask for the filling of the Holy Spirit as outlined in chapter 7. If you have already faced your weaknesses as sin, confessed them, and asked the heavenly Father by faith for victory, then why not prepare your life for service by asking for His filling, again believing that God does what you ask?

6. Walk in the Spirit and abide in Christ (Galatians 5:16; John 15:1-11).

The Lord Jesus said, "If ye abide in Me and My words abide in you, ye shall ask what ye will and it shall be done unto you." The "abiding life" is the "Spirit-filled life." Both are the way the Lord Jesus wants us to live in this generation. The following steps are suggested as a method of walking in the Spirit or abiding in Christ:

Be filled with the Holy Spirit as shown above.

Allow the Word of God to have a regular part of your life. Since the Word is a supernatural Book, it accomplishes a supernatural work in the life of the believer who reads it. A Spirit-filled Christian will read the Word of God since it is his only source of spiritual food. To be faithful in this regard, one should set aside a regular time for reading. If you are a new Christian, may I suggest that you start with the Gospel of John; read I John, Philippians and Ephesians several times; and then read the entire New Testament. Until a Christian has read through the New Testament, he should not turn to the Old Testament. Although regular reading habits are essential for long-range walking in the Spirit, avoid the danger of becoming

legalistic about your daily devotions. Certainly the Lord understands when you go to bed at 2 a.m. and have to get up at 6 a.m.
and rush out to an early appointment. He who loved us enough to
die for us understands the need of our body for rest. He also
understands the wild pace we live. Therefore, we can still enjoy the
filling of the Holy Spirit whether we have read the Word on a given
day or not. But a Spirit-filled Christian will desire to feed his soul
on the Word of God whenever possible.

Daily practice of prayer. Because prayer is communion with
God, it should also have a regular place in the life of the Christian
who is walking in the Spirit. When we speak of prayer, most people
think of protracted periods in the solitude of their room. These
protracted times of prayer are beneficial and should have a regular
part in a Christian's life, but that is not all there is to prayer. The
Bible tells us, "Men ought always to pray and not to faint" (Luke
18:1) and that we should "pray without ceasing" (I Thessalonians
5:17). The Christian walking in the Spirit will live a life of prayer.
He will commune with Christ through the Spirit about everything
in his life. He will ask His instruction about work and his family
decisions—in effect, he will follow the admonition, "In all thy ways
acknowledge Him." (Proverbs 3:6)

Continually yield yourself to the Holy Spirit. Romans 6:11-13
tells us to "yield ye your members as instruments of righteousness
unto God." The abiding Christian, or the Christian walking in the
Spirit, is one who continually yields himself to God. That is, every
plan and activity of life is conditioned on the premise, "Thy will be
done." There is nothing wrong with a Christian having a desire in a
particular direction, provided it does not violate the principles of
the Word of God, but the desire should always be patterned after
our Lord's prayer in Gethsemane: "Not my will but Thine be done."
It is only when we willfully, stubbornly demand our way that we are
on dangerous ground.

As a college student, if you desire to change colleges this year or
desire to invite a friend home for the holidays, you don't have to
fear disobeying the Lord. Our desires can very well be of God.
Always remember that God is interested in giving "good things to
them that ask Him" (Matthew 7:11). But the yielded Christian
walking in the Spirit will condition every desire on the basis, "If the
Lord will . . ." I would like to do this or that.

Serve Christ. The Lord Jesus said, "If any man serve Me, him will My Father honor" (John 12:26). He also said to His disciples, "Follow Me, and I will make you fishers of men" (Matthew 4:19), and "If any man will come after Me, let him deny himself, and take up his cross daily, and follow Me" (Luke 9:23). Jesus Christ wants us to follow Him in Christian service. All Christians are saved to serve Him. You are either serving Him or being served. As someone has said, every Christian is either a missionary force or a mission field. God uses men to do His work, and God seeks to fill your life by not only overcoming your weaknesses, but making you productive and effective in His service. This productivity is not only eternally meaningful, but it is actually therapeutic.

Man is so devised that he is frustrated when he does not serve his Creator. The happiest people in the world are those who are productive for Jesus Christ. A school teacher friend who is predominantly of the melancholy temperament and has experienced protracted periods of depression recently told me that he had one bright day during a lengthy depressed state. It was the result of a chance opportunity to witness of his personal faith in Jesus Christ to another school teacher. He enthusiastically stated, "That was the best feeling I had all week." If that dear brother had been walking in the Spirit and desiring to be available to communicate his testimony to the hundreds of other souls with whom he came in contact, he would not have had any periods of depression.

When you get right down to it, the depressed individual comes to the decision: Am I going to yield myself to Christ to serve Him, or am I going to indulge in the sin of self-pity? In short, then, the question involves self-pity or service. Your answer to that question under the filling and leading of the Holy Spirit determines your contentment of heart in this life and reward in the life to come.

Walking in the Spirit is a way of life. Admittedly, it is a supernatural way of life, but it is the result of the indwelling of God's Holy Spirit, who is supernatural. It is nothing short of what we can expect as a result of our receiving Christ, for the Word of God promises that old things pass away and "all things have become new" (II Corinthians 5:17).

The power of habit

Habit can be a vicious force that dominates many people. Do not be surprised if you find that you revert to the habit of giving in to your weakness, whether it be anger, fear, depression, or any of their derivatives. Just remember, you do not have to be dominated by that habit (Philippians 4:13). True, the devil will fight you every inch of the way, but just remember, "Greater is He that is in you, than he that is in the world" (I John 4:4). Frequently I find Christians who will try this procedure of facing their weaknesses as sin, confessing them, asking for victory, believing they have the victory, requesting the filling of the Holy Spirit, and walking in that Spirit, only to find that they revert to habit. Too often they give up because of their revision to old habit. This is a trick of the devil! A very simple cure is by faith to repeat these five steps for overcoming your weaknesses every time you sin as soon as you are conscious you have sinned, and eventually you will find that the old habits no longer dominate you.

A man once came to me who was dominated by the sin of blasphemy. As a new Christian he knew that he could no longer use the name of the Lord Jesus Christ in vain. It grieved him, and yet by force of habit he did it without thinking. In a state of deep anguish he cried out, "What can I do to overcome this awful habit?" My answer was, "Every time you use the Lord Jesus' name in vain, face the fact that it's a sin, confess it, ask your heavenly Father to remove the habit, thank Him by faith for His anticipated victory, ask for the filling of the Holy Spirit, and walk in the Spirit." Within three weeks that man came in to tell me joyfully that profanity was a thing of the past. Should the vicious habit of grieving the Spirit through anger or quenching the Holy Spirit through fear or depression be any different? Let me share with you some stories of Christians I know whom God has cured of their weaknesses.

Case histories of cured weaknesses

A young mechanic came into my office one day and told me that he had spent $250 seeing a psychiatrist and that he finally learned his problem: "I hate my mother!" This young man, after six visits to the psychiatrist, was told that because his mother had hopelessly confused his life through alcoholism and sought to turn him and his father against each other, he subconsciously hated her.

As a Christian of about four years, he had been married for a year and a half and was very happily adjusting to this new way of life when suddenly his mother was released from an institution for alcoholics. She had no sooner called him on the phone than he and his wife started having problems. He had trouble with men at work.

Everything was going wrong, and suddenly he began to develop an ulcer. All he needed to ruin his day was for mother to call him or drop by his garage. He told me that the hair on his arms stood straight up when his mother was within one hundred feet of him. I asked, "If you have been seeing a psychiatrist all this time, why have you come to me?" His answer was rather interesting. "The psychiatrist told me what's wrong, but he didn't tell me how to cure it." (About the only cure that I have seen from the school of psychiatry for intense anger came to my attention recently. A psychiatrist advised that a person should "find out what it is that annoys you and avoid it." I instantly wondered what a man does when he finds out that it's his wife that annoys him. Of course, that could be one of the contributing factors to the high divorce rate in America.)

In a sense, psychiatry has no answer because it has no supernatural source to change the angry disposition of man. Thank God, this young man knew Jesus Christ and by applying the above formula could not only come into the presence of his mother with his hair lying flat on his arms, but could talk to her kindly and graciously without grieving the Holy Spirit.

Another young man was referred to me for the counseling of his wife, who had been seeing a psychiatrist twice a week. Since neither of them came to our church, I couldn't understand how he expected me to get her to see me, so during our telephone conversation I suggested, "Why don't you come by and see me first? Then you can go home and tell your wife that you have counseled with a minister and suggest that she come in and see me also." He thought that was a good idea and made an appointment for the following Monday during his lunch hour.

I shall never forget that as he came through the door the noon siren blew, as was the custom every Monday in San Diego. He looked at his watch and very proudly announced, "I've kept my record intact. I've never been late for an appointment in my life!" As soon as he was seated, he went into an angry, 25-minute description of all the misery his wife had caused him and how psychotic she was. When he had finally unburdened himself, I began to present to him the gospel of Jesus Christ in the form of the Four Spiritual Laws which my 16-year-old daughter had introduced to me as the result of her training at a Campus Crusade for Christ conference. Because I had noticed that the Holy Spirit had used this method of presenting Christ in the lives of others, I wanted to try it.

The young engineer quickly informed me, "Well, I don't believe in Christ; it's not that I'm an atheist, I just don't believe." Squelching for the first time my ministerial inclination to present the wonderful claims of Christ and the abundant proofs for His personal deity, I ignored his statement and went right on presenting the Four Spiritual Laws. When I finished, after drawing the two circles showing the nonchristian and the Christian life, I asked, "Which of these two circles represents your life?" I was rather surprised when he replied, pointing to the nonchristian circle, "Oh, that represents my life. That's a picture of me, right there." Then rather hesitantly, because he claimed not to believe in Christ, I said, "Well, do you know of any reason why right now you couldn't invite Jesus Christ into your life?" To my utter amazement, he looked me straight in the face and said, "No, in fact, that is exactly what I need." With that he got down on his knees and began to pray. He first confessed what an angry, bitter, resentful, revengeful young man he was, and he asked Jesus Christ to forgive him and come into his life. When he finished, he sat down and began to weep. I watched him for several minutes, after which he sighed and said, "I've never felt so relaxed in all my life!" Then it was that I saw the evidence of the working of God's Spirit in his life as a new Christian, for he said, "By the way, Pastor, all those things I told you about my wife aren't really true. Forget it. Most of the problem has been me."

Two weeks later when he returned, I was intrigued by the fact that he had memorized the verses assigned him, completed a Bible study, and read his Bible every day simply because he was that kind of methodical individual. When I asked him, "How is your wife?" he again revealed the complete transformation miraculously accomplished in his life by the Holy Spirit when he said, "She's not doing too good, but I guess that's understandable. It's going to take a long time to overcome the effects of all the things that I have done to her in our married life." This loving, compassionate, gracious young man was nothing like the angry, vitriolic, bitter individual of two weeks before—another evidence of the power of the Holy Spirit to overcome man's natural weaknesses.

An interesting result of this experience appeared two months later. His wife, inspired by the transformation in her husband's life, got down on her knees in their home and invited the Lord Jesus Christ into her life. She has been delivered of her problems of fear and no longer sees a psychiatrist.

An often-depressed and fear-dominated housewife came to see me. In the course of counseling she revealed what a miserable life she lived. She had gone through shock treatments five years before and sensed herself going back into that same cycle of fear and depression that she so dreaded. She was raised in a Christian home and was married to a fine Christian businessman, but she still was dominated by her weakness of fear. One of her problems involved a particular sin committed 11 years before which she could not get out of her mind. Though she could say, "I know God has forgiven me," she would add, "But I can't forgive myself."

However, I was suspicious that she really didn't understand the extent of God's forgiveness, so I assigned her the project of doing a research study on all the biblical teaching on God's forgiveness of sin. Two weeks later she was radiant when she returned. For the first time in her life she knew what it was to have peace with God about her old sin. Gradually that sin became a thing of the past in her mind, and many of her fears vanished. Yet additional counseling was necessary because she still had long periods of depression.

One day I was able to confront her with the fact that her depression was the result of self-pity, and that just as God had cured her of her fears of the past when she recognized His forgiveness, so He could cure her of the depressed periods if she would just quit feeling sorry for herself. Being perfectionist-prone, she indulged in mental "chewing" to herself about her husband's careless habits around the house. She would often grumble to herself because he was not more expressive of his love. In fact, she acknowledged there were many areas in her life where she felt sorry for herself. When confronted with the sin involved in this deadly habit, she confessed it as a sin and went away armed with the above method for overcoming her weaknesses. It was only a few weeks before she called to tell me that she no longer needed to come in for counseling. I have received several notes of appreciation from her, and her husband thanks me regularly when we meet for "the transformation in my wife." It wasn't the counseling; it was the Holy Spirit who overcame her weakness.

These are only a few of the case histories that could be offered to illustrate the fact that God can overcome your weaknesses. We all have a tendency to exaggerate our problems, and if it is any comfort to you, remember, "There hath no temptation taken you but such as is common to man: but God is faithful, who will not suffer you to be tempted above that ye are able; but will with the temptation also make a way to escape, that ye may be able to bear it" (I Corinthians 10:13).

Whatever your weaknesses, they are "common to man" because they are a result of your temperament, your background, your training and motivation. If you have received Jesus Christ as your Savior and Lord, the Holy Spirit is now your motivation and the most important part of your character. The abundant life that Jesus Christ came to give you (John 10:10b) is yours through the filling of the Holy Spirit. If you have been dominated by your weaknesses, take heart. Jesus Christ can overcome them! A whole new way of life is now open to you as you let the Holy Spirit control your temperament.

12

SPIRIT-MODIFIED TEMPERAMENTS

When the Holy Spirit comes into a man's life, he begins immediately to modify the human temperament. As a counselor, I have had the great joy of observing the unmistakable work of the Spirit on the natural temperament of a person until it is almost impossible to see traces of the original temperament. It is particularly encouraging to observe this change when the person does not know a thing about temperament; he is just changed by the Holy Spirit.

This temperament modification is to be expected. Being "born again" is a supernatural experience and as such should have a supernatural effect upon an individual. The degree of modification in a person's temperament will be in direct proportion to the filling of his life with the Holy Spirit. The Holy Spirit will automatically introduce new traits and characteristics into an individual's nature.

The nine characteristics of the Holy Spirit as seen in Galatians 5:22-23 provide a working basis to show what God can do with the raw material of our temperament. We shall again examine each temperament and show how the Holy Spirit supplies strength for each of our natural weaknesses. This change will take place gradually and usually subconsciously.

The Spirit-filled Sanguine

Mr. Sanguine will always be an extrovert—even after he is filled with the Holy Spirit. He will also be an energetic, infectious and compassionate soul. Because he is so talkative his conversation will be one of the first apparent changes in his life. He will probably talk

just as much, but it will be far different. He will learn a new vocabulary, dropping the often used profane and dirty words that are so natural to the unsaved Sanguine. He will still tell jokes as he enlivens social gatherings, but now he will enjoy wholesome humor rather than smutty or suggestive stories. He will still feel the emotions of others but with purposeful compassion. Instead of just weeping with those that weep he will now encourage them by sharing the promises of God and pointing them to Jesus, the author and finisher of our faith.

Mr. Sanguine's weakness of will is probably his most serious problem. When filled with the Holy Spirit he will find a new strength of character that keeps him from "going along with the boys," or "following the path of least resistance." He will become

SELF-CONTROL

more consistent in his personal life, even to the point that he becomes more organized and dependable. He will learn to say "no" to some opportunities in preference to doing a good job with the responsibilities he already has. Though he is naturally receptive to his surroundings he will avoid being alone with pretty secretaries or flirting with other women. His sense of values begins to change and his own wife begins to look more attractive to him and the happiness of his family will seem more important.

This dynamic man will find a challenging new purpose in life, to be used of God. Once he has tasted the joy of seeing the Holy Spirit use his life to draw other men to the Savior, the old way of life seems very insignificant.

A salesman friend of mine took me to lunch one day and shared his problems, revealing himself as almost pure Sanguine. One quarter he led the office in sales and then he went into an apathetic period when he sold nothing. He had a problem with lust, and his past devil-may-care life was becoming attractive again. He gave up his Sunday School class and found petty excuses to skip some church services. He was thoroughly miserable!

I pointed out that the Holy Spirit was not about to let him go, for "whom the Lord loveth, he chasteneth" and his misery was of the Lord. We then discussed the Spirit-filled life, and it made sense to him. Gradually I watched this man become in practice what he was in the Spirit. A new self-control came into his life; he has been first or second in sales each month for over a year now; his family life is transformed. But even better, God has used him mightily in the lives of many business men, both churched and unchurched. Believe me, he is not about to trade his Spirit-filled experience for the old Sanguine life.

Another strength the Holy Spirit supplies Mr. Sanguine is peace. He is restless by nature but as the Spirit brings a new purpose into

PEACE

his life he also produces a relaxed peace. He will learn to commit his way unto the Lord, and instead of engendering strife and confusion he will have a more pleasing, soothing effect on people. This will help him avoid many unpleasant situations brought on by his own rash judgments.

His newfound peace and self-control will help control his fiery temper. By applying the formula for overcoming his weakness of anger as given in the preceding chapter, he will avoid excessive outbursts that often prove embarrassing and humiliating. Thus he will have many periods of peace where previously he had gone through the tortures of

HUMILITY

shame, repentance and hostility from others. Since Mr. Sanguine is inclined to be egocentric by nature, the Holy Spirit will introduce a new humility into his life. He will gradually become concerned for the needs and feelings of others. He will not ridicule some poor soul in public to get a laugh out of the group, but will be considerate of another's feelings and seek his humor elsewhere. His conversation will no longer revolve around himself, but around the Lord Jesus

Christ and Christian work. In short, his egotism will give place to a meekness foreign to his nature, and he will cease to be the braggadocio character of the past. This new humility will make new friends for him and since he is such an expressive person his faith will be contagious.

The Apostle Peter is a good example of the Spirit-filled Sanguine. After the day of Pentecost Peter used his lips to preach Jesus Christ in power. There was an apparent consistency and control in Peter's life from that point on, and absolutely no self-seeking tendencies. He was still a leader, but his conduct before the Sanhedrin in Acts 4 shows a Spirit-dominated restraint foreign to his nature. His life was used greatly to glorify Christ because he was Spirit-filled.

Many a Sanguine Christian has been used of God to share his faith as he has sought the filling of the Holy Spirit and walked in the Spirit. Great will be their reward in heaven! Sad to say, many a Sanguine Christian has gone restlessly and unproductively through life, stirring up strife, hurting other believers and actually hindering the work of their church. They will be saved, "so as by fire" (I Cor. 3:15), but have little or no reward—all because they did not heed God's command to "be filled with the Holy Spirit." (Eph. 5:18)

The Spirit-filled Choleric

The Spirit-filled Choleric will invariably produce a dynamic and effective Christian leader. His strong will power, directed by the Holy Spirit toward eternal goals, makes him very productive. He will "go the extra mile" in getting the Lord's work done. In fact,

many of the great leaders in church history possessed a heavy dose of Choleric temperament. His natural productivity is not because he has superior intelligence but is the result of his active mind and dogged determination.

A sales company years ago determined that the difference between the very successful salesman and the ordinary salesman was 17 percent greater effort. The Choleric Christian is most apt to go that extra 17 percent, and when his natural optimism is added you find a man who is willing to "attempt great things for God."

The leadership of the Choleric has proven a danger in Christian history when the Choleric gave in to the temptation to take credit for what God has done with his life, grieving the Spirit and reverting back to doing the work of the Lord in his own energy. Because of his natural abilities, it takes some time for his neglect of the Spirit to become apparent to others and they continue to follow him. Paul said, "Be ye followers of me, even as I also am of Christ." (I Cor. 11:1) We should follow Christian leaders only as they follow Christ, as he has revealed himself in his will in the Word of God.

In spite of the above mentioned good qualities of Mr. Choleric, it should be pointed out that he has the temperament with the greatest spiritual needs, but is often unaware of that fact. Frequently he is unwilling to acknowledge it even when made aware of it. He is often content to do "the work of the Lord" independent of the Holy Spirit. Happy is the Choleric (and his family) who recognizes with Paul that he must "die daily" and is willing to say, "I am crucified with Christ, nevertheless I live, yet not I but Christ liveth in me." (Gal. 2:20)

Among the first changes in the Spirit-filled Choleric will be his love for people. He will gradually look at people as individuals for

whom Christ died, and a genuine compassion for others will characterize his outlook. If properly taught, he will see the need of sending missionaries to the pagan countries of the world.

One nonchristian, upon hearing that his cousin was going to become a Bible translator and "bury his life in the jungles of Brazil," made the following statement: "I know what I would do—I'd take a machine gun and mow those natives down!" During the missionary's first term on the field, the cousin was converted. The Holy Spirit transformed him so that he met his missionary cousin at the plane when he returned after four years and outfitted the whole family with new clothes. Recently the convert told me that he and his wife are going to work for Wycliffe Bible Translators to raise money and find workers to get the gospel to the Bibleless tribes of the world! Only the Holy Spirit could put love in a heart like that!

The Spirit-filled Choleric is going to experience an enriching peace that is not limited to periods of activity. He will gradually find it easier to "wait on the Lord" for his wisdom rather than rushing off half-cocked on the basis of his intuitive judgment. As

PEACE

the peace of God replaces his innate anger he finds that he is happier and more contented. Instead of "stewing" and "churning" over some injustice done him, he learns to "cast all his care" on the Lord. If vengeance is to be taken he lets the Lord do it. In short, he comes to value the uninterrupted walk with Christ through the filling of the Holy Spirit.

In addition to gaining spiritual and emotional peace, he avoids the ulcers that he would otherwise have. In one family of four Cholerics I know, the strongest Choleric is the only one who does not have ulcers. It is no coincidence that he is the only one of the four told about the Spirit-filled life.

The other four spiritual characteristics so sorely needed by Mr. Choleric are gentleness, goodness, long-suffering and meekness. To make best use of his life and to enrich him, the Holy Spirit wants to create these characteristics in him.

GENTLENESS

GOODNESS

When filled with the Spirit, Mr. Choleric will turn from his tendency to be brusque, crude and sometimes obnoxious and be polite, gracious and courteous. Instead of ignoring his wife in public he will begin to treat her respectfully. Not because consideration and courtesy are meaningful to him, but because it is meaningful to her, and is a good testimony to Christ. It would be inconceivable to imagine the Lord Jesus walking through a door in front of a lady and letting it swing back into her face. Neither will it be a practice of his Spirit-filled servant.

When the Holy Spirit introduces a refreshing meekness and humility to the proud attitude of Mr. Choleric, he will have a natural desire to do things for others and will find a new patience in their inconsistencies and weaknesses. Instead of feeling a sense of superiority when he is confronted with another's weakness, he may thank God for the

LONGSUFFERING

MEEKNESS

gracious gift of self-control. It is a gift which he will treasure increasingly with its use.

Since the world is filled with needy people, Mr. Spirit-filled Choleric will never run out of things to do and people to help. Now, however, instead of wasting time doing those things that satisfy his quest for activity, he will be led of the Spirit to invest himself in sharing the one thing man needs most—a personal knowledge of and experience with Jesus Christ. His newfound graciousness, patience, and tact will make him a productive soul-winner. The result for him will be a rich and rewarding life invested in people for the Lord's sake, and many rewards laid up in heaven in obedience to the Lord's command.

The power of the Spirit to change the Choleric temperament was illustrated to me some years ago. We had a high school boy in our church who was downright mean. Our four-year-old girl would not go near him. During the boy's senior year, the Holy Spirit convicted him deeply, and although he had been baptized and was a member of the church, he realized that he had never really been born again. On New Year's Eve he got down on his knees and invited Jesus Christ to come into his life and become his Lord and Savior.

The change in that boy was amazing! A new gentility and kindness came into his life that was unbelievable. Two months later he was walking on the sidewalk just after church as our little daughter came down the steps from the nursery department. Smiling at her, he held out his arms, and to my utter amazement she leaped into them and gave him a big hug. I was convinced that this was not the same boy—though he looked the same outwardly!

The Spirit-filled Choleric is going to enjoy many blessings unshared by the natural Choleric. Not the least of these is love and companionship. The natural Choleric has few close friends. People respect him, often admire him, but because they are so afraid of him, very few love him. When filled with the Spirit, he will have the kind of gracious personality that draws people to him on a genuine and lasting basis. The natural Choleric, when aware that he is unloved even by his own family, may say, "I could care less." But in his heart he knows better. Mr. Choleric desperately needs the filling of the Holy Spirit.

The Apostle Paul is probably the best illustration of the Spirit-filled Choleric to be found in the Bible. We first see him in Acts 8 "consenting" to the murder of the first Christian martyr, Stephen. In chapter 9 we find him ". . . yet breathing out threatenings and slaughter against the disciples of the Lord."

If ever there was a description of a raw Choleric, this is it. Yet Bible students are thrilled to find this man so dynamically transformed that the very study of his post-conversion conduct has been used by God to lead many to acknowledge the supernatural power of Jesus Christ as the only explanation for his behavior.

The Spirit-filled Melancholy

The many talents of the Melancholy temperament are enriched and made productive by the filling of the Holy Spirit. His rich, sensitive nature will be earnestly attuned to the heart-needs of  humanity. No one can more realistically hear the pathetic cries of lost humanity like the Melancholy. When filled with the Spirit he will not just hear them, he will be available to God to do something about them. His analytical perfectionism particularly fit him for the much-needed detail work that is so often neglected by his extrovertish brethren. When filled with the Spirit, instead of being neutralized by irritation at others' disgusting carelessness, he will serve the Lord quietly, "counting it all joy" to be a part in the ongoing of the Savior's Kingdom.

The neglected corners of the world are indebted to the Spirit-filled Melancholy's self-sacrificing for their hearing of the gospel. Many a Christian can look back on a faithful, Spirit-filled Melancholy who doggedly kept after him after others had given up. Because of his great capacity to love, he loves others to the Savior, often suffering many abuses in the process.

Few Christians realize as they sing a beautiful hymn in church, read some meaningful poetry, enjoy such music as the *Messiah*, see some great work of art or read some deep truths of God in a book that they are enjoying the results of the Melancholy's talents, modified and energized by the Holy Spirit.

The self-centered characteristic of the Melancholy that so often dominates his life will give place to meekness and goodness when he is filled with the Holy Spirit. The best therapy in the world for a

GOODNESS

Melancholy person is to get his eyes off himself and involved with someone else. I don't know how this can be done without Jesus Christ! When the meekness and goodness of the Spirit take over a Melancholy he really sees that he is the "chiefest of sinners" and the recipient of the unlimited mercy of God.

Although he will never be careless in what he does, he begins to realize that the needs of others are so acute that he must offer himself to God to serve them. His perfectionism is not what really does the job—but the working of the Holy Spirit. When the Spirit finally gets through to the Melancholy that God wants his availability, not his perfectionism, he is ready to be used.

In God's hand, "any old bush will do," and as Paul said, "When I am weak then am I strong." As this meekness pervades his life he can truly enjoy other people in spite of their weaknesses, and he is not tempted to criticize them and thus grieve his sensitive conscience.

A Spirit-filled Melancholy enjoys peaceful sleep while the backslidden Melancholy's bed becomes a torture rack as he relives and rehearses the result of his uncontrolled criticism and caustic remarks. The Spirit-filled Melancholy is content to leave the results to God after doing the best he can in music, art or any field. The flesh-dominated Melancholy is never satisfied.

A Melancholy housewife complained to me about her Sanguine husband's inconsistency. Always late, quite undependable, careless with his clothes and always taking on more than he could do well, he reaped a harvest of criticism. Gently I shared with her that in spite of all her husband's weaknesses God was using him far more than her. As a young Christian, he was a dynamic testimony at work and had won several salesmen and customers to Christ. She could do anything better than he, but she had never led anyone to Christ.

Why was this? Not because he was inconsistent, but because he was available. With her, "the time is never right," she "didn't know the right Bible verses," or "maybe I will offend someone" was her response to the Spirit's leading.

But today she is a soul-winner. The reason is that now, instead of making excuses, she prays, "Lord, here are my lips; if you want to use them they are available." She isn't always just sure how the conversation gets started, but regularly the Spirit uses her. Spirit-induced meekness and goodness make any person available to God, and availability leads to fruitfulness.

The seventh characteristic of the Holy Spirit cancels the Melancholy tendency to pessimism. Pessimism is contagious; but faith cures pessimism. As the Spirit has control of a Melancholy believer, things thought impossible are looked at with the power of God in view. Through faith, Moses the Melancholy became a great leader. So today, many a believer confronted with overwhelming obstacles has looked at them by faith and God has given victory. Most Christians, like Israel of old, "limit God through unbelief." In this day God is looking for men of faith (II Chron. 16:9). He is not looking for geniuses and intellectuals, he is looking for available vessels that have faith enough to believe God for achieving the impossible.

Some years ago I broke my brown sun glasses and in looking for new ones discovered that green glasses make everything look better. The grass looks greener, the sky more blue, in fact, all colors become more vivid. Suddenly it dawned on me that when the Holy Spirit fills a believer he puts on the glasses of faith and everything looks better—the impossible becomes possible, the unattainable attainable. Happy is the Spirit-filled man in these dark days, for the

glasses of faith make everything look better. God has used all kinds of men, both in Bible days and throughout Christian history. Some were well-trained geniuses like the Apostle Paul; some were untrained, average men like Peter. But all men in every age who were used of God had one thing in common—faith.

Mr. Melancholy's natural moodiness is no match for the joy and peace of the Holy Spirit. No one can be filled with the Holy

PEACE

Spirit and be depressed at the same time, even Mr. Melancholy. That doesn't mean he won't be depressed. It does mean that when he is depressed and moody he is not filled with the Holy Spirit. If he occupies himself with the filling of the Holy Spirit instead of his circumstances or himself he will not be moody.

Joy and peace come to the Christian from two sources: the Word of God and the gift of the Holy Spirit. (Col. 3:15-17; Eph. 5:18-21) I have known moody Christians who never read the Bible for their own spiritual blessings. They would rather sit around and feel sorry for themselves than read the Word of God. Jesus said, "These things have I spoken unto you, that my joy might remain in you, and that your joy might be full." (John 15:11) The Savior also said, "These things I have spoken unto you, that in me ye might have peace. In the world ye shall have tribulation: but be of good cheer; I have overcome the world." (John 16:33)

The joy and peace of the Spirit-filled Melancholy prepare him emotionally to unlock the depth of riches God has placed within him. Gradually he will discard the old moody habits as the Joy and peace of the Holy Spirit fill his life. As one Spirit-filled Melancholy told me, "Since I have been walking in the Spirit I quit looking for happiness and it dawned on me the other day that I am happy!"

The love of God shed abroad in the believer's heart by the Holy Spirit must have an effect upon a Christian. As God's love floods the Melancholy Christian he gradually is less occupied with himself and more occupied with Christ and others. That in itself is good therapy. Under the power of this love, Mr. Melancholy becomes a different man.

The Apostle Thomas is a good New Testament example of what God can do with a Spirit-filled melancholy temperament. He is known as the doubting disciple because of his famous statement, "Except I shall see in his hands the print of the nails, and put my finger into the print of the nails, and thrust my hand into his side, I will not believe." (John 20:25) That is blatant unbelief induced by Thomas' doubts. Blatant because the words were spoken in spite of the Lord's oft-repeated promise to rise again and the ten disciples' assurance that "we have seen the Lord."

Actually, that isn't the only sample of Thomas' Melancholy pessimism. In John 11:16 Jesus insisted, in spite of his disciples' warning not to go "through Jewry" because they would kill him, that they should go to the home of Lazarus in Bethany. Seeing his Lord's determination and expressing his pessimism, Thomas said to his fellow disciples, "Let us also go, that we may die with him."

Humanly, such a man was doomed to failure, but such was not the case with Thomas. After being filled with the Holy Spirit, Thomas went out to serve the Lord faithfully. The Bible doesn't give Thomas' whole story, confining itself to the acts of Peter and Paul and their immediate associates. When I was in Madras, India, I saw the tomb of Apostle Thomas. The story of his ministry is regarded as authentic by many scholars.

It seems that after the day of Pentecost, Thomas was led of the Spirit to India where he braved all kinds of dangers and preached Christ in power. Many were converted and churches were established. Eventually, Thomas was martyred for his faith, and he died with the courage only the Holy Spirit can supply. The church in South India today is not the result of missionary labors, but dates back to the first century when doubting, Melancholy Thomas became a faithful servant of Jesus Christ through the filling of the Holy Spirit.

The Spirit-filled Phlegmatic

The least apparent change of temperament when filled with the Holy Spirit will be Mr. Phlegmatic. The reason is that by nature he

is calm, easy-going, peaceful, joyful and consistent—basically the qualities you expect in a Christian. Actually, unsaved Phlegmatics often act more like Christians than many Christians do. What then does the Holy Spirit do for the Phlegmatic?

For one thing, he will produce internally the calm, easy-going person that he appears to be on the outside. He will also overcome the weaknesses of reticence, stubbornness, fear, indifference and lack of motivation.

Mr. Phlegmatic has the capability of being a very good leader; the Holy Spirit will enable him to achieve that potential.

LOVE

The first fruit of the Spirit will go a long way toward motivating Mr. Phlegmatic. As his heart is genuinely filled with love for others he will be drawn out of his shell of self-protection and give himself more vigorously in the service of Christ. As his love for the Lord grows he will forget himself and take on, for the Lord's sake, things he previously rejected. With the Lord's power at his disposal, he will soon become a willing leader and a participant instead of a spectator. This gift of love from the Holy Spirit will take the biting edge out of his humor and he will become a source of pleasure for those associated with him. God will use him as a cheering, calming and encouraging influence on others.

The gift of faith provided to the Spirit-filled Phlegmatic will dispel one of his life-long problems—fear. Most Phlegmatics are

FAITH

unusually timid and afraid. Fear is a cruel taskmaster, and as the Spirit brings confidence and faith the Phlegmatic begins to lose many of his natural and learned inhibitions. Many a Phlegmatic has said, "I could never say anything in public," but when the Holy Spirit fills his life he finds speaking increasingly easier.

GOODNESS

The change doesn't come overnight, but gradually his concern for others and his desire to share his faith overcomes his fears. When he does speak he usually does an excellent job because he is well prepared and has his thoughts well organized. He will never be an extrovert, but he has a calm message so filled with facts and logic that it is well received by some of those missed by the loquacious extroverts.

As the Holy Spirit fills his life, the Phlegmatic gradually comes to the full realization that he "can do all things through Christ who strengtheneth." This concept propels him through open doors of service, and since he is dependable and efficient even greater opportunities confront him.

The goodness and meekness of the Holy Spirit work together on Mr. Phlegmatic, causing him to think of others instead of himself, and their needs become a source of motivation. Unselfishness multiplies and his selfishness is replaced by a growing generosity.

MEEKNESS

Most people need self-control, and that is provided by the Holy Spirit. When he fills Mr. Phlegmatic's life he inspires him to finish the job and involve himself in many forms of service previously omitted from his life. Many a productive and faithful Christian worker is a Spirit-filled Phlegmatic.

A good Bible illustration of the work of the Holy Spirit in the life of a Phlegmatic is easy-going, good-natured Abraham. This great patriarch was dominated most of his life by fear. In fact, twice in his life

SELF-CONTROL

he was so selfishly fearful that he denied his wife and tried to palm her off as his sister. She was such a beautiful woman that he thought Pharaoh and later Abimelech would kill him to marry her. This cowardly man was later transformed so much by the gift of faith it was said of him: "Abraham believed God, and it was accounted to him for righteousness." (Gal. 3:6)

Actually, the Holy Spirit has some strength for every one of man's weaknesses. God does not want us to be dominated by our weaknesses and shortcomings. That is one reason he has sent his Holy Spirit. Most people tend to wish they had some other temperament when they recognize their weaknesses. It really doesn't matter what temperament you are—God can change you and make your life usable for himself.

This can only be done by the power of the Holy Spirit in your life. The most important single thing in your Christian life is to be filled with the Holy Spirit. Go back and read chapter seven again on "How to be Filled With the Holy Spirit," and practice his filling daily.

The story is told of a young man who asked an old saint he greatly admired how long it had been since he had lived a defeated day. The old man replied, "Over 30 years." He then explained to his young friend that 30 years earlier he made a vow that he would never let an hour go by between his sin and his prayer of confession.

If you make it a point to follow that procedure with the sincere request to be filled with the Holy Spirit (Luke 11:13), you will enjoy the victory and power of the Spirit-filled life. It will take time to become consistent, but remember, you have years of habit behind you that need to be overcome. You probably won't even notice the change when it comes, but some day it will dawn on you that in daily life you are a new creature, that truly:

> "The Lord hath done great things for us;
> whereof we are glad." (Psalm 126:3)

II
Transformed
TEMPERAMENTS

1

THE BLIGHT OF FREUDIANISM

Reader response to *Spirit-Controlled Temperament* has been fascinating to see. All human beings are vitally interested in what "makes them tick," which is why psychology is a favorite subject among college students. The four-temperaments explanation of "why you act the way you do" seems to make sense to people immediately. Housewives, college students, ministers, professional men, and people from all other walks of life can easily see themselves in one of the temperaments.

We began to hear of counselors, ministers, and psychologists who recommended the book to their clients. A nationally known Christian psychologist has recommended it all across the country. Several psychology teachers in Christian colleges have used it in their courses, and I have been asked to address many such classes.

The reaction of non-Christian psychologists and psychiatrists has been less than enthusiastic, but their rejection was expected. In the first place, the concept of four temperaments is not compatible with humanistic ideas; and, second, if psychiatrists do not believe in God, they instantly reject the power of the Holy Spirit as a cure for man's weaknesses.

Such thinking strongly influences reaction to the four temperaments. I spoke to almost one thousand students from colleges and universities across the country in a two-week seminar. The first session was an in-depth presentation of the four temperaments.

Several young people were waiting for me, armed with questions, as soon as I was through. Almost all of them were "psych majors." Their main objection was, "You make it too simple" or "Your answers are simplistic."

Their response was understandable. They were absorbed in the process of learning the complex solutions to today's problems as our educators see them—not because the answers to man's problems are so complex, but because the molders of today's college curricula have rejected the Bible and God's plain cures for man's problems. Consequently, they are left with very involved solutions. The sad thing is that time does not seem to validate their solutions, and frustration sends them in search of another complex answer.

It is time for someone to point out that psychology and psychiatry are primarily based on atheistic humanism. Darwinism and Freudianism have shaped the thinking of the secular world until it builds most of its mental structure on two premises: there is no God, and man is a biological accident; man is supreme, and is sufficient to solve his problems. In philosophy studies I learned that "the validity of a conclusion is dependent on the accuracy of its premises." Since there actually is a God, the humanists' main premise is wrong; therefore we cannot expect their conclusions to be valid.

Much of the world today worships before the shrine of psychology and psychiatry. Since man must have a source of authority to lend credence to what he says, today's secularists usually quote some eminent psychologist. The fact that these authorities often contradict one another is usually not mentioned.

Do not misunderstand; I am not trying to ridicule sincere scholars. But I am calling attention to the danger of Christians being taken in by the "wisdom of the world." We need to recognize that "the wisdom of the world is foolishness with God" (1 Corinthians 1:18). The fact that men have doctoral degrees does not mean they are right. A roll call of the great philosophers of the world will show how each brilliant scholar disagreed with the great philosophers before him. A study of philosophy is frequently confusing because it is so contradictory. Experience and new knowledge have discredited the great philosophers. Christians, on the other hand, have one sure test for the accuracy of man's premises and conclusions: the Word of God! Man is right or wrong, depending on whether he agrees or disagrees with the Bible.

One senior "psych major" approached me after my final seminar and said, "I have to confess that I felt tremendous resistance against you after your first talk. You contradicted many things I have been taught, but as I listened, I came to realize that the Bible really does have the answer to man's problems! Thanks for coming here. You've been a blessing in my life." I hope this young lady and many others learned that there is nothing wrong with studying and using the valid principles of psychology and psychiatry or any other science as long as we validate them by the Word of God.

When I spoke at a couples' conference at beautiful Forest Home, high in the San Bernardino mountains, a psychologist attended all seven sessions. Because he was expressionless most of the time, I was dying with curiosity to know his reaction. Finally I got a chance to chat with him during the last meal together. He told me that he had been a counselor for almost twenty-five years. A few months previously he had received Christ as his personal Lord and Savior. Gradually be was becoming disenchanted with his techniques and the advice he had been giving for years. He had come to the conference to see if someone else had some better ideas. He concluded: "I am returning home with two clear impressions—the Bible has the answers to man's problems, and they really are quite simple."

The four temperaments seem to appeal to Christians because they are so compatible with many scriptural concepts. Just as the Bible teaches that all men have a sinful nature, the temperaments teach that all men have weaknesses. The Bible teaches that man has a besetting sin, and the temperaments highlight it. The Bible says man has "an old nature" which is the "flesh" or "corruptible flesh." Temperament is made up of inborn traits, some of which are weaknesses. The four-temperament classification is not categorically taught in the Bible, but our four biographical studies of Bible personalities will show temperamental strengths and weaknesses. The Bible shows that power over weaknesses is possible only when one receives Jesus Christ personally as Lord and Savior and yields one's self completely to his Spirit.

A psychologist friend informed me that there are twelve or thirteen theories of personality. The four-temperaments theory is probably the oldest, and many Christians consider it the best. It is not perfect—no concept of man is. It does, however, help the average person to examine himself by a process that has been systematized and improved through the centuries. It will not answer all your questions about yourself, but it will provide more answers than any other. As you study it, pause to thank God that you have access to a source of power that can change your life and make you the kind of person both you and God want you to be.

2

USE AND ABUSE OF THE TOOL

The four-temperaments theory is a valuable instrument for understanding yourself. But like any tool, it can be misused. Occasionally I meet people who have misused the concept and done a great disservice to themselves and others. The misuse usually occurs in the following ways.

Some casual observers of personality have externalized the concept, applying it indiscriminately to people they meet. And not being content just to think about it, they unceremoniously inform people what temperament they are, and outline their characteristic weaknesses. I have seen people rebuff their associates by naming their unfavorable temperament traits, exposing their weaknesses, and even humiliating them. This is dangerous. As psychologist Dr. Henry Brandt comments, "There is no nakedness comparable to psychological nakedness."

Human nature induces us to protect ourselves not just physically but psychologically. The individual who deliberately holds himself up for public ridicule is revealing a warped sense of emotional self-preservation. I suspect that such people use the exposure of lesser weaknesses as a shield for more severe but secret ones.

No Spirit-filled Christian would invade another person's privacy and expose him to psychological ridicule. It may be funny and it may spark humorous repartee at a gathering, but it may also be cruel and harmful. Anything that is not kind is not loving, and the Bible tells us to "speak the truth in love" (Ephesians 4:5). Since the indwelling Holy Spirit causes Christians to "love the brethren," we will grant them the emotional protection we cherish for ourselves.

Even when temperament analysis of others is not made public, it can be a harmful habit. A young woman revealed to me that she had rejected the friendship of a prospective suitor because she considered him an undesirable combination of temperaments. There is no such combination! No temperament is "better" than another, and temperament does not guarantee certain actions. An employer might reject a capable worker by jumping to a false conclusion about his temperament, and neither the young woman nor the employer has allowed for the transforming influence of the Holy Spirit.

The theory of the four temperaments is only a therapeutic tool. Whether used on others or on one's self, it should always be used gently, generally, and constructively. Here is a good rule to follow: don't analyze a person's temperament unless it will help you relate better to him, and don't tell a person his temperament unless he asks.

Another damaging use of the temperaments theory is to use it as an excuse for your behavior. Frequently people tell me, "The reason I do that is because I am a — temperament and can't help myself." That is self-deceit inspired by the devil. In addition, it is disbelief in God! Philippians 4:13 is either true or false: "I can do all things through Christ which strengtheneth me." If it is false, we cannot depend upon the Word of God. But since the Bible is true, God does supply all our need. Temperament may explain our behavior, but it never excuses it! Yet it is amazing how many people use it in that way. Consider the following statements made in the counseling room.

Mr. Sanguine, after an extramarital affair almost ruined his home, admitted, "I know I shouldn't have done it, but I'm a Sanguine and tend to be weak when exposed to sexual temptations." That was a cowardly way of saying: "It's God's fault—he made me this way!" Mr. Choleric, after being told that his angry outbursts had destroyed his unusual potential as a Bible teacher and Christian worker, announced: "I am a striker; I've always been a striker. When people cross me I tell them off!" That retort is characteristically choleric, but not the response of a Spirit-controlled Choleric.

Mrs. Melancholy came in for counseling after her husband left her and their three children. There was no other woman in his life— he simply felt compelled to leave. In parting he observed, "Since nothing I do ever pleases you, I've decided to get out of your life and let you find someone that doesn't have all my faults!" Through her tears this woman admitted, "I love my husband and I didn't mean to find fault with him all the time, but I'm a perfectionist and he is very careless. I feel that it's just as bad to think a thing as to say it, so I always told him when he was wrong—I just couldn't help it." A rather high price to pay for indulging in a selfish fixation, wouldn't you say?

Mr. Phlegmatic, whose desperate wife finally induced him to come for counseling, admitted that he had built a silent sound chamber for his psyche and crawled into it whenever his wife was around. Moderately friendly to others, at home he was the original "stone face." His outgoing wife found this intolerable. His response: "I'm an easygoing person that doesn't like turmoil and bickering. Rather than get into a feud, I just remain silent." This is a good way to induce ulcers not only in a mate, but in the Phlegmatic. Escape from reality behind a self-imposed wall of silence is not compatible with a father's role of leadership in the home.

These are examples of excuses used to justify self-centered behavior. Little or no cure can be effected until a person is willing to acknowledge that he has a problem. Instead of blaming one's temperament for aberrant behavior, the individual must recognize his natural weaknesses and let the Holy Spirit change them. Behavior does not reflect only temperament, but more significantly one's habit patterns. Temperament starts us out on a pattern of behavior; habit perpetuates and broadens it. A Christian is not a slave to habit! Habits—even life-long ones—can be changed by the divine Source of power within the Christian.

Discern your temperament

The best use of the temperament concept is possible only when you accurately discern your own temperament. For a complete study of the four temperaments see my book *Spirit-Controlled Temperament*.

After carefully examining the temperament chart here, you may find your dominant temperament (or temperaments) by making a list of the traits that stand out in your life. Name your strengths first because it is easier to be objective about your strengths than your weaknesses. Once you have determined your strengths, find the corresponding weaknesses on the wheel. Many people are prone to change their minds when they examine the weaknesses, but it is best to resist this temptation and realistically face your shortcomings.

There are several factors to keep in mind when trying to discern your temperament. The most important is that *no one is characterized by just one temperament.* Since our parents and even our grandparents contribute to our makeup, everyone is a blend of at least two and sometimes three temperaments. The failure of Immanuel Kant and his European followers to allow for this fact, along with the advent of Freudian psychoanalysis, caused the concept to fall into disrepute. Kant's arbitrary insistence that everyone fit into one or the other of these four temperaments did not stand up under close scrutiny.

Everyone I have ever counseled has revealed traits of more than one temperament. However, one temperament will usually be more prominent than the other. For example, a Sanguine-Choleric may be 60 percent Sanguine and 40 percent Choleric. A Melancholy-Choleric may be 70 percent Melancholy and 30 percent Choleric. It is even possible that a person may be 50 percent Phlegmatic, 30 percent Sanguine and 20 percent Melancholy. I have had no success in trying to establish amounts or percentages of temperament, but the more dominant one temperament is, the easier it is to diagnose the personality. Sometimes it is impossible to determine the secondary temperament. Naturally, a person with two prominent temperaments or a combination of three temperaments would be difficult to diagnose.

A compensating reality for a person whose blend of temperaments makes analysis difficult is that he will not be extreme in any direction. If his strengths are not too apparent, neither will be his weaknesses. Therefore, there is no need for him to be frustrated because he lacks distinctive temperament traits. Such a person is perfectly normal, although in my experience quite rare.

Spiritual maturity

One factor commonly overlooked by Christians trying to analyze their temperaments is the modifying or maturing work already accomplished by the Holy Spirit. Temperament is based on the raw material with which we were born. Consequently the more spiritually mature a Christian is, the more difficult it is to diagnose the basic temperament. It is helpful, therefore, to examine the psychic raw material as it was before the Holy Spirit began his work.

When I went to a Midwest church for a family life and prophecy

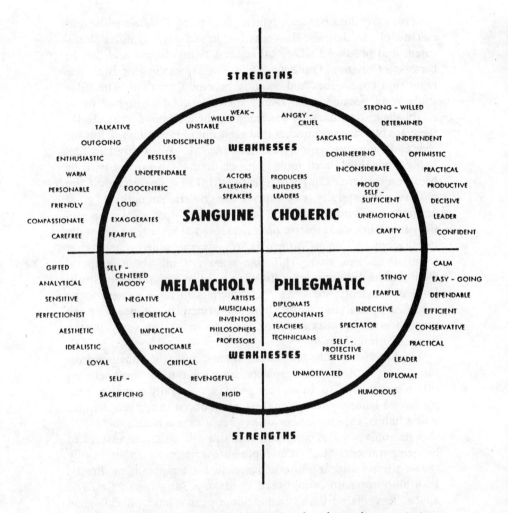

conference, the man in charge met me at the plane. At seventy-two he was the sweetest, most gracious, Spirit-filled Christian gentleman I had ever met. During the week I discovered that as president of one of the largest furniture companies in the world, he was unusually successful. The more I learned about him, the more confused I became. As a rule, phlegmatic men don't buy a bankrupt company in the middle of the depression and build it into a dynamic enterprise. That is something a Choleric would do. As I talked with his friends, the story gradually unfolded.

In his early days he was a typical, fire-eating Choleric with some melancholic tendencies. He worked night and day, organized, innovated, and produced where others had failed. In the mid-'30s he became a Christian. Quite by accident he began teaching Bible one night to a couple that had recently become Christians. The Bible study soon became a class, and then a special night had to be established. Eventually he was teaching three classes a week. Today there are two strong churches that grew out of these classes. But the change in him was equally exciting. As "the Word dwelt in him richly," the Holy Spirit molded his choleric temperament until he became a modern example of Spirit-controlled temperament. If you observe him carefully, you can see the choleric strengths of good organization and promotion ability, hard-driving, purposeful Christian work and creative optimism, even at seventy-two. Totally lacking are the anger, bitterness, resentment, cruelty, and other forms of choleric flesh. This man knew nothing about temperament, but he did know what it was to be filled with the Holy Spirit. So it isn't essential to know the principles of temperament to be modified by the Holy Spirit, but such principles will point up the greatest areas of weaknesses in our lives so we can speed up the process of modification.

Another factor to be considered when diagnosing your temperament is age. Most temperaments are easiest to discern between fifteen and thirty-five. From that point on, generally speaking, people have a tendency to become less pronounced in all their actions, unless habits, experiences, or other pressures accentuate them.

A person's physical condition will also affect the expressions of his temperament. High blood pressure can make an ordinarily sedate person appear more active than his temperament directs. Low blood pressure would tend to make a Sanguine or Choleric appear less intense than others. Some people have physiological structures that create nervous tensions—this will affect the expressions of their temperaments.

Sometimes childhood training forms early impressions and habits that make the secondary temperament seem dormant. When set free from these inhibitions by the Holy Spirit, the personality will show a marked change. My loving wife is an example.

She was raised in a rather strict environment and, during the early years of our marriage, was dominated a good deal by fear. If I had diagnosed her temperament at that time, I would have considered her about 70 percent Phlegmatic and 30 percent Sanguine. Those who knew her considered her a sweet quiet, and gracious young lady. Six years ago she had the experience of being truly filled with the Holy Spirit. The change in her has been thrilling. I have watched a very fine person become a wonderful, exciting woman. The fears that had long enslaved her have largely been laid aside, causing a new release of pent-up sanguine impulses that formerly were squelched. I have watched my timid wife, who used to say, "I would be petrified if I had to speak to an audience," or "My husband is the speaker in our family," become a dynamic women's speaker who captivates an audience. Phlegmatics don't do that, but Sanguines do. As if witnessing a rosebud open into a beautiful flower, I have watched God take my reserved wife, who went four years without being asked to address small women's groups in our own church, take speaking engagements all over the West Coast. The last time I met her at the airport coming back from another state, I remarked, "If this keeps up I will soon be known as the husband of Beverly LaHaye."

Speaking is only one area of change in this former Phlegmatic-Sanguine. Old friends who see her today can hardly believe the outgoing, dynamic person she has become. If I were to diagnose her temperament at this stage of her life, I would be inclined to say she was more a Sanguine than a Phlegmatic—perhaps 55 percent Sanguine and 45 percent Phlegmatic. Naturally, much of the change in her reflects the modification of the Holy Spirit, but part of it is due to the elimination of childhood attitudes and habits that inhibited her sanguine temperament. The reason I know this change has been accomplished by the Holy Spirit is that her sanguine modifications have all been in the direction of strength. To my knowledge she has developed none of the characteristic weaknesses of the Sanguine.

This life points up the importance of childhood training. Next to leading your child to Christ, the greatest thing you can give him is an environment of love and understanding where he is at liberty to be himself. That does not mean indulgence, nor does it preclude discipline, but it does require that parents not force upon their children their own temperament hangups, but exercise patience, love, understanding, and self-control as it comes from the Holy Spirit. Every child must be treated as an individual. Some children must be disciplined severely in love, whereas others may be brought into line with only a disapproving look. But parents in particular need to be Spirit-controlled, that their prize possessions may grow up to fulfill all the potential of their individual abilities.

Another factor that can affect a person's behavior and create an erroneous impression of his natural temperament is trauma, either from a single experience or a series of events. These are more predominant in the fear areas, causing the individual to withdraw or recoil. For instance, some people who would ordinarily speak in public have had a traumatic experience that keeps them from trying. If a child attempts a part in the school play and is ridiculed instead of commended, he may develop a lifelong inhibition. Some people, when ill at ease, react nervously through inappropriate laughter or some other form of irregular behavior.

One Sanguine on the verge of a nervous breakdown at eight years of age was completely warped in personality. Instead of being a carefree, happy-go-lucky little chap, he was sullen most of the time. Anyone examining him in that condition would have concluded immediately that he was a very melancholy child. In reality, he had little or no melancholy temperament. The problem was his traumatic home life. His parents were divorced, but before their separation he was a constant witness to their endless feuds. This broke his sense of security, and when they took out their frustrations on him by screaming every time he made a noise or did something that displeased them, he built a protective shell around himself and nursed his grudges. I saw very little hope for the boy when the mother and the new stepfather brought him in. But after the parents received Christ, and as they grew in grace and knowledge of him, they showered the boy with the love and patience he desperately needed. The transformation is a testimony to the power of God. Today he is a senior in high school, and you would never suspect that this fun-loving young man was once a withdrawn eight-year-old. Obviously the love of Christ flowing through parents to children makes a difference in the way they develop.

One harmful misconception of temperament is that one type is better than another or that one combination is preferable to another. Kant thought the choleric was the best. Preacher Alexander Whyte preferred the sanguine-phlegmatic because it was outgoing and congenial, yet controlled. But God has made us all for "his good pleasure." No matter who we are, we possess strengths and weaknesses. The greater the weakness traits, the greater the strength traits. That is why highly gifted people often have so many emotional problems. If you are a person of great strengths, you will have great weaknesses. If you have average strengths, you will have average weaknesses. In addition, because "the pasture is always greener on the other side," people tend to want to be something they are not. I have seldom talked to a person who admitted, "I'm glad I am of the temperament I am," for we are all aware of our shortcomings and weaknesses. Unfortunately, we frequently magnify them and do not appreciate our strengths. This together with the power of habit can make anyone feel that his is the least desirable temperament of all.

Actually, the nature of one's temperament is incidental. If you have received Jesus Christ as your Lord and Savior, you have his Holy Spirit within you. He can so modify your weaknesses that the positive man or woman God wants you to be will dominate. Spirit-filled Christians are walking examples of transformed temperaments.

In the revelation of God's will for man found in the Bible, we read the accounts of many spiritual leaders. Several of these characters are classic examples of God's power to transform human temperament. We shall examine four such men in the remaining chapters. Please bear in mind that the modifying work of God in each of these men is available to you. Repeatedly God said to Bible characters, "I am the God of Abraham, Isaac and Jacob . . ." meaning that his power was constant from one generation to another. In the New Testament we read that the Lord Jesus ". . . is the same yesterday, today, and forever." Since the power that transformed men in both the Old and New Testaments is available to us today, we can profit by seeing how God changed them.

3

PETER THE SANGUINE

Sanguine Peter is probably the best-loved character in the New Testament. The reason is quite simple. Because he is a complete extrovert, his shortcomings are open for everyone to see. As Peter impetuously stumbles through the pages of the Gospels, we see raw sanguine flesh. He is lovable and laughable one minute, downright disgusting the next. Peter is without question the most sanguine character in the Bible. Before proceeding farther we should examine the qualities of the sanguine temperament.

Mr. Sanguine is a warm, friendly, outgoing person who draws people like a magnet. He is a good talker, a happy-go-lucky optimist, "the life of the party." He is generous and compassionate, responsive to his surroundings and the moods or feelings of others. However, like the other three temperaments he has some natural weaknesses. He is often weak-willed, emotionally unstable and explosive, restless and egotistical. Voted "most likely to succeed" in his youth, he rarely measures up to expectations. He has great difficulty following through on details and is almost never quiet. Beneath his bold exterior he is often insecure and fearful. Sanguines make good salesmen, speakers, actors and, less frequently, leaders.

The Apostle Peter is the most prominent man in the four Gospels, aside from Jesus Christ, and is given considerable space in the first ten chapters of the book of Acts. He spoke more frequently than the other disciples and the Lord conversed more regularly with him. No disciple is given more severe reproof by our Lord, except Judas Iscariot, and, as far as we know, no other disciple had the effrontery to rebuke the Lord. On the other hand, no other disciple gave such outspoken testimony of his respect and love for Christ, and no other received such personal praise from the Savior.

Peter has a "charisma" about him that draws one to him, whether a first-century contemporary or a twentieth-century reader. That sanguine quality is probably what made Hippocrates determine that the temperament was caused by "warm blood." Certainly Peter exhibited warmth, intensity, and dynamic action. Alexander Whyte said of him, "The worst disease of the human heart is cold. Well, with all his faults, and he was full of them, a cold heart was not one of them. All Peter's faults, indeed, lay in the heat of his heart. He was too hot-hearted, too impulsive, too enthusiastic. His hot heart was always in his mouth, and he spoke it all out many a time when he should have held his peace." Peter was one of those transparent people who never kept his friends in doubt about his thoughts—he just blurted them out! This intense extrovertish tendency makes him the easiest temperament in the Bible to pick out.

The only person who finds it difficult to diagnose a sanguine temperament is Mr. Sanguine himself. He rarely scrutinizes his thoughts or actions but simply erupts as he bounds from one crisis to another. Many a Sanguine has sparked peals of laughter from his friends by declaring, "I just can't figure out which temperament I am." He is invariably the only one in doubt. Evidently he has very little analytical ability and is not given to self-examination or introspection.

Peter leaves the impression of a man of great physical stature as he strides through the first five books of the New Testament. We have no way of knowing, of course, since no description of him is given. Swashbuckling Sanguines who "make history rather than write it" usually are big men, and Peter was a swashbuckler! No matter what he did in life, Peter became the leader—he was born that way.

The completeness of the biblical record on Sanguine Peter makes him an excellent subject for this study. It is easy to diagnose his strengths and weaknesses, and the book of Acts offers enough details to demonstrate how the Holy Spirit strengthened his weaknesses. Instead of experiencing the usual frustrating futility of most Sanguines, Peter was so strengthened when filled with the Spirit that he stands as one of the most successful Sanguines we know. Not only was he the most influential man in the early church, but he continues to be a challenge to Christians as an example of what the Holy Spirit can do in the life of any man who will surrender to him.

Impulsive

When Andrew first brought his sanguine brother Simon to Jesus, he seemed anything but a promising spiritual leader. To the contrary, he was a boisterous, profane, opinionated fisherman whose most notable trait was impulsiveness. Whenever Peter acted, he acted instantaneously, now—or "straightway," as the Scripture states it. Whenever the conversational ball stopped bouncing, Peter picked it up. That is how he got his foot in his mouth so many times. He has often been called "the spokesman of the disciples." In fact, the words "then saith Peter" introduce more speeches than are recorded by all the other disciples together.

When Jesus called Peter, as described in Matthew 4:20, his impulsive response was to "straightway drop his nets and follow him." When Jesus' travels brought the disciples near Peter's home, he impulsively invited them all over to his house, not taking into consideration the fact that his mother-in-law was sick in bed (Mark 1:29). However, as so often occurs in the life of a Christian Sanguine, the Lord intervened, and this time he miraculously healed the woman, who then helped Peter's wife with the serving.

The impetuous sanguine temperament of Peter is clearly seen the night the Lord Jesus came to the disciples walking on the water. "And Peter . . . said, Lord, if it be thou, bid me come unto thee on the water. And . . . he walked on the water, to go to Jesus" (Matthew 14:28,29). Who but an impulsive, boyish Sanguine would want to leave the safety of the boat to walk on top of the water?

This story also illustrates a common but less apparent trait of the Sanguine. In spite of his loud bravado, the Sanguine is generally quite fearful. He leaps before he looks and then becomes apprehensive about the consequences. That is exactly what happened to Peter. Having taken only a few steps on the water, instead of looking at the Lord, "when he saw the wind boisterous, he was afraid; and beginning to sink, he cried, saying, Lord, save me. And immediately Jesus stretched forth his hand, and caught him, and said unto him, O thou of little faith, why didst thou doubt?"

This common tendency of the Sanguine to leap before looking and then tremble at the possible consequences will be changed when the Holy Spirit fills his life. He will become "peaceful" and "self-controlled." He will "wait on the Lord" instead of going off half-cocked in every direction. Instead of becoming fearful, he will keep his eyes on the Lord rather than on his circumstances. Anyone who looks at circumstances will have doubts, but Peter is a good example of what to do when doubt, fear, or anxiety overtake you. He cried, "Lord save me," and Christ did.

Lest we are too unkind to Peter over his unbelief in this event, I would call your attention to the fact that he had enough faith at least to climb out of the boat onto the boisterous sea. That is more than can be said for the other disciples, some of whom could have profited from a little of his venturesome spirit.

One of Peter's outbursts offers us a humorous glimpse of his compulsion to talk. As one of the three favored disciples, Peter, together with James and John, was invited by the Lord to go up the Mount of Transfiguration (Matthew 17:1-13). Jesus was "transfigured before them; and his face did shine like the sun. . . ." These three men were given the privilege of seeing our Lord's divine glory shine through his humanity. Then Moses and Elijah, two of the most respected men in the history of Israel, appeared "talking with them." Moved beyond control, as the Bible tells us, "Then answered Peter, and said unto Jesus, Lord, it is good for us to be here; if thou wilt, let us make here three tents; one for you, and one for Moses, and one for Elijah."

Whenever Mr. Sanguine doesn't know what to do, he talks. You can depend on him to break any period of strained silence with words—often ill-timed, unnecessary, or wrong. Such was the case with Peter. No one had asked him a question, yet he "answered" them. If ever there was a time for a man to keep his big mouth shut, this was it. But that didn't hinder Sanguine Peter. He had to say something, so he blurted out, "Lord, it is good for us to be here!" Isn't that classic? Here he is, treated to the rare privilege of seeing two men who died a thousand years earlier, and Peter blurts out, "It is good to be here." But that isn't enough, for our compulsive talker proceeds to suggest that they build three tents. Apparently it did not occur to him that the spirits of dead men don't need tents, and staying on top of the mountain would defeat our Lord's purpose in coming. Oh, I know Peter meant well—Mr. Sanguine usually does—but that doesn't change the fact that his ill-considered, impulsive ideas are often misdirected. On this occasion, he was so mistaken that Almighty God himself sounded from heaven the words, "This is my beloved Son, in whom I am well pleased; hear ye him!" Peter should have been listening, not talking.

The best-known illustration of Peter's impulsiveness occurred in the Garden of Gethsemane. The Lord Jesus had just drunk the "cup" of the new covenant in his blood and was ready to offer himself as the sacrifice for the sins of the world. Then "a great multitude with swords and clubs, from the chief priests and elders of the people," came out to take him by force. John tells us (18:10) that "Simon Peter, having a sword, drew it, and smote the high priest's servant, and cut off his right ear." Peter, of course, was a fisherman, not a swordsman. He probably aimed at his victim's head, but either the man ducked or Peter was out of practice, for all he got was an ear. Matthew suggests the reason for Peter's action when the Lord Jesus asked, "Thinkest thou that I cannot now pray to my Father, and he shall presently give me more than twelve legions of angels?" (26:53). That was Peter's problem—he just didn't think! Sanguines are activists, not thinkers. When the pressure is on, they must do something.

This lack of reflective thinking cheats many a Sanguine out of rich blessings in life. For instance, when Peter and the other disciples were brooding over the death of our Lord, some women came to report that they had been to the sepulcher, found it empty, and encountered an angel there who said, "He is not here; for he is risen, as he said" (Matthew 28:6). In characteristic manner, Peter rushed off to the tomb. John outran him, being a younger man, but he paused at the entrance of the empty tomb. When Peter arrived, he pushed past John and hurried into the tomb. Unlike John, who saw the evidence and believed that Christ had risen (John 20:8), Peter's emotions veiled the significance of the evidence that made a believer of John, and he went away sorrowful and confused. Only after the Lord appeared to him personally was Peter convinced that he had risen from the dead.

Another charming story which reveals Peter's impulsiveness occurred on the Sea of Galilee, after the resurrection of Christ. John tells us (21:1-11) of Peter's decision, "I go a fishing." As on a previous occasion, they "fished all night and caught nothing." Then Jesus appeared on the shore and called out to "cast the net on the right side of the boat, and ye shall find." They did, and suddenly they caught so many fish in their net that they were unable to pull it into the boat. John exclaimed, "It is the Lord!" When Peter heard that, he forgot all about the fish, cinched his cloak around him, and dived into the water to swim to Jesus. A typical Sanguine, he left the job unfinished when something more attractive appeared. We commend Peter for his love for Christ on this occasion, but he left the work to others, though he did lend them a hand when they came closer to shore. Sanguines are not lazy, but they tend to jump from one thing to another; they have a short interest span in one subject.

Uninhibited

Not all of Peter's impetuous actions were negative in effect. On several occasions he did or said the unexpectedly wonderful thing that warms your heart as you read the story. Sanguines have that pleasant capacity. Just about the time you are annoyed at their thoughtlessness, they do something that inspires your affection, and Peter was like that. It is very difficult not to love a Sanguine—often in spite of himself.

One such episode took place in the early days of our Lord's ministry (Luke 5:1-11). The people gathered close to him as he taught by the Sea of Galilee, so he stepped into Simon's boat and asked him to push it a little off shore. When he finished his message, Jesus turned to Peter and said, "Launch out into the deep, and let down your nets for a draught." Sanguine Simon, in a state of discouragement, replied, "Master, we have toiled all night, and have taken nothing." But right here one of his sanguine traits stood him in good stead, for Sanguines love to please. They delight in accommodating people and will often do anything rather than displease someone. Consequently he added, "Nevertheless, at thy word I will let down the net." No sooner had he let down his net than "they enclosed a great multitude of fishes; and their net broke . . . so that the boat began to sink."

Then it was that Sanguine Simon impulsively did something that endears him to the Christian's heart. Unashamedly and emotionally, in front of all his friends, he ". . . fell down at Jesus' knees, saying, Depart from me; for I am a sinful man, O Lord." This uninhibited bit of exhibitionism is typical of the Sanguine. Most people think Mr. Sanguine is a hypocrite or perhaps insincere because of his forthright public actions. That isn't true. He is a very uninhibited person and therefore tends impulsively to do whatever comes into his mind. It probably bothers him later, but at the moment he sincerely exhibits his internal self. Doubtless, such was the case with Simon as he forgot all others and openly worshiped the Lord. Evidence of his sincerity is found in the fact that only a short time later he heeded the Master's call to leave his nets and follow him.

Outspoken

Another positive effect of Peter's impulsive tongue is found in Matthew 16:13-20. About midway in our Lord's three and one-half-year ministry he asked his disciples who men thought he was. They responded, "Some say thou art John the Baptist; some, Elijah; and others, Jeremiah, or one of the prophets." Then Jesus asked, "But whom say ye that I am?" Simon Peter instantly responded, "Thou art the Christ, the Son of the living God." This beautiful testimony so delighted the Savior that he replied, "Blessed art thou, Simon . . . flesh and blood has not revealed it unto you, but my Father, who is in heaven." Peter's testimony to Jesus' identity was the clearest given to that point in the Lord's life. It demonstrates that even then God was speaking to Peter's heart. Because Sanguines have a great capacity to respond enthusiastically to heart motivation, their hearts will compel them to walk in God's ways, if they will let God speak to them regularly from his Word. However, since the mind as well as experiences cause the heart to feel, it is very important to check the thoughts a Sanguine permits in his mind. I doubt that Peter premeditated his answer. He was not an analyzer, but he had heard Christ's matchless teachings and had seen his uniquely holy life for almost two years. He felt in his heart that this man was more than human—he was divine. So when asked the question, Peter simply stated how he felt. We are all indebted to Sanguine Simon for his inspiring answer.

Of all the events in the life of the sanguine apostle, my favorite is found in John 6:66-69. If this were the only event given of Peter's life, I think I could love him for this alone. The Lord Jesus was divine when he walked this earth, but he was also genuinely human. He was human enough to "hunger," to be "tired," to become "sorrowful," to "weep," and to be "moved with compassion." Such a time John relates to us toward the end of his ministry.

Many wanted to follow Jesus to receive the "loaves and fishes" and his healings, whereas Jesus wanted people to worship him for who he was and the truth he gave. So he started to emphasize the difficulties his followers would encounter if they decided to truly accept and follow him. This was too hard for many of them, for we read, From that time many of his disciples went back, and walked no more with him." In what must have been a deep note of sadness, the Master turned to the twelve and inquired, "Will you also go away?" It was lovable, impulsive Peter who broke the silence with the immortal words, "Lord, to whom shall we go? Thou hast the words of eternal life! And we believe and are sure that thou art that Christ, the Son of the living God." In almost two thousand years, no man has eclipsed that classic statement.

Yes, Peter was all heart. But whenever that heart was fixed on Jesus Christ, he was 100 percent right. On the other hand, whenever his heart was fixed on others or himself, he was wrong. That problem is not limited to Sanguines! The success of any Christian's life is determined by the direction of his heart. That is why the Holy Spirit instructs us: "Set your affections on things above, not on things on the earth."

Egotistical

Another tendency of a sanguine person is egotism. Typical of the Sanguine, Peter couldn't stand success without letting it go to his head. In the very same chapter that Matthew told of Peter's excellent confession (Matthew 16), we see his tragic downfall. The Lord praised him in verse 17 for what he said and promised to give him "the keys to the kingdom of heaven." Later Peter, when filled with the Holy Spirit, used these keys in preaching the gospel to the Jews (Acts 2) and in first preaching the gospel to the Gentiles (Acts 10). But the fervent Sanguine had the gall to rebuke his Lord.

After Peter's confession, the Lord Jesus apparently began to prepare his disciples for the real purpose of his coming. He informed them that he "must go unto Jerusalem, and suffer many things from the elders and chief priests and scribes, and be killed, and be raised again the third day." Up to this point, Peter had accepted everything the Lord Jesus said, but the prospect of his death shocked Peter. He rejected the possibility so vehemently that he didn't seem to hear the Savior promise to ". . . rise again the third day." Sanguine Simon got so excited that he actually laid hands on Jesus, for it says, "Peter took him, and began to rebuke him. . . ." Whereas a few moments before he had acknowledged Jesus as the "Son of the living God," now he tried to correct him. The egotistical Sanguine proceeded to tell "the Christ, the Son of the living God" what to do. He exclaimed, "Be it far from thee, Lord; this shall not be unto thee" (Matthew 16:22). Sanguine Simon was wrong, for it did happen to him—Jesus was crucified. In fact, if it hadn't happened, we could never receive the forgiveness of sins.

Peter's impulsive action, motivated by egotism, earned him the most severe rebuke our Lord gave anyone except Judas Iscariot and the Pharisees. Turning to his sanguine disciple, the Lord charged, "Get thee behind me, Satan. Thou art an offense unto me; for thou savorest not the things that are of God, but those that are of men." Peter's spirit must have been crushed by the rebuke. The Bible doesn't tell us, but he probably moped for a while; Sanguines usually do. They tend to be easily offended, though they recover before long.

This story provides us with an excellent illustration of a common problem of the Sanguine. Peter's tendency toward egotism made him vulnerable to the devil's darts of pride. The lord revealed that Satan gave Peter those words. Years later Peter offered some instruction in his first epistle (5:5-9) that may hark back to this event. He pictures the devil as "a roaring lion" who "walketh about, seeking whom he may devour."

When we read that text we may think of the devil trying to get Christians to deny the Lord, commit adultery, or perform some other gross form of sin. But Peter was writing about humility: "Humble yourselves, therefore, under the mighty hand of God . . ." Peter realized through his experience that the devil roars around seeking to fan egotistical inclinations into pride. But "pride bringeth a snare." Peter's fall was caused by letting the devil take the Lord's words of praise and fan them into a raging fire of pride. When we harbor pride, we quench the Holy Spirit's inward working, and soon pride is expressed in action that dishonors Christ. Egotistical Simon should stand as a warning that we resist this tendency to be proud, for in doing so we also resist the devil. Incidentally, Sanguines do not have a monopoly on this weakness.

Self-seeking

By nature Mr. Sanguine is very generous. If he sees someone in need, his emotional response is usually one of compassion. During the great depression, my sanguine father, with a wife and three children at home, was so moved by a cold, hungry boy that he impulsively gave him the last quarter he had in his pocket. That was commendable generosity motivated by the heart, not the mind. No doubt Peter was like that. But there is also tendency for Mr. Sanguine to feel insecure. This anxiety, together with a desire for prominence, probably caused Peter to make a self-seeking request.

The Lord Jesus used the "rich young ruler" as an example to teach his disciples how difficult it is for people who love their possessions to enter the kingdom of heaven. The sanguine disciple then asked, "Behold, we have forsaken all, and followed thee. What shall we have, therefore?" (Matthew 19:27). This selfish thought was probably not unique to Peter, but it took a Sanguine to verbalize it. The Lord's reply reveals the nature of the true weakness when he said, "Many that are first shall be last, and the last shall be first." What was Peter's real problem? He was a first-century status seeker. There must be a little Sanguine in every man, because who can say he has never asked that very human question, "What am I going to get out of this?" Only the Holy Spirit can give us that consistent spirit of self-sacrifice so essential to an effective Christian.

Braggart

One of Mr. Sanguine's most apparent faults is his tendency to brag. Whatever he does or has is "the best." Even when he is successful, his temptation to brag or exaggerate makes his accomplishments disappointing. Give him enough rope and he will verbally hang himself. Such was the case that memorable night in the upper room when the Lord Jesus warned his disciples, "All ye shall be offended because of me this night; for it is written, I will smite the shepherd, and the sheep of the flock shall be scattered abroad" (Matthew 26:31). Blustering Peter couldn't let that prediction go unchallenged. Once again he contradicted the Lord by loudly proclaiming, "Though all men shall be offended because of thee, yet will I never be offended." The Lord then proceeded to tell Peter very pointedly that "before the cock crows, thou shalt deny me thrice." The sanguine one offered a very characteristic and vehement response: "Though I should die with thee, yet will I not deny thee." Doesn't that sound impressive? But the highway to success is not laid on a foundation of good intentions.

Peter's response on this occasion was sincere. One of the most misunderstood traits of a sanguine person is his sincerity. Have you ever noticed how quick and loud Mr. Sanguine is at making promises or commitments? When he doesn't follow through, or fails to pay, or arrives late, he gets the reputation of being insincere. Actually, he was very sincere when he made the promise—sincerely a Sanguine, that is. At the moment, in the upper room, being faithful to Jesus was all-important to Peter because he was in the Lord's presence. But Sanguines are very responsive to their environment. Away from the Lord, Mr. Sanguine was not able to keep his promise.

Weak-willed

Doubtless Mr. Sanguine usually means well. But one of his most serious difficulties is his weakness of will. Many a Sanguine is considered "a weak character" or "all mouth" by his contemporaries because he folds when the pressure is on. That weakness of will is probably what keeps him from reacting well under pressure.

Many a Sanguine will spontaneously lie under pressure rather than face shame or penalty. He will be sorry immediately, but unless strengthened by the Holy Spirit he will not have enough self-control to keep from doing the same thing again. Unaided by the power of God, Mr. Sanguine usually ensnares his carefree life with a tangled web of complexities.

Often in the counseling room, a very upset Mr. or Mrs. Sanguine has confessed a tragic series of events. Married to a loyal and faithful companion (opposites tend to attract each other), the Sanguine has committed the scarlet sin of adultery. It is an old story that comes through their tears. "I meant to keep my wedding vows!" is the piteous cry, and doubtless he did. But Mr. Sanguine's weakness of will makes it easy to forget past affirmations and intentions under the pressure of present temptation. One Sanguine businessman told me, "I love my wife and kids, but they were at home and that beautiful secretary was with me all day!" One thing I have noticed about sexual sins—they are invariably followed by lies and all kinds of deception. One lie leads to another, and it isn't long before Mr. Sanguine's short memory causes him to contradict himself. As the Bible says, "Be sure your sins will find you out."

Interestingly, Mr. Sanguine is usually relieved when he finally gets caught. The reason is quite simple: he can't stand pressure. The tangled web woven by unfaithfulness in marriage creates more guilt-pressure than the Sanguine can take. Being an emotional person, his repentance is accompanied by profuse weeping. Like Peter, Mr. Sanguine repents sincerely, and when he is filled with the Holy Spirit, tragedy can result in a life-changing experience; however, it is very important for him to realize that it isn't his strong resolutions or good intentions that produce consistency in his life. It is the Holy Spirit! Without the Holy Spirit, Mr. Sanguine cannot be trusted; but worse than that, he cannot trust himself.

Simon's denial

It is tragically true that the good things people do are not as well known as the bad. The one event best known in the life of our Lord's sanguine friend is his betrayal of the Savior. As Judas is known as "the disciple who betrayed him," Peter is known as "the disciple who denied him." All four Gospels tell us the shameful story. It may be that the Holy Spirit gave it four times to impress on us that God can take the most inconsistent and spineless lump of clay and fashion it into a mighty man of God.

A careful analysis of the events that surrounded Peter's denial supplies many interesting clues to the weakness of Mr. Sanguine. No one is more easily influenced by his environment than a Sanguine. That fact is not apparent when you first meet him. He comes on strong, almost overpowering sometimes, and gives the impression that he can master any situation. But that is not the case. Mr. Sanguine desperately needs the warmth of Christian fellowship.

In Peter's case, his troubles began when he left the disciples and joined the company of the enemy. "And the servants and officers stood there, who had made a fire of coals; for it was cold, and they warmed themselves; and Peter stood with them, and warmed himself" (John 18:18). It is always dangerous for a Christian to warm his hands at the enemy's fire, but particularly is that true of a Sanguine. He is sensitive to his associates and tends to adapt to their ways rather than stand alone in a crowd. Sanguines can act one way with one group of friends and quite another with a different group.

Matthew tells us that as Peter warmed his hands, a maid came by and said, "Thou also wast with Jesus of Galilee. But he denied it before them all, saying, I know not what thou sayest" (Matthew 26:69-70). The pressure of the group was too much for Sanguine Peter, and thus he denied the Lord whom he loved. He left the fire and walked out on the porch while Jesus was being tried inside. Then, "another maid saw him, and said unto them that were there, This fellow was also with Jesus of Nazareth. And again he denied with an oath, I do not know the man."

Many Sanguines since Peter have entertained the idea that if they could get off the hook just this once, then they would submit to God. Unfortunately, compromise never meets the standard. A small compromise may initiate a big compromise. Sooner or later we have to resist the pressure around us and take a stand, Happy is the man who learns that the sooner he faces the issue, the better off he is. Peter's instinctive desire to escape danger provoked him not only to repudiate allegiance to Christ, but to deny him "with an oath." He used a sign of honesty to cover his bald lie!

A short time later, others came to Peter. "Surely thou also art one of them; for thy speech betrayeth thee. Then began he to curse and swear, saying, I know not the man. And immediately the cock crowed." Peter's compulsion to talk kept him from being silent even while mingling with his enemies. Most of the people were city folk from Jerusalem, whereas Peter, from Galilee, had a different accent which "betrayed him."

An illustration of the progressive nature of sin is seen as the sanguine one, having denied his Lord twice, adds to the third denial the sin of cursing and swearing. Evidently, before his salvation Peter was a blasphemous character, often typical of the sanguine temperament. Most Sanguines tend to speak faster than they think, and in order to fill in the blank spaces they accumulate pet expressions that are often profane. Doubtless Peter did not use such language in the presence of the Lord, and possibly he had not used it for some time. But under group pressure and in a typical craving to be accepted by the people around him, Peter reached into his past and unconsciously resorted to his old language habit. When such a thing happens, a Sanguine is quick to explain, "Oh, I don't mean anything by it," but that does not change the fact that he has sinned with his tongue and publicly dishonored God.

Sanguine Simon, characteristically motivated by external stimuli, suddenly "remembered the word of Jesus" when he heard the cock crow. His reaction, recorded by all four of the Gospel writers, is typically sanguine: "And he went out, and wept bitterly." Only two temperaments in men are given to weeping: the sanguine and the melancholy. Contrary to popular notions, this does not lessen their manhood but reveals the depth of their feelings and the ability to express emotion.

Peter's bitter tears at the end of this tragic drama illustrate a typically sanguine trait. Sanguines are easy repenters. When Mr. Sanguine sins grievously, he is thoroughly remorseful when confronted with his sin or ensnared by the effects of it. Many modern Sanguines find their way to confession and sincerely weep in their expression of remorse. Observers sometimes think that depth of repentance is measured by the quantity of tears, whereas the tears only mean that Mr. Sanguine is sincere at that very moment. If he goes away to "warm his hands at the enemy's fire" again, it will be just a matter of time before he falls again.

The depth of Peter's remorse is evident in the tender scene recorded in the last chapter of the Gospel of John. After Jesus' resurrection he came to Peter and asked, "Simon Peter, lovest thou me more than these?" Peter responded, "Yes, Lord, you know that I love you." An important play on the Greek words originally used by our Lord and his sanguine apostle is not apparent in the English translation. The Lord Jesus used the word "*agape*," which is the highest form of love used in the New Testament. In fact, it is the word used in describing the love of God for man. Peter, evidently because of great remorse at his tragic denial, was reluctant to use that word. His word for love is more akin to our word "like." In fact, some translators have rendered his reply, "You know, Lord, that I am very fond of you."

The Lord Jesus asked him again, "Simon, lovest thou me? He saith unto him, "Yea, Lord, thou knowest I am fond of thee." This response is identical to the first. But the third time the Lord Jesus changed his word in the original to Peter's word and asked, "Peter, are you fond of me?" "Peter was grieved because he said unto him the third time, Lovest thou me? And he said unto him, Lord, thou knowest all things; thou knowest that I am very fond of thee." It seems that the wound of Peter's great denial was so fresh and so deep that the sanguine apostle had finally learned an invaluable lesson. Peter had discovered that he could not trust himself. The only hope for a Sanguine is in a life dependent on the Holy Spirit. Peter seemed to realize that he could not trust his emotions, therefore he was reluctant to give a glib answer and excessively commit himself. Instead, he wanted to prove his love by his actions. This life-hanging decision seems to characterize most of Peter's life from this point on, evidence that even an inconsistent Sanguine can become a stable, usable instrument when filled with the Holy Spirit.

Simon's inconsistency

The previous story and many other events in the life of Peter indicate that one of Mr. Sanguine's greatest problems is inconsistency. His life seems to be a paradox of extremes. He is hot one minute and cold the next. That Mr. Sanguine himself is displeased with this tendency and disgusted with himself because of it I have no doubt. The Lord Jesus seemed to know that the longing of Simon's sanguine heart was to be a stable individual. For that reason, he prophetically changed his name, saying, "Thou art Peter . . ." meaning, thou art a stone. That Peter became strong when filled with the Holy Spirit is now history.

When a man receives Jesus Christ into his life he becomes a "new creature." Thus he has two natures, the old and the new. Peter's two names are typical of the two natures of every believer. "Simon" represents the old sanguine nature, whereas "Peter" represents the new rocklike nature, the stable consistent man molded by the Spirit of God out of the sanguine temple of clay. However, as illustrated in the life of Peter, this change is not immediate; it is a matter of growth.

John tells us in the second chapter of his first epistle, "I have written unto you, young men, because ye are strong . . . and ye have overcome the wicked one." Baby Christians do not overcome the old nature. Only as we mature in Christ and are controlled by the Holy Spirit does the new man control the old. This change is more evident in the sanguine temperament than in any other. The reason for that is quite simple: everything the Sanguine does, whether good or bad, is conspicuous. The other, less volatile, temperaments are less noticeable in behavior. In fact, sometimes wrong conduct is not recognized as such, because it is not extreme. God, however, looks on the heart. The changing of Peter's name by the Master Changer of men is a good example of what he wants to do for every human being. The Spirit-controlled man will not cease to be "himself." We shall see that the change that eventually came into Peter's life did not eliminate his temperament, but modified it. After the filling of the Holy Spirit, Sanguine Simon no longer erupts in uncontrolled behavior. Instead, as Sanguine Peter he is controlled in his actions. The dynamic, lovable, magnetic characteristics of Sanguine Peter are still evident, as we shall see, but the weaknesses are modified by the strengths, and God is glorified in the transformation.

Peter's filling

As one of his promises to his disciples, our Lord said, "But ye shall receive power, after that the Holy Spirit is come upon you. . . ." We usually think of this power in the framework of witnessing, and certainly it means that. But that is not all it means. The power of the Holy Spirit in the life of the sanguine apostle was an obvious influence for good. That power, available to every believer today, so modified Peter that it obscured his weaknesses and revealed his strengths. As we study this Spirit-controlled Sanguine in the book of Acts, let us keep in mind that God is no respecter of persons. What he did for his sanguine apostle he will do for you if you are willing to cooperate with the Holy Spirit and let his power strengthen your weaknesses.

The first sign of change in the Apostle Peter is seen in Acts 1:15, even before the Day of Pentecost. He "stood up in the midst of the disciples" when they were gathered together for prayer while awaiting the coming of the Holy Spirit. This is Peter's first recorded sermon, apparently a funeral message for Judas Iscariot.

As we scrutinize the message we find no exaltation of Peter but, instead, a Spirit-filled message based on the Word of God, offering a practical solution to the vacancy of the traitor Judas. Peter then proposed a very practical standard for his replacement: ". . . Of these men who have companied with us all the time that the Lord Jesus went in and out among us, beginning from the baptism of John unto that same day that he was taken up from us; must one be ordained to be a witness with us of his resurrection." In other words, the twelfth apostle should have been with the other apostles all during Jesus' ministry. He then prayed and asked the Lord for wisdom. They selected two candidates and, as was their custom, relied on the Holy Spirit to choose the right one through the casting of lots. We no longer cast lots in such matters, for since the Day of Pentecost we have the indwelling Holy Spirit to guide us in making our decisions, but on that side of Pentecost, Peter's action was commendable and in keeping with Old Testament practice.

On the Day of Pentecost we get another thrilling insight into the transformation of the sanguine apostle. When the Holy Spirit came upon men, they spoke in the languages of foreign visitors to Jerusalem so that everyone heard God's message in his "own tongue." The Jerusalemites, who could not understand these languages, began to mock the disciples and jumped to the conclusion that "these men are full of new wine."

It was a Spirit-controlled Sanguine Peter who, "standing up with the eleven, lifted up his voice, and said unto them, Ye men of Judaea, and all ye that dwell at Jerusalem. . . ." and preached the first gospel sermon of the church age. His sermon is a masterpiece that cannot be explained by three years of association with Jesus Christ. Peter was an uneducated fisherman. He was not an intellectual; Sanguines rarely are. This sermon was the message of God through the instrument of Sanguine Peter, a classic example of the way God wants to use men today. As you well know if you have studied the second chapter of Acts, the result was that "the same day there were added unto them about three thousand souls. And they continued steadfastly in the apostles' doctrine and fellowship." The stumbling, inconsistent, emotionally unstable Sanguine Simon was transformed into a Spirit-controlled Sanguine Peter, a mighty preacher of the gospel.

Sanguine men usually make good speakers, but only Spirit-controlled Sanguines make good preachers. Sanguine preachers have a built-in danger. It is easy for them to speak whether or not they have anything substantial to say, for a natural Sanguine has the ability of making anything sound interesting. But a Spirit-controlled Sanguine can be a mighty influence for God.

It is not too difficult to tell when Mr. Sanguine is speaking by Spirit or the "flesh." Speaking under the influence of his sanguine temperament, he will emphasize "I" and the message will remind hearers of Shakespeare's "Words, Desdemona, words!" Like Peter on the Day of Pentecost, Mr. Sanguine under the controlling influence of the Holy Spirit will glorify Jesus Christ. The Spirit-controlled sanguine pastor will overcome his great temptation of flitting here and there in restless activity and discipline himself for sufficient study of the Word of God to deliver a message from God rather than a charismatic, spontaneous sanguine speech. Spiritually astute listeners will notice the difference.

Peter's consistency

The third chapter of Acts assures us that Peter's power on the Day of Pentecost was not an emotional outburst or a fleeting trust in God. Instead, we find Peter and John going together "into the temple at the hour of prayer." Spiritual discipline is very difficult for Mr. Sanguine, but that is the only way his inconsistency will be eliminated. Melancholy John would naturally do the right thing in going up to the house of prayer at the designated hour. But a prayer meeting is only attractive to Mr. Sanguine when he is controlled by the Holy Spirit.

Another characteristic of the Spirit is seen in this story. When he controls our lives, we are not going to be "up tight" or fearful. A fruit of the Holy Spirit is "peace." This means in a practical sense that we will be flexible and "available" to whatever the Holy Spirit would have us do. Peter and John went to the temple to pray, relaxed in the Spirit, but when they saw the crippled man begging at the gate, they were moved with compassion and their plans changed entirely. As a matter of fact, they didn't get to the temple to pray. For Peter, "fastening his eyes upon him, with John, said, Look on us. . . . Silver and gold have I none, but, such as I have, give I thee. In the name of Jesus Christ of Nazareth, rise up and walk. And he took him by the right hand, and lifted him up; and immediately his feet and ankle bones received strength."

What is missing in this story? Close scrutiny will reveal the absence of Sanguine Simon. Spirit-controlled Peter in no way seeks to glorify himself but gives all glory to the Lord Jesus Christ in the healing of this man. This seems to be a hallmark for Sanguine Peter. Led by the Holy Spirit, Peter seizes the opportunity presented by the crowd that gathers to see the healed man leaping and shouting for joy, and he preaches a marvelous sermon, showing unusual depth and understanding. The Holy Spirit's participation is seen in the results: "Many of them who heard the word believed; and the number of the men was about five thousand" (Acts 4:4).

Peter's courage

The news that thousands of people who had clamored for the death of Jesus Christ a few weeks earlier were now repenting of that sin and openly confessing him as Lord and Savior did not set well with the Jewish officials. The chief priests summoned the apostles before them for interrogation. It was Spirit-controlled Sanguine Peter who answered their charges, giving all glory to Jesus Christ. The Scripture tells us that "when they saw the boldness of Peter and John, and perceived that they were unlearned and ignorant men, they marveled; and they took knowledge of them, that they had been with Jesus."

A short time before, cowardly Peter had denied his Lord three times. Now, under even greater pressure, he boldly acknowledged Jesus Christ. His remarks do not reveal sanguine bravado, but instead a fearless commitment to a condemned Man. What made the difference in Peter's reactions under pressure? Acts 4:8 explains it clearly: "Then Peter, filled with the Holy Spirit, said unto them. . . ." Peter did not strive to gain boldness under pressure; instead he relaxed and was impelled by the Holy Spirit. This should always be the case with a Christian facing a witnessing opportunity.

A college student asked me: "Why do I always get up tight and nervous when I go to witness to someone on campus?" I explained that this common experience occurs when we are relying on our own gifts and skill, though we may be sincerely concerned. The best way to witness to our faith comes through yielding ourselves to the Holy Spirit.

If you are on an elevator with a person who may need to hear about Christ, you are not responsible to force a conversation. You are responsible, however, to make your lips available to the Holy Spirit. I used to struggle with introductory clichés or "door openers," but with very little success. The most thrilling conversions that I have witnessed have resulted from a simple prayer in the presence of a sinner, "Lord, here are my lips; if you want to use them to share Christ with this person, I'm available." I would relax, and if I found myself conversing and we verged on spiritual things, as frequently happens, I was confident the Holy Spirit was making a witness. But if the conversation didn't move into spiritual matters, though I was willing, I was equally confident that I was led by the Holy Spirit. I don't always know the mind of the Holy Spirit and what he does in and through my life, nor am I responsible for what he does. I am responsible, as Sanguine Peter was, to be available, and so are you. This kind of witnessing is more effective because it permits control by the Holy Spirit. If there must be pressure, put the "pressure" on the Holy Spirit by yielding yourself to him. He can stand pressure—you can't.

The most remarkable illustration from my own life of the Holy Spirit's using my available lips took place on a 707 jet between Chicago and San Diego. Dog-tired after a week of meetings, I boarded the plane, hoping to sleep all the way home. It was very crowded, and I happened to see a man who vaguely recognized me. He invited me to sit next to him and then suddenly turned pale, for he recalled that I was the minister who had prayed at a public meeting about a year before. If he had remembered that sooner, he never would have invited me to sit next to him.

This aeronautical engineer, who had been a squadron commander in the Air Force and was spared from death many times, was returning from a ten-day inspection tour. The last thing he wanted to do—I found out later—was talk to a minister, but he bravely and politely made the best of the situation. During the first of the four hours on that flight we got into an in-depth political conversation, one of my few secular hobbies. The conversation was so far removed from anything spiritual that I prayed, "Lord, I know you had me meet this man for a reason, but how in the world I will get the conversation around to spiritual things I cannot imagine. Here are my lips. I am available for whatever you have for us."

Within five minutes that man jumped a conversational ocean and said, "Say, you're a theologian; I wonder if you would answer a question for me. My brother-in-law has been talking to me about religion and I don't understand what he is trying to say. Would you explain to me what it means to be born again?" In more than twenty-five years of sharing Jesus Christ with individuals, I have never had a better opportunity, and it came exclusively through the power of the Holy Spirit. Long before we got to San Diego, this veteran flyer bowed his head and invited Jesus Christ into his life. The Holy Spirit isn't looking for clever people, but for available people.

Peter's wisdom

Most individuals do not think well under pressure. Usually our best ideas come long after an argument. But this was not the case with Sanguine Peter when controlled by the Holy Spirit. Under the pressure of interrogation by religious authorities, whom he had held in high esteem all his life, Peter's mind was clear as a bell. Then the authorities commanded Peter and John "not to speak at all nor teach in the name of Jesus." Peter and John did not vacillate and stammer before these brilliant leaders, nor did Peter emotionally utter things detrimental to his testimony. Instead, he said to them, "Whether it is right in the sight of God to hearken unto you more than unto God, judge ye. For we cannot but speak the things which we have seen and heard." This wisdom and emotional control is foreign not only to Sanguine Peter, but to any Sanguine. The disciples left their oppressors, celebrated by conducting a prayer meeting, and did not cease to speak "the word of God with boldness" (Acts 4:31).

Further evidence of the divine perception given to Sanguine Peter, the leader of the early Church, is seen in the unique way he handled the Ananias and Sapphira affair in Acts 5. There was no bitterness nor animosity in the way he dealt with them, but these two who had defrauded the Spirit before the people were exposed and slain as an example to the early Church. The whole thing was handled in a moderate manner that was foreign to Sanguine Simon but a common experience to Spirit-controlled Sanguine Peter.

Another example of Spirit-inspired wisdom occurred when Peter stood before the council and was rebuked by the high priest for trying to "bring this man's blood upon us." Peter did not become angry, as was his sanguine inclination, but instead, under the control of the Spirit, he wisely answered, "We ought to obey God rather than man."

Even when pressured by man to do wrong, the Spirit-controlled Christian does not have to get upset, resentful, or vitriolic. He can always do right without grieving the Holy Spirit. Sanguines must bear this in mind concerning flesh-motivated anger. Since "God's grace is sufficient for you" under all circumstances, you never have to "blow your top" or ruin your testimony by other hostile conduct. Your victory does not depend on someone else's behavior! Humanly speaking, you may have several reasons to get angry, but you have divine resources within you to respond in peace. The secret is in recognizing you are sunk the moment you indulge yourself by thinking: "He has no right to do that to me." Never respond in kind, but in the Spirit.

Even when Mr. Sanguine is controlled by the Holy Spirit, he is going to be enthusiastic and extrovertish. God made him that way. But sometimes his forceful response to situations is erroneously interpreted as hostility. He will have to be watchful of this, particularly around non-Christians because they expect Christians to be calm and serene.

Peter's joy

Joy is a natural tendency of the sanguine temperament. Ordinarily Mr. Sanguine not only takes pleasure in what he does but he has a way of making folks around him enjoy life. However, he does have a tendency to be easily offended, and his enjoyment may be turned into grousing or griping about the way people have treated him or the way things have turned out. This will produce a period of depression which is usually dissipated by the first external object that comes into view.

Peter's reaction to being severely beaten by the Sanhedrin officials is the reverse of what we would expect from a Sanguine. In Acts 5:41 we read, "And they departed from the presence of the council, rejoicing that they were counted worthy to suffer shame for his name." This reaction is evidence of Spirit-control. In Ephesians 5 we find that one of the first characteristics of the Spirit-filled life is a rejoicing heart. That is the reason Peter went on his way "rejoicing" instead of grumbling. Any Christian seeking to walk in the Spirit will examine his speech. When you find yourself griping, criticizing, grumbling, or using other verbal expressions of complaint, it is evidence that you are not controlled by the Spirit. The Holy Spirit will give us a spontaneous inclination to rejoice, thus fulfilling "the will of God in Christ Jesus concerning you" (1 Thessalonians 5:18).

Peter's humility

Humility is definitely not a characteristic of the Sanguine. Mr. Sanguine's natural egotistical traits cause him to be a glory seeker. For that reason be rarely does anything obscurely just to help people, but accomplishes everything with fanfare and staging to give him as much recognition as possible. This is certainly not the case with Spirit-controlled Sanguine Peter. An excellent illustration is found in Acts 9:36-42. Dorcas, a woman "full of good works and almsdeeds," became ill and died. As Peter was in Joppa, her home city, the leaders of the church sent for him. Peter's conduct, recorded in verses 39-42, is a classic example of how the Holy Spirit modifies a sanguine egotist.

"Then Peter arose and went with them. When he was come, they brought him into the upper chamber; and all the widows stood by him weeping, and showing the coats and garments which Dorcas made, while she was with them. But Peter put them all forth, and kneeled down, and prayed; and turning to the body said, Tabitha, arise. And she opened her eyes; and when she saw Peter, she sat up. And he gave her his hand, and lifted her up; and when he had called the saints and widows, presented her alive. And it was known throughout all Joppa; and many believed in the Lord."

What could bring more glory to one's reputation than raising the dead? Yet Peter insisted that they all leave the room so that no one could observe what he did. He enjoyed the privacy that gave the glory exclusively to God. Such conduct is so foreign to a man of Peter's native temperament that it has to be the work of the Holy Spirit.

Peter's prayerfulness

A perennial difficulty with most sanguine Christians is a lack of consistency in their devotional habits. Restless by nature, they find it easy to flit around, engaging in all kinds of "activities for the Lord," without spending much time with him personally in prayer and Bible study. In themselves many sanguine Christians are very shallow and prone to be carnal in their decisions, but time spent in daily Bible study and prayer seems to make a strong impact on them.

The tenth chapter of Acts reveals an exciting experience in the life of Spirit-controlled Sanguine Peter. Little did he know as he went on the housetop to pray that this would lead to his second use of the "keys of the kingdom"—the opening of heaven to the Gentiles through the gospel. As he prayed, he had a vision of a sheet lowered from heaven bearing all kinds of four-footed beasts, and he was instructed to "kill and eat." Verse 19 tells us, "While Peter thought on the vision, the Spirit said unto him . . ." Many a sanguine Christian lacks guidance by the Spirit because his restless activity keeps him from talking to and hearing from the Lord.

Peter's love

This same story reveals another modification of Sanguine Peter by the Holy Spirit. Sanguines are prone to be opinionated and biased. One rarely has to guess the degree of their bigotry, for they are prone to blurt it out. Frequently they welcome a chance to argue with such outbursts. Once having made up their minds, they tend to refuse evidence to the contrary, and thus it is difficult to get them to alter their opinions. Before Pentecost, Peter revealed these characteristics abundantly, but now, controlled by the Holy Spirit, things were different. As a good Israelite he had an ingrained antagonism toward all Gentiles, particularly Roman soldiers. Now the Spirit of God was instructing him to go to Cornelius, a Roman centurion, and tell him the gospel. Peter's response was one of immediate obedience (verse 21).

Cornelius, deeply convicted by the Holy Spirit, welcomed Peter "and fell down at his feet, and worshiped him. But Peter took him up, saying, Stand up; I myself also am a man." This humble reaction by Peter testified again to the controlling influence of the Holy Spirit.

Even before Peter knew the nature of his errand or the deep change God had wrought, he revealed his objective concern for the alien Gentiles. He said, "Ye know that it is an unlawful thing for a man that is a Jew to keep company, or come unto one of another nation: *but God* has shown me that I should not call any man common or unclean. Therefore came I unto you without objection as soon as I was sent for" (verses 28, 29). This story illustrates that it was not just Peter's mouth that was sanctified, but his entire attitude and motivation. Peter was determined to be completely available to the living God. Verse 28 conveys the key to such temperament modification: "*but God.*" These two words guarantee help for every undisciplined, opinionated, egotistical, weak-willed Sanguine. God the Holy Spirit proves a strength for every human weakness.

Because he was available to the Holy Spirit, Peter preached a Spirit-filled message that offered salvation to these Gentiles. The response was electrifying! "The Holy Spirit fell on all them who heard the word." Even though the Jews who accompanied Peter were astonished, he led the new converts into water baptism; "And he commanded them, to be baptized in the name of the Lord."

Peter's gentleness

The characteristic sanguine tendency to be rough, impatient, and much like the proverbial "bull in the china shop" had left Peter. He was so Spirit controlled that we find nothing but grace and gentleness. When he returned to Jerusalem, "they that were of the circumcision (Jewish legalists) contended with him." Typical of flesh-controlled Christians, they couldn't see over their critical bias to the harvest of souls. Instead of lashing out at them, the normal reaction of Sanguine Simon, we find that Peter gently "reviewed the matter from the beginning, and expounded it in order unto them." And he gave them all the details.

Because of Spirit-controlled and gentle explanation, they responded to this first harvest of Gentile outsiders, for the Scripture tells us, "When they heard these things, they held their peace, and glorified God, saying, 'Then hath God also to the Gentiles granted repentance unto life." Sanguine Simon knew nothing about the principle that grace and gentleness turn away angry criticism, but the Holy Spirit did. Instead of inciting a fight and division, Peter drew the people closer together. We cannot help but ask ourselves if many of the shameful conflicts of the past nineteen hundred years of church history would have been avoided had the leaders faced their critics under the controlling influence of the Holy Spirit. This challenge, of course, is not limited to those of sanguine temperament.

Peter's faith

One of the nine characteristics of the Spirit-filled life, according to Galatians 5:22, 23, is faith. As we have already seen, Mr. and Mrs. Sanguine have a tendency to be fearful. This is particularly true when they must face decisions alone. The twelfth chapter of Acts presents Sanguine Peter in a completely different light. Herod the King had imprisoned some of the leaders of the church because he wanted to "vex" them. Peter, alone and in jail, was sent for by Herod (12:6). Instead of fretting and fuming because of the confinement or worrying about his security, Peter was peacefully sleeping when the angel suddenly appeared to set him free. To sleep under such conditions could only mean that Peter was relaxed and fearless in the care of his heavenly Father.

Peter's patience

Sanguine people have a tendency to be sarcastic to the point of emotional injury of their friends. As a counselor I have come to believe that most people have sarcastic thoughts but tend to keep them to themselves. Not so Mr. Sanguine. He blurts out almost everything that comes into his head.

After Peter's miraculous delivery by the angel, he "came to the house of Mary, the mother of John . . . where many were gathered together praying. And as Peter knocked at the door of the gate, a maid came to hearken, named Rhoda. And when she knew Peter's voice, she opened not the gate for gladness, but ran in, and told how Peter stood before the gate. And they said unto her, Thou art mad.

But she constantly affirmed that it was even so. Then said they, It is his angel." What was the naturally impatient Peter doing while the unbelieving prayer warriors were doubting the answer to their own prayers? Patiently, "Peter continued knocking."

Instead of greeting them with a blast of sarcasm, the Scripture tells us that Peter, "beckoning unto them with the hand to hold their peace, declared unto them how the Lord had brought him out of the prison." If ever there was an opportunity for a church leader to slash his friends this was it. But Peter was more concerned about their spiritual encouragement and the grace of God than in ridiculing others' weakness. Chapter 12 is a vivid demonstration of the work of the Holy Spirit in a sanguine temperament.

Peter's leadership

The Spirit-inspired leadership of the sanguine apostle becomes apparent in the 15th chapter of Acts at a crucial moment in the early Church's history. Paul and Barnabas had just returned from their first missionary journey among the Gentiles. The reaction of legalistic Christians was bitter, creating "no small dissension and disputation with them." Paul and Barnabas appeared before the elders, declaring "all things that God had done with them. But there rose up certain of the sect of the Pharisees who believed, saying that it was needful to circumcise them and to command them to keep the law of Moses. . . . And when there had been much disputing, Peter rose up." The speech of Peter in the face of these hostile circumstances was used of the Holy Spirit to bring unity again to the early Church. For we read that when he had finished, "then all the multitude kept silence, and listened to Barnabas and Paul, declaring what miracles and wonders God had wrought among the Gentiles by them."

One of the things that keeps most Sanguines from being good leaders over a long period of time is their immaturity. It is difficult for them to be objective, and in the heat of battle they get so involved that instead of acting as oil on the water they become a source of irritation. This usually limits the effectiveness of their leadership. However, such natural tendencies are excluded from this record of Peter's behavior. The only explanation for Peter's acting in such an unusual manner is the control of the Holy Spirit.

Proof that Peter was an effective leader in the early days of the young Church is supplied for us by the Apostle Paul in Galatians

2:8. Paul was an intellectual with superb training, yet in these words he paid high tribute to the leadership ability of his sanguine friend, the Apostle Peter. "For he that wrought effectually in Peter to the apostleship of the circumcision . . ." offers a contemporary testimony to the miraculous results in Peter's Spirit-modified temperament.

Peter's lapse

It would be a mistake to think that after the Day of Pentecost Peter was always Spirit controlled. Idealistic Christians tend to set up standards so unreal that it is impossible to maintain them. Then in discouragement some stop trying to walk in the Spirit. As we shall see, the New Testament shows that Peter was not always controlled by the Holy Spirit after the Day of Pentecost.

Although God is interested in every experience of our lives and commands us to walk in holiness, he is not waiting to punish us for failure. King David is known in the Bible as "the man after God's own heart," not because he was perfect, but because he repented after sinning and turned contritely to God for forgiveness and restoration of grace. God did not cease blessing the king after his gross sins, but he sent conviction through Nathan the prophet and welcomed David back into fellowship. Even Elijah became so depressed that he asked God to let him die. God forgave the great prophet and used him mightily afterward. Because Christians cannot escape "flesh" impulses, Galatians 5:16 urges us: "Walk in the Spirit, and ye shall not fulfill the lust of the flesh." This challenge was not given to godless people but to Christians. Instead of becoming depressed over our sins and perpetuating carnality by self-abasement, erring Christians should immediately invoke the confession of 1 John 1:9 and enjoy God's complete forgiveness and forgetfulness of sin.

Peter's reversion to Sanguine Simon is recorded by the Apostle Paul in Galatians 2. It seems that when Peter was with Paul at Antioch, "he did eat with the Gentiles," because the church of Antioch contained a large number of Gentile converts. But when "certain men came from James . . . he withdrew and separated himself, fearing them who were of the circumcision." The Apostle Paul said that in doing so "they walked not uprightly according to the truth of the gospel" (Galatians 2:14). Somehow Sanguine Peter turned back to Sanguine Simon because of "fear." The fear of man is particularly characteristic of the Sanguine. Peter did not want to receive the displeasure of his friends, so he separated himself from his Gentile brethren and no doubt offended them. This certainly did not indicate that God ceased to use Peter's life, for his two epistles were written long after this event. It does, however, suggest that even mature, Spirit-filled Christians must "take heed to themselves" lest they, too, walk in the flesh momentarily.

Peter's maturity

The apostle's spiritual maturity is seen in a number of events that took place after this. But perhaps the outstanding occasion was his meekness after the Apostle Paul had "withstood him to the face" (Galatians 2:11). Instead of resenting Paul's rebuke, Peter demonstrated loving appreciation. In his second epistle, written near the end of his life, we find this whole-hearted tribute to the Apostle Paul as it came from the pen of Sanguine Peter: "The longsuffering of our Lord is salvation, even as our beloved brother, Paul, also according to the wisdom given unto him, hath written unto you" (2 Peter 3:15). Peter further commends the epistles of Paul, and in verse 16 puts them on a par with the Old Testament Scriptures. This is probably the greatest tribute one Jewish Christian could pay to another—acknowledging the work of God in Paul's life as in the life of Moses, David, Daniel, and Samuel.

The transformation of the sanguine apostle graphically demonstrates that God is able to make *you* the kind of person he wants you to be. It also shows that for every inherited weakness, even those increased in intensity through habit, there is a cure. God the Holy Spirit has a strength for every one of the weaknesses of the Sanguine. Mr. Sanguine, like every other Christian, continually needs to heed the admonition: "Be filled with the Spirit" (Ephesians 5:18).

4

PAUL THE CHOLERIC

The best illustration of choleric temperament among Bible characters is found in the Apostle Paul. He is also the best illustration of transformed choleric temperament. In fact, he is an excellent example of the way the Holy Spirit modifies a strong-willed person after conversion. Very few of Saul's pre-Christian activities are revealed in Scripture, and over 95 percent of his recorded experiences took place after he was filled with the Holy Spirit. Nevertheless, he walks through the pages of the book of Acts with a heavy choleric foot. A modified Choleric, yes, a Spirit-controlled Choleric, yes, but every inch a Choleric. Before we make a detailed study of this choleric apostle, let's examine the characteristics of a choleric person.

Mr. Choleric is a practical activist. All of life is utilitarian to him. He is strong willed, a natural leader, and very optimistic. His brain is filled with ideas, projects, or objectives, and he usually sees them through. Like Mr. Sanguine, he is extrovertish, but not nearly as intense. Although very productive in life, he has serious natural weaknesses. He is self-sufficient, impetuous, hot-tempered, and has a tendency to be harsh or cruel. No one can be as cutting and sarcastic as a Choleric. They make good supervisors, generals, builders, crusaders, politicians, or organizers, but are not usually able to do precise detail work.

Saul of Tarsus was not only raw choleric temperament, but a well-educated and very religious Choleric. So it should not surprise us that the first time Saul of Tarsus comes on the scriptural scene he is participating in the stoning of Stephen, the first recorded Christian martyr.

After a magnificent sermon by Stephen, the Spirit-filled "deacon," the antagonistic religious leaders lashed out against him. "When they heard these things, they were cut to the heart, and they gnashed on him with their teeth" (Acts 7:54).

When Stephen revealed his vision of heaven and the Lord Jesus standing at the right hand of the throne of God, the Scripture tells us that "they cried out with a loud voice, and stopped their ears, and ran upon him with one accord, and cast him out of the city, and stoned him; and the witnesses laid down their clothes at a young man's feet, whose name was Saul." Some have suggested that placing their clothes at Saul's feet indicated his leadership of the group. Some scholars further suggest that Choleric Saul was a member of the Sanhedrin, the select council of seventy elders in Israel. It was an esteemed honor to be on this council, and for a young man it was particularly unusual. Such suggestion is taken from Acts 26:10, where the choleric apostle acknowledges that in his younger years he had testified against the Christians in Jerusalem before the chief priests. Saul voted there that they "be put to death." In any case, Acts 8:1 shows that "Saul was consenting unto his death"—referring to Stephen.

Cruel

From this hostile beginning Saul continued his harsh, cruel way so characteristic of the choleric temperament. Most of the world's cruel dictators and criminals have been predominantly of the choleric temperament. One of the hardest things for a Christian Choleric to learn is to exhibit the "milk of human kindness." He is often blunt, verbally sarcastic, and cutting with his tongue.

Two couples at a fair decided to have their handwriting analyzed by an IBM computer, and the Choleric in the group was the first to volunteer. His wife and friends of over twenty years erupted in peals of laughter when they saw his card which read: "You have a strong tendency to be blunt and sarcastic." Their spontaneous laughter verified that the computer was right on target. Ordinarily it is easy to tell when a Choleric is Spirit-filled, because his speech will be flavored with Spirit-motivated kindness and grace instead of cutting, biting, or nasty remarks. This is true also of his deeds.

Choleric Saul tramples his cruel way through the early chapters of the book of Acts, leading the "great persecution against the Church which was at Jerusalem." Seemingly his hatred for Christians and his ruthless attempt to destroy them was inspired by religion. History reveals that many a Choleric has perpetrated inhuman deeds in the name of religion. Some have even used Christianity as a cloak to hallow their wrath and justify their hateful deeds.

The Scripture describes Choleric Saul as "breathing out threatenings and slaughter against the disciples of the Lord." Like most Cholerics who have a tendency to be cunning and crafty when motivated by hatred and ruthlessness, Saul "went unto the high priest, and desired of him letters to Damascus to the synagogues, that if he found any of this way [Christians in the early days of the Church] whether they were men or women, he might bring them bound unto Jerusalem" (Acts 9:1-2). With these documents of authority in his hands, Saul was a fire-breathing vigilant with the power of life or death for enemies of the people. One of the men who lived in Damascus at this time, Ananias, acknowledged that he knew how "much evil (harm) he had done." In fact, because of Saul's former brutality, Ananias hesitated to believe the Holy Spirit's message that this powerful enemy had been converted.

This is almost the extent of our knowledge of Saul's pre-Christian activities, but it is sufficient to establish his native temperament as choleric. No doubt he had a secondary temperament, as do all people. It is sometimes difficult to determine the secondary temperament, as we mentioned in chapter 3, but in Paul's case it was probably melancholy. This is suggested by his brilliant mental gifts, as reflected primarily by his writings. Unlike many melancholy theologians who followed him, however, Paul's writings were highly practical, suggesting that his choleric temperament predominated. Temperaments that are basically melancholy, as we shall see, are usually more theoretical or philosophical and border on being impractical.

From the passages already examined, we can deduce several distinctly choleric tendencies in Saul of Tarsus. He was a leader by natural instinct, he was very zealous and activity prone, he was an angry, hostile, bitter individual, "breathing out threatening and slaughter." In addition, he was ruthless and cruel. In all probability, Saul of Tarsus would have been a great leader whether or not he became a Christian. His encounter with Jesus Christ on the Damascus road changed the direction of his leadership but did not lessen it. In fact, the Holy Spirit used this leadership ability as a dynamic force to glorify Jesus Christ. It is important to keep in mind that God does not obliterate temperament when we are Spirit filled, for each person retains his distinctive individualism. Instead, the Holy Spirit redirects our strengths to glorifying God and tempers our weaknesses by overcoming them with the characteristics of the Spirit-filled man. Saul-turned-Paul became a classic example of the Spirit-controlled choleric temperament.

Strong-willed

One of the best assets of a Choleric's temperament is his strong willpower. If pointed in the right direction, it makes him a most successful person. As a rule, Cholerics are successful in any vocation they select, but not because they have more mental gifts than other temperaments. Their success can be attributed to determination rather than native ability. When others have abandoned some endeavor or project, Mr. Choleric continues tenaciously until he reaches his goal. The Apostle Paul refers to this in 1 Corinthians 9:24-27 when describing standards of self-discipline.

"Know ye not that they who run in a race run all, but one receiveth the prize? So run, that ye may obtain. And every man that striveth for the mastery is temperate in all things. Now they do it to obtain a corruptible crown, but we, an incorruptible. I, therefore, so run, not as uncertainly; so fight I, not as one that beateth the air. But I keep under my body, and bring it into subjection, lest that by any means, when I have preached to others, I myself should be a castaway."

This text gives us several insights into the strength of will of the choleric apostle. He indicates that he was "temperate in all things." His activity was not that of the Sanguine, who needs no purpose to satisfy him because the sheer joy of being active is sufficient satisfaction. The choleric apostle ran "not as uncertainly," indicating that he knew where he was, where he had been and where he was going; everything he did had purpose and meaning. He also indicates here that he did not abuse his body: "I keep under my body, and bring it into subjection." One can scarcely imagine the Apostle Paul being obese or intemperate even in today's affluent society.

It is the same choleric apostle who revealed an important secret from his personal life on how to live victoriously over weaknesses. He knew that self-discipline begins in the mind. If you don't determine in your mind to do something hard, it probably will not get done. In 2 Corinthians 10, Paul describes the spiritual power residing in the Christian's "flesh," meaning the body, that is "bringing into captivity every thought to the obedience of Christ." The disciplined Christian has a good purpose in his mind which produces positive feelings in his heart. This is very important, for the Lord Jesus said, "As a man thinketh in his heart, so is he." Success in the Christian life begins in the mind, and that is shaped by the will. If you indulge your weaknesses, excusing them and pampering yourself, you will not change. Only by acting on the truth that "I can do all things through Christ who strengtheneth me" will you be victorious in the warfare of the temperament (Philippians 4:13).

This strong willpower made the choleric apostle a very dynamic and exciting person. He was decisive and highly motivated, possessing the ability to lead and motivate others. He was seemingly indefatigable and full of faith. Strong will-power, however, has some subtle weaknesses and dangers. Many times a Christian Choleric is considered a great man of faith when in reality his faith is an exaggerated form of self-confidence. One of Mr. Choleric's greatest difficulties is to trust in the Lord and not in his choleric temperament. He must remember that success is not by his might nor his power, but "by my Spirit, saith the Lord." Paul had a very acute awareness of his need for divine resources.

The hallmark of the choleric apostle—his persistence—is an admirable characteristic when directed by the Holy Spirit. But persistence can also get a choleric Christian far out of the will of God. Although some of my respected Christian friends tend to think the Apostle Paul revealed no grievous fault after his conversion, I believe the Bible relates an incident of his misguided persistence.

Toward the close of Paul's third missionary journey, recorded in Acts 20, he decided "if it were possible for him, to be at Jerusalem the day of Pentecost." We have no indication that this was of the Holy Spirit. It was a strong desire and a doubtful goal, but it grew to become a resolute, driving desire. Instead of visiting the church at Ephesus, he invited the elders to meet him in Miletus. Verse 22 says he was "bound in the spirit to go unto Jerusalem." This was Paul's spirit, indicating his determination to get to Jerusalem. We do not find that he asked the Lord about this, but arranged his plans according to his wishes.

This story indicates that even a mature Christian can get himself out of the will of God by setting his will above God's. Verse 23 shows that Paul had already been warned of unpleasant consequences, for "the Holy Spirit witnesseth in every city, saying that bonds and afflictions await me." But Paul would not be deterred, for he said, "But none of these things move me, neither count I my life dear unto myself, so that I might finish my course with joy, and the ministry, which I have received of the Lord Jesus. . . ."

The Lord wanted Paul to finish his course joyfully, but the time and place had not been revealed to Paul. If God wanted Paul to go to Jerusalem, his grace would assure it, not Paul's determination. Whether or not Paul actually got out of God's will by going to Jerusalem is a subject upon which I would not be dogmatic, although I personally think he did. But there is no question that his attitude was that of the flesh, not of the Spirit. Sometimes I think Christians have a tendency to lose much spiritual enjoyment, not because they do the wrong thing, but because they do it in the wrong way. That is, they set their minds on something, but they don't ask God because they're afraid he will say "no," so they just proceed on their own. Even though things may work out in the end, we may certainly wonder if such people wouldn't be much happier if they would heed the admonition, "In all thy ways acknowledge him, and he shall direct thy paths," instead of arching their choleric backs and setting their stubborn jaws to follow their own wills.

The Holy Spirit certainly revealed his will to Paul concerning the trip to Jerusalem, for the 21st chapter indicates that when he had come to Tyre, the Holy Spirit warned him through the disciples "that he should not go up to Jerusalem." But again Paul steadfastly persisted. A few days later, after arriving at Caesarea, they stayed in the home of Philip the evangelist. A Judean prophet named Agabus came and, taking Paul's belt, bound his hands and feet, saying, "Thus saith the Holy Spirit, So shall the Jews at Jerusalem bind the man that owneth this belt, and shall deliver him into the hands of the Gentiles." When the believers heard this they "besought him not to go up to Jerusalem." But Paul refused to heed their warnings. The Scripture tells us, "When he would not be persuaded, we ceased, saying, The will of the Lord be done." Either all these disciples and prophets were wrong or Paul was wrong. Hardheaded, self-willed Cholerics need to learn that when spiritually motivated people recommend a change in direction, they had better seek the will of the Holy Spirit on the matter. This is difficult for Cholerics because they thrive on opposition. The more we oppose a Choleric and attempt to hinder his activities, the more he lowers his shoulder and pushes.

A Christian doctor analytically described two different reactions to opposition shown by two minister friends of his. When the sanguine minister was opposed or threatened, he wanted to "take the threatener out for a cup of coffee and have fellowship with him." His insecurity made him want to use his charismatic gifts in charming his opposition into a spirit of cooperation. But the choleric minister reacted to opposition by "pushing that much harder."

The besetting temptation of choleric Christians is to set their minds on doing something and persistently push without knowing whether or not it is really the will of God. This may produce a seemingly productive Christian worker, but it does not make a happy Christian, nor does it make the best use of his talents. A Spirit-filled Choleric will always out-perform a carnal Choleric. Like every other temperament, Mr. Choleric desperately needs the filling of the Holy Spirit. To be otherwise is to incur many unnecessary difficulties, as did the Apostle Paul.

It is well known what happened to the choleric apostle who, more choleric than apostle, refused the admonitions of the Holy Spirit and went up to Jerusalem anyway. One sin leads to another, and we find Paul shaving his head and taking an Israelite vow in an attempt to please the Jews. Ordinarily compromise is not a temptation to Cholerics, but they are vulnerable to compromise when they think they may do a little thing wrong to do a big thing right. This may have been the apostle's thinking when he went up to Jerusalem and observed this Jewish custom, for he had a tremendous burden on his heart to reach the Jews.

God had called Paul to a great ministry among the Gentiles, which he fulfilled, but Paul's nationalistic spirit gave him a great burden for his own people, which is understandable and commendable. No doubt he thought that if he went through this Jewish rite, which to him was meaningless, it would put him in good with the Jews of Jerusalem so that he could preach the gospel to them. He learned—and all Christians should learn from this experience, recorded in Acts 21 and 22—that it is never right to do wrong to get a chance to do right. It is always wrong to do wrong! In reality, disobedience is a form of unbelief, a lack of trust that if God wants us to preach in Jerusalem or witness to a great crowd or to a certain person, he can work it out. God is able to use the wrath of men to praise him; he does not need our sin to reveal his grace.

The choleric apostle paid dearly for his brief period of self-will. He was incarcerated in Jerusalem and then transferred to Caesarea, where he remained for approximately two years. He learned a valuable lesson through this personal experience from which all Christian Cholerics may profit: to turn their strong will over to God, who makes no mistakes in the direction of their lives.

This period of self-will must have been confessed, although Scripture does not indicate so, for we find that Paul goes on after this period of stumbling and is again very productive and usable in the hands of the Spirit of God. As we saw in the life of Sanguine Peter, we now see in the life of the choleric apostle that God does not carry a grudge, even when we sin. For God went on to use this man mightily in prison as a witness to governors, kings, and finally to Caesar himself. Many of Paul's epistles were written after this display of flesh-dominated temperament. Reinstatement with God is an instant experience for any believer who acknowledges his sin and yields himself again to God.

Hostile

The hostility and anger that characterizes the choleric temperament is not very apparent in the life of the Apostle Paul after his conversion. We have seen it motivate him prior to his conversion, but after his conversion it rarely appears. One such case is recorded in the 15th chapter of Acts at the outset of the second missionary journey. It seems that Paul and Barnabas had taken young John Mark, a nephew to Barnabas, with them on their first journey, but he turned back when they came to Perga (Acts 13:13). For that reason Paul was determined that Mark would not accompany them on their second journey. A Choleric could not tolerate quitters. By nature he would be intolerant of those who did not share his stamina and fortitude in the face of adversity. But Melancholy-Phlegmatic Barnabas insisted that his nephew join them. This is typical of his temperament for he was a loyal friend, a sacrificing individual who would be prone to give the lad another chance.

Paul was absolutely inflexible. Verse 39 indicates that "the contention was so sharp between them that they departed asunder one from the other; and so Barnabas took Mark, and sailed unto Cyprus." Some Christians like to pass this off as a wonderful way for the Holy Spirit to get two missionary journeys started instead of one, but that is aside from the real point. The Holy Spirit doesn't need an argument between brothers to accomplish his will. When Spirit-filled, we are not contentious, angry, hostile, and unforgiving. It may not have been God's will for Barnabas and Paul to leave on this trip together, for certainly he blessed the second journey and Paul's new companion, Silas. But we can be certain that the Holy Spirit did not need a typically choleric explosion by the Apostle Paul to precipitate such a decision.

Another eruption of the choleric apostle's anger is found in the 23rd chapter of Acts. Paul had been arrested and taken before the Sanhedrin council. He had just begun his defense speech, "I have lived in all good conscience before God until this day," when the high priest, Ananias, commanded the men who stood by Paul to "smite him on the mouth." Paul's instinctive reaction was to retort: "God shall smite thee, thou whited wall; for sittest thou to judge me after the law, and commandest me to be smitten contrary to the law?" Now it is true that Paul apologized when he realized he had reviled the high priest, but his outburst against injustice was the spontaneous expression of choleric hostility.

This episode is not repeated here to discredit the great apostle, but to show that a Christian Choleric has a problem with anger. He does not have to be dominated by it, for he can have victory over anger through the power of the Holy Spirit whenever he is willing to face it as a sin, confess it, and ask God to remove it. And he must repeat this action whenever he gets angry. When, like the Apostle Paul, he acts in self-will, he is vulnerable to the resurrection of the flesh. This can only be remedied by walking in the Spirit. Happy is the Choleric (and those around him) who is willing to label his anger immediately as sin, refuse the temptation to excuse it, and ask God to give him the peace of the Spirit-filled life.

Self-sufficient

As a result of his strong willpower, Mr. Choleric is very self-sufficient and independent. The more successful he becomes, the more his self-sufficiency will reveal itself. The self-sufficiency of the choleric apostle is seen in the fact that he refused payment for his

Christian work though he acknowledged it was right and permissible to be paid. Whenever he went into a town or city to serve, he would ply his trade as a tent-maker (20:34). There is nothing wrong with a man's earning his own way, but this is a typical choleric reaction. Seldom is a Choleric found on the welfare rolls. In this instance I am reminded of my father, who had no small supply of choleric temperament. During the days of the great depression it was impossible for him to secure a job. Not only was his talent for machine repair useless to closed automobile plants, his handicap of having only one leg made finding employment more difficult. During the ten months we were on city welfare, my father refused to take the money unless he could work for it. The welfare agency let him deliver government food to welfare recipients who had no transportation, and then he accepted help.

Because of this feeling of independence and self-sufficiency, Mr. Choleric is not afraid to be alone; in fact, he is often called "a loner." It's not that he dislikes other people, but many times he would just rather do things by himself. This trait seen in the Apostle Paul, who found himself alone in the city of Athens, a skeptical community filled with idolatry. Most people would sink into obscurity and wait until reinforcements arrived—but not the Apostle Paul. Acts 17 indicates that his heart burned so fiercely at the Athenians' plight that he entered into debates with the people, and when a crowd gathered he was brought to the Areopagus on Mars' hill to address the elite of the city.

I have been to Athens and have seen the ruins of the Acropolis, a magnificent center of pagan worship when Paul was there. Slight of stature at best, Paul must have looked minuscule beside the towering rock structures of the Acropolis as he declared the truth about the "unknown God." Undaunted by his lonely position, the choleric apostle proclaimed what is considered a classic example of pulpit oratory. Although the hearers' response was not overwhelming, the Scripture says: "Nevertheless, certain men joined him, and believed . . ." (Acts 17:34).

The spirit of self-sufficiency and independence may limit the effectiveness of the Christian Choleric because he does not readily sense the need for a personal devotional relationship to God and dependence on the ministry of the Holy Spirit. He is often so effective and capable in his own right that the plaudits of people fan his ego and he is tempted to proceed in Christian work without the

power of God. Only when Mr. Choleric recognizes his utter useless-
ness without the Holy Spirit can he summon his strong willpower to
a disciplined devotional life that produces a power-filled servant of
God.

Choleric Saul's conversion is typical of the extreme measures that
are often necessary to force the adult Choleric to humble himself
and receive Jesus Christ. We do not know for certain that Paul had
heard the gospel prior to Stephen's sermon; however, it seems likely
that he had gained some knowledge of what was taught in order to
have developed the intense hatred that led him to persecute the
Christians. This is implied also by our Lord when he said to Paul:
"It is hard for thee to kick against the pricks," indicating that he
had been under conviction for some time. Choleric-induced self-
sufficiency seems to provide amazing stamina and resistance
against the conviction of the Holy Spirit in adult Cholerics. The late
Henrietta C. Mears, one of the finest Christian educators of our
time, used to say, "Never let a junior out of the department who
doesn't know Jesus Christ." She knew that many boys, especially
Cholerics, who do not know Christ by the time they finish the sixth
grade, are not likely to respond to the Savior until the complexities
of life drive them to their knees. That may explain the extreme
measures the Lord took in sending a "light from heaven," blinding
Paul, and then speaking to him audibly (Acts 9:1-8). Only when
humbled by adversities will a Choleric respond to the gracious
invitation to receive God's gift of eternal life.

Dynamic

Another characteristic of the choleric temperament that is apparent in the Apostle Paul is his native leadership ability. This was
exhibited in his activities on the Jerusalem council, and it was also
apparent on the first missionary journey. Barnabas and Paul com-
prised the first missionary team (Acts 13). Barnabas was the senior
Christian who had invited Saul, the young convert, to work with
him in the church at Antioch (Acts 11:25, 26). However, by the time
they left the Isle of Cyprus, the group was designated "Paul and his
company" (Acts 13:13), indicating that the reins of leadership had
changed hands. From that point on it was "Paul and Barnabas."
This leadership flashed on many occasions, one being when Paul
and Silas confronted a young woman possessed with "a spirit of
divination." "Paul, being grieved, turned and said to the spirit, I

command thee, in the name of Jesus Christ, to come out of her. And he came out the same hour" (Acts 16:18). This aggressive leadership, obviously initiated by the Holy Spirit, is characteristic of this choleric apostle's ministry. Another illustration is found in Acts 27:21-25. Paul was a prisoner on board a ship bound for Rome. In the midst of a furious storm, the Roman guards were about to kill all their prisoners because of the Roman custom that required a guard to pay the price of the prisoners who escaped. Paul said: "Sirs, ye should have hearkened unto me, and not have loosed from Crete, and to have gained this harm and loss. And now I exhort you to be of good cheer; for there shall be no loss of any man's life among you, but only of the ship. For there stood by me this night an angel of God, whose I am, and whom I serve, saying, Fear not, Paul, thou must be brought before Caesar; and, lo, God hath given thee all them that sail with thee. Wherefore, sirs, be of good cheer; for I believe God, that it shall be even as it was told me." Only a Spirit-filled Choleric could react like this! The prisoner assumed authority of his captor's ship and saved their lives. This was more than an intuitive response to a challenging situation; it was supernaturally induced confidence from God.

Such boldness characterized the apostle all his life. He is perhaps the boldest witness recorded in the annals of the Church. Acts 22 relates how he boldly proclaimed his relationship to Jesus Christ in the face of Christ-hating Jews in Jerusalem who interrupted his sermon in a fit of anger and created a riot that was squelched only by the presence of the chief captain of the Romans. As a prisoner, Paul forthrightly defended himself before Tertullus, the governor; before Felix, who replaced Tertullus; and before Agrippa, king of the Herodians. In each case he personally challenged the king or governor with his message. Paul was a powerful preacher of the Word of God.

A thrilling illustration of the choleric apostle's bold witness occurred when, as a prisoner in Rome, he witnessed constantly to his captors and anyone else who would give him a hearing. In Philippians 4:22, while sending greetings to the church of Philippi, he stated, "All the saints greet you, chiefly they that are of Caesar's household." We could well ask how some of Caesar's household were made saints. Since all saints are fashioned through the hearing and receiving of the gospel, we perhaps can assume that some were converted through Roman soldiers who were chained to Paul during his imprisonment in Rome. While awaiting trial a prisoner customarily had a jailor chained to his wrist. One can scarcely imagine the Apostle Paul failing to boldly proclaim his faith to the guards. Such bold witness, inspired by the Holy Spirit, certainly brought fruit, perhaps in the very household of Caesar.

Practical

Cholerics as a rule have few aesthetic characteristics, but are highly practical. To them, life's decisions must be made with utilitarian purposes in view. That is one reason it is very difficult for a Choleric to relax and enjoy leisure time with his family. Many a modern Choleric is willing to work his fingers to the bone and provide the very best material benefits for his family, whereas the thing they desire most is his love, expressed by the time he spends with them.

The writings of the Apostle Paul abound in practical comments, as you will see by reading the last two or three chapters of Paul's epistles. His letters usually follow a pattern of doctrinal instruction in the first portion, answers to questions believers may have asked, and practical exhortation at the end. My color coding system for marking my Bible uses orange to indicate commands, and the last chapters of Paul's epistles are almost covered with orange. These commands have highly practical implications for the believer.

It is not difficult to pick out a choleric preacher, because his sermons abound in practical implications. Melancholy preachers are prone to emphasize theology and deal in the abstract. Sanguine preachers are known for their oratory and emotion. We happen to live in a day tuned to the practical side of life, and this may explain why most of the growing churches across the country are pastored by Cholerics. There are some noteworthy exceptions, but people readily gravitate to the man who teaches the Word of God in simple terms with practical applications to life.

The practical characteristics of choleric preachers may make them longer-winded than others. They frequently get by with it because they talk rapidly and maintain sufficient interest so that even self-indulgent Christians will sit through their lengthy sermons. This inclination makes them "compulsive communicators" because they know from the practical point of view that the gospel alone will solve the problems of mankind.

Such must have been the motivation of the Apostle Paul in Troas on his third missionary journey. On Sunday, when the disciples gathered together to break bread, "Paul preached unto them, ready to depart on the next day, and continued his speech until midnight" (Acts 20:7). Since Sunday was probably a work day, they may have met in the early evening and Paul preached four or five hours. A man named Eutychus, we're told, dozed off "and fell down from the third loft, and was taken up dead." The choleric apostle, undaunted by this tragedy, "went down, and fell on him, and embracing him said, Trouble not yourselves; for his life is in him." Preaching this man "to death" did not stop the compulsive, communicating choleric apostle! Instead, he went right back to preaching: "When he, therefore, was come up again, and had broken bread, and eaten, and talked a long while, even till break of day, so he departed."

One of the leaders in our church rather facetiously—though perhaps seriously—suggested that my sermon the previous Sunday night had been quite lengthy. My wife also clocked me at one hour and ten minutes, which was unusual for me. I responded, "I'm not as bad as the Apostle Paul; I've never killed anyone with my preaching." My friend wisely replied, "Pastor, when you can do what Paul did after he killed him through preaching, then you can preach that long too." Paul was obviously not just a choleric apostle, but a Spirit-filled Choleric with a deep desire to teach the truths of God to people he would never see again on this earth.

Crusading

Cholerics are born crusaders. They are the first in any community to instigate reform movements. When they observe social injustice, they are not just concerned, they immediately respond, "Let's get organized and do something about this." After observing Cholerics for many years, I concluded their crusades are not motivated so much by compassionate feelings as by their penchant for action. Usually the crusading Choleric is a tough-skinned individual, impervious to the opinions and feelings of others. He is the one temperament type who really doesn't care what other people think. This tendency becomes more pronounced as time goes on, particularly if he experiences a degree of success in his field. Christian Cholerics are prone to decide what is right and proceed to do it regardless of whose toes they step on or whom they offend. This can be a commendable trait if it is motivated by the right power, but sometimes it is a self-indulgence made to appear Christian.

Galatians 2 gives us an insight into the crusading, tough-skinned conduct of the choleric apostle. We saw this same experience earlier from the viewpoint of Sanguine Peter, who fellowshiped with the Gentiles until the Christian Jews arrived from Judea. Then, for fear of offending them, he separated himself from his Gentile brethren and their ways. The fact that Paul was among the youngest of the believers, that he was in the presence of the Church's leaders, and that his words would be closely examined did not deter the choleric apostle from taking action. Noting that the Gentile believers were affronted by Peter in a way contrary to the "truth of the gospel," Paul "withstood him to the face, because he was to be blamed." Paul further stated that he did this "before them all, saying, If thou, being a Jew, liveth after the manner of Gentiles, and not as do the Jews, why compellest thou the Gentiles to live as do the Jews?" The fact that he might be ridiculed or in some other way rebuked by these "elders" was immaterial to Paul. He saw an injustice and he was moved to rectify it.

I cannot help but feel that the "great cloud of witnesses," who have a better understanding of truth since they have gone on to be with the Lord, were cheering Paul on. Most Christians in such circumstances are prone to keep their mouths sealed when rebuke is needed or to go away and criticize behind a person's back. It is always best to be straightforward with brethren in Christ. We often do more good to our brethren in rebuke than in silence. Naturally, care must be taken that our action is motivated by the Holy Spirit and not our selfish nature.

Controversial

Anyone with an abundance of choleric temperament is bound to be controversial, even when filled with the Holy Spirit. When Spirit-filled, he will be controversial for righteousness' sake; when he walks in the flesh, he will be controversial because of his choleric qualities. Everywhere Paul went, he was controversial. People either loved him or hated him. The zealous Jews, of course, hated him. A delegation would follow him from one city to another to stir up trouble and persecute him. They stoned him and left him for dead in Iconium. Some Jews in Jerusalem so hated Paul that their conduct was irrational. One group banded together and made a vow that they would neither eat nor drink until they had killed him.

All the reaction to the choleric apostle, however, was not hostility. He also motivated people to an intense feeling of love and loyalty. For instance, Timothy and Luke followed him halfway around the world.

Those who loved the Lord and were filled with the Spirit seemed to love Paul fervently. Throughout the book of Acts we find people who wept when he left town. This man who moved across the Middle East and southern Europe, leading thousands of people to a saving knowledge of Jesus Christ, is probably one of the most loved men in all of Christendom. Those who hated him did so because he was a powerful Christian.

Don't expect everyone to love you if you walk in the Spirit, but profit by the attitude of the Spirit-filled choleric apostle who was determined to please God, not man. A greater than the Apostle Paul was hated for righteousness—the Lord Jesus Christ. If he could not please mankind, don't expect that you will. However, if you find yourself abrasive among Christians, you had better take stock to see whether your choleric traits are overriding the Spirit or the Spirit is truly controlling your temperament.

Paul's motivation

The choleric apostle was probably the world's most optimistic human being. That optimism produced the motivation that is unsurpassed in the history of the Church. Without access to human resources, the choleric apostle optimistically set out for parts unknown with only the assurance that the Spirit of God had sent him. He went through more suffering than any man known in church history. In 2 Corinthians 11 the apostle gives a report of some of his sufferings as a servant of Jesus Christ.

". . . In stripes above measure, in prisons more frequently, in deaths often. Of the Jews five times received I forty stripes, save one. Thrice was I beaten with rods, once was I stoned, thrice I suffered shipwreck, a night and a day I have been in the deep; in journeyings often, in perils of waters, in perils of robbers, in perils by mine own countrymen, in perils by the Gentiles, in perils in the city, in perils in the wilderness, in perils in the sea, in perils among false brethren; in weariness and painfulness, in watchings often, in hunger and thirst, in fastings often, in cold and nakedness. Beside those things that are without, that which cometh upon me daily, the care of all the churches." This is not a complete listing of the sufferings of Paul, for it was given long before his imprisonment in

Jerusalem and subsequent shipwreck in the Mediterranean Sea en route to Rome. Little did he know when he wrote these words that he would be in prison at least three more times.

Humanly speaking, the natural temptation in adversity is to give up. Not so the Spirit-filled choleric apostle. Probably the best illustration of his optimism is seen after he was stoned and left for dead at Iconium on the first missionary journey (Acts 14:19-21). Most Christians would have fled to their homeland and never again embarked on a ministry to such ungrateful heathen. We sometimes read the words glibly: ". . . having stoned Paul, drew him out of the city, supposing he had been dead," and give little thought to the deep suffering of the apostle. We are not sure God brought Paul back from death, but the antagonists quit stoning him because they thought he was dead, so at least he was near death. This meant he suffered severe lacerations, bruises, and possibly broken bones. But instead of quitting, he "rose up, and came into the city; and the next day he departed with Barnabas to Derbe. And when they had preached the gospel in that city, and had taught many, they returned again to Lystra." What could possibly motivate a man to rise up from a rock pile of death, proceed to preach the gospel in Derbe, and shortly come back to Lystra and the rock throwers again? There is no human explanation, but there is a scriptural one. Paul had found the secret of motivation that many depressed and apathetic people of our society have failed to discover. The Old Testament tells us, "Where there is no vision, the people perish" (Proverbs 29:18). No man can be motivated without a vision. That is the reason a basically well-adjusted human being can lose all interest in life. Because changes come in life, he may realize a goal too soon or find that a goal is impossible. If he does not set another goal, he will ultimately waste away. Optimistic people continually maintain goals.

The choleric apostle's secret of motivation was given him by the Holy Spirit. He revealed it to the church of Philippi in the third chapter, verses 13 and 14, where he acknowledged that, although he was not perfect, he had learned to do one thing: "Forgetting those things which are behind, and reaching forth unto those things which are before, I press toward the mark for the prize of the high calling of God in Christ Jesus."

The Apostle Paul could forget the stonings, shipwrecks, hunger, beatings, and rejection by men because he didn't look back; instead, he always looked forward to the ultimate goal when he would stand before Jesus Christ to give an account of himself. Next to the filling of the Holy Spirit, that is the greatest secret of motivation in the world. Actually, the two go hand in hand.

Whenever a Christian mopes, gripes, and feels sorry for himself, he is looking back to personal affronts, deprivations, sufferings, or rebukes. That is never productive, healthful, or helpful to the Christian. In fact, it is deeply demoralizing. The Apostle Paul, like Abraham before him, looked for a city whose builder and maker is God. He looked especially for the Savior and lived his life under the motivation that Jesus Christ was coming back, when he wanted to hear Jesus say, "Well done, thou good and faithful servant."

If you are an unmotivated, frustrated, ineffective Christian, I suggest that in addition to checking your life for habits that grieve the Spirit of God, you should also examine your goals. Man is a goal-striving being; if he has no goal he does not strive. Have you ever noticed how on a day off work you have little motivation unless you are going somewhere or doing something special? The anticipation of engaging in a specific project motivates you.

Extensive experiments on motivation show that "as a man think-eth in his heart, so is he," and particularly at night. If you want to be motivated tomorrow, go to bed tonight thinking positively and optimistically about what God is going to do with and through you tomorrow. Think specifically, anticipating what you expect God to do and how you expect to face challenges and opportunities. Evangelist John Hunter has said, "Christians do not have problems when they face the issues of life, but if they do not face them in faith, they become problems." The night before your day off, sit down and write out a list of all the things you want to accomplish the next day, placing the items in an order of priority. Then pray about it. You will be amazed how much easier it is to awaken the next day, how much happier you will feel during the day, and how satisfied you will go to bed. But if you retire thinking how tired you are, you are likely to be tired the next morning.

During the past two years I have been experimenting with this, primarily because I have been preaching as many as five sermons on Sunday, three in the morning and two in the evening. At the close of the first Sunday on that schedule I was completely exhausted and could scarcely pull my feet into bed at the end of the day. The last thing I said to my wife was, "Don't wake me; I'm just going to sleep until I wake up." I slept until 10:30 the next morning and was absolutely miserable when I awakened. For weeks I kidded myself that I needed Monday to "recuperate from Sunday's preaching schedule." Each Sunday night I programmed into my brain the fact that I was completely exhausted and I would relax and recuperate the next day. It didn't take my wife long to get me out of the habit of sleeping until 10:30, but she couldn't get me into a good mood on Monday.

Fortunately, the Lord took care of it, because with the resignation of a Bible teacher in our Christian high school, I agreed to teach the early morning Bible class in his place, forgetting that the class met the first thing Monday morning. Once having committed myself to the responsibility, I wasn't about to turn back. As I crawled into bed Sunday night after preaching five times, I studied my Bible in preparation for teaching the young people the next morning. To my amazement, Mr. Lethargy turned into Mr. Vitality. As I watched myself carefully through the next few months, I found that my attitude at night determined how I awakened the next day. We had an off-Monday from school two months later, and again I awakened feeling miserable. That's when the Holy Spirit revealed to me that for years as a minister I had pampered myself into thinking that I had to take a day off Monday in order to recuperate from Sunday. My wife and I had a family conference, and we decided that since our children were teen-agers and out of the home five days a week at school, I should quit taking Monday off and choose Saturday as my day for maximum sharing with the family. For over two years now I have been enjoying a highly motivated work schedule on Mondays in direct proportion to my mental optimism on Sunday night.

The Apostle Paul, of course, had far greater goals than these. He dragged his tired, aching body from Iconium because the city of Derbe was desperately in need of the gospel of Jesus Christ. That was the short-range goal which motivated him to walk those weary miles to the next harvest field. If you would be a motivated, Spirit-filled Christian, ask the Spirit of God to give you short-range, medium-range, and long-range goals. You will complete the short-range and medium-range in this life, but only when we stand before the Lord Jesus will we reach the eternal goal he has set for the child of God.

A lack of goal-setting accounts for the early deaths of many retired people. Although a man can be very productive in his field with the ultimate goal of retirement at sixty-five, he may die before his retirement is two years along. It may not be poor health that kills him, but poor "vision." As long as the goal of relaxing and retiring is ahead, he has something to work for. But after the novelty of relaxed living wears off, he is left without any specific purpose and consequently declines in energy. Unless a retired person is able to program a new goal and a new vision for leisure hours, he will shorten his life.

I mention this in the midst of the study of the choleric apostle, who "died with his boots on," because many Christians get to the age of maximum opportunity to serve Jesus Christ and then decide to retire. I have seen people in their late forties, with their children married or off to college, drop all forms of Christian service, much to their own loss. No Christian is going to be happy and confident unless his life is consistently available to the Holy Spirit.

A lady once asked me, "What is the age of retirement from Christian service?" I replied, "There is none!" As long as there is one sinner in this world and one Christian to convey the message of Christ to him, that Christian has no right to retire. Any pastor will tell you that the most disgruntled, cantankerous, unhappy people are elderly Christians who have no purpose in life. The happiest senior Christians I have met are those who constantly invest themselves in the service of our Lord and Savior.

When my wife and I were in Hong Kong several years ago, we took a tour of the Oriental Boat Mission's "field" in the Hong Kong harbor. There we met the most motivated and interesting octogenarian I have ever seen. She was an 82-year-old missionary from England whose board had said she was too old to return to the field. After being forced into retirement, she decided that God had called her to the mission field for life, so under his orders she went out again, depending on him for support. This dear lady was actively engaged in the thing she enjoyed best, sharing Jesus Christ with the refugees from Red China who, possessing no homes, lived in rickshaws or in Chinese junks tied together and docked in the harbor. After a lifetime of motivation this saint of God could say with the apostle, "I have fought a good fight, I have finished my course, I have kept the faith; henceforth there is laid up for me a crown of righteousness, which the Lord, the righteous judge, shall give me at that day; and not to me only, but unto all them also that love his appearing" (2 Timothy 4:7, 8).

What was her secret? Like the apostle, she had a lifetime goal: "the prize of the high calling of God in Christ Jesus," for which she was actively striving. What is your goal? The quality and definiteness of your goal will determine your motivation. The Holy Spirit has a goal for every Christian; let him motivate you.

Paul's transformation

Much of the Holy Spirit's transformation of the choleric apostle's temperament had to do with directing him in the way God wanted him to go. We shall now examine some of the characteristics of the Apostle Paul revealed in the Scripture that are completely contrary to the natural choleric temperament. Paul's instant obedience, after his conversion to Christ, is predictable, because Cholerics are prone to be decisive and act intuitively. But the humility that came into this haughty, aristocratic Pharisee's heart cannot be explained by natural means.

In spite of the potential effectiveness of the Choleric, he is probably by nature in need of more of the Spirit-filled characteristics than any of the other temperaments. Galatians 5:22, 23 reveals the following characteristics needed by the choleric temperament. All of them are found in the life of the Apostle Paul after his conversion.

Love. The first characteristic of the Spirit-filled life is love, which is probably the greatest single need of the choleric believer. By nature Cholerics are unfeeling, hard, unemotional individuals who find it very difficult to express love. Even when they do, it is often mistakenly directed into doing things for other people and expecting them to interpret that as a demonstration of love. Compassion is naturally foreign to a Choleric.

As we read the life of the Apostle Paul, we find him to be a loving Choleric. The Holy Spirit thrillingly transformed him from an angry, bitter, persecuting individual to a compassionate, warm-hearted person. He retained the strength of character and innate sternness of the Choleric, but he consistently conveyed the compassionate, loving interest in other people that is needed in an effective Christian.

There are many illustrations in Paul's writings and in the book of Acts to illustrate our point, but one will suffice. In the book of Romans, the choleric apostle writes, "Brethren, my heart's desire and prayer to God for Israel is, that they might be saved" (10:1). "I say the truth in Christ, I lie not, my conscience also bearing me witness in the Holy Spirit, that I have great heaviness and continual sorrow in my heart. For I could wish that I myself were accursed of God for my brethren, my kinsmen according to the flesh" (9:1-3). No natural Choleric, knowing about eternal damnation and loss of heaven, would be willing to make the sacrifice Paul refers to here. He was actually declaring that he would exchange his place in heaven for hell if the nation Israel could be saved. The self-love of the Choleric renders this absolutely supernatural, possible only by the Holy Spirit. This compassion by the choleric apostle is not exceptional, for we also find it in his attitude toward entire churches, toward individuals, and even toward some of his enemies.

We have a right to expect that a Spirit-filled, choleric Christian will have a compassionate heart towards others. This compassion should begin in his own family and extend to his relatives, his neighbors, and to the most remote peoples of the earth.

It is from the experienced pen of the same choleric apostle that the Holy Spirit admonishes all believers to "rejoice in the Lord always, and again I say, Rejoice" (Philippians 4:4). He also instructed us, "See that none render evil for evil unto any man, but ever follow that which is good, both among yourselves, and to all men. Rejoice evermore. Pray without ceasing. In everything give thanks; for this is the will of God in Christ Jesus concerning you. Quench not the Spirit" (1 Thessalonians 5:15-19). More of God's people quench the Spirit of God by griping and chafing than by anything else. Paul, by example and commandment, admonishes us to "rejoice evermore," and in everything to give thanks—thus we fulfill the will of God. If you are not a rejoicing Christian, you are not a Spirit-filled Christian. Instead of griping and fuming over annoyances, get down on your knees and confess your thankless spirit or persecution complex to God as sin. Ask him to take it away and fill you with his Spirit, then the joy of the Lord will be your experience.

Sometimes we understand the dealings of God with his people; sometimes we do not. You will find when you come to one of those perplexing circumstances that you rejoice anyway. How? By faith through the Holy Spirit. When circumstances look bleak, remember that God is in control and we can rejoice by faith through the ministry of the Holy Spirit in us. Expressing our joy lifts us; expressing our gripes depresses us. It is God's will that we rejoice both in the things we understand and the things we do not. Obedience to this one command will tremendously exhilarate and purify our emotional life.

Peace. Peace in heart is foreign to the carnal Choleric. Not only is he not at peace, but he resents others' having peace. The only sense of peace he experiences is absorption in whirlwind activities; the moment he stops, he is restless to be up and doing, envisioning and prodding something else.

We might expect that the highly motivated and aggressive choleric apostle would find peace only in action. But the record indicates otherwise. The Holy Spirit had so modified the Apostle Paul that he knew peace was not dependent on ideal circumstances. Happy is the Christian who recognizes that heart peace and outward circumstances need not be related. We have not experienced spiritual victory when peace of heart accompanies a pleasant situation. But when things are going wrong and we still have peace, the controlling presence of the Holy Spirit is bearing fruit. Such was the modified character of the choleric apostle.

Nothing could be worse for the dynamic preacher of the gospel than confinement and curtailment of his public ministry. A zealous preacher can bear almost any trial if he can regularly and effectively preach the Word of God. But when the Apostle Paul was imprisoned for proclaiming the gospel of Jesus Christ, a supernatural sense of peace invaded his being. It was this same choleric apostle who said, "Not that I speak in respect of want; for I have learned, in whatsoever state I am, therewith to be content. I know both how to be abased, and I know how to abound; everywhere and in all things I am instructed both to be full and to be hungry, both to abound and to suffer need" (Philippians 4:11, 12).

One day while visiting a discouraged church member confined to bed for a few weeks, I tried to lift her spirit by sharing Paul's challenge to rejoice evermore and experience peace of heart in spite of the circumstances. I read Paul's testimony, "I have learned in whatsoever state I am, therewith to be content," and she retorted, "Well, Paul had never been in a state like this!" I looked at this woman who knew nothing about suffering compared with the apostle, and asked, "Do you know where he was when he made that statement?" "No," she replied. "In jail, waiting to be brought before Caesar and possibly executed for the cause of Christ." Quite embarrassed, she admitted her impulsiveness and entered into prayer in a new spirit. If we chafe and fume in our circumstances, we cannot have the peace of God.

Some Christians fret and worry until they lose control of themselves. The Bible tells us, "Be anxious for nothing; but in everything by prayer and supplication with thanksgiving, let your request be made known unto God. And the peace of God, which passeth all understanding, shall keep your hearts and minds through Christ Jesus" (Philippians 4:6, 7). This statement also was made by the Holy Spirit through the pen of the Apostle Paul while he was in prison. If you lack peace and contentment, confess your self-centered bitterness or fear and ask the Spirit of God to give you his peace.

Gentleness. Carnal Cholerics, by nature, know nothing of gentleness—at least not in the sense the Bible means gentleness. Most translators indicate that the word means "kindness." Can you imagine a thick-skinned, hardnosed, square-jawed but gentle Choleric? Can you further imagine him as polite, gracious, and considerate, performing gentle acts of kindness for others? These stem from a compassionate, tender heart, and that comes only by the filling of the Holy Spirit.

The Apostle Paul exhibited all of these gentle characteristics. The book of Philemon was written as an expression of gentleness, pleading for the welfare of a fellow Christian. An evidence of spontaneous gentleness is recorded in the last written words of the choleric apostle. We have already seen how he blasted Barnabas for insisting on taking young John Mark on the second missionary journey, but in 2 Timothy 4:11 we find these words: "Take Mark, and bring him with thee; for he is profitable to me for the ministry." Paul was big enough to acknowledge that Mark had become a faithful servant of God. This same gentleness, motivated by compassion, is also seen in the apostle's treatment of women. By nature choleric men are not usually very thoughtful of women. And choleric women can be downright nasty to other women, almost as if they resent being women and are scornful of other women who lack their drive and initiative.

Christian Cholerics should go out of their way to be gentle to other people, particularly to women. The self-confidence of a Choleric often creates a feeling of inferiority or insecurity in others. Because he is usually quick of tongue and prone to be sharp and sarcastic, he tends to incite fear in others. From my experience in the counseling room, I would say that more Christian women married to Cholerics have suffered emotional shock than women married to the other three temperaments combined. This is quite understandable when Cholerics do not know Jesus Christ and are not filled with the Holy Spirit, but such mistreatment of the gentler sex is shameful in a Christian companion.

Cholerics tend to dominate every area of activity; consequently, they do not permit others to use their talents and gain self-confidence from personal achievement. Christian Cholerics would be wise to go out of their way to commend others and to show their approval in commendable things. I have observed that, as a rule, Cholerics are very hard to please. Since they are highly opinionated, they easily overlook good and show disapproval because of a minor failure. Yet approval and encouragement is necessary to enhance respect and love. When the Holy Spirit fills a Choleric's life, he will be more concerned about the feelings of others than in letting off steam or expressing himself; this is seen in his gentleness.

A most commendable treatment of women was exhibited by the Apostle Paul in the 16th chapter of Acts. He had been summoned to Macedonia by a man in a vision, but the first devout people he met there were women. At a women's prayer meeting he gave his first message in Europe, and the first convert was Lydia, a seller of rich linen. The entire story shows Paul's gentle concern and respect for womanhood, which was not only contrary to the custom of the day but also opposed to his choleric temperament. Men who are not gentle toward women in general, and their own wives in particular, are not Spirit-filled. The best solution to marital disharmony is the filling of the Holy Spirit. This benefit, of course, is not limited to the marriage relationship but is healing in any conflict arising between people.

Meekness. In his writing on the temperaments, theologian Alexander Whyte offers this prayer that should be the attitude of the choleric Christian: "Lord, let me be ever courteous, and easy to be entreated. Never let me fall into a peevish or contentious spirit. Let me follow peace with all men, offering forgiveness, inviting them by courtesies, ready to confess my own errors, apt to make amends, and desirous to be reconciled. Give me the spirit of a Christian, charitable, humble, merciful and meek, useful and liberal, angry at nothing but my own sins, and grieving for the sins of others, that, while my passion obeys my reason, and my reason is religious, and my religion is pure and undefiled, managed with humility, and adorned with charity, I may escape thy anger, which I have deserved, and may dwell in thy love, and be thy son and servant forever, through Jesus Christ our Lord, Amen."

Faith. Faith is another spiritual trait greatly needed by the carnal Choleric. Oh, he has plenty of faith in himself, which we call self-confidence, but he desperately needs to believe God and trust God for everything. The Apostle Paul is a classic example of a Spirit-filled Choleric who no longer trusts in himself but relies implicitly on the living God. One of many passages that reveals this is Paul's extraordinary statement spoken on a ship in the midst of a storm: "Sirs, be of good cheer; for I believe God, that it shall be even as it was told me" (Acts 27:25). This faith comes from knowing the Word of God and being controlled by the Holy Spirit. It is sometimes difficult to tell whether a choleric Christian is placing his faith in himself or in God. But he knows. If he is trusting in himself, he is not Spirit-filled.

Humility. Many passages in the book of Acts and in Paul's epistles reveal a surprising humility in a choleric temperament. One such passage is Acts 14 where Paul and Barnabas receive acclaim as gods by the people of Lystra. Immediately the apostles tore their clothes in revulsion and asserted that they were just human beings. Shortly after this Paul was stoned and left for dead, perhaps because some people were disillusioned or vengeful at discovering that the miracle-working men were only flesh and blood. Such an opportunity to masquerade as a god would have been seized and exploited by a carnal Choleric.

The Holy Spirit was aware of Paul's need for humility, for after his vision of heaven recorded in 2 Corinthians 12, he noted in verse 7: "And lest I should be exalted above measure through the abundance of the revelations, there was given to me a thorn in the flesh, the messenger of Satan to buffet me, lest I should be exalted above measure." Although Paul prayed that this "thorn" of affliction be removed, God promised his grace would be sufficient for Paul's need, and the thorn remained. This is an example of a Spirit-approved (and Satan-inspired!) physical adversity to maintain a Christian's humility and dependence on God. Since God never does anything not for good (Romans 8:28), we may conclude that Paul had a struggle with the trait of humility—as does every Choleric. Many a Christian Choleric is proud and domineering of his natural temperament. As he refuses to change, he perpetuates his spiritual immaturity and restricts God's use of his life.

Jacob Behman, as quoted by Alexander Whyte, made the following statement concerning the Choleric's need of humility. "That man, who has his soul compassed about with a choleric complexion, must above all things practice at every turn and exercise himself like an athlete in humility. He must everyday pour the cold water of humility on the hot coals of his own complexion. Take all thy might after meekness in word and thought, and so shall not thy temperament inflame thy soul. Choleric man, mortify thy temperament and thy complexion, and do all to the glory of God."

Who can doubt after reading 2 Corinthians and understanding the events that inspired it that the choleric apostle had learned to humble himself? When his own spiritual children rebuffed him and rejected his first epistle because he named their sin, he spoke endearingly, patiently, and graciously, without the sarcastic barbs that characterize the natural Choleric. This can only be attributed to the modifying ministry of the Holy Spirit.

When the Lord Jesus spoke to Paul from heaven and said, "I am Jesus, whom thou persecutest; it is hard for thee to kick against the goads," Paul instantly answered, "Lord, what wilt thou have me to do?" (Acts 9:5, 6). When the Lord instructed him to arise and go into the city, he immediately obeyed. From that point on, his life was characterized by prompt obedience, indicating his complete yieldedness to the Holy Spirit.

On the Damascus road Paul surrendered his strong choleric will to Jesus Christ. Only rarely did he retake that will from his Master. So he could counsel others in Romans 6:13, "Neither yield ye your members as instruments of unrighteousness unto sin, but yield yourselves unto God, as those that are alive from the dead, and your members as instruments of righteousness unto God."

God has given to every man a free will which he can use as he sees fit. Paul chose to reject self-will and its brittle potentialities, and accept the perfect will of Jesus Christ. We cannot imagine all that was involved in that instant decision. As a member of the select Sanhedrin, Saul the Pharisee had a glittering future. Starting out at such a young age on the council, he would likely have become a prominent leader of Israel and might have become the high priest. When he yielded himself to Jesus Christ he was in effect saying, "I am giving up all efforts for personal glory, all opportunities for personal power, and am turning my back on everything I previously worked for because it was all opposed to the will of Jesus Christ." There were no strings on Paul's commitment, but perfect yieldedness.

Some Christians think that such a decision is a great sacrifice. A young person may fear that if he surrenders his life to Jesus Christ he will end up in a jungle wilderness or a position alien to his interests. This betrays a twisted conception of God's love. Our heavenly Father wants us to be happy more than we do. I have yet to meet a miserable Christian who is fully surrendered to God's will, but I know many frustrated Christians who will not yield their lives to God.

At the time Paul made his dynamic decision, it seemed as though he were giving up a great deal. He was unceremoniously expelled from the Sanhedrin council and his name became despised in Israel. But as the Apostle Paul he proceeded under the controlling power of the Holy Spirit to become the greatest name in Christian history. How many of the other Sanhedrin members can you remember? Most of the world knows about the choleric Apostle Paul. Certainly fame doesn't come through dedication to Christ, but personal fulfillment comes only in this way. Paul's life is a classic example of Jesus' words: "He that findeth his life shall lose it; and he that loses his life for my sake shall find it" (Matthew 10:39). What are you doing with your life? If it isn't yielded to the Lord Jesus Christ, I suggest that you give it to him and receive a hundredfold in return.

5

MOSES THE MELANCHOLY

The richest of all temperaments is the melancholy. It is usually blessed with a gifted mind and a tremendous capacity to experience the complete spectrum of emotions. Its greatest danger is in giving in to negative thinking patterns that exaggerate its pessimistic tendencies. Some of the world's greatest geniuses have been gifted Melancholies who squandered their talents in the slough of despondency and became apathetic and unproductive. This should never happen to a Christian Melancholy, for he has a source of power within him to change a negative thinking pattern to positive and motivate him to the maximum use of his talents. The secret of motivation is one's thinking pattern, and the key to a proper thinking pattern is the Spirit-filled life. A simple rule that will help a Christian Melancholy is to question the validity of every negative thought, counter it with positive thought, and claim Philippians 4:13. Amazing results will follow.

Evidence that melancholic Christians have abundant potential is seen in the lives of great men of God in the Bible who were more often melancholy than any other temperament. The Melancholies' "hall of fame" would include Jacob, Solomon, Elijah, Elisha, Jeremiah, Isaiah, Daniel, Ezekiel, Obadiah, Jonah, John the Baptist, the Apostles John and Thomas, and many others. Heading this list of famous servants of God is the greatest man in the history of Israel, Moses the Melancholy.

In order to evaluate the temperament of Moses we should first examine the strengths and weaknesses of the melancholy temperament. Mr. Melancholy is the most talented of all the temperaments. He is a natural perfectionist, very sensitive and appreciative of the fine arts, analytical, self-sacrificing, and a faithful friend. He is not outgoing as a rule and rarely pushes himself forward. With his exceptional gifts come equally complex weaknesses that often neutralize his effectiveness. He tends to be moody, critical, pessimistic, and self-centered. The world's great artists, composers, philosophers, inventors, and theoreticians have usually been Melancholies.

Melancholy Moses provides an excellent study in temperament analysis because so much information is given about him in Scripture. Certain factors, however, make it difficult to determine whether some activities were motivated by the power of God or the variations of his temperament. First, he lived before Pentecost when the Holy Spirit did not indwell believers as he does today. Even more important, a melancholy person experiences a variety of mood fluctuations that are sometimes confusing. It is easy to diagnose his dark moods as flesh motivated, but sometimes his bright moods make him appear Spirit-led when he is not. One can only determine his real source of control by his actions over a period of time.

The melancholy leader of Israel is a classic illustration of the difference which the power of God makes in a man's life. After forty years of education in the center of Egyptian culture, this brilliant Melancholy spent forty years tending animals in a remote desert. At eighty he heard God from a burning bush, and during the next forty years he was one of the greatest leaders in the history of the world. The change in this melancholy servant of Jehovah was gradual, sometimes sporadic, occasionally electrifying, but in some cases regressive. All of this establishes him as quite human and provides us with a typical illustration of Spirit-directed melancholy temperament when he was yielded to the Holy Spirit and raw melancholy temperament when he was not. Like any other Christian, Moses was productive for God only when he was controlled by the Holy Spirit.

Gifted

The inherent talent and gifts of Moses the Melancholy are apparent throughout the entire scriptural narrative. In Acts 7, Stephen, the first Christian martyr, informs us that Moses "was learned in all the wisdom of the Egyptians, and was mighty in words and in deeds" (Acts 7:22). Egypt was a leading center of civilization in Moses' day, apparently, and he absorbed the knowledge of the Egyptians without being dominated by it. The concepts of the Egyptians were heavily inculcated with superstition, none of which taints the writings of Moses. This is not only a testimony to his ability, but a confirmation of the power of the Holy Spirit within him as he wrote. The tremendous gifts of character and the Holy Spirit are graphically illustrated in his writings in the first five books of the Bible. Granted, the Holy Spirit gave these Scriptures to Moses, but the personality of Moses shines through the scriptural narrative, establishing him as the outstanding intellect of the Old Testament, just as the Apostle Paul's writings confirm him as the outstanding scholar among New Testament writers.

Melancholy people have a capacity for the dramatic and rise to great heights on occasion. Moses was never better cast than when he appeared before the Egyptian Pharaoh, unemotionally delivered the warning of God, and eventually convinced the stubborn king with ten miraculous plagues to let God's people go free. As a general rule, melancholy people excel under this kind of pressure because external motivation spurs their latent talents. Once the pressure is off, however, they tend to recede into apathy unless motivated by the Holy Spirit.

The ability of Moses to lead three million people on a wilderness journey and control them as judge, prophet, and mediator with God reflects his exceptionally gifted nature. Even acknowledging the special guidance of God and his divine enabling in his melancholy servant, we are confronted with a man of tremendous gifts. Secular historians agree that Moses was one of the superior men of his time.

Self-sacrificing

One of the hallmarks of a melancholy temperament is a desire to be self-sacrificing. Strongly melancholy individuals find it difficult to enjoy ease or success without a guilty conscience. They are often prone to dedicate themselves to some sacrificial cause. This usually is on a personal basis with a high personal cost. Dr. Albert Schweitzer was a good example of such a gifted, self-sacrificing temperament. He had already distinguished himself as an exceptional musician and able philosopher when he took up medicine and devoted his life to healing the sick in a remote area of Africa. Typical of his temperament, he chose an area where the people could never adequately compensate him for his services.

One of the values of a temperament study for Melancholies is its help for decision-making. Melancholies should carefully check their tendency to be "sacrificial" for selfish reasons! Sometimes they cramp and misdirect their lives in a self-sacrificing endeavor that actually is self-serving—a means of heightening pride through self-abasement. Some humanitarian enterprises are compensations for self-deficiencies, and therefore are not as noble as they appear. Service and sacrifice must not be disparaged, but the melancholy person should examine his decisions to see that they are God-directed, not self-centered.

Very little is known about the life of Moses between his adoption by Pharaoh's daughter and his identification with his own people forty years later. The book of Hebrews, however, reveals how Moses came to his crucial decision. "By faith Moses, when he was come to years, refused to be called the son of Pharaoh's daughter, choosing rather to suffer affliction with the people of God than to enjoy the pleasures of sin for a season, esteeming the reproach of Christ greater riches than the treasures in Egypt; for he had respect unto the recompense of the reward. By faith he forsook Egypt, not fearing the wrath of the king; for he endured, as seeing him who is invisible" (11:24-27).

Jewish historians suggest on the basis of tradition that Moses was the prime minister of Egypt and as the adopted son of Pharaoh's daughter he was second only to the Pharaoh himself. But he chose to "suffer affliction with the people of God"—a very self-sacrificing decision. We realize from this passage that Moses had the spiritual capacity to understand the transient value of this world and the enduring riches of the life to come. On that basis he was willing to sacrifice the "pleasures of sin for a season" that he might be God's man and earn an eternal reward.

To one degree or another, all Christians face this decision. It seems easier for a melancholy person to see through the sham and the shallow material rewards this world offers and to rightly evaluate eternal things. I have observed that many missionaries going to the foreign field have a higher-than-average degree of melancholy temperament. This characteristic accounts for the fact that many gifted missionaries are willing to renounce the pleasures and possessions of this life to serve Jesus Christ here and anticipate his "Well done, thou good and faithful servant," plus the reward that "fadeth not away, reserved in heaven for you." Moses' life proves that no man loses who gives his life to God.

Self-depreciating

Although the Melancholy may possess the greatest native talents of any of the temperaments, these talents are often neglected because of an inordinate feeling of inferiority. Melancholy people are perfectionists; consequently, they are rarely satisfied with anything they do or anyone else does because it fails to measure up to their high standards of perfection. It is almost impossible for a Melancholy who is unaided by the Holy Spirit to graciously receive commendation or congratulations. Whether directing an orchestra or quarter-backing a football team, he remembers his mistakes rather than the overall success.

A publisher and I discussed the writings of one of the great Bible scholars of our day who possesses no small degree of melancholy temperament. His work is so excellent that the published books instantly become outstanding sellers. Yet they reach the reader only after long delays. Printing deadlines have to be pushed back because the author constantly revises his work. The first draft of his writing looks eloquent to other people, but the gifted Melancholy is dissatisfied.

Parents must be especially considerate of this tendency in a melancholy child, for criticism makes a deep impression on his sensitive nature and may discourage further effort. When asked to undertake a project, the strong Melancholy activates his inferiority complex with a series of excuses. If he can be persuaded to try, he usually does an excellent job. When stripped of his excuses, Mr. Melancholy begins to realize that his reluctance stems from his self-protective instinct. His aversion to criticism—by himself or others—is greater than his desire to see the job done.

The excuses Moses gave to Almighty God during their conversation at the burning bush are a classic example of Melancholies' low esteem for themselves. We will look at each of them in detail to see how a gifted and sincere man can live far below his potential. Fortunately, Moses responded in spite of his excuses, and later events proved Moses could do what he thought he couldn't. A melancholy person should never trust his feelings to guide him through a door of opportunity for God. Instead, he should commit himself to God's sure leading. Then he can claim Philippians 4:13 and know that God will supply his needs, and remind himself that "If God be for us, who can be against us?" (Romans 8:31).

1. *I don't have any talent!* After appearing to Moses in the burning bush and revealing his long-range plan of leading the Jews out of Egypt and into "a land flowing with milk and honey," God said to Moses, "Come now therefore, and I will send thee unto Pharaoh, that thou mayest bring forth my people the children of Israel out of Egypt" (Exodus 3:10). Moses unfurled his inferiority complex by replying, "Who am I, that I should go unto Pharaoh and that I should bring forth the children of Israel out of Egypt?" In other words, Moses was protesting: "I don't have any talent." Though secretly proud, as a typical Melancholy, Moses depreciated his personal ability. So he shrank from making his talent available to God.

Many melancholy Christians do the same thing today. When challenged by a Sunday school superintendent or pastor, they draw back, thinking: "Who am I?" or "I don't have any talent." God's answer to Moses is as valid for twentieth-century Christians as for the chosen leader of Israel. God promised, "Certainly I will be with thee!" What more did Moses need!

Of tremendous help to every melancholy Christian would be a study in the Bible concerning God's provision. Reading through the Scriptures, we find that whether God is speaking to Adam and Eve, Noah, Abraham, Moses, the prophets, or the kings, he always promises to keep and strengthen them. And the Lord Jesus promised his disciples the same just before he left this world.

In Matthew 28:18-20, after issuing the Great Commission, which commanded believers to go into all the world and preach the gospel to every creature, Jesus concluded, ". . . and, lo, I am with you always, even unto the end of the age." What greater assurance could a Melancholy ask who is struggling with an inferiority complex? If you as a Christian Melancholy have a tendency to reject opportunities for Christian service, may I suggest that you remind yourself that God has promised, "Certainly I will be with thee!" Actually, since God indwells our lives in the person of his Holy Spirit, we don't even need talent to serve him—we simply need to be responsive to his directing.

2. *I don't know theology.* Melancholy Moses' second excuse for not serving God was as ill founded as the first. He assumed that when he went to lead Israel out of Egypt the people would question his commission from God, and so he weakly inquired, "What shall I say unto them?" Moses was trained in the arts of the Egyptians, but he was not yet instructed in the principles of God and he knew that many of the Israelites raised in the land of Goshen were educated in the faith of their fathers.

Many modern-day Christians claim ignorance as an excuse for failing to witness for Christ. Before they share what Jesus Christ has done for them, they imagine a skeptic concocting a philosophical or theological question they cannot cope with and so they refuse to try. Jesus prepared the seventy messengers of his kingdom by assuring them: "It shall be given you in that same hour what ye shall speak. For it is not ye that speak, but the Spirit of your Father who speaketh in you" (Matthew 10:19, 20).

The Lord God revealed himself to Moses as the omnipotent, unchangeable Sovereign by saying: "I am that I am." He then proceeded to inform Moses that he is the God of Abraham, Isaac, and Jacob, that he promised to deliver Israel, and that Moses should give them the promises of God.

In a vital way, this is what Christians do today in sharing their faith, ministering to needs, and standing for righteousness in society. We reveal the nature of God as revealed to us in the Word of God and convey the promises of God to spiritually lost men. With the Holy Spirit as our personal instructor and the Word of God in an easily understood version, any Christian can serve Christ before mastering the Bible. One need not be a Bible school or seminary graduate to introduce a person to Jesus Christ. Any true believer who knows John 3:16 and companion verses can do that. It is not a question of how much we know, but how much we care. Someone has said, "The key to success in the Christian life is not ability but availability."

3. *No one will believe me!* "Moses answered and said, But, behold, they will not believe me, nor hearken unto my voice" (Exodus 4:1). Fear of rejection is part of the inferiority complex of the melancholy temperament. Moses clearly reveals this fear in his excuse, and he does so in direct contradiction to God's promise. In chapter 3, verse 18, God had promised, "And they shall hearken to

thy voice. . . ." What could be more explicit! God had assured Moses that the people of Israel would believe him, but Moses chose to remember his rejection forty years earlier by some Israelites he tried to help (Exodus 2:11-15). Naturally, he felt he would be repulsed again.

Failure is often devastating to Melancholies. From that point on, their feelings of inferiority increase and they dread to attempt anything lest they repeat their disastrous performance. Right here Mr. Melancholy should take a good look at a very natural habit, that of thinking more of himself than the cause of Christ and the needs of others. One of the best escapes from this mental prison is to focus attention on the ripe harvest field of the world that Jesus said is waiting for spiritual laborers.

Doubtless the judgment seat of Christ will reveal a grievous number of Christians who quenched the Holy Spirit's leading to share their faith because "they will not believe me." This fear is completely selfish! The sooner we recognize and confess it as a sin, the sooner we will experience the power of the Holy Spirit in our lives. We are not responsible for the success or failure of our witness; we are responsible only to give that witness.

4. *I can't speak in public!* Moses' fourth excuse is used by Christians repeatedly. In Moses' words, "I am not eloquent . . . but I am slow of speech, and of a slow tongue." Every pastor and Sunday school teacher has heard this excuse in one form or another. God's answer to Moses is as pertinent today as it was then. "And the Lord said unto him, Who hath made man's mouth? Or who maketh the dumb, or deaf, or the seeing, or the blind? Have not I the Lord? Now therefore go, and I will be with thy mouth and teach thee what thou shalt say" (Exodus 4:11, 12). The question, God said, is not what you can do but what I can do. As is often the case, gifted, scholarly people are not loquacious, but neither are they guilty of saying meaningless things. Though Melancholies may not be dynamic and charismatic like Sanguines, the Holy Spirit certainly can make them effective speakers.

Moses' lame excuse not only slighted the power of God, it saddled him with an assistant, his brother Aaron, who often was a hindrance rather than a help. Moses was not a gifted speaker, but a call to preach or teach the Word of God is not concerned with eloquence—it asks obedience. The Lord's answer to Moses reveals unequivocally that the power of God, not our talents and potential, gains spiritual success. The Christian Melancholy, like Moses, can prove the power of the living God by trusting his direction rather than his own feelings of inadequacy.

As pastor of a church with an active youth ministry, I have gone out of my way to encourage melancholic young men to consider the gospel ministry. We don't need more ministers of melancholy temperament than others, but melancholy youths are prone to think they are unqualified for preaching because they are more inhibited than their sanguine and choleric friends. Such young men need encouragement that speaking competence can be acquired. As sanguine and choleric students have to discipline themselves to learn *what* to say, the Melancholy requires training in learning *how* to say it. By nature, he will set a high standard for study and will strive for superior sermons.

An older minister who had a profound influence on my life surprised me by revealing that as a lad he resisted God's call to preach the gospel because he stuttered severely. He went to college finally with faith that God would remove his impediment. When I met him years later and heard him preach repeatedly, not once did I detect a speech impediment. It would never have been known if he had not mentioned it. Man's inabilities are no measure of God's provision.

5. *I don't want to go.* The irresolute, impractical tendency of a Melancholy is revealed in the last excuse of Moses that incurred the anger of the Lord. "And he said, O my Lord, send, I pray thee, by the hand of him whom thou wilt send" (4:13)—in other words, "I'd appreciate it if you sent someone else." This bares Moses' real reason for not accepting the leadership of Israel—he just didn't want to do it. Melancholy people have a tendency to clutch preconceived prejudices in the face of contrary facts. Once they make up their minds they can't do something, even good reasoning will not change their minds. God had performed miracles for Moses, had answered every one of his doubts, and had even given him the power to perform miracles, but Moses asked God to send someone else because he didn't want to go. He was on the verge of turning down the greatest opportunity he would ever receive. Only God's insistence and the provision of an assistant persuaded Moses to be available.

It is possible that the fifth excuse of Moses reveals his pent-up hostility and bitterness from forty years of isolation in the wilderness. Humanly speaking, we can understand that when he was willing to give up the pleasures and prestige of Egyptian leadership for his people, only to be rejected by them, he would develop deep resentment. I am inclined to believe this is one of the underlying factors in his rejection of God's call. Sensitive, melancholy people brood and indulge in persecution complexes to their own detriment. Moses' inability to make a common sense decision in the very presence of God was probably caused by a faulty thinking pattern that had persisted for forty years. This poisons the emotional well-being of any temperament, but particularly of a Melancholy. Such feelings are sin and have no place in the heart of a believer. They must be confessed and replaced with thanksgiving by faith in order to maintain fellowship with God (1 Thessalonians 5:18).

Good mental and spiritual hygiene for every temperament, particularly the melancholy, is to refuse to coddle negative and critical thoughts. Since the Melancholy by temperament is a perfectionist, he severely criticizes those who disagree with him. No one can breed bitterness or nurse a grudge like a Melancholy. Such thanklessness not only grieves the Holy Spirit, it produces a very unpleasant personality.

The bitterness of Moses points up the power of forgiveness. I have known many people who were so filled with hatred that they could not think rationally, and some people have unconsciously turned their hatred for one person toward people they really loved. One of the leading causes of sexual impotence in biologically normal men is hatred. It may be subconscious aversion to a domineering, critical mother or a woman who spurned their love, but it can deaden the normal mating drive with a wife they truly love. I have known men that were immediately healed when they got down on their knees and confessed their hatred and asked God to give them a forgiving heart. Forgiveness removed a spiritual cancer.

The remedy for negative, stultifying thinking is not difficult for a Christian. He simply acknowledges bitter thoughts, hostile feelings, and "evil imaginations" about others as sin and confesses them, then he will be released from their power and forgiven by God. A new thinking pattern is built by concentrating on good things and God's good purpose for all. We should not be discouraged if this change does not come immediately, for a pattern is made up of many pieces. An excellent verse of Scripture to memorize and follow is Philippians 4:8: "Finally, brethren, whatever things are

true, whatever things are honest, whatever things are just, whatever
things are pure, whatever things are lovely, whatever things are of
good report; if there be any virtue, and if there be any praise, think
on these things."

The excuses of Moses the Melancholy that reveal his inferiority
complex are all based on lies. Although they seemed reasonable to
him, none was valid—nor helpful. Such feelings limit the effectiveness of any individual. If you are ruled by an inferiority complex,
you are limiting God through unbelief. One of your great needs,
therefore, is faith, and faith comes through the Word of God, by the
Holy Spirit. It is a gift for your taking, and it increases "from faith
unto faith" as we obey God's leading step by step to his destination
for us.

Moses' anger

In addition to fear, repressed anger often stalks the temperament
of a Melancholy. Moses' propensity for anger seared several epi-
sodes of his life. His failure to gain control over this emotion cost
him the satisfaction of leading his people into the Promised Land.
This deep-running anger, which not only grieves the Spirit of God,
but sometimes destroys one's health, is fertile soil for irritability.

As you read through Scripture, note such reports as "Moses was
angry with them" (Exodus 16:20) and "Moses' anger burned"
(Exodus 32:19). Not all anger is wrong, but self-indulgent anger
displeases God and leads to serious overt sins.

Moses' anger flared surprisingly after he had experienced many
days in the presence of God on the mountain where God wrote the
Ten Commandments and gave him Israel's laws. When Moses
rejoined the people and saw them indulging in pagan, immoral
revelings, he was so angry that he "cast the tables out of his hands,
and broke them" (Exodus 32:19). This may have been righteous
anger toward evil, but Moses' propensity for wrath produced sin
when not controlled.

Anger-motivated actions usually cause problems and intensify
difficulties. James 1:20 tells us, "the wrath of man worketh not the
righteousness of God." Anger must lead to righteous action for God
to be served.

We can appreciate the enormous emotional pressure on Moses in
the wilderness. The hot, hungry, disgruntled Israelites took out
their frustrations on Moses, complaining bitterly against him when-

ever they were dissatisfied with God's provisions for them. Few men have faced the pressures he did for such a long period of time. No understanding person would criticize Moses for becoming vexed at these ungrateful people, but the all-sufficient God did. God had offered Moses all the guidance and power he needed, and Moses' neglect of it resulted in sinful self-assertion that matted his testimony and invoked God's judgment.

Toward the end of their exile in the wilderness, when Moses' irritability was at an all-time high, the people besieged him with complaints. Numbers 20:3-5 records their savage verbal assault: "Would God that we had died when our brethren died before the Lord! And why have ye brought up the congregation of the Lord into this wilderness, that we and our cattle should die there? And wherefore have ye made us to come up out of Egypt, to bring us in unto this evil place? It is no place of seed, or of figs, or of vines, or of pomegranates; neither is there any water to drink."

Moses' initial reaction is portrayed in the next verses. "And Moses and Aaron went from the presence of the assembly unto the door of the tabernacle of the congregation, and they fell upon their faces; and the glory of the Lord appeared unto them. And the Lord spoke unto Moses, saying, Take the rod, and gather thou the assembly together . . . and speak ye unto the rock before their eyes; and it shall give forth its water, and thou shalt bring forth to them water out of the rock: so thou shalt give the congregation and their beasts drink."

Then the melancholy nature of Moses erupted in anger. "And Moses took the rod from before the Lord, as he commanded him. And Moses and Aaron gathered the congregation together before the rock, and he said unto them, Hear now, ye rebels; must we fetch you water out of this rock? And Moses lifted up his hand, and with his rod he smote the rock twice; and the water came out abundantly, and the congregation drank, and their beasts also. And the Lord spoke unto Moses and Aaron, Because ye believed me not, to sanctify me in the eyes of the children of Israel, therefore ye shall not bring this congregation into the land which I have given them" (Numbers 20:9-12).

Though Moses' vehemence may seem insignificant, he flagrantly disobeyed the express command of God to speak to the rock. God's plan was to show his gracious provision in response to the people's needs, but Moses' impetuous action ruined all that! With an imperious denunciation of the people, he struck the rock twice and the water gushed out. Instead of conveying God's grace and power, Moses communicated his own rage and self-righteousness. His poor example shortened his life and his leadership as God decreed he could not enter the Promised Land. He was given a mountaintop view of the land just prior to his death, but a new, unsullied leader took his place at the front of Israel's army.

Unconfessed anger still causes many heartaches in the lives of God's people. It grieves and suppresses the Spirit, cheats Christians of eternal rewards, and even shortens lives (1 Corinthians 11:30-32). I know a missionary of melancholy temperament who died many years before his time because be refused to admit that his anger was sin. He blamed everyone around him, stewed in his own misery, and died from an overdose of black bile before he reached the normal halfway mark in life! It isn't worth it! We may profit from Moses' experience and enjoy the maximum blessings of God in this life and the life to come by seeking the transforming grace of the Holy Spirit for all forms of angry hostility.

Moses' depression

Moses is one of three great servants of God who became so depressed that he despaired of life and asked God to let him die. The others were Elijah (1 Kings 19) and Jonah (Jonah 4:1-3). Of all the temperaments, melancholy people have the greatest problem with depression. Some very impressive excuses are given to justify depression, but, as I pointed out in the chapter on the subject in *Spirit-Controlled Temperament*, depression is the emotional result of *self-pity*. It doesn't matter what temperament you are, if you indulge in self-pity you will be depressed. Melancholy people experience more depression because they tend to indulge in self-pity more than others. They can be gracious and kind outwardly but be suffering in self-pity which if indulged long enough, will develop into a persecution complex or apathetic state.

The account of Moses' depression is given in Numbers 11:10-15 for our admonition and profit. In the account we find Moses' angry thinking pattern going from bad to worse. Instead of looking to God for his needs when the people complained about the heaven-sent bread called manna, he began to feel sorry for himself. "Wherefore hast thou afflicted thy servant . . . that thou layest the burden of all this people upon me?" Moses moaned. How human; and how wrong! God never asked Moses to bear all this burden or responsibility; it was God's! Moses cultivated so much pity for himself that he asked God: "Kill me, I pray thee, out of hand."

Have you ever felt so burdened that you wanted to die? If so, I suggest that it wasn't the size of your burdens that crushed you, but your attitude toward them. Attitude forms your thinking patterns which produce your feelings. If your attitude is consistently thankful to God, you cannot become depressed. But if you focus on unfavorable circumstances around you, you will frequently be depressed. Remember, Moses' reaction to the situation caused his depression, not the circumstances in themselves. God promises to sustain us at all times, and since he cannot fail it is our refusal to believe him and appropriate his supply that produces self-pity and depression.

One reassuring aspect of this story is that God disregarded Moses' request to die. Evidently the melancholy servant confessed his sin of self-pity, for God went on to use him for many years. This should bring hope to depressed saints who, like Moses, have prayed for death. God forgives us and uses our lives. He did the same to Elijah and Jonah. If, however, you are in severe depression, you face a decision. Will you give thanks no matter what the outlook, as commanded by God, or will you go right on indulging your self-pity? You decide whether or not you will be healed, and Christ waits to heal you.

Moses' perfectionism

As a Melancholy, Moses was a perfectionist. In spite of those moments of carnality mentioned above, Moses' talents were yielded to God. If you read the latter half of Exodus and the books of Numbers and Leviticus, you will see how God used this characteristic. God gave Moses the meticulously minute details of his law: the ceremonial law, the governmental law, and the instruction of the priesthood. He also gave Moses the specific measurements and materials for building the tabernacle, the Israelites' center of worship for hundreds of years. God's standard of righteousness is so exact that only a Spirit-filled Melancholy like Moses could have been his instrument for such an undertaking. One of the outstanding instruments of blessing to the people of God in Old Testament days was the tabernacle, provided by the grace of God through the perfectionist traits of Moses which were yielded to the Holy Spirit. God is ever seeking such traits to bless the lives of men.

Probably as a product of this perfectionist ability, Melancholies have a difficult time delegating authority and responsibility. A prime illustration of that in Moses' life is found in the 18th chapter of Exodus. His father-in-law, Jethro, who came to visit Moses and his daughter, found his son-in-law so busy administering laws that he couldn't spend any time with his family. Moses was so conscientious that he was trying to help everyone who wanted to come to him. Working from morning to night, he returned home exhausted. Jethro counseled: "The thing that thou doest is not good. Thou wilt surely wear away, both thou, and this people that are with thee; for this thing is too heavy for thee; thou art not able to perform it thyself alone" (18:17, 18). He then advised Moses to select qualified men to divide the populace into small groups and rule over their affairs. Moses heeded this advice and helped everyone!

This story is used in business management courses as an illustration of how to cure an organizational problem. Much of the creative genius of a melancholy person is lost because he is reluctant to assign to others the work that needs to be accomplished. As a rule, he has an innate distrust for the abilities of others, and thus tends to do everything himself. D. L. Moody used to advise: "Instead of doing the work of ten men, get ten men to work." When motivated by the Holy Spirit, Mr. Melancholy will tend to get his eyes off details and onto important projects. As the vision of a lost world burns into his heart and mind, he will tend to put a premium on motivating others instead of being a one-man band. He may have to settle for work beneath his standard of perfection, but the net result will be far greater productivity in the cause of Christ. Moses' reorganization program freed him from details, thus reserving his time for things of major importance.

Some men will admit, "But I like to do these things myself." Although they do a terrific job by themselves, it is only a fraction of what they could accomplish had they trusted God and other people. I know a man who does the work of three people, but if he were not afraid of rejection and didn't have a low esteem of others' capabilities, he could delegate authority and accomplish the work of ten. When this is pointed out to him, he gets defensive and protests, "But we can't find adequate help," or, "I'm afraid other people will do it wrong and I'll have to do it over anyway." By contrast, the Spirit-filled Melancholy will think big. Most people by nature have too little vision, and this is particularly a weakness of Mr. Melancholy.

Moses' loyalty

One of the most admirable traits of a Melancholy is his loyalty and faithfulness. Although he does not make friends easily he is intensely loyal to those he acquires. This characteristic makes him particularly devoted to God when filled with the Spirit. When Moses turned his life over to God, he became an example of this dedication, directed by the Holy Spirit. He was so transformed that he changed from an insecure, doubtful, pessimistic, compulsive, depressed man to the responsible father-image for the people, who responded to his leadership. As Moses walked with God, so the Israelites walked.

Moses' devotion seems to have grown through the forty years he served God. As problems arose, he turned to God for guidance. When the people complained of hunger, Moses prayed and God answered with manna from heaven (Exodus 16). When they needed water, he struck the rock and God supplied an abundance of water (Exodus 17). When they needed the waters of the Red Sea rolled back, he struck them with his rod in the name of the Lord and God miraculously separated the waters (Exodus 14). The man's faith is a tribute to what God can do with a fearful, negative, melancholy temperament dedicated to his will.

The information is so complete concerning the life and ministry of Moses that the reader would be wise to study Exodus 1–20; 24:9–18; 32–34; and the book of Numbers. The transforming power of the Holy Spirit is demonstrated on almost every page. This does not mean that Moses was perfect. You will come upon several failures in his life that indicate be was very human during the years he served God. That, of course, is what makes the Bible such a believable book: it portrays both the successes and failures of its heroes because, as they say today, "That's the way it is." God doesn't use perfect men—there aren't any. He uses men who trust him. Every successful servant of God has had to get up off the canvas of failure at some time in his life, confess his unbelief, and ask God to use him again.

Even the greatest of Spirit-filled Christians have proved their humanity by failure. Almost every great saint I know admits to apologizing to some brother for something said or done. Moses is a good example of Spirit-filled temperament, not because he was perfect, but because most of the time he was pliable in the hand of God. Melancholy Christians' failure to be perfect often digs another pitfall: "If I can't be perfect, I won't try at all." And they quit. To Moses' credit, although he fell many times, each time he confessed his sin, re-yielding his life to God, and went on as a transformed Melancholy. God wants to do the same in every life. Right now, instead of fretting over your weaknesses, thank God for his power in your life and trust him to transform you.

6

ABRAHAM THE PHLEGMATIC

The easiest people to get along with in life are Phlegmatics. Their calm, easygoing nature makes them well liked by others, and their clever wit and dry humor makes them a joy to have around. They qualify for the "Mr. Nice Guy" label wherever they go. In fact, Phlegmatics are usually such good people that they act more like Christians before their salvation than other temperament types afterward.

Mr. Phlegmatic, in addition to being calm and easygoing, is a cheerful fellow who works well with others. He is an efficient, conservative, dependable, witty person with a practical turn of mind. Since he is quite introvertish, as a rule, his weaknesses, like his strengths, are not as readily perceptible as those of the more expressive temperaments. But he does have some, the greatest of which is lack of motivation. He can ignore work graciously and is prone to be stubborn, stingy, and indecisive. He has an ability to look at life through the eyes of a spectator and seek to avoid "getting involved" with anything. Phlegmatics make good diplomats since they are natural peacemakers. Many are teachers, doctors, scientists, comedians, and magazine and book editors. When externally motivated they make very capable leaders.

As a professional observer of people, I have concluded that when filled with the Spirit, and thus properly motivated, Phlegmatics make unusually successful servants of Christ. They never volunteer to serve as leaders, but they have latent leadership capabilities and, because of their efficient, gracious way with others, do not seem to create friction.

Several years ago I elected to have a professionally trained school teacher lead our vacation Bible school program during the summer. She was predominantly choleric in temperament and tackled the job with characteristic intensity. We enjoyed a very good school that year, exceptionally efficient and well run. However, she tended to be sharp and abrasive with people. In fact, the next year we experienced a very difficult time securing workers. About that time I was in the midst of my first serious studies of temperament. As a result, I developed a growing respect for the phlegmatic temperament as a source of untapped help. Rather than give up my idea of having a professionally trained educator run our VBS program, I urged the Christian education board to seek a Phlegmatic to take the job. Naturally she was reluctant—Phlegmatics usually are—but we persisted. Finally she agreed, and we have been delighted with the results. Not only have we enjoyed a well-planned and efficient school, but a director who is so easy to work with that we have little trouble getting others to participate when they discover that Mrs. Phlegmatic is the superintendent.

One important thing to keep in mind when trying to motivate a Phlegmatic—don't take no for an answer. At the same time, don't be obnoxiously forceful or he will stiffen his back and stubbornly, though graciously, resist your most aggressive entreaties. Present your case and expect to be refused—the first time around. Gently leave the door open and draw back, allowing him sufficient breathing room to think calmly and to pray about it. Occasionally approach him, but don't press him for a quick decision. Give him plenty of encouragement and be as factual as you can. You can't trick or "psych" him, but if you appeal to his sense of Christian responsibility, he will gradually respond.

For years I disdained enlisting Phlegmatics because they did not seem to respond to my enthusiasm. I erroneously interpreted this as disinterest. In actuality, they just don't get enthusiastic about much of anything, but that is *not* the measure of their capability.

Looking back over the last five years since I have consistently tried to employ Phlegmatics in the work of the Lord, I must say I am very pleased with the results. Although it took a little longer to get them committed, most of them are still consistently turning out effective work. The Sanguines have enthusiastically rushed in but, like whipping cream, have been inclined to melt under the heat of routine service. The Cholerics have volunteered their services and done a good job, but we have treated some emotionally scarred victims of their caustic tongues all over the church. Melancholies who could be persuaded to think of others long enough to accept a place of service have often been short termers also. They are critical of the way we do things because we don't measure up to their standards or they are offended by the hustle and bustle of Sunday school or youth hijinks and ride the first black mood back out of circulation.

Not so the Phlegmatics! Week after week they are in their place in the department or youth group, quietiy organizing and efficiently serving with good humor. That is, if you can get them motivated at the outset. Oh, yes, there are outstanding exceptions to this negative catalog of temperament failures. These are the Spirit-controlled Sanguines, Cholerics, Melancholies, and Phlegmatics. As the Spirit of God transforms them, they show a consistency and fruitfulness foreign to their temperament. That is what makes working with Christians in the local church such an exciting and rewarding experience.

For the benefit of the Phlegmatics who read this section, I would like to offer a special suggestion. So far, I have yet to find a Phlegmatic who has taken on more than he can accomplish. Since it is your natural inclination to be overprotective of yourself, pray earnestly about an opportunity before you decide to turn it down. Examine your excuses for noninvolvement to see if it is the Holy Spirit's leading or your own selfishness. Telling yourself, "There are so many others who can do a better job than I," can be a form of selfishness. Since most Phlegmatics have a fear of failure before others, they are reluctant to launch out on seas of service where others can watch them sink. Forget that selfish thinking pattern! Ask God for his leading, and if he gives you a burden for that work, take the responsibility and trust him to supply the ability to do the job. Philippians 4:13 says you can do it. Since most Phlegmatics tend to underestimate their abilities, you should memorize that verse and learn to trust God's power instead of your phlegmatic fears. You will be thrilled at what God can do with a Phlegmatic who is fully yielded to his will.

"Likewise reckon ye also yourselves to be dead indeed unto sin, but alive unto God through Jesus Christ our Lord. Let not sin therefore reign in your mortal body, that ye should obey it in the lusts thereof. Neither yield ye your members as instruments of unrighteousness unto sin, but yield yourselves unto God, as those that are alive from the dead, and your members as instruments of rightcousncss unto God" (Romans 6:11-13).

The lack of motivation so characteristic of the phlegmatic temperament is discussed with clever satire by Alexander Whyte in his notes on the temperaments. We include his lengthy quotation here for your interest.

"Sloth sums up, in one short and expressive word, the bad side of this temperament. Some part of what we call sloth in some men is, no doubt, in fairness to be set down to such a Phlegmatic constitution that it would take the will and the energy of a giant to overcome it. There are men of such a slow-working heart, their blood creeps through their veins at such a snail's pace, their joints are so loosely knit, and their whole body is so lethargic, that both God and man must take all into consideration before they condemn them. And when we must say sloth in his case, we still take into account all that can be said in extenuation, and the Phlegmatic man will not be blamed for what he could not help. He will be blamed and chastised only for what he could quite well have helped if only he had resolved to help it. At the same time, sloth is sloth, laziness is laziness, whatever your temperament may be. Laziness, indeed, is not of the body at all; it is of the mind. It is not their temperaments that make shipwrecks of so many of our students' and of our ministers' lives.

"The Phlegmatic minister has not worked harder on Sabbath than some of his people have worked every day of all the week. But he is a minister, and he has no master beside him but his own conscience, and so he spends all Monday on the sofa with a newspaper and a novel. He will read for his pulpit tomorrow forenoon, and visit his sick in the afternoon. But tomorrow he is not very well in the morning, and it rains in the afternoon. On Wednesday he still has four whole days before Sabbath, and besides, his letters are in terrible arrears; he has not had time to answer a note for a fortnight. A friend drops in to spend Thursday with him, but what of that? He has all Friday and Saturday to be kept shut up and absolutely sacred. On Friday afternoon he is told that his old elder, who was so ill, is dead, and he is as unhappy a man all that day as you could wish him to be. And he has a very unhappy errand before him that afternoon in having to explain to the bereaved family how busy he was all the beginning of the week. He sits into Saturday morning seeking for his Sabbath text, but has to go to bed before he has found it. All Saturday he has his meals at his desk, and he is like a bear robbed of her whelps if anybody but looks at him or speaks to him. On Sabbath morning he takes an old rag out of his drawer, and his people look at one another, as he cannot even read it. Brother minister, of the most remote and illiterate congregation in Scotland, sit down to thy desk early every day, and if God has made thee of a slothful, lethargic, phlegmatic temperament, only sit down to thy desk doggedly. Let every lazy student of divinity, and with him every waiting, complaining, postponing probationer, go drown himself at once."

Actually, there is a better solution to the phlegmatic temperament's natural sloth or lack of motivation than drowning. One of the nine strengths of the Holy Spirit (Galatians 5:22-23) is "self-control." Therefore the filling of the Holy Spirit will keep the Phlegmatic from indulging the flesh and will motivate him to service. As he feeds on the Word and yields his mind to the Holy Spirit, he will be given goals and plans that motivate him. The secret of motivation is not high blood pressure, enthusiasm, or energy. It is vision! Whenever a person has goals and objectives he is motivated. Consequently, the Spirit-filled Phlegmatic will be a motivated person and his daily life will be a demonstration of transformed temperament. Phlegmatics concerned about a greater motivation to glorify God should study the goal-setting techniques of the Apostle Paul described in Chapter 5.

Several of the men God used in Bible days seem to possess a high degree of phlegmatic temperament: Noah, Samuel, Daniel, Joseph (the husband of Mary), Nathaniel, Philip, and the Apostle James. The best illustration for the purposes of our study is Abraham. Revered by more people than any man except the Lord Jesus, Abraham would never have achieved greatness without the transforming power of the Holy Spirit. His lifetime struggles with a phlegmatic temperament provide us with an ideal illustration of what God can do with a phlegmatic yielded to his will and filled with his Spirit. When he walked in the Spirit, depending on the Lord, he was highly successful. But when he grieved the Spirit through fear and doubt he was a total failure. It is the same with us today. Hopefully, we will profit by the experiences of Abraham the Phlegmatic.

Cautious

The natural hesitancy, indecision, and fear of a Phlegmatic are seen in Abraham the first time he appears in the Bible. He was a resident of Ur of the Chaldees, shortly after the days of Nimrod and the destruction of the tower of Babel. Archeological research indicates that Ur was a highly developed city, comparable to Babylon in the days of Nebuchadnezzar 1,000 years later. It also was heavily influenced by the idolatrous religion of Babylon begun by Nimrod and his mother Semiramis.

This evil city located in "the cradle of civilization" was no place for the young man and his wife whom God had selected to be the ancestors of his chosen people. For that reason God called Abram (as he was known then) out of that country, saying, "Get thee out of thy country, and from thy kindred, and from thy father's house, unto a land that I will show thee" (Genesis 12:1). But Abram was so dependent on his father and relatives that instead of going all the way with God, he stopped in Haran with his family. Not until his father Terah died and God spoke to him again did Abraham obey, and even then he took his nephew Lot with him.

It seems to be very difficult for Phlegmatics to trust God fully. This is probably because fear is one of their most common problems. Their tendency to be anxious for everything and to become professional worriers is not as severe as for those of the melancholy temperament, but it does tend to limit them. Many Christian Phlegmatics are reluctant to enter the door of opportunity when it opens. It is not lack of capability that keeps Phlegmatics from the upper echelon of success, but reluctance to venture out onto the uncharted seas of the unknown. Quite characteristic is Abram's reluctance to leave his father, and then he took along his nephew Lot as a sort of "security blanket" to this unknown land God had promised him. The Phlegmatic becomes dynamically usable in the hands of God only when he learns to trust God alone. His security blanket usually turns out to cause an unnecessary problem in his life, as Lot was to Abraham.

The promises of God as given to Abraham in Genesis 12:1-3 are in the past tense, indicating that God had already made these promises to him and is now reiterating them. It took several years for Phlegmatic Abraham to learn to trust in God. God extended six promises to him: (1) "I will make of thee a great nation," (2) "I will bless thee," (3) "I will make thy name great," (4) "Thou shalt be a blessing," (5) "I will bless them that bless thee and curse him that curseth thee," (6) "In thee shall all families of the earth be blessed."

If Abraham had taken God at his word, he would have experienced much less heartache and confusion. Faith is simply taking God at his word and launching out upon his promises. God has never proven unfaithful to anyone, but every generation of Christians, particularly those of the phlegmatic temperament, have to learn Abraham's lessons all over again. Later God spoke to Abraham and gave him another promise which specifically said, "Unto thy seed will I give this land" (12:7). Abraham was seventy-five years of age, so fathering children was unlikely but still humanly possible; therefore, God chose to let time elapse until it became biologically impossible, and then he miraculously fulfilled his promise as an illustration of his faithfulness, not only to Abraham but to Christians of all generations.

The Bible teaches us that God increases our faith by testing. James 1:2-4 states, "My brethren, count it all joy when ye fall into various trials, knowing this, that the testing of your faith worketh patience. But let patience have her perfect work, that ye may be perfect and entire, lacking nothing." This principle of God operated in the life of Abraham, and it teaches us that we should expect our faith to be tested, and instead of grumbling or seeking a human solution, we should thank God for the testing and trust him for the solution. This formula always succeeds.

Shortly after God gave his promises to Abram, he tested the pioneer. Genesis 12:10 states, "And there was a famine in the land; and Abram went down into Egypt to sojourn there, for the famine was grievous in the land." Egypt, like Lot, was a false security blanket for Abram. Having come from a center of civilization to a wilderness area seared by famine, Abram looked to the nearest proven area of supply, the land of Egypt. Without consulting God for direction, he took his family into that pagan land, similar to the one from which God had called him. His disgraceful failure in Egypt, which we will examine later, would never have occurred had he waited for his deliverance, which would have come in the land of Canaan. All fear-prone Christians should claim the promise,

"Faithful is he that calleth you, who also will do it" (1 Thessalonians 5:24).

Peaceable

One of the most admirable characteristics of Phlegmatics is their love for peace. They tend to exhibit a serenity and calmness that is soothing to others. Usually their desire for peace and harmony is greater than their desire for personal possessions, a trait revealed in Abraham when his herdsmen and the herdsmen of Lot began to strive with each other. Since both were heads of families and had servants, they kept their flocks and herds separated. But without fences, it was natural that conflict arose over grazing land and water sources. Abram offered a solution by saying to Lot: "Let there be no strife, I pray thee, between me and thee, and between my herdsmen and thy herdsmen; for we are brethren. Is not the whole land before thee? Separate thyself, I pray thee, from me; if thou wilt take the left hand, then I will go to the right; or if thou depart to the right hand, then I will go to the left" (13:8, 9). This seems a pleasant solution for a trying situation. But it is likely that Abram suffered much heartache by separating himself from his human security blanket. That Lot proved unworthy of such reliance did not lessen Abram's pain.

It seems no coincidence that "after that Lot was separated from him" God gave Abram the specific title deed for the land of Canaan. God wants to bless his children, but he requires absolute faith, for "without faith it is impossible to please him" (Hebrews 11:6).

If we are unwilling to trust the Lord completely, we lose blessings he has in store for us or he permits trials to come our way to bring us to rely upon him. If Abram and Lot had not separated, it seems that God could not have promised the following blessing: "Lift up now thine eyes, and look from the place where thou art northward, and southward, and eastward, and westward: For all the land which thou seest, to thee will I give it, and to thy seed forever. And I will make thy seed as the dust of the earth: so that if a man can number the dust of the earth, then shall thy seed also be numbered. Arise, walk through the land in the length of it and in the breadth of it; for I will give it unto thee" (Genesis 13:14-17).

Many a Christian worker has come to the place where he must separate himself from loved ones and friends in order to enter the appointed place of God's blessing. Practically every missionary and most ministers of the gospel have faced that traumatic decision; and many laymen must likewise face it, for God has a particular plan for all of his children. Many a young person has chosen to attend a college that was convenient rather than a Christian school that required extra cost or sacrifice. Most pastors can produce a list of "shipwrecked" young people whose faith foundered on a secular campus. This is not to imply that God wants all Christian young people to attend a Christian college. But most pastors and counselors believe God has led far more to Christian colleges than have gone, and the failure is usually unbelief on the part of the parents or the student.

One of the hardest decisions I ever made was to send my eighteen-year-old daughter 2,500 miles away from home to a Christian college. I well remember thinking at the time that it was like cutting one-fourth of my heart out of my body and sending it far from me. Only two years later another fourth of my heart had to be cut away when my son made the same decision. No doubt the day will come when the two younger children will face the same decision. In retrospect, I have no misgivings. It cost us the enjoyment of their presence and many happy hours and days of fellowship, but it has been well worth it. Both young people are walking with God and preparing to serve him, which has more than compensated for the "heart surgery" this loving father experienced. Their mother and I thank God regularly that we did not limit his use of their lives by clinging to them, but abandoned them to his perfect will.

Reliable

"What you are under pressure is what you are!" is one of my longstanding convictions. Pressure does not change our character—it just identifies its true nature. Of all the temperament types, Mr. Phlegmatic by nature comes out best under pressure. Sanguines often run off half-cocked in the wrong direction, and Melancholies may go to pieces under pressure, but Cholerics and Phlegmatics both rise to occasions of difficulty. The Choleric tends to rely on intuitive judgment in such emergencies and many times lacks the organization and efficiency that is a hallmark of the Phlegmatic. One of the behavioral surprises in a study of human nature is the calm, efficient reaction of the Phlegmatic in a time of great crisis. The fourteenth chapter of Genesis recounts such an experience in the life of Abraham.

Shortly after Lot became a resident of Sodom, war broke out among the kings of Canaan. Chedorlaomer, king of Elam, and several other kings conquered Sodom and Gomorrah and took many inhabitants as slaves, including Lot and his family. One of the captives escaped and revealed the disaster to Abram. The Bible describes Abram's reaction in these words: "And when Abram heard that his brother was taken captive, he armed his trained servants, born in his own house, three hundred and eighteen, and pursued them unto Dan. And he divided himself against them, he and his servants, by night, and smote them, and pursued them unto Hobah, which is on the left hand of Damascus. And he brought back all the goods, and also brought again his brother Lot, and his goods, and the women also, and the people" (14:14-16).

This exciting story reveals several things about Phlegmatic Abraham and others of his temperament. Their concern for loved ones in an emergency takes precedence over their love for personal safety and emotional protection. When motivated to action and committed to the battle, Phlegmatic Abraham revealed latent leadership characteristics that were extremely effective. His method of attacking an army of superior forces is a model that has been used many times since in the annals of warfare. By dividing his small band and using the cover of darkness and the element of surprise, he not only overcame a superior army but relentlessly pursued them until he was victorious. His calm, unemotional response to victory is also characteristic of the Phlegmatic. We do not find a single illustration of braggadocio in the life of Abraham. This is not only a tribute to his spiritual life, but a distinctive of Phlegmatics in general, who are prone to be conservative about everything, including self-praise. Abraham knew—as Melchizedek, the priest of Salem, later pointed out—that victory was really due to the blessing of God, who delivered him from his enemy. For that reason he faithfully gave tithes of all he possessed to God through the priest.

If the truth were known and the financial records of evangelical churches could some day be computed, I am confident that Phlegmatics would be accounted the most consistent in the practice of tithing. Doubtless they are not the ones who talk about it most, but when once committed to a principle of God, they are prone to be the most regular. Sanguines are ever making new vows of faithfulness whereas Cholerics are usually so overcommitted financially they keep putting off gifts to the Lord, which is tantamount to not doing it at all. Melancholies are likely to be fearful that they cannot live on the rest of their income and so are reluctant to commit themselves to tithing. Phlegmatics, more than any other temperament, are inclined to do the "acceptable thing." They are the most prone of all the temperaments to obey what God expects of a Christian. However, once having committed themselves to tithing, their somewhat thrifty nature makes them least spontaneous in giving offerings. The other temperaments would be more susceptible to spontaneously responding to a particular need. Not so the Phlegmatic, who is regular and consistent in his giving habits. When truly transformed by the Holy Spirit, however, his liberated emotions will open his pocketbook.

Passive

The natural tendency of the Phlegmatic to be a peacemaker, as already illustrated, carries with it a tendency to be passive in the face of conflict unless crisis is involved. This often results in male Phlegmatics being "henpecked" by their wives. In the early days of his marriage Abram seemed to be no exception. The sixteenth chapter of Genesis shows Sarai's great influence over her husband. Becoming impatient for God to fulfill his promise of a son to perpetuate their seed, Sarai devised her own plan. Since she was unable to bear him children, she suggested that he take her Egyptian maid named Hagar and "obtain children by her." Abram's agreement produced one of the most regrettable events in the Bible, for it brought into the family of nations a people who would perpetually be in conflict with the promised people of God.

The Bible tells us, "And Abram hearkened to the voice of Sarai." The tragedy of Hagar's pregnancy, her rejection by Sarai, and her ultimate expulsion from the family in order to keep peace is a sad picture of Abram's henpecked state. He loved Ishmael, his son by Hagar, but did not have the strength to resist his wife even after the mistake was made. It would be hard to describe the emotional trauma that must have been Abram's when, after Isaac was born, he sent away Ishmael, whom he loved, to please his wife.

One of the lessons which peace-loving Phlegmatics need to learn is that nothing is ever accomplished by compromise. Peacemaking is admirable if it can be done legitimately, but if it requires compromise of principle it must be paid for in the long run. Many a phlegmatic man, in order to keep peace at home, has allowed his wife to "rule the roost." It is impossible for him to have a spiritual home or develop an effective Christian testimony unless he is the head of his house. Young people who grow up in feminine-dominated homes are emotionally unprepared to face society. Most feminine domination could have been averted if the young husband had assumed the dominant role in his home immediately in obedience to God's will.

I have interviewed Phlegmatics in the counseling room who hated their wives and accordingly had no spiritual vitality whatsoever. Through the years they had acquiesced to their wives' leadership, but resentment had mounted in direct proportion to their own loss of authority. Ultimately this resentment will destroy love because it is unnatural for a woman to dominate a man. Such a situation is not only undesirable for the husband, but will become a source of misery for the wife, who cannot truly respect a mate she does not look up to. Phlegmatic Abraham offers a good example in this respect because the New Testament reveals that God modified his temperament and he became the dominant leader in his home. Ultimately Sarai acknowledged him as her spiritual leader and the family head (1 Peter 3:1-6).

Many a strong-willed woman rebels at the biblical concept of the wife's being in submission to her husband, for by nature she finds it much easier to take over the situation, make the decisions, and boss everyone in the house including her husband. Invariably this withers happiness.

Fearful

It is almost impossible to exaggerate the negative, destructive effects of fear. Hundreds of books have been written on overcoming fear and anxiety. The widespread use of such books and the repeated admonitions of "fear not" in the Word of God mark fear as a universal problem. Of the four temperaments, the one least predisposed to fear is the choleric. Mr. Sanguine, in spite of his false bravado, possesses an underlying insecurity and fear that occasionally bother him. Both Mr. Melancholy and Mr. Phlegmatic have a generous dose of fear, and thus Moses and Abraham had no small problem from innate fears. The only true cure for this temperament predisposition is the supernatural power of God. Moses and Abraham are prime illustrations that this negative aspect of our temperament is transformed when God has control of our lives.

In spite of many of the positive things we have said about Phlegmatic Abraham, he nevertheless committed two reprehensible acts of cowardice under the influence of fear.

The first is recorded in the twelfth chapter of Genesis. Because there was famine in the land, Abram forsook God's will and went to Egypt. Knowing that the king of Egypt owned a large harem and did not discriminate, in his selection of wives and concubines, between married and single women, Abram became fearful. As Abram considered Sarai, he realized she was very beautiful and he feared the Egyptians might kill him for his beautiful wife. Therefore he suggested, "Say, I pray thee, thou art my sister; that it may be well with me for thy sake; and my soul shall live because of thee." Sure enough, beautiful Sarai was noticed and ushered into the presence of the king. Thinking that Abram was her brother, he treated Abram well for her sake. Only through a plague from God did Pharaoh become aware of the truth and Abram and his wife were spared serious sin. Abram's cowardly fear resulted in his banishment from the country and a very poor witness for God in the pagan nation. This blemish on Abram's life would not have occurred had he trusted God for his food and safety.

Once was not enough for Abram to betray Sarai out of fear. Many years later, as revealed in the twentieth chapter, Abraham again asked Sarai to acknowledge him as her brother in an attempt to curry favor with the heathen king Abimelech. Again she was selected for her beauty and was almost added to the king's harem. Had God not warned Abimelech in a dream, Abraham and Sarai would have been involved in a tragic sin. God was prepared to slay Abimelech to prevent the nullification of his promises to Abram and Sarai. God's standards of morality include no exceptions—lying is sin and adultery is sin, even when thought necessary to spare life. Our pretexts and compromises never improve on God's plan and provision.

Unbelief was the greatest problem of Abram, or Abraham, as he was renamed. As he grew in grace and knowledge of the Lord, he was so transformed that this tendency was obliterated from his thinking.

As we look carefully into the story, we find that God cured Abraham's fear by revealing himself in greater measure. The more

Abraham learned about God, the more he trusted him—the less fearful he was. The Lord spoke to Abraham in a vision and said, "Fear not, Abram: I am thy shield, and thy exceedingly great reward" (Genesis 15:1). At first Abraham was reluctant to use God as his protector and ultimate rewarder. Instead he looked around for human solutions. Whenever he followed human ingenuity, he stumbled into failure, but when he acted on the promises of God he experienced miracles. Eventually God performed a biological miracle on the bodies of aged Abraham and Sarah so that they became the parents of Isaac and, through him, of the Israelite nation.

Until the birth of Isaac, Abraham's faith was a growing experience, sometimes faltering and then forging ahead. Ultimately he became known as the "father of the faithful," the forebear of those who have put their faith in God.

This does not mean that Abraham invariably obeyed God. It means that his faith became the example of true, unconditional submission to God for all who would know the Savior. God uses a yielded vessel despite lapses when failures are confessed. The key to consistent faith is hearing God's Word, obeying it as the reliable guide of a loving Father, and confessing and forsaking every lapse.

Abraham's transformation

The strength of Abraham's faith is dramatically illustrated in his sacrifice of his son Isaac at God's command. Genesis 22 tells us "God did test Abraham" by instructing him to take the son whom he loved and "offer him for a burnt offering upon the mountains which I will tell thee of." Abraham took his son up Mount Moriah and prepared to sacrifice him. When young Isaac asked about a lamb for the burnt offering, Abraham replied, "My son, God will provide himself a lamb for a burnt offering." Then he bound his son and placed him upon the altar, with knife raised to execute Isaac as God had ordered. But God only wanted Abraham's supreme loyalty, not his son's body. He stopped Abraham and said, "Now I know that thou fearest God, seeing thou hast not withheld . . . thine only son from me." God provided a ram as a substitute offering, for Isaac's death, a picture of the manner in which Jesus Christ many generations later would become the perfect offering for the sins of all mankind. Abraham, the father of the faithful, was asked to be willing to give his son; God actually gave his only begotten Son.

The growth of Abraham's faith illustrates the gradual growth of faith that God provides every believer. We see him transformed from the man in the twelfth chapter who did not have faith enough to trust God for food to the unwavering servant who, as the Holy Spirit reveals in Hebrews 1:19, believed God so implicitly that he expected God to resurrect Isaac if he died on the altar.

Where did Abraham get that faith? By taking God at his word and acting on his promises. God had explicitly promised a posterity to Isaac, and Abraham believed death could not prevent it. Faith does not need answers, but only direction. Many Christians say, "If I knew how this would turn out, I could trust God." This is unbelief. The transformation of Abraham made him one of the greatest men who ever lived, not because he had a phlegmatic temperament but in spite of it. Transformation of temperament is available for every child of God who will be filled with the Spirit and directed by the Word of God.

III
Why You Act
THE WAY YOU DO

ONE

THE POWER OF TEMPERAMENT

1

TEMPERAMENT INFLUENCES
EVERYTHING YOU DO

When I was in high school, there was a pair of identical twins in my class. We could hardly tell them apart. They tested out identically on their IQ scores (128). But that is where the similarities stopped. One was personable; the other withdrew from people. One loved sports, history, and literature; the other preferred math, physics, and language. Interesting to me was the fact that their grade-point averages were almost identical at the end of their four years in high school. Yet they did not get the same grades in most subjects. What made the difference between these young men? Their temperaments!

Temperament influences everything you do—from sleep habits to study habits to eating style to the way you get along with other people. Humanly speaking, there is no other influence in your life more powerful than your temperament or combination of temperaments. That is why it is so essential to know your temperament and to be able to analyze other people's temperaments, not to condemn them, but so you can maximize your potential and enable them to maximize theirs.

Sit with me in the counseling room and you will see what I mean. The sanguine talks about the weather, friends, and a hundred things before facing the real problem. The choleric gets right to the point. He (or she) wants you to straighten out his partner so he can have a good home life. The melancholy sighs deeply as he sits down with depression, self-pity, and unhappiness etched on his face. The phlegmatic rarely gets around to making an appointment, and when she does it takes most of the first half hour just to prime her conversational pump.

These people are not the temperament they are because they do these things. Rather, they act the way they do because of their temperaments. Some of our acts are subtle, like tastes or preferences, while others involve outlooks and attitudes or even styles of thinking. There is hardly a function in life that is not influenced by temperament Thus, you had better determine your temperament and consistently direct it into the best life-style for you and your family. Otherwise your temperament will subconsciously direct you.

Temperament and eating habits

I can almost judge a man's temperament by his eating habits. Sanguines eat everything in sight—and usually look it. In a restaurant they so enjoy talking that they almost never look at a menu until the waitress arrives. Cholerics—stereotyped eaters—seldom vary their menu from one day to the next; and when it arrives, they bolt it down in big chunks, often talking while chewing their food. Melancholies are very picky eaters. It takes them forever to make up their minds about what to order, but once it arrives they savor every bite. Phlegmatics are the most deliberate eaters of all and are invariably the last ones through eating. That is the main reason they rarely gain weight. (All weight specialists warn obese patients to eat slowly, for it takes twenty minutes for food passing into the mouth to shut off hunger pangs.)

Temperament and driving skills

Sanguines are erratic drivers. Sometimes they speed, then for no apparent reason lose interest in driving fast and slow down. They are so people-oriented that they want to look you in the face when talking, even while driving.

Cholerics are daring speed demons who dart in and out of traffic constantly. They always try to get more accomplished in a given period of time than is humanly possible and attempt to make up time by driving furiously between appointments.

Melancholy motorists never leave home without preparing for the trip well in advance. They study the map and know the best route from A to Z. Of all the temperaments, they are the most likely to keep a complete log of their driving history, including gas and oil consumption and car repairs. Legalists by nature, they rarely speed.

Phil Phlegmatic is the slowest driver of all. The last one to leave an intersection, he rarely changes lanes and is an indecisive danger when joining the flow of freeway traffic from an entrance ramp. He is a pokey "Sunday driver" seven days a week. He gets few tickets and rarely has accidents, but he can be a road hazard.

Temperament and the way you shop

Sanguines are not price conscious, but select for visual satisfaction. They are drawn by colorful packaging and advertising. In the grocery store, theirs is the most overloaded cart.

Cholerics, particularly men, are not fond of shopping. They only go to the store when they need something and want to purchase it and get out. Like sanguines, they usually overbuy but not quite as much.

Melancholies are deliberate and decisive shoppers who compare prices and quality quite carefully. They run their hands over the item, try it on two or three times, leave the store a time or two, and if it isn't sold by the time they return, they buy it. They create traffic jams waiting to make up their mind. In the grocery store they know where everything is and save all the coupons from every manufacturer.

Phlegmatics, particularly women, enjoy shopping. They take longer, shop slower, and are probably more frugal than any other type. They are almost as indecisive as the melancholy. They have to shop more frequently than any other type because they don't get enough on the first trip.

Temperament and yard care

As incredible as it may seem, you can almost decipher a person's temperament by the way he does the yard work around his home. Sparky Sanguine gets up early Saturday morning to fix his yard. With great gusto he lines up all his tools (he has every gadget known to man because he totally lacks sales resistance) and prepares to cut, trim, shear, and prune. However, within thirty minutes he is chatting joyfully with a neighbor. Before the day is over, he orders his son to "put my tools away" and decides to fix the yard next week. Sparky is clearly one of the world's great procrastinators.

Rocky Choleric hates yard work, and therefore when he does it at all it is with a vengeance. He works at a frenzied pace in order to get the job done, and neatness is not his hallmark. One can usually spot the choleric's yard while driving through the neighborhood. Just look for miniature hedges and dwarf trees.

Martin Melancholy has a natural aptitude for growing things and usually maintains the best yard in the neighborhood. He is the one who talks to and babies his plants, and on almost any weekend we will find him on hands and knees, "manicuring" his lawns and hedges.

The phlegmatic's lawn usually suggests that its owner is still in the house late on a Saturday morning, sipping his third cup of coffee—because he is. Capable of superior lawn care, Phil will scrupulously attend to "the old plantation," however, because his desire to rest is overcome by his drive to do the accepted thing.

Temperament and study habits

Melancholies are usually good students who enjoy learning. They have inquisitive minds and if taught to read well will have a ferocious appetite for books. They are blessed with keen retentive minds that enable them to remember a multitude of details. As a rule they are good spellers because they take mental pictures of each word. Although they have messy files and a desk top that is impossible to organize, they have an amazing concentration regardless of the mess, interruptions, or noise going on around them.

Phlegmatics can be good students if their procrastination doesn't catch up with them. They need a series of short-term assignments rather than long-term projects. They work best under pressure, though they claim they don't like it. They have orderly minds capable of analysis and deductions. They are prone to get their news more from TV than magazines and newspapers. They have good memories and can be intelligent people if somehow motivated to learn.

Cholerics are clever as a rule but not brilliant. They like the people-oriented subjects such as history, geography, literature, and psychology. They may not be good spellers, because they skim over things so quickly. They are adept at speed-reading and have curious minds. They constantly ask "Why?" Cholerics love charts, diagrams, and graphs; they like to know where everything fits in the main scheme of things. They may have a difficult time concentrating on anything that reminds them of other goals or projects that get their minds off on a tangent and then may have a difficult time getting back to the subject at hand.

Sanguines, unless endowed with a high IQ, are not usually good students. They can be if they are motivated, because they are often bright enough, but they are very restless and undisciplined. They have a short interest span and anything can be a distraction, from a bird flying overhead to a picture on the wall. These people have incredible potential but usually squander it because they don't discipline themselves. Concentration for long periods of time is difficult for them.

Handwriting and your temperament

I am not an authority on handwriting, but l have observed that temperament and handwriting analysis are very similar. Our penmanship usually follows our temperament. Everything a sanguine does is expressive and flamboyant, and he writes that way. The choleric usually has poor handwriting. Everything he does is fast; consequently, he does not take time to write legibly. The phlegmatic usually has small but neat handwriting. Melancholies have the most unpredictable handwriting of all. They are extremely complex people and usually write that way.

Communication skills and temperament

Thinking skills and communication skills are not based solely on the brain. They also involve temperament. Sanguines are intuitive speakers. They are overly expressive and use exaggeration freely. Cholerics are extroverted enough to speak freely, but usually are more deliberate than sanguines. They are debaters and arguers; no one can be more biting or sarcastic. Melancholies never start talking until they have thought out precisely what they want to say. They don't like to interrupt others, but once they get started they go on until they have unloaded their entire message. Phlegmatics are quiet about everything and seldom enter into debates or thrust themselves into conversations. They will respond to questions with wit and good humor, but rarely volunteer anything unless asked.

Peter was told, "Your speech betrays you" (Matt. 26:73). That is often true of your temperament; your speech patterns are a give-away of your temperament.

Bill paying and temperament

Paying bills is a necessary part of life, and it seems to get more complex all the time. Believe it or not, unless you are a trained bookkeeper, the way you tackle that problem will be a reflection of your temperament.

Sanguines are terrible record-keepers. They dislike detail and can get momentarily depressed with their overspending habits. Their method of handling deficit spending is rarely to cut down on their standard of living, but simply to try to make more money. They pay their bills, but it usually takes several reminders.

Cholerics like to pay bills on time. They aren't very detailed unless they have a melancholy or phlegmatic secondary temperament, but they like things orderly. Their style is to put all the bills in one place and pay them all the same night each month. They aren't "bugged" if their checkbook doesn't balance, just so they keep the bank honest. For $5 or $10 they will accept the bank's balance— they figure their time spent hassling over the details is more than that.

Melancholies are perfectionists. Their conscientious nature makes them difficult to live with if they don't pay all their creditors on time. Their bill cabinet is a mess, but they know what each statement and receipt is. They usually have every receipt for the past five years, but in no set order. They pride themselves on balancing their checkbook to the penny. If there is a mistake, it will be the bank's. They usually have a triple "A" credit rating.

Phlegmatics systemize everything. They have a detailed budget and keep matching records. They not only pay bills on time, they like to get them in early wherever it saves an additional 2 or 4 percent. (Sanguines don't even realize there are companies that do this.) To some phlegs, balancing their checkbook is the highlight of their month. It is the one clear signal that their life is in order and they are ready to launch into the next month.

Child discipline and your temperament

Child discipline is largely a result of family tradition, religious training, culture, and temperament. In recent years there have been a number of books written on this subject, some good, some very harmful. Those who base their philosophy on humanistic values or humanistic psychology have produced a permissive society that tends toward lawlessness. Books based on biblical principles have, on the other hand, been very valuable. My three favorite books on child discipline are two by my friend Dr. James Dobson (*Dare to Discipline* and *The Strong-Willed Child*) and one by my wife, Beverly: *How to Develop Your Child's Temperament*. These three books should be in every Christian parent's library. If you study them, you will be equipped to be a maximum parent.

Having said all of that, however, you will find that unless you learn what is right in disciplining your children, you will respond to them according to your temperament. Even when you know what to do, your temperament will influence the way you do it. Consider these four familiar styles.

Everything a sanguine does in life is spontaneous, and discipline is usually no exception. He is loud in his instruction and correction, and a woman sanguine is apt to be a screamer. Since sanguines are not disciplined themselves, their threats are rarely carried out, so Johnny knows he never has to answer the first time he is called or told to do something. He waits until the pitch of the scream or the volume of the call gets to a certain intensity before he comes home.

When it comes to spankings, sanguines must do it immediately, while they are angry or frustrated, or they probably won't do it at all. Their tender heart and forgiving spirit make delayed punishment no punishment. Their leniency leads to permissiveness, which in turn encourages lawlessness. And inconsistent parents usually raise inconsistent children.

One thing is commendable about sanguines: after they have disciplined their children, they take time to love and comfort them. Sanguines never carry grudges (we could all do with a bit of that). Another thing about these fun-loving people is that they will often take time to play with their children, particularly as they get older.

Cholerics, being authority-prone, want to run their homes like a Marine boot camp. This may produce good robots, but it doesn't do much for kids. The child of a choleric parent never lacks knowledge of what his parent requires in the way of obedience and rules—he is told regularly. Cholerics love to give out orders. Choleric spankers tend to spank too hard too often and too many spanks per discipline. Masters of the overkill in all that they do, their motto is, "If a little helps, a lot will cure." (In reality, no parent should spank a child when angry. He makes the child feel he is just a release valve for the parent's frustration.)

Cholerics can be good parents, but they have to work at it. They are hard to please at best, and if a child is a "late bloomer" or of a less activist temperament, such parents are apt to make her feel inferior and constantly disapproved. Such parents need to encourage their children, approve them, and build up their self-image, going out of their way to show their love.

Melancholy parents were perfectionists before they became parents, and having children won't change that. They have high-to-unreal expectations for their young and dole out praise sparingly (although most children need it lavishly). Academically, their children know that anything less than an "A" is a failure—in every subject. Legalistic by nature, they usually have rules for everything and procedures that must be followed. If they say they will spank for a particular offense, they usually follow through; but rarely do they overspank, unless they see their own shortcomings in their child. Then they may take out on the child the frustrations they have toward themselves.

It is hard for melancholies to be approving because their standard is so high and because they are afraid their child will become complacent with approval. They are the last temperament to learn that everyone needs praise and that most people thrive better on approval than on condemnation. They have a great capacity to love their children, but they need to learn how to express it. One of the biggest parental failings is that they never forget anything wrong the child has done, and if not trained out of the habit will bring it up again and again.

Phlegmatics can be good parents if they learn to be more assertive and confrontational when necessary. They are patience personified. They love children and probably feel more comfortable with little children than anyone else. They take time with them, play with them, and can be patient trainers. As choleric children get older, phlegmatic parents may be intimidated by them and look the other way, thus undermining in the teen years the good training they gave in childhood. However, the one thing they may indulge in (melancholies can be guilty of this also) is to permit their children to sass them. No parent should accept this. The Bible says children are to honor their parents. If they don't honor them with their mouths, they must at least be forced not to dishonor them. Parents who lose that battle in childhood seldom gain control in the teen years.

The phlegmatic is the least likely to spank. He usually waits until the more extroverted parent does it. When the teen years come and the child needs a forceful father figure, it is sad when Dad goes to the garage and putters at his workbench to avoid unpleasant confrontations. I once counseled a phlegmatic man whose conflict with his wife arose because she wouldn't forbid the kids to watch certain TV shows he felt were objectionable. Children need two parents to agree on rules and to enforce them, applying whatever punishment is appropriate or promised. Phlegmatics can be good parents but, like the rest of us, they have to work at it.

Summary

We could go on giving illustrations of how temperament influences the way you exercise, sleep, decorate, select clothes, have hobbies, and do everything else in your life. But these are enough to get you started in the right direction. As you become more familiar with the temperament theory, you will see it at work in your own life and that of your friends.

TWO

WHAT TEMPERAMENT ARE YOU?

2

THE TWELVE BLENDS OF TEMPERAMENT

The chief objection to the theory of the four temperaments as advocated by the ancients is that it was overly simplistic in assuming every person could be characterized by only one of the four temperaments. As I have said in my previous books on temperament, that just is not true. We are all a blend of at least two temperaments; one predominates, the other is secondary. In an attempt to make the temperament theory more practical and true to life, we shall briefly examine twelve possible blends of temperament. In all probability, it will be easier for you to identify yourself in one of the blends than in one of the four basics.

A variety of blends

Essentially, each person is capable of possessing twenty strengths and twenty weaknesses to one degree or another (ten for the predominant and ten for the secondary temperament). Some of them, as we shall see, cancel each other out, some reinforce each other, and some accentuate and compound others, accounting for the varieties of behavior, prejudices, and natural skills of people with the same predominant temperament but with different secondary temperaments. This will become clearer as you study the following twelve blends of temperament.

THE SANCHLOR   The strongest extrovert of all the blends of temperaments will be the SanChlor, for the two temperaments that make up his nature are both extro-

verted. The happy charisma of the sanguine makes him a people-oriented, enthusiastic, salesman type; but the choleric side of his nature will provide him the necessary resolution and character traits that will fashion a somewhat more organized and productive individual than if he were pure sanguine. Almost any people-oriented field is open to him, but to sustain his interest it must offer variety, activity, and excitement.

The potential weaknesses of a SanChlor are usually apparent to everyone because he is such an external person. He customarily talks too much, thus exposing himself and his weaknesses for all to see. He is highly opinionated. Consequently, he expresses himself loudly even before he knows all the facts. To be honest, no one has more mouth trouble! If he is the life of the party, he is lovable; but if he feels threatened or insecure, he can become obnoxious. His leading emotional problem will be anger, which can catapult him into action at the slightest provocation. Since he combines the easy forgetfulness of the sanguine and the stubborn casuistry of the choleric, he may not have a very active conscience. Consequently, he tends to justify his actions. This man, like any other temperament, needs to be filled daily with the Holy Spirit and the Word of God.

Simon Peter, the self-appointed leader of the twelve apostles, is a classic example of a New Testament SanChlor. He obviously had mouth trouble, demonstrating this repeatedly by speaking up before anyone else could. He talked more in the Gospels than all the others put together—and most of what he said was wrong. He was egotistical, weak-willed, and carnal throughout the Gospels. In Acts, however, he was a remarkably transformed man—resolute, effective, and productive. What made the difference? He was filled with the Spirit.

THE SANMEL

SanMels are highly emotional people who fluctuate drastically. They can laugh hysterically one minute and burst into tears the next. It is almost impossible for them to hear a sad tale, observe a tragic plight of another person, or listen to melancholic music without weeping profusely. They genuinely feel the griefs of others. Almost any field

is open to them, especially public speaking, acting, music, and the fine arts. However, SanMels reflect an uninhibited perfectionism that often alienates them from others because they verbalize their criticisms. They are usually people-oriented individuals who have sufficient substance to make a contribution to other lives—if their ego and arrogance don't make them so obnoxious that others become hostile to them.

One of the crucial weaknesses of this temperament blend prevails in SanMel's thought-life. Both sanguines and melancholies are dreamers, and thus if the melancholy part of his nature suggests a negative train of thought, it can nullify a SanMel's potential. It is easy for him to get down on himself. In addition, this person, more than most others, will have both an anger problem and a tendency toward fear. Both temperaments in his makeup suffer with an insecurity problem; not uncommonly, he is fearful to utilize his potential. Being admired by others is so important to him that it will drive him to a consistent level of performance. He has a great ability to commune with God, and if he walks in the Spirit he will make an effective servant of Christ.

King David is a classic illustration of the SanMel temperament. An extremely likable man who attracted both men and women; he was colorful, dramatic, emotional, and weak-willed. He could play a harp and sing, he clearly demonstrated a poetic instinct in his Psalms, and he made decisions on impulse. Unfortunately, like many SanMels, he fouled up his life by a series of disastrous and costly mistakes before he gained enough self-discipline to finish out his destiny. All San Mels, of course, are not able to pick up the pieces of their lives and start over as David did. It is far better for them to walk in the Spirit daily and avoid such mistakes.

THE SANPHLEG   The easiest person to like is a SanPhleg. The overpowering and obnoxious tendencies of a sanguine are offset by the gracious, easygoing phlegmatic. SanPhlegs are extremely happy people whose carefree spirit and good humor make them lighthearted entertainers sought after by others. Helping people is their regular business, along with sales of various kinds. They are the least extroverted of any of the sanguines

and are often regulated by their environment and circumstances rather than being self-motivated. SanPhlegs are naturally pro-family and preserve the love of their children—and everyone else for that matter. They would not purposely hurt anyone.

The SanPhleg's greatest weaknesses are lack of motivation and discipline. He would rather socialize than work, and he tends to take life too casually. As an executive remarked about one, "He is the nicest guy I ever fired." He rarely gets upset over anything and tends to find the bright side of everything. He usually has an endless repertoire of jokes and delights in making others laugh, often when the occasion calls for seriousness. When Jesus Christ becomes the chief object of his love, he is transformed into a more resolute, purposeful, and productive person.

The first-century evangelist Apollos is about as close as we can come to a New Testament illustration of the SanPhleg. A skilled orator who succeeded Paul and others who had founded the churches, he did the work of stirring the churches with his Spirit-filled preaching and teaching. Loved by all, followed devotedly by some, this pleasant and dedicated man apparently traveled a great deal but did not found new works.

THE CHLORSAN

The second-strongest extrovert among the blends of temperament will be the reverse of the first—the ChlorSan. This man's life is given over completely to activity. Most of his efforts are productive and purposeful, but watch his recreation—it is so activity-prone that it borders on being violent. He is a natural promoter and salesman, with enough charisma to get along well with others. Certainly the best motivator of people and one who thrives on a challenge, he is almost fearless and exhibits boundless energy. His wife will often comment, "He has only two speeds: wide open and stop." Mr. ChlorSan is the courtroom attorney who can charm the coldest-hearted judge and jury, the fund-raiser who can get people to contribute what they intended to save, the man who never goes anywhere unnoticed, the preacher who combines both practical Bible teaching and church administration, and the politician who talks his state into changing its constitution so he can represent them one more time. A convincing debater, what he lacks in facts or arguments he makes up in bluff or bravado. As a teacher, he is an excellent communicator, particularly in the social sciences; rarely is he drawn to math, science, or the abstract. Whatever his professional occupation, his brain is always in motion.

The weaknesses of this man, the chief of which is hostility, are as broad as his talents. He combines the quick, explosive anger of the sanguine (without the forgiveness) and the long-burning resentment of the choleric. He is the one personality type who not only gets ulcers himself, but gives them to others. Impatient with those who do not share his motivation and energy, he prides himself on being brutally frank (some call it sarcastically frank). It is difficult for him to concentrate on one thing very long, which is why he often enlists others to finish what he has started. He is opinionated, prejudiced, impetuous, and inclined doggedly to finish a project he probably should not have started in the first place. If not controlled by God, he is apt to justify anything he does—and rarely hesitates to manipulate or walk over other people to accomplish his ends. Most ChlorSans get so engrossed in their work that they neglect wife and family, even lashing out at them if they complain. Once he comprehends the importance of giving love and approval to his family, however, he can transform his entire household.

James, the author of the biblical book that bears his name, could well have been a ChlorSan—at least his book sounds like it. The main thrust of the book declares that "faith without works is dead"—a favored concept of work-loving cholerics. He used the practical and logical reasoning of a choleric, yet was obviously a highly esteemed man of God. One human weakness he discusses— the fire of the tongue and how no man can control it (James 3)— relates directly to this temperament's most vulnerable characteristic, for we all know the ChlorSans feature a razor-sharp, active tongue. His victory and evident productiveness in the cause of Christ is a significant example to any thoughtful ChlorSan.

THE CHLORMEL   The choleric/melancholy is an extremely industrious and capable person.

The optimism and practicality of the choleric overcome the tendency toward moodiness of the melancholy, making the ChlorMel both goal-oriented and detailed. Such a person usually does well in school, possesses a quick analytical mind, yet is decisive. He develops into a thorough leader, the kind whom one can always count on to do an extraordinary job. Never take him on in a debate unless you are assured of your facts, for he will make mincemeat of you, combining verbal aggressiveness and attendance to detail. This man is extremely competitive and forceful in all that he does. He is a dogged researcher and is usually successful, no matter what kind of business he pursues. This temperament probably makes the best natural leader. General George S. Patton, the great commander of the U.S. Third Army in World War II who drove the German forces back to Berlin, was probably a ChlorMel.

Equally as great as his strengths are his weaknesses. He is apt to be autocratic, a dictator type who inspires admiration and hate simultaneously. He is usually a quick-witted talker whose sarcasm can devastate others. He is a natural-born crusader whose work habits are irregular and long. A ChlorMel harbors considerable hostility and resentment, and unless he enjoys a good love relationship with his parents, he will find interpersonal relationships difficult, particularly with his family. No man is more apt to be an overly strict disciplinarian than the ChlorMel father. He combines the hard-to-please tendency of the choleric and the perfectionism of the melancholy. When controlled by the Holy Spirit, however, his entire emotional life is transformed and he makes an outstanding Christian.

There is little doubt in my mind that the Apostle Paul was a ChlorMel. Before his conversion he was hostile and cruel, for the Scripture teaches that he spent his time persecuting and jailing Christians. Even after his conversion, his strong-willed determination turned to unreasonable bullheadedness, as when he went up to Jerusalem against the will and warning of God. His writings and ministry demonstrate the combination of the practical-analytical reasoning and the self-sacrificing but extremely driving nature of a

ChlorMel. He is a good example of God's transforming power in the life of a ChlorMel who is completely dedicated to God's will.

THE CHLORPHLEG

The most subdued of all the extrovert temperaments is the ChlorPhleg, a happy blend of the quick, active, and hot with the calm, cool, and unexcited. He is not as apt to rush into things as quickly as the preceding extroverts because he is more deliberate and subdued. He is extremely capable in the long run, although he does not particularly impress you that way at first. He is a very organized person who combines planning and hard work. People usually enjoy working with and for him because he knows where he is going and has charted his course, yet is not unduly severe with people. He has the ability to help others make the best use of their skills and rarely offends people or makes them feel used. The ChlorPhleg's slogan on organization states: "Anything that needs to be done can be done better if it's organized." These men are usually good husbands and fathers as well as excellent administrators in almost any field.

In spite of his obvious capabilities, the ChlorPhleg is not without a notable set of weaknesses. Although not as addicted to the quick anger of some temperaments, he is known to harbor resentment and bitterness. Some of the cutting edge of the choleric's sarcasm is here offset by the gracious spirit of the phlegmatic; so instead of uttering cutting and cruel remarks, his barbs are more apt to emerge as cleverly disguised humor. One is never quite sure whether he is kidding or ridiculing, depending on his mood. No one can be more bullheadedly stubborn than a ChlorPhleg, and it is very difficult for him to change his mind once it is committed. Repentance or the acknowledgement of a mistake is not at all easy for him. Consequently, he will be more apt to make it up to those he has wronged without really facing his mistake. The worrisome traits of the phlegmatic side of his nature may so curtail his adventurous tendencies that he never quite measures up to his capabilities.

Titus, the spiritual son of the Apostle Paul and leader of the hundred or so churches on the Isle of Crete, may well have been a ChlorPhleg. When filled with the Spirit, he was the kind of man on whom Paul could depend to faithfully teach the Word to the churches and administrate them capably for the glory of God. The book which Paul wrote to him makes ideal reading for any teacher, particularly a ChlorPhleg.

Now we turn to the predominantly introverted temperaments. Each will look somewhat similar to one we have already examined, except that the two temperaments making up their nature will be reversed in intensity. Such variation accounts for the exciting individuality in human beings.

THE MELSAN

Mr. MelSan is usually a very gifted person, fully capable of being a musician who can steal the heart of an audience. As an artist, he not only draws or paints beautifully but he can sell his own work—if he's in the right mood. It is not uncommon to encounter him in the field of education, for he makes a good scholar and probably the best of all classroom teachers, particularly on the high school and college level. The melancholy in him will ferret out little-known facts and be exacting in the use of events and detail, while the sanguine will enable him to communicate well with students.

Mr. MelSan shows an interesting combination of mood swings. Be sure of this: he is an emotional creature! When circumstances are pleasing to him, he can reflect a fantastically happy mood. But if things work out badly or he is rejected, insulted, or injured, he drops into such a mood that his lesser sanguine nature drowns in the resultant sea of self-pity. He is easily moved to tears, feels everything deeply, but can be unreasonably critical and hard on others. He tends to be rigid and usually will not cooperate unless things go his way, which is often idealistic and impractical. He is often a fearful, insecure man with a poor self-image which limits him unnecessarily.

Many of the prophets were MelSans—John the Baptist, Elijah, Jeremiah, and others. They had a tremendous capacity to commune with God, were self-sacrificing people-helpers who had enough charisma to attract a following, tended to be legalistic in their teachings and calls to repentance, exhibited a flair for the dramatic, and willingly died for their principles.

THE MELCHLOR

The mood swings of the melancholy are usually stabilized by the MelChlor's self-will and determination. There is almost nothing vocationally which this man cannot do—and do well. He is both a perfectionist and a driver. He possesses strong leadership capabilities. Almost any craft, construction, or educational level is open to him. Unlike the MelSan, he may found his own institution or business and run it capably—not with noise and color but with efficiency. Many a great orchestra leader and choral conductor is a MelChlor.

The natural weaknesses of MelChlors reveal themselves in the mind, emotions, and mouth. They are extremely difficult people to please, rarely satisfying even themselves. Once they start thinking negatively about something or someone (including themselves), they can be intolerable to live with. Their mood follows their thought process. Although they do not retain a depressed mood as long as the other blends of the melancholy, they can lapse into it more quickly. The two basic temperaments haunted by self-persecution, hostility, and criticism are the melancholy and the choleric. It is not uncommon for him to get angry at God as well as his fellowman, and if such thoughts persist long enough he may become manic-depressive. In extreme cases, he can become sadistic. When confronted with his vile thinking pattern and angry, bitter spirit, he can be expected to explode.

His penchant for detailed analysis and perfection tends to make him a nitpicker who drives others up the wall. Unless he is filled with God's Spirit or can maintain a positive frame of mind, he is not enjoyable company for long periods of time. No one is more painfully aware of this than his wife and children. He not only "emotes" disapproval, but feels compelled to castigate them verbally for their failures and to correct their mistakes—in public as well as in private. This man, by nature, desperately needs the love of God in his heart, and his family needs him to share it with them.

Many of the great men of the Bible show signs of a MelChlor temperament. Two that come to mind are Paul's tireless traveling companion, Dr. Luke, the painstaking scholar who carefully researched the life of Christ and left the church the most detailed account of our Lord's life, as well as the only record of the spread of the early church, and Moses, the great leader of Israel. Like many MelChlors, the latter never gained victory over his hostility and bitterness. Consequently, he died before his time. Like Moses, who wasted forty years on the backside of the desert, harboring bitterness and animosity before surrendering his life to God, many a MelChlor never lives up to his amazing potential because of the spirit of anger and revenge.

THE MELPHLEG

Some of the greatest scholars the world has ever known have been MelPhlegs. They are not nearly as prone to hostility as the two previous melancholies and usually get along well with others. These gifted introverts combine the analytical perfectionism of the melancholy with the organized efficiency of the phlegmatic. They are usually good-natured humanitarians who prefer a quiet, solitary environment for study and research to the endless rounds of activities sought by the more extroverted temperaments. MelPhlegs are usually excellent spellers and good mathematicians. These gifted people have greatly benefited humanity. Most of the world's significant inventions and medical discoveries have been made by MelPhlegs.

Despite his abilities, the MelPhleg, like the rest of us, has his own potential weaknesses. Unless controlled by God, he easily becomes discouraged and develops a very negative thinking pattern. But once he realizes it is a sin to develop the spirit of criticism and learns to rejoice, his entire outlook on life can be transformed. Ordinarily a quiet person, he is capable of inner angers and hostility caused by his tendency to be vengeful.

MelPhlegs are unusually vulnerable to fear, anxiety, and a negative self-image. It has always amazed me that the people with the greatest talents and capabilities are often victimized by genuine feelings of poor self-worth. Their strong tendency to be conscientious allows them to let others pressure them into making commitments that drain their energy and creativity. When filled with God's Spirit, these people are loved and admired by their family because their personal self-discipline and dedication are exemplary in the home. But humanitarian concerns can cause them to neglect their family. Unless they learn to pace themselves and enjoy diversions that help them relax, they often become early mortality statistics.

The most likely candidate for a MelPhleg in the Bible is the beloved Apostle John. He obviously had a very sensitive nature, for as a youth he laid his head on Jesus' breast at the Lord's Supper. On one occasion he became so angry at some people that he asked the Lord Jesus to call fire from heaven down on them. Yet at the crucifixion he was the lone disciple who devotedly stood at the cross. John was the one to whom the dying Jesus entrusted his mother. Later the disciple became a great church leader and left us five books in the New Testament, two of which (the Gospel of John and the Book of Revelation) particularly glorify Jesus Christ.

THE PHLEGSAN

The easiest of the twelve temperament blends to get along with over a protracted period of time is the PhlegSan. He is congenial, happy, cooperative, thoughtful, people-oriented, diplomatic, dependable, fun-loving, and humorous. A favorite with children and adults, he never displays an abrasive personality. He is usually a good man who enjoys a quiet life and loves his wife and children. Ordinarily he attends a church where the pastor is a good motivator, there he probably takes an active role.

The weaknesses of a PhlegSan are as gentle as his personality— unless you have to live with him all the time. Since he inherited the lack of motivation of a phlegmatic and the lack of discipline of a sanguine, it is not uncommon for the PhlegSan to fall far short of his true capabilities. He often quits school, passes up good opportunities, and avoids anything that involves "too much effort." Fear is another problem that accentuates his unrealistic feelings of insecurity. With more faith, he could grow beyond his timidity and self-defeating anxieties. However, he prefers to build a self-protective shell around himself and selfishly avoids the kind of involvement or commitment to activity that he needs and that would be a rich blessing to his partner and children. I have tremendous respect for the potential of these happy, contented people, but they must cooperate by letting God motivate them to unselfish activity.

The man in the Scripture that reminds me most of the PhlegSan is gentle, faithful, good-natured Timothy, the favorite spiritual son of the Apostle Paul. He was dependable and steady but timid and fearful. Repeatedly, Paul had to urge him to be more aggressive and to "do the work of an evangelist" (2 Tim. 4:5).

THE PHLEGCHLOR

The most active of all phlegmatics is the PhlegChlor. But it must be remembered that since he is predominantly a phlegmatic, he will never be a ball of fire. Like his brother phlegmatics, he is easy to get along with and may become an excellent group leader. The phlegmatic has the potential to become a good counselor, for he is an excellent listener, does not interrupt the client with stories about himself, and is genuinely interested in other people. Although the PhlegChlor rarely offers his services to others, when they come to his organized office where he exercises control, he is a first-rate professional. His advice will be practical, helpful, and—if he is a Bible-taught Christian—quite trustworthy. His gentle spirit never makes people feel threatened. He always does the right thing, but rarely goes beyond the norm. If his wife can make the adjustment to his passive lifestyle and reluctance to take the lead in the home, particularly in the discipline of their children, they can enjoy a happy marriage.

The weaknesses of the PhlegChlor are not readily apparent but gradually come to the surface, especially in the home. In addition to the lack of motivation and the fear problems of the other phlegmatics, he can be determinedly stubborn and unyielding. He doesn't blow up at others, but simply refuses to give in or cooperate. He is not a fighter by nature, but often lets his inner anger and stubbornness reflect itself in silence. The PhlegChlor often retreats to his "workshop" alone or nightly immerses his mind in TV. The older he gets, the more he selfishly indulges his sedentary tendency and becomes increasingly passive. Although he will probably live a long and peaceful life, if he indulges these passive feelings it is a boring life—not only for him, but also for his family. He needs to give himself to the concerns and needs of his family.

No man in the Bible epitomizes the PhlegChlor better than Abraham in the Old Testament. Fear characterized everything he did in the early days. For instance, he was reluctant to leave the security of the pagan city of Ur when God first called him; he even denied his wife on two occasions and tried to palm her off as his sister because of fear. Finally, he surrendered completely to God and grew in the spirit. Accordingly, his greatest weakness became his greatest strength. Today, instead of being known as fearful Abraham, he has the reputation of being the man who "believed in the Lord; and he counted it unto him for righteousness."

THE PHLEGMEL

Of all the temperament blends, the PhlegMel is the most gracious, gentle, and quiet. He is rarely angry or hostile and almost never says anything for which he must apologize (mainly because he rarely says much). He never embarrasses himself or others, always does the proper thing, dresses simply, is dependable and exact. He tends to have the spiritual gifts of mercy and help, and he is neat and organized in his working habits. Like any phlegmatic, he is handy around the house and as energy permits will keep his home in good repair. If he has a wife who recognizes his tendencies toward passivity (but tactfully waits for him to take the lead in their home), they will have a good family life and marriage. However, if she resents his reticence to lead and be aggressive, she may become discontented and foment marital strife. He may neglect the discipline necessary to help prepare his children for a productive, self-disciplined life and so "provoke his children to wrath" just as much as the angry tyrant whose unreasonable discipline makes them bitter.

The other weaknesses of this man revolve around fear, selfishness, negativism, criticism, and lack of self-image. Once a PhlegMel realizes that only his fears and negative feelings about himself keep him from succeeding, he is able to come out of his shell and become an effective man, husband, and father. Most PhlegMels are so afraid of over-extending themselves or getting overinvolved that they automatically refuse almost any kind of affiliation.

Personally I have never seen a PhlegMel overinvolved in anything—except in keeping from getting overinvolved. He must recognize that since he is not internally motivated, he definitely needs to accept more responsibility than he thinks he can fulfill, for that external stimulation will motivate him to greater achievement. All phlegmatics work well under pressure, but it must come from outside. His greatest source of motivation, of course, will be the power of the Holy Spirit.

Barnabas, the godly saint of the first-century church who accompanied the Apostle Paul on his first missionary journey, was in all probability a PhlegMel. He was the man who gave half his goods to the early church to feed the poor, the man who contended with Paul over providing John Mark (his nephew) another chance to serve God by accompanying them on the second missionary journey. Although the contention became so sharp that Barnabas took his nephew and they proceeded on their journey by themselves, Paul later commended Mark, saying, "He is profitable to me for the ministry" (2 Tim. 4:11). Today we have the Gospel of Mark because faithful, dedicated, and gentle Barnabas was willing to help him over a hard place in his life. PhlegMels respond to the needs of others if they will just let themselves move out into the stream of life and work with people where they are.

Additional variables to consider

With twelve temperament blends to choose from, it should be easier for you to identify with one of them than it was when only the four basic temperaments were presented. Don't be discouraged, however, if you find that you don't quite fit into any one of the twelve either. No two human beings are exactly alike. Consequently, other variables could alter the picture sufficiently so that you will not fit any model precisely. Consider the following:

1. Your percentages may be different from the 60/40 I arbitrarily chose as a basis for this section. I think you will agree that it would be nearly impossible to detail all the conceivable mixtures of temperament. I leave that to the reader. For example, a MelChlor of 60/40 will be significantly different from an 80/20 MelChlor. Or consider the disparity between a 55/45 SanPhleg and an 85/15 SanPhleg. Only detailed scientific testing can establish an accurate diagnosis.

2. Different backgrounds and childhood training alter the expressions of identical temperament blends. For example, a San-Phleg raised by loving but firm parents will be much more disciplined than one raised by permissive parents. A MelPhleg brought up by cruel, hateful parents will be drastically different from one raised by tender, understanding parents. Both will share the same

strengths and talents, but one may be overcome with hostility, depression, and self-persecution, so that he will never use his strengths. Although upbringing wields a powerful influence on the child, it is all but impossible to assess a wide variety of backgrounds in such a temperament analysis as this. I can only suggest that if the reader cannot identify his temperament blend readily, he will consider this variable.

3. You may not be objective when looking at yourself. Therefore, you may wish to discuss your temperament with loved ones and friends. All of us tend to view ourselves through rose-colored glasses. To paraphrase the yearning of the poet Robert Burns: "Oh, to see ourselves as others see us."

4. Education and IQ will often influence the appraisal of a person's temperament. For example, a MelSan with a very high IQ will appear somewhat different from one who is average or lower in intelligence. An uneducated person takes longer to mature than an educated man, as a rule, because it may take much longer to excel at something and thus "find himself." By "educated" I include the trades. It is not uncommon for a man who learns a skill (such as plastering, plumbing, and so on) to be more outgoing, confident, and expressive than he would be otherwise. Even so, if you carefully study the strengths and weaknesses of people of a particular temperament blend, you will find, in spite of the IQ, education, or experience levels, they will be basically similar in their strengths and weaknesses.

5. Health and metabolism are important. A ChlorPhleg in top physical condition will be more aggressive than one with a faulty thyroid gland or other physical ailment. A nervous PhlegMel will also be more active than one who is suffering from low blood pressure. Recently I worked with a hyperactive SanChlor minister who is a charming, superaggressive charger who made me tired just being around him. He was too powerful even to be a SanChlor. It didn't come as a surprise to learn that he had high blood pressure, which often produces the "hyper" dimension to any temperament.

6. Three temperaments are sometimes represented in one individual. In doing the research for my temperament test, I discovered a small percentage of people who have one predominant temperament with two secondary temperaments.

7. Motivation is the name of the game! "Out of [the heart] are the issues of life" (Prov. 4:23). If a person is properly motivated, it

will have a marked impact on his behavior regardless of his temperament blend. Actually, that is why I have written this book—so people who are improperly motivated at present will experience the power of God to completely transform their behavior. I have heard testimonies that this has happened to thousands as a result of reading my other books on temperament or attending my lectures on the subject. I trust God will use this book with its greater detail and suggestions to help an even greater number of people.

8. The Spirit-controlled life is a behavior modifier. Mature Christians whose temperament has been modified by the Holy Spirit often find it difficult to analyze their temperamental makeup because they make the mistake of examining the temperament theory in light of their present behavior. Temperament is based on the natural man; there is nothing spiritual about it. That is why we find it so much easier to diagnose and classify an unsaved person or a carnal Christian than a dedicated, mature Christian. Because such a person has already had many of his natural weaknesses strengthened, it is difficult to assess his temperament. He should either concentrate only on his strengths or consider his behavior before he became a Spirit-controlled believer.

Temperament theory—a useful tool

The temperament theory is not the final answer to human behavior, and for these and other reasons it may not prove satisfactory to everyone. But of all behavior theories ever devised, it has served as the most helpful explanation. Additional factors could be included to explain some of the other differences in people, but these will suffice. If you keep them in mind, you will probably find that you and those you try to help in life fall into one of the twelve blends we have studied. Now a question arises: What can be done about it?

3

EVALUATING YOUR STRENGTHS
AND WEAKNESSES

Dr. Henry Brandt, a Christian psychologist, has probably helped more people than any other person in that profession. He certainly has a profound influence on this writer's life, both personally and in my role as a family counselor. He made a profound statement that I have never forgotten in relation to maturity. He defines a mature person in relation to his attitude toward his own strengths and weaknesses: "A mature person is one who is sufficiently objective about himself to know both his strengths and his weaknesses and has created a planned program for overcoming his weaknesses."

The Bible says, ". . . we are more than conquerers through him [Jesus Christ] that loved us" (Rom. 8:37). He has given us his Holy Spirit to strengthen our weaknesses so he can use us. We will now examine both your potential weaknesses and your potential strengths. Knowing both your strengths and weaknesses is the first giant step toward that mature person you have always wanted to be.

The chart we studied earlier listed several strengths and the most prominent weaknesses for each temperament. There are more, but based on my counseling, testing of thousands of people, and many years of observations I have selected these as the most common. First let's examine the strengths of each temperament.

SPARKY
SANGUINE'S
STRENGTHS

Sparky is not just an extrovert, he is a super-extrovert. Everything he does is superficial and external. He laughs loudly

and dominates every conversation whether he has anything meaningful to say or not. He loves the limelight and excels at public speaking. He rarely waits for others to speak first, but usually is the first to initiate a conversation.

Mr. or Ms. Sanguine's ability to respond to others is instantaneous. If he catches another person looking at him, he always responds with a nod, wink, or greeting. No one enjoys life more than Sparky Sanguine. He never seems to lose his childlike curiosity for the things that surround him. Even the unpleasant things of life can be forgotten by his change of environment. It is a rare occasion when he does not awaken in a lively mood, and he will often be found whistling or singing his way through life.

The natural trait of Mr. Sanguine that produces both his hearty and optimistic disposition is defined by Dr. Hallesby, a European authority on this subject: "The sanguine person has a God-given ability to live in the present." He easily forgets the past, and is seldom frustrated or fearful of future difficulties. The sanguine person is optimistic.

He is easily inspired to engage in new plans and projects, and his boundless enthusiasm often carries others along with him. If yesterday's project has failed, he is confident that the project he is working on today will definitely succeed. The outgoing, handshaking, backslapping customs of the cheerful sanguine stem basically from his genuine love for people. He enjoys being around others, sharing in their joys and sorrows, and he likes to make new friends. No one makes a better first impression.

One of the greatest assets of Mr. Sanguine is that he has a tender, compassionate heart. No one responds more genuinely to the needs of others than the sanguine. He is able to share the emotional experiences, both good and bad, of others. By nature, he finds it easy to obey the scriptural injunction, "Rejoice with those that do rejoice, and weep with those who weep."

The sincerity of Mr. Sanguine is often misunderstood by others. They are deceived by his sudden changes of emotion, and they fail to understand that he is genuinely responding to the emotions of others. No one can love you more nor forget you faster than sanguines. The world is enriched by these cheerful, responsive people. When motivated and disciplined by God, they can be great servants of Jesus Christ.

ROCKY CHOLERIC'S STRENGTHS

Mr. Choleric is usually a self-disciplined individual with a strong tendency toward self-determination. He is very confident in his own ability and very aggressive.

Once having embarked upon a project, he has a tenacious ability that keeps him doggedly driving in one direction. His singleness of purpose often results in accomplishment.

The choleric temperament is given over almost exclusively to the practical aspects of life. Everything to him is considered in the light of its utilitarian purpose, and he is happiest when engaged in some worthwhile project. He has a keen mind for organization but finds detail work distressing. Many of his decisions are reached by intuition more than by analytical reasoning.

Mr. Choleric has strong leadership tendencies. His forceful will tends to dominate a group, he is a good judge of people,

and he is quick and bold in emergencies. He not only will readily accept leadership when it is placed on him, but will often be the first to volunteer for it. If he does not become too arrogant or bossy, others respond well to his practical direction.

When Rocky sets his mind to do something, he never gives up. Just about the time his optimism has come home to engulf him in impossibility, he doggedly burrows out another way. And if the people don't agree with him, that's just too bad—he is going to do it with or without them. What other people think of him or his projects makes very little difference to him.

No one is more practical than a choleric. He seems to have a utilitarian mentality. He has strong workaholic tendencies. Mr. Choleric's outlook on life, based on his natural feeling of self-confidence, is almost always one of optimism. He has such an adventuresome spirit that he thinks nothing of leaving a secure position for the challenge of the unknown. Adversity does not discourage him. Instead, it whets his appetite and makes him even more determined to achieve his objective.

MARTIN MELANCHOLY'S STRENGTHS

Usually melancholies have the highest IQ of any member in their family. They may be musical, artistic, or athletic. Sometimes you will find all these traits in one individual.

Mr. Melancholy has by far the richest and most sensitive nature of all the temperaments. A higher percentage of geniuses are melancholy than any other type. He particularly excels in the fine arts, with a vast appreciation for life's cultural values. He is emotionally responsive,

but unlike the sanguine is motivated to reflective thinking through his emotions. Mr. Melancholy is particularly adept at creative thinking, and during high emotional peaks will often launch into an invention or creative production that is worthwhile and wholesome.

Mr. Melancholy has strong perfectionist tendencies. His standard of excellence exceeds others', and his requirements of acceptability in any field are often higher than either he or anyone else can maintain. The analytical abilities of the melancholy, combined with his perfectionist tendencies, make him a "hound for detail." Whenever a project is suggested, Mr. Melancholy can analyze it in a few moments and pick out every potential problem.

A melancholy person can always be depended upon to finish his job in the prescribed time or to carry his end of the load. Mr. Melancholy rarely seeks the limelight, but prefers to do the behind-the-scenes task. He often chooses a very sacrificial vocation for life, for he has an unusual desire to give himself to the betterment of his fellowmen.

He is prone to be reserved and seldom volunteers his opinion or ideas. Melancholy temperaments are extremely self-disciplined individuals. They rarely eat too much or indulge their own comforts. When they engage in a task, they will work around the clock to meet deadlines and their high self-imposed standards. One of the reasons they can go into a deep depression after completion of a big project is because they have so neglected themselves while seeing the task to com-

pletion by going without sleep, food, and diversion that they are literally exhausted physically and emotionally.

PHIL PHLEGMATIC'S STRENGTHS

Just because they are super-introverts does not mean phlegmatics are not strong. Actually the phlegmatic's calm and unexcited nature is a vital asset. There are things he can do and vocations he can pursue that extroverts could never do. Phlegmatics rarely, if ever, leap before they look. They are thinkers and planners.

Phil is a born diplomat. Conciliatory by nature, he does not like confrontation and would rather negotiate than fight. He has a knack for defusing the hostile and excitable types and is a walking example that "a soft answer turns away wrath."

The unexcited good humor of the phlegmatic keeps him from being intensely involved with life so that he can often see humor in the most mundane experiences. He seems to have a superb inborn sense of timing in the art of humor and a stimulating imagination.

Mr. Phlegmatic is dependability itself. Not only can he be depended upon to always be his cheerful, good-natured self, but he can be depended upon to fulfill his obligations and time schedules. Like the melancholy, he is a very faithful friend, and although he does not get too involved with others he rarely proves disloyal.

Mr. Phlegmatic is also practical and efficient. Not prone to making sudden decisions, he has a tendency to find the practical way to accomplish an objective

with the least amount of effort. He often does his best work under circumstances that would cause other temperaments to "crack." His work always bears the hallmark of neatness and efficiency. Although he is not a perfectionist, he does have exceptionally high standards of accuracy and precision.

The administrative or leadership capabilities of a phlegmatic are seldom discovered because he is not assertive and doesn't push himself. But when once given the responsibility, he has a real ability to get people to work together productively and in an organized manner.

Summary

The variety of strengths provided by the four temperament types keeps the world functioning properly. No one temperament is more desirable than another. Each one has its vital strengths and makes its worthwhile contribution to life.

Someone facetiously pointed out this sequence of events involving the four temperaments: "The hard-driving choleric produces the inventions of the genius-prone melancholy, which are sold by the personable sanguine and enjoyed by the easygoing phlegmatic."

The strengths of the four temperaments make each of them attractive, and we can be grateful that we all possess some of those strengths. But there is more to the story! As important as are the temperament strengths, even more important, for our purposes, are their weaknesses. It is our intent to contrast the strengths of the temperaments with their weaknesses. Our purpose in so doing is to help you diagnose your own weaknesses and develop a planned program for overcoming them.

Don't be afraid to be objective about yourself or to face your weaknesses. Many people have decided what basic temperament they are at this point in the study, then changed their mind when confronted with their unpleasant weaknesses. Strengths carry corresponding weaknesses, so face them realistically, then let God do something to improve them.

Temperament weaknesses

This will doubtless be the most painful section in this book, for no one likes to be confronted with his weaknesses. But if we think of ourselves only in terms of the strengths of our temperament, we will develop a faulty view of ourselves. Everyone has weaknesses.

THE SANGUINE WEAKNESSES

Sanguines are voted "most likely to succeed" in college, but often fail in life. Their tendency to be weak-willed and undisciplined will finally destroy them unless it is overcome. Since they are highly emotional, exude considerable natural charm, and are prone to be what one psychologist called "touchers" (they tend to touch people as they talk to them), they commonly have a great appeal for the opposite sex and consequently face sexual temptation more than others. Weakness of will and lack of discipline make it easier for them to be deceitful, dishonest, and undependable. They tend to overeat and gain weight, finding it most difficult to remain on a diet. Someone has said, "Without self-discipline, there is no such thing as success." Lack of discipline is Mr. Sanguine's greatest weakness.

The only temperament more emotional than a sanguine is a melancholy, but he isn't anywhere near as expressive as Sparky Sanguine. Not only can Sparky cry at the drop of a hat (one pro football player's wife won't watch a sad film on TV with her husband because "his blubbering embarrasses me!"), but his spark of anger can instantly become a raging inferno.

A lack of emotional consistency usually limits him vocationally, and it certainly destroys him spiritually. When filled with the Spirit, however, he becomes a "new creature," an emotionally controlled sanguine.

Every human being is plagued with ego-

tism, but sanguines have a double dose of the problem. That's why a Spirit-filled Sparky is easily detected; he will reflect an unnatural spirit of humility that is refreshing.

Sanguines are notoriously disorganized and always on the move. They seldom plan ahead but usually take things as they come. They rarely profit by past mistakes and seldom look ahead. As one man said, "They are a disorganized accident waiting to happen."

Wherever Sparky works or lives, things are in a disastrous state of disarray. He can never find his tools, even though they are right where he left them. Sparky's garage, bedroom, closet, and office are disaster areas unless he has an efficient wife and secretary willing to pick up after him. His egotism usually makes him a sharp dresser but if his friends or customers could see the room where he dressed, they would fear that someone had been killed in the explosion. How does Sparky get by with that kind of living? The way Mr. Sanguine handles all confrontations caused by his temperament—a disarming smile, a pat on the back, a funny story, and a restless move to the next thing that sparks his interest. The sanguine will never become a perfectionist, but the Spirit of God can bring more planning and order into his life. And when that happens, Sparky is a much happier person—not only with others but also with himself.

Behind that superextroverted personality that frequently overpowers other people, giving him a false reputation as a very self-confident person, Sparky Sanguine is really quite insecure. His insecurity is often the source of his vile profanity.

Sanguines are not usually fearful of personal injury and often resort to outlandish feats of daring and heroism. Their fears most often arise in the area of personal failure, rejection, or disapproval. That's why they often follow an obnoxious display of conversation with an equally mindless statement. Rather than face your disapproval, they are hoping to cover up the first goof with something that will gain your approval.

Perhaps the sanguine's most treacherous trait, one that really stifles his spiritual potential, is his weak or flexible conscience. He usually is able to talk others into his way of thinking, earning him the reputation of being the world's greatest con artist. When things go wrong, he has no difficulty convincing himself that whatever he did was justified. He "bends the truth" until any similarity between his story and the facts is totally coincidental; yet this rarely bothers him, for he cons himself into believing that "the end justifies the means."

Others often find it incredible that he can lie, cheat, or steal, yet seldom endure a sleepless night. That is why he frequently walks over the rights of others and rarely hesitates to take advantage of other people.

Sooner or later, Sparky Sanguine will weave a web of deceit that will produce his own destruction. The Bible says, "Be not deceived; God is not mocked: for whatsoever a man soweth, that shall he also reap" (Gal. 6:7). The only way to conquer that problem is to concentrate on truth and honesty. Every time a man lies or cheats, it becomes easier—and the next temptation is bigger.

Sparky Sanguine's penchant for exaggeration, embellishment, and plain old-fashioned deceit catches up with him most quickly in his marriage and family. While he may fool those who see him occasionally, it is impossible for him to cheat and deceive his way through life without teaching his wife and children that they cannot depend on his word. One of the nine necessary building blocks in any love relationship (according to 1 Cor. 13:4-8) is trust. Part of the reason our Lord and the Scriptures speak so frequently on the subject of truth or honesty is that it not only produces the necessary clear conscience all men need, but it creates the kind of foundation on which lasting and enjoyable interpersonal relationships are made.

THE CHOLERIC WEAKNESSES

Cholerics are extremely hostile people. Some learn to control their anger, but eruption into violence is always a possibility with them. If their strong will is not brought into control by

proper parental discipline as children, they develop angry, tumultuous habits that plague them all through life. It doesn't take long to learn that others are usually afraid of their angry outbursts and thus they may use wrath as a weapon to get what they want—which is usually their own way. The choleric can cause pain to others and enjoy it. His wife is usually afraid of him, and he tends to terrify his children.

Rocky Choleric often reminds me of walking Mount Vesuvius, constantly gurgling until, provoked, he spills out his bitter lava all over someone or something. He is a door slammer, table pounder, and horn blower. Any person or thing that gets in his way, retards his progress, or fails to perform up to the level of his expectations will feel the eruption of his wrath.

No one utters more caustic comments than a sarcastic choleric! He is usually ready with a cutting comment that can wither the insecure and devastate the less combative. Even Sparky Sanguine is no match for him, because Sparky isn't cruel or mean. Rocky will rarely hesitate to tell a person off or chop him to bits. Consequently, he leaves a path of damaged psyches and fractured egos wherever he goes. It is a happy choleric (and his family members) who discovers that the tongue is either a vicious weapon of destruction or a tool of healing. Once he learns the importance of his verbal approval and encouragement to others, he will seek to control his speech—until he gets angry, whereupon he discovers with the Apostle James that "the tongue can no

man tame; it is an unruly evil, full of deadly poison" (James 3:8). Ready speech and an angry spirit often combine to make a choleric very profane.

The milk of human kindness has all but dried up in the veins of a choleric. He is the most unaffectionate of all the temperaments and becomes emotionally spastic at the thought of any public show of emotion. Marital affection to him means a kiss at the wedding and on every fifth anniversary thereafter. His emotional rigidity rarely permits him the expression of tears. He usually stops crying at the age of eleven or twelve and finds it difficult to understand others when they are moved to tears.

Similar to his natural lack of love is the choleric's tendency to be insensitive to others' needs and inconsiderate of their feelings. When a choleric is sensitive and considerate, he can be a great blessing to others, for as we have seen, what he thinks of others is of vital importance to them. By nature Rocky Choleric has the hide of a rhinoceros. However the Spirit of God will make him "kind, tenderhearted. . . ."

The choleric's natural determination is a temperament asset that stands him in good stead throughout life, but it can make him opinionated and bullheaded. Since he has an intuitive sense, he usually makes up his mind quickly (without adequate analysis and deliberation), and once made up, it is almost impossible to change. No temperament type more typifies the old cliché: "Don't confuse me with the facts; my mind is made up."

One of the undesirable characteristics of the choleric involves his inclination to be crafty if necessary to get his own way. He rarely takes no for an answer and will often resort to any means necessary to achieve his ends. If he has to juggle his figures and bend the truth, he rarely hesitates, for to him the end justifies the means.

Since he easily comes to conclusions, he finds great delight in making decisions for other people and forcing them to conform to his will. If you work for a choleric, you rarely wonder what he wants you to do, for he tells you five times before eight-thirty in the morning—and usually at the top of his lungs.

The Rocky Cholerics of life are very effective people if their weaknesses are not indulged until they become a dominating lifestyle. When they are filled with the Spirit, their tendencies toward willfulness and harshness are replaced by a gentleness which verifies clearly that they are controlled by something other than their own natural temperament. From the days of the Apostle Paul until the present, both the church of Jesus Christ and society have benefited much from these active, productive people. Many of our great church institutions were founded by venturous cholerics. But to be effective in God's service, they must learn the divine principles of productivity.

THE MELANCHOLY WEAKNESSES

The admirable qualities of perfectionism and conscientiousness often carry with them the serious disadvantages of negativism, pessimism, and a spirit of criticism. Anyone who has worked with a gifted melancholy can anticipate that his first reaction to anything will be negative or pessimistic. This one trait limits a melancholy's vocational performance more than any other. The minute a new idea or project is presented, his analytical ability ignites and he begins to concoct every problem and difficulty that may be encountered in the effort.

The most damaging influence upon a person's mind, in my opinion, is criticism; and melancholies have to fight that spirit constantly. I have observed that the most psychologically disturbed children come from homes of predominantly melancholy or choleric parents. Cholerics are hard to please; melancholies are impossible to satisfy. Even when the children bring home B's and B-pluses, the parent will grimace with dissatisfaction because they don't get A's. Instead of commending their wives and encouraging them, melancholies criticize, carp, and censure. Even when they realize the importance of their approval to both wife and children, it is hard for them to offer it because they cannot endure the hypocritical taint of saying something that isn't 100 percent true.

The same high standard is usually turned inward by a melancholy, making him very dissatisfied with himself. Self-examination, of course, is a healthy thing for any Christian who wants to walk in

the Spirit, for through it he gains the realization that he must confess his sins and seek the Savior's forgiveness (1 John 1:9). But the melancholy is not satisfied to examine himself he dissects himself with a continuing barrage of introspection until he has no self-confidence or self-esteem left. Everything in life is interpreted by the melancholy in relation to himself. He tends to compare himself with others on looks, talent, and intellect, invariably feeling deficient because it never occurs to him that he compares himself to the best of another's traits and fails to evaluate their weaknesses.

He is ever examining his spiritual life and typically coming up short in his own mind. This keeps him from enjoying confidence before God. A melancholy finds it difficult to believe he is "approved of God," basically because he can seldom approve himself.

This self-centered trait, together with his sensitive nature, makes a melancholy thin-skinned and touchy at times. Although not as expressive of his anger as the sanguine or choleric, he is very capable of long-term seething and slow-burning anger in the form of revengeful thinking patterns and self-persecution reveries. If indulged long enough, this can make him manic-depressive or at least erupt into an angry outburst that is unlike his normally gentle nature.

One of the most prominent characteristics of a melancholy's temperament concerns his mood swings. On some occasions he is so "high" that he acts like a sanguine; on others he is so "down" that he feels like sliding under the door rather than opening it. The older he gets (unless transformed by a vital relationship to Jesus Christ), the more he is prone to experience dark moods. During such times he is gloomy, irritable, unhappy, and all but impossible to please. Such moods make him particularly vulnerable to depression.

Three years ago I read an article on depression in *Newsweek* magazine that stated: "Depression is the emotional epidemic of our times. Fifty thousand to seventy thousand depressed individuals commit suicide annually." Having counseled over one thousand depressed people by that time, I felt compelled to write a book, *How to Win over Depression*; it became a best-seller in only three months.

Anyone with a depression problem, particularly a melancholy, should make 1 Thessalonians 5:18 a way of life: "In every thing give thanks: for this is the will of God in Christ Jesus concerning you." You cannot rejoice and give thanks over something while maintaining a state of depression.

No other temperament is so apt to be rigid, implacable and uncompromising to the point of unreasonableness as the melancholy. He is intolerant and impatient with those who do not see things his way; consequently he finds it difficult to be a team player and is often a loner in the business world, but at home it is a different matter. A wife and children subjected to such rigid standards will often become insecure and unhappy and sometimes give up on him. Once he learns that flexibility and cooperation are the oil that makes interpersonal relationships run smoothly, he is a much happier person and so are those around him.

We have already seen that the melancholy is an idealist, a trait we list as a strength. However, on the other side of that characteristic, he is apt to be impractical and theoretical, often campaigning for an ideal that is so altruistic it will never work. A melancholy should always subject his plans to the practicality test.

God has used many melancholies who made their talents available to him. In fact, many of the characters recorded in the Bible were melancholies. However, the key to their success was not their temperament, talents, or gifts, but their commitment to the Holy Spirit.

THE PHLEGMATIC
WEAKNESSES

The most obvious of Phil Phlegmatic's weaknesses and that which caused Hippocrates (who originated the idea of the four temperaments) to label him phlegm (slow or sluggish) is his apparent lack of drive and ambition. Although he always seems to do what is expected of him, he will rarely do more. Rarely does he instigate an activity, but thinks up excuses to avoid getting involved with the activities of others.

More than any other temperament, the phlegmatic is vulnerable to the law of inertia: "A body at rest tends to stay at rest." He needs to reverse that trend with premeditated activity. Both he and his family will benefit by such efforts.

No one likes to be hurt, and that is particularly true of Phil Phlegmatic. Although not as sensitive as a melancholy, he does have a thin skin and accordingly learns early in life to live like a turtle— that is, to build a hard shell of self-protection to shield him from all outside griefs or affronts. But even a turtle could give Phil a valuable piece of advice: "You can never go anywhere unless you stick your neck out." Nor will you ever help anyone else unless you risk the possibility of an emotional injury.

One of the less obvious weaknesses of the phlegmatic is his selfishness. Every temperament faces the problem of selfishness, but Phil is particularly afflicted with the disease, though he is so gracious and proper that few people who don't live with him are aware of it. Selfishness makes him self-indulgent and unconcerned about his family's need for activity.

No one can be more stubborn than a phlegmatic, but he is so diplomatic about it that he may proceed halfway through life before others catch on. He almost never openly confronts another person

or refuses to do something, but he will somehow manage to sidestep the demand. In church administration I have found this gracious, kindly, placid individual to be most exasperating at times. He will smile as I detail the program, even nod his head as if he understands, and then walk away and ignore the mandate. He simply will do it his way—quite affably and with less contention than any other temperament, but definitely his way. In a family situation, phlegmatics never yell or argue; they just drag their feet or set their legs and will not budge.

Beneath the gracious surface of a diplomatic phlegmatic beats a very fearful heart. He is a worrier by nature who erroneously seems to misinterpret Philippians 4:6 as: "Be anxious for everything, and by worry and fear let your requests be made known unto God." This fear tendency often keeps him from venturing out on his own to make full use of his potential.

Fear keeps phlegmatics from being used in the church. I'm convinced that they would like to teach, sing in the choir, or learn to share their faith, but fear stifles them. One of the strengths of the Holy Spirit is faith, which dissolves our fears. A salient result of reading and studying the Word of God is a growing faith. Most people are fearful of failure, but those who succeed in effectively serving God replace their fears with faith.

I have found it well worth the time to try motivating phlegmatics to work in the church. They make good board members and policymakers as well as excellent Sunday school teachers and department superintendents. Once committed, they become very dependable workers for many years. The difficult task is to get them to agree to an assignment in the first place.

Summary

Now you have the bad news—all temperaments have weaknesses—at least ten according to their temperament. But there is a power that can enable you to improve your temperament. Read on.

4

STRENGTHENING YOUR WEAKNESSES

One thing about temperament—it never changes. If your parents' genes combined to make you a ChlorSan, a MelPhleg, or a San-MelPhleg, you will never be anything else. Like your appearance, height, and IQ, your temperament will be a part of you as long as you live. And remember, your temperament probably has more to do with your current behavior than anything else in your life. The rest is the result of your childhood training, home life, education, motivation, and other things. The following formula will put it all together for you.

As you look over this list, you are probably stuck with the realization that you have very little control over most of the ingredients in this formula. Don't be deceived! It is true that you cannot change your temperament, but there are three things in that formula that you do control and so can improve your temperament and change your life: motivation, mental attitude, and habit.

BEHAVIOR FORMULA

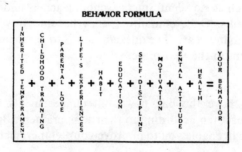

Your motivational potential

When God created Adam, he made him unique from all other living creatures. He gave him a "soul." This soul not only has a capacity for God but is a source of external motivation that is all but untapped by most people today. But it does account for the tremendous transformation that occurs in people when they have a "born again" experience with Jesus Christ. To understand this, you must visualize the four parts of human nature as described in the Bible.

Jesus Christ knew more about human nature than anyone who has ever lived. (He should, for he was the Creator of man in the first place.) And he said, "Thou shalt love the Lord thy God with all thy heart, and with all thy soul, and with all thy mind, and with all thy strength" (Mark 12:30). Notice carefully the four aspects of human nature: heart, soul, mind, strength. Notice these on the following chart.

Your inherited temperament probably resides in the heart, where it influences the method of your thinking—not the content. It can be influenced by the mind, soul, and heart. It is what the Bible means when it speaks of "the flesh" or "nature" or "natural man."

Christ is not the natural man; he is outside man's life. He knocks at the door of our life through the convicting of the Holy Spirit in preaching, tracts, radio, television, personal witness, etc. If God's Spirit is not *within* him, he will experience the guilt, fear, emptiness, misery, purposelessness, confusion, and other negative things pictured above. The amount of negative feelings will depend on his willfulness and sin. His greatest need is his emptiness—his unfilled "God-shaped vacuum" that Pascal said was in the heart of every man and can be filled with no one save Jesus Christ. This emptiness that plagues mankind all through life cheats man not only out of God's daily presence in his life but also out of His power to improve his temperament.

God never forces his way into a person's life; he leaves it to an individual to decide whether or not to receive Christ as his Savior and Lord. But if you believe Jesus Christ died for your sins and rose again the third day, you can humbly repent of your sins and submit your will to him by praying a simple but beautiful prayer like this: "O God, I know I am a sinner and have willfully disobeyed you many times. I believe Jesus died for my sins and rose again that I

THE NATURAL MAN

1) Heart: The emotional center—source of feeling and motivation. "As a man thinks in his heart so is he."

2) Soul: Source of human life and the will. God has given each person sovereignty over his own will. Your self is by nature the control mechanism of your will.

3) Mind: The most incredible organ in the body. It contains twelve billion brain cells, and how you fill those cells influences your feelings, which in turn influences everything you do.

4) Strength: This refers to the perishable part of man, or that which we see the most.

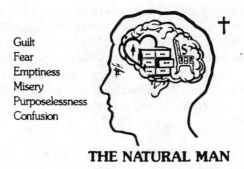

Guilt
Fear
Emptiness
Misery
Purposelessness
Confusion

THE NATURAL MAN

might have eternal life. Therefore, I invite you to come into my life to both save me from my sins and to direct my future. Today I give myself to you."

"As many as received him [Jesus], to them gave he power to become the sons of God" (John 1:12). All who believe in him are born again and have two natures. The new one is the new man in Christ, opening up a whole new source of power. The old nature still wants to sin.

Both natures are alive. Which one is dominant depends on which one you feed the most. If you feed the old nature the food of the sin-sick culture that surrounds us, don't be surprised when the weaknesses of your temperament dominate you. If, however, you feed your new nature the spiritual food of the Word of God and things pertaining to God, your new nature will become so dominant it will overcome the natural weakness of your temperament, enabling God to make maximum use of your inherited strengths or talents.

Who's in control?

We hear a lot in our humanistic culture about "taking control of your life." That sounds good at first, but if you look deeper into this cult of the self-actualizers, you will find the worst sin of all—selfishness.

God wants to control your life. He makes no secret of that. He challenges us, "Therefore, I urge you, brothers, in view of God's mercy, to offer your bodies as living sacrifices, holy and pleasing to God—this is your spiritual act of worship. Do not conform any longer to the pattern of this world, but be transformed by the renewing of your mind. Then you will be able to test and approve what God's will is—his good, pleasing and perfect will" (Rom. 12: 1-2, NIV). Who controls your life? It is not hard to tell. Ask yourself, "Do I do what Jesus Christ wants or what I want?" Jesus said, "If you love me keep my commandments." It is ridiculous to sing "Oh, How I Love Jesus" while doing as you please with your life. When Christ is in control, you will do what he tells you in his Word.

Three modern life-styles

There are only three possible life-styles today. You should analyze which is yours and see if the results of that kind of life are what you really want.

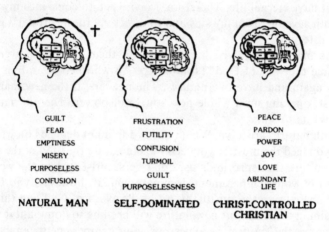

GUILT	FRUSTRATION	PEACE
FEAR	FUTILITY	PARDON
EMPTINESS	CONFUSION	POWER
MISERY	TURMOIL	JOY
PURPOSELESS	GUILT	LOVE
CONFUSION	PURPOSELESSNESS	ABUNDANT LIFE
NATURAL MAN	**SELF-DOMINATED**	**CHRIST-CONTROLLED CHRISTIAN**

Note the similarity of results in the two life-styles pictured above where self is on the throne. The only real difference between 1 and 2 is that Christ was at one time invited into the Christian's life and he will go to heaven when he dies. But he is as miserable as the individual who doesn't know Christ. In fact, sometimes he is more miserable because the Holy Spirit can convict him from within. Both of these individuals will be dominated by their natural temperament weaknesses.

The third drawing illustrates the individual who has surrendered the center of his life to Christ (or most of the time lives this way—no one is perfect). We all give in to the flesh on occasion, but at least this person has the capability of living up to his divine potential.

How to strengthen your weaknesses

"Therefore, if anyone is in Christ, he is a new creation; the old has gone, the new has come!" (2 Cor. 5:17, NIV).

One of the fundamental premises of the Christian life is, "When a natural individual is indwelt by a supernatural power, he ought to be different!" Think about that. If God is *really* in your life, you will be different than if he were not.

But it is also true that growth takes place *slowly*. You don't see much growth in a fruit tree on a daily basis, but there is growth if the tree is alive. So it is with a Christian. The growth in us is painfully slow sometimes, but it does take place.

The power to change

What will be different after the Holy Spirit of God comes to reside in you? Your looks? Unfortunately not. Will you get smarter? No! What changes? Your *emotions*. The Holy Spirit of God brings emotional stability into our lives.

Paul describes it in these words: "The fruit of the Spirit is love, joy, peace, patience, kindness, goodness, faithfulness, gentleness and self-control" (Gal. 5:22-23, NIV). As you study these verses, you discover nine specific strengths that God provides the Christian to enable him to overcome his emotional weaknesses. The Spirit-controlled Christian will be an emotionally controlled Christian.

The nine emotional strengths of the Spirit-filled temperament make any temperament what God originally intended. It does not matter what one's natural temperament is. Any man filled with the Holy Spirit, whether sanguine, choleric, melancholy, or phlegmatic, is going to manifest these nine spiritual characteristics. He will have his own natural strengths and maintain his individuality, but the Spirit will transform his weaknesses.

These nine characteristics represent what God wants each one of his children to be. We shall examine each in detail. There is a longing in the heart of every child of God to live this kind of a life. It is not the result of man's effort, but the supernatural result of the Holy Spirit controlling every area of a Christian.

LOVE   The first characteristic in God's cata-
              log of Spirit-filled temperament traits is
love—love for God and for our fellowmen. The Lord Jesus said, "Love the Lord your God with all your heart and with all your soul

and with all your mind and with all your strength. . . . Love your neighbor as yourself" (Mark 12:30, NIV).

A love for God that causes a man to be more interested in the kingdom of God than in the material kingdom in which he lives is supernatural, for man by nature is a greedy creature.

The Christian who says he is "filled with the Spirit," but is unmoved by the suffering of others, is kidding himself. If we have the love of God flowing through us, it will benefit others around us.

I must also point out that the love God's Spirit provides makes us want to obey him. If you would like to test your love for God, try this simple method given by the Lord Jesus: "If ye love me, keep my commandments." Just ask yourself, "Am I obedient to his commandments as revealed in his Word?" If not, you are not filled with the Holy Spirit.

JOY

The second temperament characteristic of the Spirit filled man is joy. One theologian gave this comment concerning the gracious emotion of joy; "Yes, joy is one of the cardinal Christian virtues; It deserves a place next to love. Pessimism is a grave fault. This is not fatuous joy such as the world accepts; it is the enduring joy that bubbles up from all the grace of God in our possession, from the blessedness that is ours, that is undimmed by tribulation. . . ."

The joy provided by the Holy Spirit is not limited by circumstances. No Christian can have joy if he depends upon the circumstances of life. The Spirit-filled life is characterized by a "looking unto Jesus the author and finisher of our faith," which causes us to know that "in all things God works for the good of those who love him, who have been called according to his purpose" (Rom. 8:28, NIV).

In the Scriptures, "joy" and "rejoicing" are not the result of self-effort, but are the work of the Holy Spirit in your life. "You have filled my heart with greater joy than when their grain and new wine abound" (Ps. 4:7, NIV). The Apostle Paul, writing from a prison dungeon, said, "Rejoice in the Lord always. I will say it again: Rejoice!" (Phil. 4:4, NIV). Any man who can rejoice in prison has to have a supernatural source of power!

This supernatural joy is available for any Christian regardless of his basic or natural temperament. Jesus said, "These things have I spoken unto you, that my joy might remain in you, and that your joy might be full" (John 15:11). This is only possible as we are filled with the Holy Spirit.

Martin Luther said, "God does not like doubt and dejection. He hates dreary doctrine, gloomy and melancholy thought. God likes cheerful hearts. Christ says: 'Rejoice, for your names are written in heaven.'"

PEACE

The third temperament trait of the Spirit-filled man is peace. The preceding verses in Galatians 5 describe not only the works of the natural man without the Spirit, but also his emotions. His emotional turbulence is described by ". . . hatred, variance (strivings), emulations, wrath, strife, seditions, heresies." We see that the further man gets from God, the less he knows of peace.

The "peace" spoken of here is really twofold. It is peace with God and the peace of God. The Lord Jesus said, "Peace I leave with you, my peace I give unto you" (John 14:27). The peace he leaves us is peace with God. "My peace I give unto you" is the peace of God, for in the same verse he defines it as the peace of an untroubled heart: "Let not your heart be troubled, neither let it be afraid." And the preceding verse describes the coming of the Holy Spirit. The Holy Spirit is the source of peace.

Peace with God is the result of salvation by faith. Man outside of Jesus Christ knows nothing of peace in relationship with God, because his sin is ever before him and he knows he is accountable before God at the Judgment. However, when this individual takes Jesus Christ at his word and invites him into his life as Lord and Savior, Jesus Christ not only comes in as he promised to do (Rev. 3:20), but immediately cleanses all his sin (1 John 1:7, 9). "Therefore being justified by faith, we have peace with God through our Lord Jesus Christ" (Rom. 5:1).

The peace of God, the antidote to worry, is not as automatically possessed by Christians as the peace with God. This peace, enabling one to be untroubled in the face of difficult circumstances, is illustrated by the Lord Jesus who was sound asleep in the lower part of the ship while the twelve disciples were frightened beyond rationality. Many are prone to worry, further complicating their emotional, physical, and spiritual life. While those who believe God get a good night's sleep, awaken refreshed and available for God's use the next day.

Just becoming a Christian does not spare us from the difficult circumstances of life. However, the Holy Spirit's presence in our lives can supply us with one of life's greatest treasures: the peace of God, in spite of any circumstances. The Apostle Paul had this in mind when he wrote the words, "Be careful [worried or anxious] for nothing; but in every thing by prayer and supplication with thanksgiving let your requests be made known unto God. And the peace of God, which passeth all understanding, shall keep your hearts and minds through Christ Jesus" (Phil. 4:6-7). The Holy Spirit longs to give such peace to every believer.

LONG-SUFFERING

The fourth temperament trait of the Spirit-filled man is longsuffering (also known as patience or endurance). It can be characterized by an ability to bear injuries or suffer reproof or affliction without answering in kind. As the Apostle Peter said about the Lord Jesus, ". . . who, when he was reviled, reviled not again." A long-suffering person is one who can do the menial, forgotten, and difficult tasks of life graciously—as unto the Lord—without complaining or seething. He finishes his task or suffers affronts while manifesting the loving Spirit of Christ.

GENTLENESS

The fifth characteristic of the Spirit-filled temperament is described in the King James Version as gentleness. This is a thoughtful, polite, gracious, considerate, undersanding act of kindness stemming from a tender

heart. The world in which we live knows little of such tenderheartedness. It is the result of the compassion of the Holy Spirit for a lost and dying humanity.

The Lord Jesus' gentle spirit contrasted sharply with the disciples' cruel attitude toward the children who had been brought by their parents to be blessed by him. The Scripture tells us that the disciples rebuked those who brought them, but Jesus said, "Suffer the little children to come unto me, and forbid them not" (Mark 10:13-14).

This gentle characteristic of the Holy Spirit never asks such questions as, "How often must I forgive my brother when he sins against me?" or, "Isn't there a limit to how much a person can stand?" The Holy Spirit is able to give gentleness in the face of all kinds of pressures.

Jesus, who possessed the Holy Spirit "without measure," pictured himself as a shepherd gently caring for injured sheep; and he, through his followers, tenderly cares today.

GOODNESS

The sixth characteristic of the Spirit-filled man is called "goodness." This is benevolence in its purest sense. It includes hospitality and all acts of goodness that flow from an unselfish heart that is more interested in giving than receiving

Instead of bringing joy to someone else's life by an act of kindness, the self-centered person sinks deeper and deeper in the slough of despondency and gloom. D. L Moody once stated that it was his custom, after presenting himself to the Holy Spirit and asking to be led of the Spirit, to act upon those impulses which came to his mind, provided they did not violate any known truth of Scripture. Generally speaking, that is a very good rule to follow, for it pays rich dividends in mental health in the life of the giver.

FAITH

The seventh trait of the Spirit-filled man is faith, a complete abandonment to God and an absolute dependence upon him. This is a perfect

antidote to fear, which causes worry, anxiety, and pessimism. Some commentators suggest that more than faith is involved—namely, faithfulness or dependability. A man who has Spirit-inspired faith will be faithful and dependable.

Many of God's people, like the nation of Israel, waste years in the desert of life because they do not believe God. Far too many Christians have "grasshopper vision." They are like the ten faithless spies who saw the giants in the land of Canaan and came home to cry, "We are as grasshoppers in their sight."

The Bible teaches that there are two sources of faith. The first source is the Word of God in the life of the believer. Romans 10:17 states, "Faith cometh by hearing, and hearing by the word of God." The second is the Holy Spirit. Faith is a fruit of the Spirit. If you find that you have a temperament that is conducive to doubts, indecision, and fear, then as a believer you can look to the filling of the Holy Spirit to give you a heart of faith which will dispel the emotions and actions of your natural nature, including fear, doubt, and anxiety. It will take time, however; habits are binding chains; but God gives us the victory in Christ Jesus. "Wait on the Lord: be of good courage, and he shall strengthen thine heart: wait, I say, on the Lord" (Ps. 27:14).

MEEKNESS

The eighth temperament trait of the Spirit-filled man is meekness. The natural man is proud, egotistical, and self-centered; but when the Holy Spirit fills the life of an individual, he will be humble, mild, submissive, and easily entreated.

The greatest example of meekness is the Lord Jesus Christ himself. He was the Creator of the universe, and yet was willing to humble himself, take on the form of a servant, and become subject to the whims of humanity, even to the point of death, that he might purchase our redemption by his blood. Here we see the Creator of man buffeted, ridiculed, abused, and spat upon by his own creation. Yet he left us an example of not reviling again.

Meekness is not natural for us. Only the supernatural indwelling Spirit of God could cause any of us to react to physical or emotional persecution in meekness. It is a natural tendency to assert oneself, but even the most angry temperament can be controlled by the filling of the Holy Spirit and made to manifest this admirable trait of meekness.

SELF-CONTROL

The final temperament characteristic of the Spirit-filled believer is self-control. The King James Version translates it "temperance." Someone has defined it as "self controlled by the Holy Spirit."

Self-control will solve the Christian's problem of emotional outbursts such as rage, anger, fear, and jealousy, and cause him to avoid emotional excesses of any kind. The Spirit-controlled temperament will be one that is consistent, dependable, and well-ordered.

It has occurred to me that all four of the basic temperament types have a common difficulty that will be overcome by the Spirit-filled trait of self-control. That weakness is an inconsistent or ineffective devotional life. No Christian can be mature in Christ, steadily filled with the Holy Spirit, and usable in the hand of God unless he regularly feeds on the Word of God.

Mr. Sanguine is too restless and weak-willed by nature to be consistent in anything, much less in getting up a few minutes early to have a regular time of Bible reading and prayer. Mr. Choleric is by nature such a self-confident individual that even after he is converted it takes some time for him to realize what the Lord Jesus meant when he said, "Without me, ye can do nothing." Mr. Melancholy is perhaps the most likely of the four to be regular in his devotional life, except that his analytical ability often sends him off in the quest of some abstract, theologically hair-splitting truth rather than letting God speak to him concerning his personal needs. Mr. Phlegmatic is prone to recommend a regular quiet time as a necessary part of the Christian life, but if his slow, indolent, and often indifferent inclination is not disciplined by the Holy Spirit he will never quite get around to a regular feeding on God's Word.

As you look at these nine admirable traits of the Spirit-filled man, you not only get a picture of what God wants you to be, but what he is willing to make you in spite of your natural temperament. It should, however, be borne in mind that no amount of self-improvement or self-effort can bring any of these traits into our lives without the power of the Holy Spirit. From this we conclude that the most important single thing in the life of any Christian is to be filled with the Holy Spirit.

It is my conviction that God has given us at least one strength of the Spirit for every human weakness.

The needs of the Sanguine temperament

Sparky Sanguine needs at least six fruits or strengths of the Spirit to be the man or woman God wants him to be. He is by nature loving or compassionate, so he doesn't need that, though the Spirit of God will direct and purify that love. He also is by nature joyful, so the Spirit doesn't have to supply joy. He also has a natural "goodness" trait; that is, he loves to do good things for other people.

Peace, however, is another matter. Sanguines are so restless by nature that they need the supernatural peace of God that only the Holy Spirit can supply. Whenever you see a combustible sanguine face pressure in an attitude of peace, you are looking at a miracle of God.

Long-suffering, which basically means endurance, is foreign to the nature of a sanguine. He usually leaves a sea of unfinished projects behind him unless filled with the Spirit.

The bull-in-the-china-shop traits of sanguines are somehow replaced by the *gentleness* of the Spirit of God. One evidence of this is in their conversation. By nature they are blunt, loud, hurtful in their humorous treatment of others, seldom aware of how they have injured those who bear the brunt of their jokes. The gentleness of the Spirit of God will soften their injurious tongue.

One of the chief problems of Sparky Sanguine is ego. To him, by nature, he is the greatest. But when the spirit of *meekness* controls his life, the sanguine ceases to think more highly of himself than he ought to, but rather has a streak of humility burning in his soul, another evidence of the supernatural power of God.

Some of the lesser traits of a sanguine personality are his secret fears and insecurities. To such individuals faith is a wonderful source of blessing. I have seen God's Spirit not only supply the love-starved spirit of a sanguine, but give him courage in the face of adversity.

The number one need of the sanguine is *self-control.* We have seen that his natural problem of lack of self-discipline usually proves his undoing. We all know capable, lovable, charismatic sanguines who never live up to their potential and destroy themselves by lack of discipline.

The needs of the Choleric temperament

If you listen to the hard-driving, activity-prone choleric you might get the feeling he doesn't have emotional needs. Don't you believe it. These insensitive, caustic people have many needs and everyone around them wishes they would get help somewhere. I have noticed that the choleric is the only one of the temperaments that has a specific need for seven of the nine "fruits" or strengths of the Holy Spirit.

We have already seen that the choleric is self-disciplined and long-suffering by nature. You will recall we said he was strong-willed, determined, goal-oriented, and persistent. These traits stand in good stead when controlled by the Holy Spirit, for he is more likely to follow Jesus fully, energetically, and consistently. But even here he is vulnerable to mistaking his self-will for the will of God.

The besetting temptation of choleric Christians is to set their minds on doing something and persistently push for it without knowing whether or not it is really the will of God. This may produce a seemingly productive Christian worker, but it does not make a happy Christian, nor does it make the best use of his talents. A Spirit-filled choleric will always outperform a carnal choleric. Like every other temperament, Mr. Choleric desperately needs the filling of the Holy Spirit.

The first and primary need of a choleric's temperament is love and compassion. His insensitive and underdeveloped emotional nature is a real challenge to the work of the Holy Spirit. Love is not a static emotion. That is, you cannot love without being motivated to do something to express it; and the object of our expression when that love comes from the Holy Spirit will always be other people. The choleric who manifests love to his family and associates is manifesting the supernatural strength of the Holy Spirit in control of his temperament.

Although cholerics are extremely hard to please by nature, they are not an unhappy lot as long as they're busy working toward one of their goals in life. The *joy* the Holy Spirit supplies is not related to man's effort, but will characterize the choleric even in the face of adversity.

When the Holy Spirit fills cholerics' lives, they will still be activity-bound, but there is a sense of *peace* and a loss of that frenetic force that often drives them to an early grave. Cholerics desperately need peace with God.

Whenever you find a *gentle* choleric, you find a walking illustration of the supernatural power of the Holy Spirit of God, for that is not their natural forte.

The best place to manifest that Spirit-induced gentleness is in their speech patterns. No one can be more caustic and cutting than a choleric. And when the choleric tongue is modified to gracious speech and gentle approval, you know he is controlled by the Holy Spirit.

Cholerics need *goodness*. That is, they need to be involved in the goodness of God. It is important to them to invest their lives in something so worthwhile it lifts them into a new dimension of effectiveness and productivity. The Spirit of God alone provides that for a Christian choleric.

Interestingly enough, cholerics are not fearful people; they have tons of self-confidence. However, one of the lessons they must learn early in their Christian life is, "not by might, nor by power [nor even by their choleric spirit], but by my Spirit, saith the Lord."

I have found that the temptation to which many cholerics give vent is to rush off in their own direction instead of putting their faith in the living God and following him.

A choleric is not meek by nature. Cholerics universally equate meekness and weakness. It is a happy day for the choleric who understands that God will not tolerate a haughty, proud spirit, but will bring such individuals down and humble them. It is much better for a choleric to humble himself under the mighty hand of God and to develop meekness before the Holy Spirit has to do it for him.

The needs of the Melancholy temperament

God used more melancholies in the Bible than all the other temperaments put together! That should be good news to the average melancholy individual who is often plagued by feelings of inadequacy in spite of recognized talents and creativity. It has long been a mystery to me that those melancholy individuals who are endowed by their Creator with the greatest number of talents seem to have the least confidence in themselves. This is probably due to their everlasting tendency toward self-criticism and self-condemnation.

In spite of that, however, down through the years, both in the Old and New Testaments and in the history of Christianity, God has transformed many a self-sacrificing, gentle melancholy into a faithful, consistent servant when once filled with the Holy Spirit. Melancholies don't need a great deal of long-suffering and self-control, for if their motivation is oriented by the Spirit of God and they are instructed by the Word of God, they make extremely effective Christian workers known not for their flamboyant style, but for their self-sacrificing consistent spirit. It seems easier to challenge a melancholy to a lifetime of service for Jesus than any other temperament. That, too, is probably because of their natural tendency toward self-sacrifice. The genuineness of making a lifetime investment in a cause greater than oneself is probably what does it. However, I'm not blind to the fact that they nevertheless are in need of five specific fruits from the Holy Spirit.

Nothing turns a melancholy's life around like the *love* that is characteristic of the Spirit-filled life. By nature a melancholy is self-centered; his tendency toward perfectionism makes him very impatient with the idiosyncrasies and carelessness of his fellowmen. But when the Holy Spirit fills him with the love of Christ, love literally transforms his nature.

Joy is an absolute necessity for every melancholy, to replace his naturally morose, moody, griping spirit. It seems difficult for melancholies to understand that they must reflect the joy of the Lord. However, once that concept grips their heart, it can have a transforming effect on their entire being and make them delightful individuals to be around.

The *peace* of the Holy Spirit is a welcome tonic to the melancholy, whose inner thoughts fluctuate from criticism and condemnation, to hostility and revenge, and back to suspicion and fear. You can well imagine the influence of the pervading Spirit of God's peace that strengthens this aspect of the melancholy temperament.

It is absolutely essential for the melancholy to invest his life sacrificially in the doing of *goodness* for other people. Fortunately, once he is filled with love that gets his eyes off himself, his next objective is to apply this new strength or compulsion within him to acts of kindness to other souls on behalf of the gospel and the Lord Jesus Christ. In so doing, he brings fulfillment to himself.

There is a trace of the haughty spirit in a melancholy. The Spirit-filled life, however, injects a meekness or humility that, although foreign to his natural characteristics, brings great balance to his life and makes him less critical of others and easier to get along with.

The sixth strength of the Holy Spirit needed so desperately by the melancholy is *faith*. This will get him out of his ever-present tendency to limit himself by unbelief and will inspire him to take steps of faith in the use of his natural characteristics. Most melancholy temperaments immobilize themselves by fear (of the future, for example). What they need desperately from God is the realization that he is with them constantly to supply their every need.

One of the things I hope you have noticed about these spiritual strengths provided by the Holy Spirit is how very practical they are for everyday living. Every temperament has a besetting sin or an area of weakness that so easily besets him or causes him to stumble. The Holy Spirit fortifies this area of the person's weakness, and though he doesn't change the person's temperament from its basic root, he so strengthens it in the areas of weakness that it seems that person has been transformed by walking under the control of the Spirit.

The needs of the Phlegmatic temperament

Phlegmatics are nice people by nature. I have often said in public that phlegmatics act more like Christians *before* they become Christians than most of the rest of us do afterwards. They are quiet, gentle, gracious people. And yet, phlegmatics are as needy as any of the other temperaments.

Their natural tendency to be gentle should not be confused with the gentleness or kindness of the Holy Spirit of God. Phlegmatics are gentle in the treatment of other people regardless of their spiritual motivation. When filled with the Holy Spirit, however, that gentility characterizes itself in a motivated servant spirit that makes them a great asset to any family, church, or organization.

Like all other temperaments, the primary need of the phlegmatic is *love* and compassion for other people. The most underdeveloped part of a phlegmatic's nature is motivation. The love of the Holy

Spirit motivates him to utilize his gracious gentle spirit in the service of Christ.

Endurance is one of the great needs of the phlegmatic. He finds it only in the power of the Holy Spirit. Not only are phlegmatics good procrastinators, but they are also respectable quitters. The Holy Spirit will prompt them to keep on. Every church has more than its share of nice, kind, gentle people who warm the pews, but never get involved in the work of the Lord.

The antidote to that is the fruit of goodness—that is, good acts of service for Jesus Christ. Once they have committed themselves to a Sunday school class, a department superintendentship, Monday night church visitation, or some other form of Christian service, they do an excellent job, if they will accept the assignment in the first place.

One of the principal needs of the phlegmatic is *faith* to overcome his fears and worry. No one can be a more professional worrier than the phlegmatic; but when filled with the Holy Spirit he will have faith to trust God to do the impossible, even for him.

Phlegmatics without the Holy Spirit tend toward an increasing life-style of passivity until they are motivated by the self-control of the Holy Spirit and recognize their self-indulgent attitude. The self-control of the Spirit of God will tend to cure their tendency toward procrastination. Our fulfillment in life comes in direct relationship to our being filled with the Holy Spirit of God.

How to be filled with the Holy Spirit

One of the things I have tried to communicate in all of my books on temperament is that far more important than what is your personal temperament is the question, "Are you filled with the Holy Spirit?" It is almost impossible to exaggerate how dependent we are on the Holy Spirit. We are dependent on him for convicting us of sin before and after our salvation, for giving us understanding of the gospel, causing us to be born again, empowering us to witness, guiding us in our prayer life—in fact, for everything. It is no wonder that evil spirits have tried to counterfeit the work of the Holy Spirit and confuse his work.

There is probably no subject in the Bible upon which there is more confusion than that of being filled with the Holy Spirit. There are many fine Christian people who seem to equate the filling of the Holy Spirit with external signs. There are other Christians who because of excesses observed or heard of in this direction have all but eliminated the teaching of the filling of the Holy Spirit from their experience. They do not recognize his importance in their lives.

Satan places two obstacles before men: he tries to keep them from receiving Christ as Savior; and if he fails in this, he then tries to keep men from understanding the importance and work of the Holy Spirit.

One of the false impressions gained from people and not from the Word of God is that there is some special "feeling" when one is filled with the Holy Spirit. Before we examine how to be filled with the Holy Spirit, let us examine what the Bible teaches we can expect when we are filled with the Holy Spirit.

Four major results of being filled with the Holy Spirit

There are four specific results of the Spirit-filled life—all guaranteed by the Bible. Consider them carefully, for they are the true marks of being a Spirit-controlled Christian.

1. *The nine temperament strengths of the Spirit-filled life (Gal. 5:22-23).* We have already examined these traits in detail and have seen that they provide a strength for every natural weakness. Any individual who is filled with the Holy Spirit is going to manifest the characteristics of love, joy, peace, longsuffering, gentleness, goodness, meekness, faith, and self-control. He does not have to act out a role; he will be this way when the Spirit has control of his nature—regardless of his original temperament.

When the Holy Spirit fills your life, you will still be yourself minus the domination of your weaknesses. When filled with the Spirit, we all are able to be used of God in the areas of our natural talents or strengths as given to us by him.

2. *A joyful, thankful heart and a submissive spirit (Eph. 5:18-21).* When the Holy Spirit fills the life of a believer, the Bible tells us he will cause that believer to have a singing, thankful heart and a submissive spirit.

> And be not drunk with wine, wherein is excess; but be filled with the Spirit; speaking to yourselves in psalms and hymns and spiritual songs, singing and making melody in your heart to the Lord; giving thanks always for all things unto God and the Father in the name of our Lord Jesus Christ; submitting yourselves one to another in the fear of God.

A singing, grateful heart and a submissive spirit, independent of circumstances, are so unnatural that they can only be ours through the filling of the Holy Spirit. The Spirit of God is able to change the gloomy or griping heart into a song-filled thankful heart. He is also able to solve man's natural rebellion problem by increasing his faith to the point that he really believes the best way to live is in submission to the will of God, God's Word, and God's Spirit.

The same three results of the Spirit-filled life are also the results of the Word-filled life, as found in Colossians 3:1-18:

> Let the word of Christ dwell in you richly in all wisdom; teaching and admonishing one another in psalms and hymns and spiritual songs, singing with grace in your hearts to the Lord. And whatsoever ye do in word or deed, do all in the name of the Lord Jesus, giving thanks to God and the Father by him. Wives, submit yourselves unto your own husbands, as it is fit in the Lord.

It is no accident that we find the results of the Spirit-filled life and those of the Word-filled life to be one and the same. The Lord Jesus said that the Holy Spirit is "the Spirit of Truth. " He also said of the Word of God, "Thy word is Truth." It is easily understood why the Word-filled life causes the same results as the Spirit-filled life, for the Holy Spirit is the author of the Word of God. The Christian who is Spirit-filled will be Word-filled, and the Word-filled Christian who obeys the Spirit will be Spirit-filled.

3. Power for our witness about Jesus Christ (Acts 1:8). The Lord Jesus told his disciples that "It is expedient [necessary] for you that I go away: for if I go not away, the Comforter [Holy Spirit] will not come unto you" (John 16:7). That explains why the last thing Jesus did before he ascended into heaven was to tell his disciples, "But ye shall receive power, after that the Holy Ghost is come upon you: and ye shall be witnesses unto me . . ." (Acts 1:8).

Even though the disciples had spent three years with Jesus, had heard his messages several times, and were the best trained witnesses he had, he still instructed them "not [to] depart from Jerusalem, but wait for the promise of the Father" (Acts 1:4). All of their training obviously was incapable of producing fruit without the power of the Holy Spirit. And when the Holy Spirit came on the day of Pentecost, they witnessed in his power and three thousand persons were saved.

Power to witness in the Holy Spirit is not always discernible, but must be accepted by faith. When we have met the conditions for the filling of the Holy Spirit, we should be careful to believe we have witnessed in the power of the Spirit whether or not we see the results. It is possible to witness in the power of the Holy Spirit and still not see an individual come to a saving knowledge of Christ. For in the sovereign plan of God he has chosen never to violate the right of man's free choice. We cannot always equate success in witnessing with the power to witness!

4. *The Holy Spirit will glorify Jesus Christ (John 16:13-14).*

Howbeit when he, the Spirit of truth, is come, he will guide you into all truth: for he shall not speak of himself, but whatsoever he shall hear, that shall he speak: and he will shew you things to come. He shall glorify me: for he shall receive of mine, and shall shew it unto you.

A fundamental principle should always be kept in mind regarding the work of the Holy Spirit: he does not glorify himself, but the Lord Jesus Christ.

The late F. B. Meyer told the story of a missionary who came to him at a Bible conference after he had spoken on the subject on how to be filled with the Holy Spirit. She confessed that she was never consciously filled with the Holy Spirit and was going to go up to the prayer chapel and spend the day in soul-searching to see if she could receive his filling.

Late that evening she came back just as Meyer was leaving the auditorium. He asked, "How was it, sister?"

"I'm not quite sure," she responded, explaining her day's activities of reading the Word, praying, confessing her sins, and asking for the filling of the Holy Spirit. She then stated, "I do not feel particularly filled with the Holy Spirit, but never have I been so conscious of the presence of the Lord Jesus in my life." To which Meyer replied, "Sister, that is the Holy Spirit. He glorifies Jesus."

Let us summarize what we can expect when filled with the Holy Spirit. Very simply, the nine temperament characteristics of the Spirit; a singing, thankful heart that gives us a submissive attitude; and the power to witness. These characteristics will glorify the Lord Jesus Christ. What about certain feelings or ecstatic experiences?

The Bible does not tell us to expect these things when we are filled with the Holy Spirit, and we should not expect what the Bible does not promise.

The infilling of the Holy Spirit

The filling of the Holy Spirit is not optional equipment in the Christian life, but a command of God! Ephesians 5:18 tells us, "And be not drunk with wine, wherein is excess; but be filled with the Spirit." Since God commands us to be filled with the Holy Spirit, it must be possible for us to be filled with his Spirit. I would like to give five simple steps for being filled with the Holy Spirit.

1. *Self-examination (Acts 20:28; 1 Cor. 11:28).*

The Christian interested in the filling of the Holy Spirit must regularly "take heed" to "examine himself," not to see if he measures up to the standards of other people or the traditions and requirements of his church, but to the previously mentioned results of being filled with the Holy Spirit. If he does not find he is glorifying Jesus, if he does not have power to witness, or if he lacks a joyful, submissive spirit or the nine temperament traits of the Holy Spirit, then his self-examination will reveal those areas in which he is deficient and will uncover the sin that causes them.

2. *Confession of all known sin (1 John 1:9).*

If we confess our sins, he is faithful and just to forgive us our sins, and to cleanse us from all unrighteousness.

After examining ourselves in the light of the Word of God, we should confess all sin brought to mind by the Holy Spirit, including those characteristics of the Spirit-filled life that we lack. Until we acknowledge as sin our lack of compassion, our lack of self-control, our lack of humility, our anger instead of gentleness, our bitterness instead of kindness, and our unbelief instead of faith, we will never have the filling of the Holy Spirit. However, the moment we recognize these deficiencies as sin and confess them to God, he will "cleanse us from all unrighteousness." Until we have done this, we cannot have the filling of the Holy Spirit, for he fills only clean vessels (2 Tim. 2:21).

3. *Submit yourself completely to God (Rom. 6:11-13).*

Likewise reckon ye also yourselves to be dead indeed unto sin, but alive unto God through Jesus Christ our Lord. Let not sin therefore reign in your mortal body, that ye should obey it in the lusts thereof. Neither yield ye your members as instruments of unrighteousness unto sin: but yield yourselves unto God, as those that are alive from the dead, and your members as instruments of righteousness unto God.

Do not make the mistake of being afraid to give yourself to God! Romans 8:32 tells us, "He that spared not his own Son, but delivered him up for us all, how shall he not with him also freely give us all things?" If God loved us so much as to give his Son to die for us, certainly he is interested in nothing but our good; therefore, we can trust him with our lives. You will never find a miserable Christian in the center of the will of God.

Ephesians 5:18 says, "Be not drunk with wine . . . but be filled with the Spirit." When a man is drunk, he is dominated by alcohol. So with the filling of the Holy Spirit, man's actions must be dominated by and dictated by the Holy Spirit. For consecrated Christians this is often the most difficult thing to do, for we can always find some worthy purpose for our lives, not realizing that we are often filled with ourselves rather than with the Holy Spirit as we seek to serve the Lord.

When you give your life to God, do not attach any strings or conditions to it. He is such a God of love that you can safely give yourself without reservation, knowing that his plan and use of your life is far better than yours. And remember, the attitude of yieldedness is absolutely necessary for the filling of God's Spirit. Your will is the will of the flesh, and the Bible says that "the flesh profiteth nothing."

Someone has suggested that being yielded to the Spirit is being available to the Spirit. Peter and John in Acts 3 make a good example of that. They were on their way to the temple to pray when they saw the lame man begging alms. Because they were sensitive to the Holy Spirit, they healed him "in the name of Jesus Christ of Nazareth." The man began leaping about and praising God until a crowd gathered. Peter, still sensitive to the Holy Spirit, began preaching; "many of them which heard the Word believed; and the number of the men was about five thousand" (Acts 4:4).

Many times I fear we are so engrossed in some good Christian activity that we are not available when the Spirit leads. When a Christian yields himself unto God "as those that are alive from the dead," he takes time to do what the Spirit directs him to do.

4. *Ask to be filled with the Holy Spirit (Luke 11:13).*

> If yet then, being evil, know how to give good gifts unto your children: how much more shall your heavenly Father give the Holy Spirit to them that ask him?

When a Christian has examined himself, confessed all known sin, and yielded himself without reservation to God, he is then ready to do the one thing he must do to receive the Spirit—very simply, to ask to be filled with the Holy Spirit.

The Lord Jesus compares this to our treatment of our earthly children. Certainly a good father would not make his children beg for something he commanded them to have. How much less does God make us beg to be filled with the Holy Spirit. But don't forget Step 5.

5. *Believe you are filled with the Holy Spirit! And thank him for his filling.*

> And he that doubteth is damned if he eat, hecause he eateth not of faith: for whatsoever is not of faith is sin. (Rom. 14:23)
> In every thing give thanks: for this is the will of God in Christ Jesus concerning you. (1 Thess. 5:18)

For many Christians the battle is won or lost right here. After examining themselves, confessing all known sin, yielding themselves to God, and asking for his filling, they are faced with a decision: to believe they are filled, or to go away in unbelief, in which case they have sinned, for "whatsoever is not of faith is sin."

The same Christian who tells the new convert to "take God at his Word concerning salvation" finds it difficult to heed his own advice concerning the filling of the Holy Spirit. If you have fulfilled the first four steps, then by faith thank God for his filling. Don't wait for feelings or for physical signs; fasten your faith to the Word of God, which is independent of feeling. Believing we are filled with the Spirit is merely taking God at his Word, and that is the only absolute this world has (Matt. 24:35).

A common question

The most common question I am asked after my lectures on the Spirit-filled life for overcoming temperament weaknesses is, "How often should I ask to be filled with the Holy Spirit?"

My answer is: every time you think you are not! Some Bible teachers think the Spirit's filling is automatic whenever we ask forgiveness for our sins (1 John 1:7-9). Personally I am not convinced. I like to make sure by asking. In fact, I ask for his filling when I awaken in the morning and many times through the day. The Greek in Ephesians 5:18 literally means, "Keep on being filled with the Spirit."

Occasionally someone protests, "But that is all too simple; being filled with the Spirit must be much more complex!" Why? As an eight-year-old boy I asked the Lord Jesus to come into my heart. He instantly answered my request Why should he not answer when I ask to be filled with the Holy Spirit? A. B. Simpson used to say, "Being filled with the Spirit is as easy as breathing; you can simply breathe out and breathe in."

One of the reasons some Christians are reluctant to think they are filled with the Spirit is that they don't see an immediate change in their lives, or the change is of short duration. Two factors have an important bearing on this: temperament and habit, and they work together. The weaknesses of our temperament have created strong habits that involuntarily recur.

For illustration, let us consider a fear-prone melancholy or phlegmatic Christian. These people have a deeply ingrained habit of doubt, negativism, worry, and anxiety. I can predict the thinking pattern of such a person after he follows the five steps of being filled with the Spirit. Before long his negative thinking habit will stir doubts: "Am I filled with the Spirit? I don't feel any different. I'm still afraid." This mental attitude is sin, and the Spirit's filling and control ends.

What such people need to realize is that our feelings are the result of thought patterns. We need to learn that feelings are reliable only when they are based on truth and righteousness. God's people need to fill their minds with the Word of God so their feelings will correspond to God's.

The feelings of the perennial doubter who is filled with the Spirit will gradually change, but it will take time. If he looks to the Lord for mercy and forgiveness each time he feels doubtful or unbelieving, he will *gradually* be assured by the Lord. But if he continues to think negatively or doubtfully and justifies it by saying, "I've always been this way," he will remain that way. Or he may get worse, because he is quenching the Holy Spirit by indulging in this sin and etching the habit deeper on his mind.

Mr. Sanguine and Mr. Choleric have a similar problem with their pet sin of anger. It isn't long after they are filled with the Holy Spirit that their ingrained anger feelings rise up to grieve the Holy Spirit. Unless they immediately confess this sin, they will no longer be filled with the Spirit and the old feelings will control them. Each time they think self-righteously of how they have been offended or insulted or cheated, they cultivate feelings of hostility. These easily-triggered feelings are the result of years of hostile thoughts that can be overcome only as the Spirit of God is given access to and control of the conscious and subconscious mind. He replaces these hostile thoughts with love, kindness, and gentleness, but it will take time for a permanent change to be accomplished.

How to walk in the Spirit

"Since we live by the Spirit, let us keep in step with the Spirit" (Gal. 5:25, NIV).

Walking in the Spirit and being filled by the Holy Spirit are not one and the same thing, though they are very closely related. Having followed the five simple rules for the filling of the Holy Spirit, it is then essential to learn how to walk daily in the Spirit.

Being filled with the Spirit is just the beginning of Christian victory. We must "walk in the Spirit" to be effective (Gal. 5:16). It is one thing to start out in the Spirit-filled life and quite another to walk day by day in the control of the Spirit. The following procedure for walking in the Spirit can be a practical tool for victorious daily living.

1. *Make the filling of the Holy Spirit a daily priority.* You cannot walk in the Spirit unless you sincerely want to and unless you have his filling. As we have already seen, old habit patterns sneak back to haunt us. If we enjoy them more than the peace of God, we will indulge the sins of the flesh. Let's be honest—lust, worry, self-pity, and anger are fun, temporarily. Only when we want the filling of the Holy Spirit more than anything else in the world are we willing to give up lesser emotional satisfactions of lust, worry, self-pity, and anger.

2. *Develop a keen sensitivity to sin.* Sin short-circuits the power of the Holy Spirit in us. The moment we are conscious of any sin, we should confess it immediately, so the time between grieving, or

quenching, the Spirit and reinstatement is minimal. The main advantage to the study of temperaments is that we can diagnose our most common weakness. Consequently we are on our guard for "the sin that doth so easily beset us." When it rears its ugly head, confess it, forget it (God does, so you might as well), and press on toward the fulfillment of the will of God for your life. The main secret to victorious living among those I have counseled has been the practice of instant confession.

3. *Daily read and study God's Word.* It is my conviction after a good deal of observation that it is impossible for a Christian to "walk in the Spirit" unless he develops the habit of regularly feeding his mind and heart upon the Word of God. One of the reasons Christians do not "feel" as God does about life issues is that they do not know God's way from his Word.

Since our feelings are produced by our thought processes, we will feel as carnal worldlings do if we feed our minds on the "wisdom of the world." If we feed our minds on the Word of God, we will feel as the Spirit does about life issues. (Remember that it takes some time to reorient our minds from human wisdom to divine wisdom. So regular reading is essential.)

Sometimes Christians object that this will make them legalists. Yet they don't seem to view coming to the table three times a day as legalistic. We do it because we sense a need and enjoy eating. In the same way we can feed spiritually on God's Word from a sense of need, but it takes time to build our spiritual appetite. Many Christians feel something is very wrong if they miss reading the Word of God, but they didn't start out that way.

A consistent feeding of one's mind upon the Word of God produces some interesting results. Consider the following revolutionary benefits.

Joshua 1:8	It makes your way prosperous and gives success.
Psalm 1:3	It produces fruitfulness.
Psalm 119:11	It keeps us from sin.
John 14:21	God reveals himself increasingly to keepers of his Word.
John 15:3	The Word cleanses us.
John 15:7	The Word produces power in prayer.
John 15:11	The Word brings joy to our hearts.
1 John 2:13-14	The Word gives victory over "the wicked one."

With these transforming results from filling our minds with God's Word, it is a tragedy that so many Christians live a second-rate life with feelings of insecurity, uncleanness, discontent, anxiety, and impotence. The character of our feelings depends on the character of our thoughts, and the sincere Christian should ask himself, "What is shaping and filling my thoughts?"

A careful comparison of the Spirit-filled life (Eph. 5:18-21) with the Word-filled life (Col. 3:15-17) is revealing. Both passages promise a song in your heart, a thanksgiving attitude, and a submissive spirit. A mind that is filled with and yielded to the Word of God will produce the same effects on the emotions as the mind filled with and yielded to the Holy Spirit. We may legitimately conclude from this that the filling of the Spirit and walking in the Spirit depend upon our being filled with the Word of God!

Reading the Bible at night is especially helpful. The mind digests the events and thoughts of the day, particularly the last things we think about before going to sleep. For that reason it is very profitable to read God's Word just before retiring—that way you can go to sleep thinking about the things just read. It is amazing how this helps us awaken with a positive outlook for the day. Get into the habit of reading the Word just before sleeping, and your subconscious mind will mold your feelings in God's patterns.

Another valuable habit is meditation. The mind is always working, and our will determines whether our mind works for or against us. To work for good, the mind must meditate on the truths and insights of God's Word. There is one catch: you must memorize in order to meditate profitably, because you can't meditate on what you don't know intimately. Whether it is a phrase, concept, or whole verse of Scripture, you must memorize it in order to meditate on it.

A simple method I use to inspire meditation is to write down verses that bless my soul, then put the sheet of paper in my Bible or notebook. I learn at least one of these verses every week. It is hard work, but I don't know any mentally lazy Christians who walk in the Spirit.

4. *Guard against grieving the Holy Spirit.* The next step for walking in the Spirit is an extension of step two—developing a sensitivity to sin. Ephesians 4:30-32 makes it clear that all forms of hostility, including anger, bitterness, and enmity, grieve the Holy Spirit. All anger-prone believers should memorize those three

verses and develop a particular sensitivity to hostility. In addition to making instant confession, they should resolve to be loving, kind, tenderhearted, and forgiving toward others. This grace is markedly unnatural for a sanguine or a choleric, but the Holy Spirit will develop in the believer a new capacity for thoughtfulness and love.

The importance of our will becomes apparent at this point of walking in the Spirit. When we feel the bludgeon of injustice or someone's wrath, we can hate the offender or forgive and pray for him. Our overall feelings as well as our walk in the Spirit depend upon our decision. Don't be surprised if you fail repeatedly at first. But be sure to confess the sin as soon as you are aware of grieving the Spirit, and let him reestablish your walk. As you choose to forgive and to let the Holy Spirit react through you with patience and love, you will find your temperament weakness changing into a strength.

5. *Avoid quenching the Spirit through fear and worry.* According to 1 Thessalonians 5:16-19, we quench the Holy Spirit when we doubt and resist his dealings in our lives. When a Christian says, "I don't understand why God let this awful thing happen to me," he has already quenched the Spirit through fear. The Christian who is trusting God could face the same circumstances and say, "I thank God he is in control of my life! I don't understand his dealings with me right now, but I trust his promise that he will never leave me and he will supply my every need."

We have seen that melancholy and phlegmatic people have a predisposition toward fear, just as the more extrovertive temperaments have a predisposition toward anger. Some people possess both introvertive and extrovertive temperaments, and consequently may have deep problems with both fear and anger. God's grace is sufficient to cure both problems through his Holy Spirit. But if you have these tendencies, you need to watch carefully your reaction to seemingly unfavorable events. If you groan or complain inwardly, you have already quenched the Holy Spirit. This can be remedied immediately if you are willing to call your doubt-induced complaining exactly what it is—sin—and ask God to transform this habit pattern and fill you with his Spirit.

God is not nearly so interested in changing circumstances as he is in changing people. It is no victory to live without worry when there is nothing to worry about, and becoming a Christian did not exempt you from trouble. Job said, "Yet man is born unto trouble, as the sparks fly upward" (Job 5:7). Jesus warned us we would face tribulation in this world, and the Bible tells us God sends testings to strengthen us. Many Christians flunk the tests by seeking their removal rather than rendering obedience in the Spirit.

It is impossible for a fear-prone Christian to walk in the Spirit any length of time without strong infusions of God's Word to encourage his faith. The more God's Word fills his mind, the more his feelings will abound in faith. But worriers usually enjoy wallowing in their misery, especially with God watching the piteous scene. All worriers should memorize Philippians 4:6-7: "Do not be anxious about anything, but in everything, by prayer and petition, with thanksgiving, present your requests to God. And the peace of God, which transcends all understanding, will guard your hearts and your minds in Christ Jesus" (NIV).

These verses direct prayer to be made "with thanksgiving." You cannot genuinely pray with thanksgiving and finish with the same burdens you started with. Consider the following two prayers—and the emotions they create—offered by Christian parents with a sick child.

"Dear Lord, we come to you on behalf of our little girl so near death. The doctor tells us there is no hope for her. Please, dear Lord, heal her. You know how much she means to us. If this sickness is caused by sin in our lives, forgive and cleanse us that she may live. After all the other tragedies in our lives, we do not think we can bear another. In Jesus' name. Amen."

"Dear Heavenly Father, we thank you that we are your children and can look to you at this time of need. You know the report of the doctors, and you have promised that all things work together for good to folks like us. We don't understand our dear child's sickness, but we know you love us and are more than able to heal her. We commit her little body to you, Father, asking for her healing according to your perfect will. We dedicated her to you before she was born, and we thank you that you are able to supply all her needs right now, as well as ours. In Jesus' name. Amen."

It is obvious which set of parents will feel the "peace of God" and which couple will wring their hands in anguish during this time of deep need. The difference comes in learning the attitude of thanksgiving from the Word of God. Lest you think the above prayer is hypothetical or idealistic, let me share a personal experience. The blonde, blue-eyed cutie named Lori that God sent to us is the apple of my heart. Several years ago I stood at her bedside in Children's Hospital and prayed that prayer. Frankly, I don't know how people without Jesus Christ go through such trials. My wife and I can testify that in spite of Lori's raging fever and delirium, and no known hope, God imparted peace to our troubled hearts. However, not until we prayed with thanksgiving beside her oxygen tent did we receive that peace.

If you tend to worry or grumble, you will find that you are not a very thankful person. You may be a fine person in many other respects, but unless you learn to be thankful you can never walk far in the Spirit, nor will you be consistently happy. The secret to a thankful attitude is in coming to know God intimately as he reveals himself in his Word. This will require consistent Bible reading, studying, and meditation. When your faith is established through the Word, it is easier to give thanks, but it is still an act of the will. If you have not accepted his full leading for your life, you will complain because you doubt things will turn out all right. And doubt quenches the Spirit and sidetracks your real progress.

One last practical suggestion for walking in the Spirit is in order. Although mental attitude is important at all times, prayer is of paramount importance twice during each day: when we go to bed and when we arise. It is very important to pray "with thanksgiving," as well as to read the Scriptures, at night. Though it may be hard, the other strategic time to give thanks is the first thing in the morning. The psalmist helps us: "This is the day which the Lord hath made; we will rejoice and be glad in it" (Ps. 118:24).

After beginning your day with thanksgiving, yield youself anew to God according to Romans 6:11-13. Tell him you are available to share your faith with the needy one he sends to you. Yield your lips to the Holy Spirit and let him open the conversation. Walk in the Spirit, and you will bear fruit for God. As soon as you sense you have grieved or quenched the Spirit, confess your sin and again ask for his filling. If you follow these steps, your spirit will improve regardless of your temperament. And when you improve your spirit, you permit God to make the most out of your life.

5

GIVE YOURSELF A TEMPERAMENT TEST

One day an industrial psychologist from the Midwest was visiting San Diego and attended our Sunday morning church service. Afterwards he invited me to lunch with his family and, since my wife was out of town speaking at a women's conference, I accepted. We had barely returned from the buffet with our food when he said, "I have used your temperament theory in vocational counseling for ten years and find it the most helpful tool for vocational guidance I have ever seen."

Here was a man with a Ph.D. in psychology who served as a consultant to the major aircraft companies of the nation and recognized that the four-temperament theory is the best single theory of human behavior yet devised. It isn't perfect, and it is not accepted universally, but it is an excellent aid to many things, particularly vocational guidance.

My psychologist friend then asked, "Have you developed a temperament test? If so, I'd like to see it." At that time I had to respond, "Not yet. I'm working on one, but I'm not satisfied with it." That was seven years ago and five temperament tests back. I am very satisfied with the one I now use—The LaHaye Temperament Analysis—which is extremely thorough. But I also developed a simple test you can give yourself or have some of your friends give you.

Through the years I have received at least a dozen tests worked out by some of the enthusiasts of my other temperament books. Some were extremely complex and others worthless. All were sincere attempts to help people. Two professors at Andrews University in Berrien Springs, Michigan, contacted me about collaborating with them on such a test. One was a statistician and the other a computer science and testing professor. Together we worked up a test they were extremely enthused about. I administered it to several people I knew well and was not satisfied with the results. I found too many phlegmatics coming out like cholerics. These good men refined their test and later marketed it.

I went on to develop my own tests which I administered to volunteers in my congregation, among my acquaintances, and to over one thousand missionaries encountered on a world missions tour. Finally, I came up with the LaHaye Temperament Analysis, which I believe is over 92 percent accurate. We have given it to almost 20,000 people and have received very few complaints. In fact, those who have taken the test are quite amazed at its thoroughness and professionalism.

One of the tests I did not use in my analysis is the simple test enclosed in this chapter. I do not claim 92 percent accuracy for it because it is a simple, one-celled test. The LaHaye Temperament Analysis consists of four tests in one to allow for comparison and both a lie scale and mood scale. For interestingly enough, any subjective test like this will be influenced heavily by both your mood and how honest you are when looking at yourself (or should I say, how objective you are). In any case, to get a good handle on your primary and perhaps your secondary temperament you will enjoy the tests on the following pages.

A double check

Five temperament charts are given for your personal use. Chart 1 is to determine how you see yourself. Charts 2-4 are to give your best friends to do on you. Chart 5 is for you to average the scores of your friends. Then you can compare the average of your friends' charts with your own temperament blob chart to see if your perception of you is similar to the way your friends see you. If not, then you need to ask yourself if you really are objective about yourself or if you project a face to others so they see you as you want them to rather than as you really are.

The following test should not take more than twenty-five minutes.

Assessing the results

Chart 5 now contains two blobs of different colors. Ideally the blobs will be identical. In most cases there will be some variation. However your primary temperament should stand out as the larger blob. Hopefully, both large blobs will be in the same temperament zone. If they are not, something for you to think about is, "Do my friends see me as I see myself, or is there a great difference?" If two of your friends' scores were quite similar to your own, then disregard the third chart altogether. Some people read too much into a simple test like this. Consequently, their excessive scores will completely alter the averages of your other friends.

On the other hand, if your score and that of your friends is in marked contrast, then it may mean you are trying to make yourself something God never intended you to be—in which case you need to realistically face yourself as you really are and be yourself as controlled by the Holy Spirit.

Further tests to give yourself

If you are not satisfied with the accuracy of the above temperament blob, here are some questions to ask yourself to at least identify your primary temperament.

1. Are you an extrovert or an introvert?
2. Are you a spontaneous quick-talker?
3. Do you have to apologize frequently?
4. Do you have high emotional responses?
5. Are you quiet and slow of speech?
6. Are you a good speller?
7. Do you do well at math and detail?
8. Do you get depressed easily?

If your answer to question 1 is extrovert and you answered yes to 2-4, your primary temperament is probably sanguine. If only one of 2-4, you are probably a choleric temperament.

If you answered 1 that you're an introvert and yes to 6-8, your primary temperament is probably melancholy. But if you said yes to 5 and you do not get depressed very often, your predominant temperament is probably phlegmatic.

CHART 1

Your Personal Profile Blob Chart

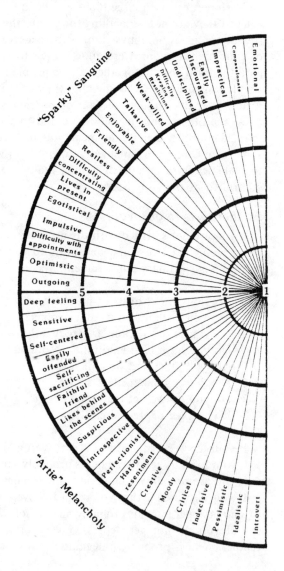

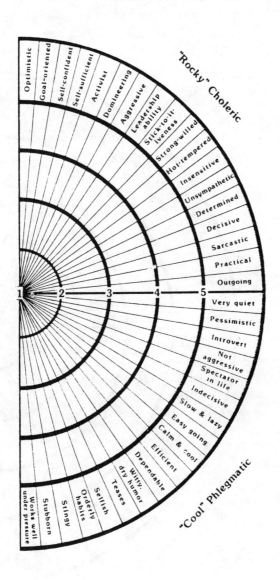

CHART 5

Scoring Your Temperament Blob

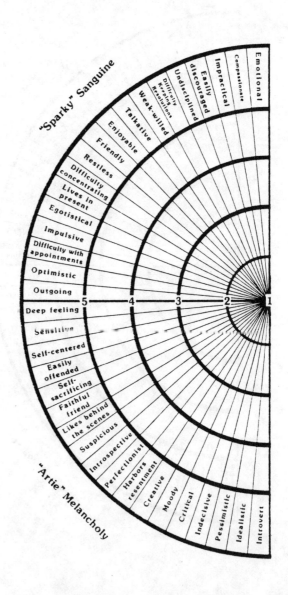

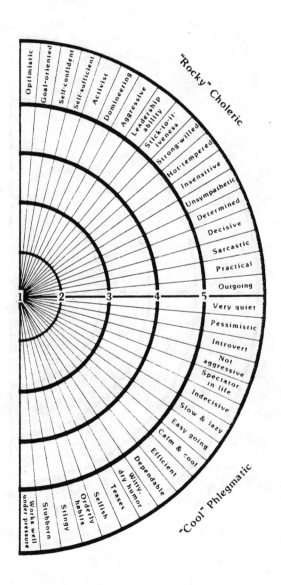

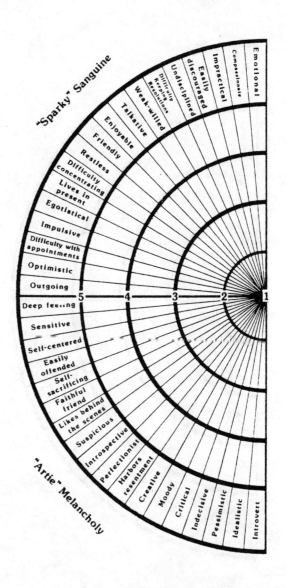

Instructions: 1. Relax, get in a quiet place, and read the entire chart before making any markings. **2.** After each word on the circle below, place a dot on the number that best describes you, 5 being *most* like you and 1 being *least* like you. Try to be objective!

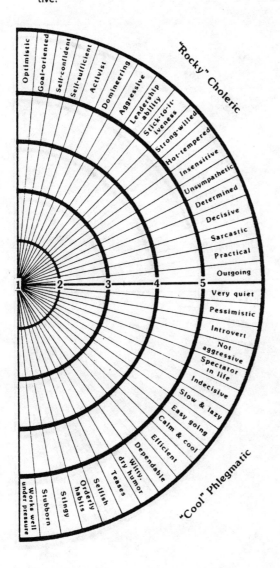

CHARTS 2 - 4

Your Friends Analyze You

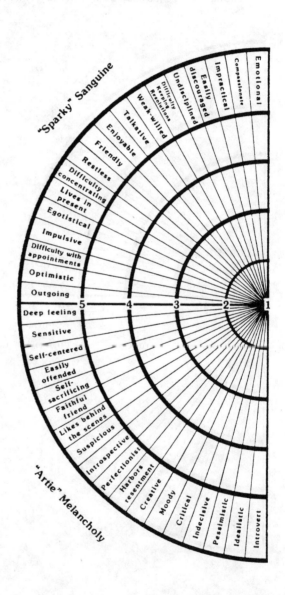

The following blob charts are for three of your best friends to use in "analyzing" you. Ask each friend to fill out one blob chart with *your* characteristics, strengths, and weaknesses. Have each friend read the following instructions: **1.** Read all the adjectives below before making a mark.   **2.** After each word on the chart, place a dot on the number that best describes your friend — 1 being *least* like him and 5 being *most* like him.   **3.** Try to be objective, indicating what he is like most of the time.

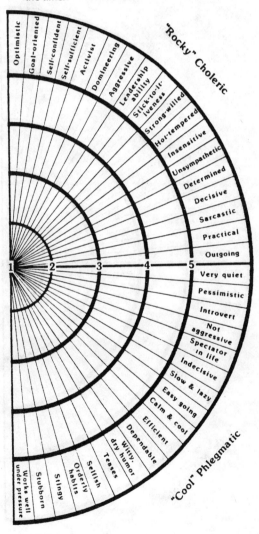

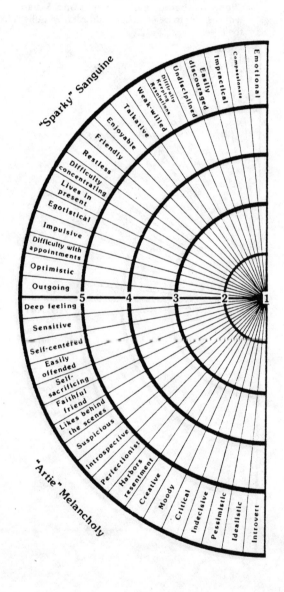

Instructions: **1.** Average only the 3-5 dots listed in Charts 2-4 (omit the 1's and 2's—they are of such low intensity that they do not influence this test). **2.** Place the average totals from Charts 2, 3, and 4 on the circle below. **3.** Connect the dots by drawing curved lines paralleling the basic circles from dot to dot except when nothing appears in a temperament quadrant. Follow the outer edge of the quadrant to the center, then return to the next dot. **4.** Now with a *different color pencil* transfer all 3-5 dots from your test in chart 1. **5.** Connect your dots as in Step 3.

Obviously this is a very casual analysis, but it can serve as an interesting check on the accuracy of the predominant temperament in your blob chart.

Take this test in two years

One exercise you will find very interesting is to concentrate on walking in the Spirit on a daily basis as outlined earlier. Then retake the above test and see how God has modified your temperament. You will find lower scores in the weakness areas of your temperament.

If you wish a new set of these testing charts, just send one dollar to: Family Life Seminars, PO. Box 2700, Washington, D.C. 20013-2700.

Unfortunately, all that the above test will do for you is reveal your primary and secondary temperaments. It does not provide specific vocational aptitudes and the other information found in the more complete testing instrument—The LaHaye Temperament Analysis. You may wish to send for that. (However, once you have determined your primary and secondary temperaments you will be prepared to evaluate whether or not you are presently pursuing the right vocation. The next chapters will be helpful in that determination.)

THREE

TEMPERAMENT AND YOUR VOCATION

6

DISCOVERING YOUR VOCATIONAL APTITUDES

Human beings were designed by God with a special capacity for productivity. It is one of those inherited traits unique to human beings that separates mankind from animals.

Even in the Garden of Eden, God gave man responsibility and duties. Note these words: "The Lord God took the man and put him in the Garden of Eden to work it and take care of it . . ." (Gen. 2:15, NIV). It should be remembered that this whole scene took place *before* sin occurred and before the fall. Work, a command from God, has nothing to do with the fall—though that made it more difficult. Evidently weeds did not grow in the Garden of Eden until the curse came, but man still had to work. Now man's work is compounded by thorns, weeds, disease, bugs, etc.

After the fall, man was also told by God that work was his lot in life.

> To Adam he said, "Because you listened to your wife and ate from the tree about which I commanded you, 'You must not eat of it,' cursed is the ground because of you; through painful toil you will eat of it all the days of your life. It will produce thorns and thistles for you, and you will eat the plants of the field. By the sweat of your brow you will eat your food until you return to the ground, since from it you were taken; for dust you are and to dust you will return." (Gen. 3:17-19, NIV)

All through the Bible the work ethic is exalted. Many references are given in the book of Proverbs calling the lazy "sluggards" and challenging both men and women to be workers. This concept is also fostered in the New Testament, which proclaims that "If a man will not work, he shall not eat" (2 Thess. 3:10).

All the commands of God work for the good of man. By that I mean that no one is left psychologically unfulfilled or warped by obeying the commands of God. Quite the opposite, mankind is fulfilled in the obeying of God's instructions.

We need to work because it is good for us. There is something self-enriching in a job well done. The unemployed are miserable not just because they are out of money, but because they do not have the opportunity to work productively. We have all known hard-working individuals who quit working at sixty-five and died before their sixty-seventh birthday. The real reason, not the one that appears on their death certificate, is that they could not handle the emotional vacuum that results from lack of productivity.

Vocational frustration

Next to lack of employment, the worst thing that can happen to a person is to have the wrong job. It is incredible how many people despise their work. No wonder it becomes such drudgery to them. And as technology advances, increasing numbers of people will discover they are ill-fitted for the vocation in which they find themselves. This is particularly true of the unskilled or those whose area of skill is automated out of existence. All vocational experts warn that this will be an increasing problem in the years ahead.

One of the ways to avoid vocational frustration, or feeling like a round peg in a square hole, is to know your temperament and its natural vocational possibilities, then find work or a profession that allows you to express your natural temperament characteristics. Examine this brief exposure to the four temperaments' vocational aptitudes and see if they sound familiar.

Sparky Sanguine's vocational aptitudes

The world is enriched by sanguines with their cheeriness and natural charisma. They usually make excellent salesmen and more than any other seem attracted to that profession. Sparky is so convincing that he could sell rubber crutches to people who aren't even crippled. If you ever want to watch Mr. Sanguine in action, just visit your local used-car dealer. Two-thirds of his salesmen are probably sanguines.

In addition to being good salesmen, sanguines make excellent actors, entertainers, and preachers (particularly evangelists). They are outstanding masters of ceremonies, auctioneers, and sometimes leaders (if properly blended with another temperament). Because of our mass media today, they are increasingly in demand within the political arena, where natural charisma has proven advantageous (sanguines have charisma to burn).

In the area of helping people, sanguines excel as hospital workers. Doctor Sanguine always has the best bedside manner. You may be on the verge of death, as white as the sheet you are lying on when he bubbles into the room, but before he leaves, he will lift your spirits by his natural charm. His obvious compassion in response to your tale of woe will almost make paying his exorbitant bill easy. (Sanguines are never moderate about anything.) Nurse Sanguine is equally enthusiastic about helping sick folk, and her radiant smile as she enters the room always gives you a pickup. In fact, most sick people respond to the sanguine's question of "How are you today?" by saying, "Fine," whereas Nurse Melancholy asking the same question would probably receive the self-pitying lament of "Miserable."

No matter what work the sanguine enters, it should always give him extensive exposure to people. I think his chief contribution to life lies in making other people happy. Certainly someone should be assigned that task in these uncertain times.

It is well known that sanguines are not too swift on detail. One of their biggest frustrations is the sales manager that wants them to use "purchase orders" or "fill in all the blanks on contracts." Most sanguines can't even remember where they put the contracts, much less fill them out. They would much rather be out on the golf course with a client than strategizing, analyzing, or filling out forms. Most sanguines lament, "Paperwork is the bane of my life."

While it is true sanguines are not *natural* detail hounds, they can do better. It is all a matter of self-discipline. That seems to be the most self-limiting thing a sanguine does: indulge his weaknesses and refuse to discipline himself. It is sad to have to say it, but sanguines usually limit their ultimate potential by their failure to discipline themselves. Every job has something undesirable about it, and changing jobs won't change that. Sooner or later you will find something in your new job that you don't like to do.

When my wife and I launched a national television program, we thought it would be an exciting way to serve our Lord. We thoroughly enjoyed the filming of the programs, the meeting of new people, the exciting experience of learning a new field, and, of course, helping millions of people instead of thousands. But I had not counted on the 224 fund-raising meetings all over the country during a recessionary year. I hated them! I love to teach and preach the Bible, but asking people for money to finance even this effective ministry? It was the hardest thing I have ever done in the work of God. In fact, I was tempted to quit 223 times.

Now that such meetings are behind us, I'm glad we didn't quit under fire. A long time ago I learned that God is interested in *finishers*, not starters. Sanguines are so capable they look for instant success, but are not used to putting their head down and ploughing on in the face of difficulty, opposition, or frustration.

Once they learned that lesson, there is no limit to what God can do with them vocationally.

Rocky Choleric's vocational potential

Any profession that requires leadership, motivation, and productivity is open to a choleric, provided it does not require too much attention to details and analytical planning. Committee meetings and long-range planning bore him, for he is a doer. Although he is not usually a craftsman (which requires a degree of perfection and efficiency usually beyond his capability), he often serves as a supervisor for craftsmen. He usually enjoys construction because he is so productive and will frequently end up as a foreman or project supervisor.

Rocky is a developer by nature. When he and his wife drive through the countryside, he cannot share her enjoyment of the "beautiful rolling hillsides," for he envisions road graders carving out streets and builders constructing homes, schools, and shopping centers. Most of today's cities and suburbs were first envisioned by a choleric. You can be sure, however, that he hired a melancholy as the architect with the analytical and creative ability to draw the plans he has outlined, for he could never do that himself. He still can't understand why a few lines on the back of an envelope aren't sufficient to gain the city planning department's approval. No one fights City Hall harder than a choleric, who bitterly laments, "Why all this business of detailed plans, anyway? I've built enough projects to know that the best plans have to be modified during construction; so why not make up your mind as you go along on the little issues? I know what I want to accomplish!" It is a wise choleric who hires a melancholy as his assistant or goes into business partnership with a melancholy. Together they make an unbeatable team. Of course, since everyone has both a primary and secondary temperament, occasionally one meets a person with both traits.

Most entrepreneurs are cholerics. They formulate the ideas and are venturesome enough to launch out in new directions. They don't limit themselves to their own ideas either, but sometimes overhear a creative idea from someone who is not sufficiently adventurous to initiate a new business or project. Once Rocky has started a new business, however, it is not unlike him to get bored soon after it is succesful. There are two reasons for this. First, as the business grows under his dynamic leadership, of necessity it creates more detail work. But since cholerics are not by nature good delegators of responsibility (although with proper training they can learn) and tend to prefer the fruits of their own productive and capable industry, the efforts of others are evaluated as somewhat inadequate. Consequently, they end up trying to do everything themselves. Second, when visionary Rocky finds himself so inundated with the mass of details this successful venture has spawned, he looks for a buyer to assume those responsibilities in order to free his own time to launch something new. Thus, the average choleric can be expected to start four to ten businesses or organizations in a lifetime.

Once a choleric learns to delegate responsibility to others and discovers that he is able to accomplish more through other people, he can complete an amazing amount of work. Other people cannot believe that he can be involved in so many things and keep his sanity, but to Rocky Choleric it is really very simple. Since he is completely performance-conscious and has no perfectionist hang-ups, he will reason, "I'd rather get a number of things finished 70 to 80 percent than a few things 100 percent." As Charlie "Tremendous" Jones says in his talks to businessmen, "Your motto should be: From production to perfection." Cholerics love that philosophy; perfectionist melancholies reject it vigorously.

Rocky Choleric is a natural motivator of other people. He oozes self-confidence, is extremely goal-conscious, and can inspire others to envision his goals. Consequently, his associates may find themselves more productive by following his lead. His primary weakness as a leader is that he is hard to please and tends to run roughshod over other people. If he only knew how others look to him for approval and encouragement, he would spend more time patting them on the back and acknowledging their accomplishments, which would generate even greater dedication from his colleagues. The problem is, however, the choleric subconsciously thinks that approval and encouragement will lead to complacency, and he assumes that an employee's productivity will fall off if he is too complimentary. Thus he will resort to criticism and fault-finding, in the hope that this will inspire greater effort. Unfortunately, he must learn that criticism is a demotivator. Once Rocky discovers that people require reassurance and stimulation in order to perform at the height of their potential, his role as leader radically improves.

Learn a lesson from football's middle linebackers just before a crucial play. They walk up and down the line patting their teammates encouragingly. That touch silently urges, "I'm counting on you to do your best; don't let me down." As one lineman said of his defensive captain, "I'd lay down my life for that man!" Interestingly enough, the captain was a perennial back-patter.

In the early days of American industry, when business production and manufacturing were not so technical, our industrial complexes were largely built by cholerics. In these days as technology demands greater sophistication and creativity, it is gradually turning for leadership to melancholies or at least choleric/melancholies or melancholy/cholerics. Today cholerics are more apt to build the factory buildings or the streets and highways which furnish the supply routes used by industry, whereas complex organization increasingly requires a more analytical leader.

Don't feel sorry for the choleric of the future; he will figure out something worthy of his talents. He always lands on his feet. Cholerics have a built-in promotional ability and do well in sales, teaching (but always practical subjects), politics, military service, sports, and many other endeavors. Like the sanguine, Rocky Choleric makes a good preacher in the pulpit. Not only is he a dynamic Bible teacher, but his organization and promotional ability together with his strong leadership gifts make it hard for the average fearful congregation to slow him down. According to an old saying, "Fools rush in where angels fear to tread." No one ever accused a choleric of being an angel. He launches into many projects and, with proper motivation and the blessing of God, usually enjoys a successful ministry.

Western civilization has benefited much from its Rocky Cholerics (Nordic, Teutonic, Germanic, Gallic, or Frankish people often had a high degree of choleric temperament). But it has suffered much from them also. The world's greatest generals, dictators, and gangsters have been mainly cholerics. What made the difference? Their moral values and motivations. If there is such a thing as a "success tendency," cholerics have it. That doesn't mean they are smarter than other people, as is often assumed, but that their strong will and determination drive them to succeed where other more gifted people are prone to give up in the midst of their superior projects. If a job requires industry, hard work, and activity, Rocky Choleric will usually outperform the other temperaments. If it demands analysis, long-range planning, meticulous skills, or creativity, that's a different ballgame. Rarely will you find a predominant choleric as a surgeon, dentist, philosopher, inventor, or watchmaker. Rocky's interests thrive upon activity, bigness, violence, and production. He is so optimistic, rarely anticipating failure, that he seldom fails— except at home.

Vocational possibilities of Martin Melancholy

As a general rule, no other temperament has a higher IQ, creativity, or imagination than a melancholy, and no one else is as capable of perfectionism. Most of the world's great composers, artists, musicians, inventors, philosophers, theoreticians, theologians, scientists, and dedicated educators have been predominantly melancholies. Name a famous artist, composer, or orchestra leader and you have identified another genius and an often eccentric melancholy. Consider Rembrandt, Van Gogh, Beethoven, Mozart, Wagner, and a host of others. Usually the greater the degree of genius, the greater will be the predominance of a melancholy temperament.

Any vocation that requires perfection, self-sacrifice, and creativity is open to a Martin Melancholy. However, he tends to place self-imposed limitations on his potential by underestimating himself and exaggerating obstacles. Almost any humanitarian vocation will attract melancholies to its staff. For years I have watched doctors, and although there are bound to be exceptions, almost every doctor I know is either predominantly or at least secondarily a melancholy.

It would almost require a melancholy's mind to get through the rigors of medical school, for a doctor has to be a perfectionist, an analytical specialist, and a humanitarian propelled by a heart that yearns to help other people.

The analytical ability required to design buildings, lay out a landscape, or look at acreage and envision a cohesive development usually requires a melancholy temperament. In the building trades the melancholy may want to supervise construction. However, he would be better off hiring a project supervisor who works better with people and then spend his own time on the drawing board. He becomes frustrated by the usual personnel problems and, with his unrealistic perfectionist demands, adds to them.

Almost every true musician has some melancholy temperament, whether he be a composer, choral conductor, performing artist or soloist This often accounts for the melancholy's lament that seems to find its way into so much of our music—both in and out of the church. Just yesterday my wife and I were driving to the airport when a country-western tune was crooned (or warbled, depending on your point of view) over the radio. We looked at each other and laughed as the wail of the obvious melancholy became so apparent—and that song is one of today's top tunes.

The influence of temperament on a person's musical ability was apparent several years ago as our church evaluated a very gifted minister of music and his piano playing wife, obviously a choleric. On the way home I reflected to my wife that I couldn't understand how a choleric could be such a good pianist. Beverly replied, "She is a mechanical musician. By strong willpower she forced herself to play the piano well, but she doesn't feel her music." As it turned out, the fantastic arrangement used that night had been written by her husband, a melancholy. Although he was not a pianist, he could feel music.

Not all melancholies, of course, enter the professions or arts. Many become craftsmen of a high quality—fine carpenters, brick-layers, plumbers, plasterers, scientists, nurserymen, playwrights, authors, mechanics, engineers, and members of almost every profession that provides a meaningful service to humanity. One vocation that seems to attract the melancholy, surprisingly enough, is acting, though we tend to identify this profession with an extrovert. On stage, the melancholy can become another person and even adopt that personality, no matter how much extroversion it requires; but as soon as the play is over and he comes down from his emotional high, he reverts back to his own more introverted personality.

Vocational aptitudes of the Phlegmatic

The world has benefited greatly from the gracious nature of Phil Phlegmatic. In his quiet way he has proved to be a fulfiller of the dreams of others. He is a master at anything that requires meticulous patience and daily routine.

Most elementary school teachers are phlegmatics. Who but a phlegmatic could have the patience necessary to teach a group of first-graders to read? A sanguine would spend the entire class period telling stories to the children. A melancholy would so criticize them that they would be afraid to read aloud. And I can't even imagine a choleric as a first-grade teacher—the students would leap out the windows! The gentle nature of the phlegmatic assures the ideal atmosphere for such learning. This is not only true on the elementary level but in both high school and college, particularly in math, physics, grammar, literature, language classes, and others. It is not uncommon to find phlegmatics as school administrators, librarians, counselors, and college department heads. Phlegmatics seem drawn to the field of education.

Another field that appeals to phlegmatics is engineering. Attracted to planning and calculation, they make good structural engineers, sanitation experts, chemical engineers, draftsmen, mechanical and civil engineers, and statisticians. Most phlegmatics have excellent mechanical aptitude and thus become good mechanics, tool-and-die specialists, craftsmen, carpenters, electricians, plasterers, glassblowers, watch and camera repairmen.

The biggest problem faced by industry pertains to personnel. With wages for many jobs skyrocketing, disharmony in a department can so demotivate employees that the employer may lose millions of dollars in productivity. In recent years, management has begun to discover that experienced phlegmatics in their employ often make excellent foremen, supervisors, and managers of people. Because they are diplomatic and unabrasive, people work well with them. When given positions of leadership, they seem to bring order out of chaos and produce a working harmony that is conducive to increased productivity. They are well organized, never come to a meeting unprepared or late, tend to work well under pressure, and are extremely dependable. Phlegmatics often stay with one company for their entire working career.

An interesting aspect of their leadership ability is that they almost never volunteer for authoritative responsibilities, which is why I labeled them "reluctant leaders." Secretly a phlegmatic may aspire for a promotion, but it would be against his nature to volunteer. Instead, he may patiently wait until more discordant and inept personalities make a mess out of things and then assume the responsibility only after it is forced upon him. Unfortunately, in many instances phlegmatics wait their lives away and opportunity never knocks—because although employers appreciate their capabilities, they don't envision them as leaders. Consequently, both the company and the employees lose. Rarely does a phlegmatic either live up to his full capabilities or fail in life.

Phlegmatics may take a job with retirement or security benefits in mind. Therefore, civil service, the military, local government or some other "good security risk" will attract them. Rarely will they launch out on a business venture of their own, although they are eminently qualified to do so. Instead they usually enhance the earning power of someone else and are quite content with a simple life-style.

Temperament test

You will find the self-scoring temperament test on pages 328-329 very interesting now that you realize your temperament is the key to your vocational aptitude. You may even be more interested in the more professional temperament test which I developed over a fifteen-year period to help Christians find the right vocation and the best place in their own local church to serve the Lord. In the personalized analysis, which gives a thorough appraisal of your primary and secondary temperament, I included fifty vocational aptitudes which would fit your unique combination of temperaments. You also will find helpful the thirty possible places of service in your local church to which you would be best suited, based on your temperament combination.

How to find the right job

Next to salvation, marriage, and your family, your vocation is the most important thing in your life. For that reason I would like to give you some of the practical suggestions I have personally shared with hundreds of men and women about how to change jobs, find one, or evaluate a new one.

Finding a lifetime vocation is really not too difficult *if* you're a Christian and *if* you're committed to seeking the Lord's will for your life. But don't expect it to be the dramatic thing it is for some people. I find that the narration of a dynamic experience of finding God's will to be very inspirational in a church service, but with most of us it is a slow, step-by-step process. While it is still true that God speaks to us today, it is rarely in the audible voice with which he spoke to Abraham, Isaac, and Moses. Most of us hear God by the gentle urging of our heart, or a "burden" that he puts into our hearts to do something. As we walk by faith, moving in the direction of that burden, we gradually find ourselves doing that will. For most of us, finding the will of God is not the electrifying experience of a moment, but a continuing process over a long period of time. We climb the mountain at hand only to find it leads to the next mountain. Then when we get to a central point we can look back and say, "Thank you, God, for your faithful leading."

God is interested in directing your life into the most productive and effective place where you can serve him. But he is first and foremost interested in you as a person. Most Christians have the attitude about finding God's will that was reflected by one man's honest but somewhat irreverent prayer, "Dear Lord, please write out on paper your plan for my life during the next ten years and if I like it, I'll do it!" Naturally we would never say such a thing, but often Christians act that way. Instead, God wants us to walk in unbroken fellowship with him so he can lead us in the making of the thousands of decisions in life that ultimately lead us to fulfill the perfect will of God.

The problem with most of us is that we are always in a hurry. God never rushes. He is more interested in our daily dependence on him than in all of the specifics. The reason he seldom gives us much advance warning or leading about his will is because he knows that even if we saw a ten-year blueprint, we would be off trying to do it and seldom check in at headquarters until we completed it or ran into a problem. Finding God's will for your life is not only the best possible way to live; it should also bring you closer to him in the process. My favorite verses in the Bible on this subject are:

Trust in the Lord and do good; dwell in the land and enjoy safe pasture. *Delight yourself in the Lord*, and he will give you the desires of your heart. *Commit your way to the Lord; trust in him* and he will do this: He will make your righteousness shine like the dawn, the justice of your cause like the noonday sun. *Be still before the Lord* and *wait patiently for him*; do not fret when men succeed in their ways, when they carry out their wicked schemes. (Ps. 37:3-7, NIV, emphasis mine)

Trust in the lord with all your heart and lean not on your own understanding; in all your ways acknowledge him, and he will make your paths straight. (Prov. 3:5-6, NIV)

Once you have committed yourself to live the kind of life described above, you cannot go wrong. That doesn't mean you won't have problems or face obstacles. I have never known anyone who accomplished anything for God, great or small, who didn't find obstacles in his path. But it is end-results with which we are concerned. The following steps will guide you to finding the Lord's direction in your vocation.

Seven steps to finding the right vocation

1. Establish your *primary* purpose in life according to Matthew 6:33.

What is your *real* purpose in changing jobs or finding a new vocation? It should be the same as your life's motivation which Jesus outlined for every Christian—"But seek first his kingdom and his righteousness, and all these things will be given to you as well" (Matt. 6:33, NIV). Once you have determined that *your primary purpose* is to seek first the kingdom of God, then and only then are you ready to find a different position.

"More money," "better opportunity for advancement," or "more enjoyable work" are not good answers in themselves. Settle the matter of who is first in your life, whose servant you are (see 1 Cor. 6:19-20); then you can get on with what is second. You may need more money, better opportunity, etc., and God knows that. But you need to know that your primary desire is to seek *first* the advancement of the kingdom.

That principle alone will save you many headaches. For example, all through the years of my counseling I have said, privately and publicly, that "anyone who has a job that requires they work every

Sunday so they can rarely, if ever, attend church has the wrong job." God's will on Sunday is that we attend church; there is no question on that. If your job will not permit you to obey God, then you have the wrong job.

Twenty years ago a personable supermarket manager with a wife and three small girls told me, "I can't come to church because I work on Sundays; that way I get double-time pay." I told him that was wrong motivation for working on Sunday. Once in a while is understandable. Even in the Old Testament, when the ox got into the ditch on the Sabbath day, it had to be pulled out. Jesus also endorsed that plan. Obviously, someone is going to have to work on the Sabbath and get dirty. But God said OK because it was only occasional or an emergency. But every Sabbath day was different. So it is with the Lord's day. I watched that man lose his wife and three girls to a carnal, southern California life-style. His double-time pay cost him far more than it gained him. And now that it is too late, he has realized it.

This same principle will help guide you in the kind of employment you seek. If it involves illegal or harmful products, that is not seeking the kingdom of God. A woman told me she turned down "$20,000 a year and perks" as an executive secretary because it involved all-night entertaining of some of the firm's out-of-town customers. There are some things more important in life than money—Matthew 6:33 makes that clear.

2. Analyze your temperament.

The simple temperament test on pages 328-329 will help you determine your temperament, which is a key to your vocational aptitude. We have already gone into detail on the vocational capabilities of each of the four temperaments. The following rule of thumb will give you general guidance, although you would really benefit from taking the temperament test described in the back of this book.

Sanguines	are people-oriented salesman types who excel in public relations, people-helping, or anything that requires charisma.
Cholerics	are strong natural leaders that are goal- or project-oriented individuals who like to manage people.

Melancholies   are creative, analytical individuals with strong perfectionist tendencies who often have aesthetic
traits.

Phlegmatics   are cool, detailed individuals who tend to limit
themselves. They can do statistical, microscopic
work that would drive others berserk.

With that brief overview you can tell generally what kind of
vocation best suits your needs. If you are discontent in your present
employment, your temperament test may reveal you are in the
wrong type of work.

3. Pray.

The introductory verse at the beginning of this section covered
the key words, "pray," "trust," "commit," and "acknowledge" God.
That is what prayer is. It is what asking God is based upon. If you
are unemployed or dissatisfied where you are employed, then pray
about it. God will either remove your discontentment or open the
door to a new opportunity—*if* you give him time and draw closer to
him during the waiting period.

4. Share your concern with others you can trust.

Regardless of your temperament, you will find it helpful to share
your burden with a friend. That's what friends are for. As the
Scripture says, "Bear one another's burdens and fulfill the law of
Christ." How can a friend share a burden unless you let him?
Usually it is helpful just to verbalize to another person your inner-
most thoughts. And those who find that kind of talk the most
difficult are the very ones who need it most.

Be sure the friend with whom you seek counsel shares your spiritual values. Psalm 1:1 says, "Blessed [happy] is the man who does not
walk in the counsel of the wicked" (NIV). That is so important! Many
a Christian has sought counsel from a professional counselor or
vocational counselor and failed to filter that counsel in the light of the
fact that the individual did not share his eternal perspective in relation
to God, life, death, or eternity. As a pastor, I saw many individuals
heed the advice of non-Christians at their peril.

Talking out your burden or sharing it with your friends does
more than just help you clarify your thinking. It puts others on the
alert for opportunities. I have been amazed at the way God opens
doors through other people.

5. Investigate.

Don't plan to sit back after you have prayed about it and expect God to send down a job on a white cloud. Prayer usually motivates us to do something, like look in the want ads. I have a friend who while praying about her need felt the urge to read the want ads and found a local Christian doctor looking for help. He had prayed for guidance three days before and felt led to call the newspaper. His ad was only in the paper three days. She caught it the first day, and now two Christians who wanted to work with a Christian both got the answer to their prayer.

Oftentimes the biblical directive, "you have not because you ask not" seriously limits our lives vocationally.

Some reading this may be entirely unskilled. You may have married young thinking "it will all work out" and now find yourself unemployable. You may well need to go back to school. An industrial arts program or some other specialized training plan may be your need.

Make a list of the kind of jobs you think you would enjoy doing and that pay what you feel you will need for your family to live on. Then prioritize those on the top of your list and start contacting them. If you need to take night school or specialized training, do it. It is becoming increasingly necessary that everyone going out into the work force be trained in some area. Even the Bible says a "workman" is one who "studies" (2 Tim. 2:15). There are very few positions that do not require "study." If that's what it takes, do it!

When I was forty-eight years old, I enrolled in graduate school at Western Conservative Bible Seminary, through their San Diego satellite program. It took four long years and lots of hard work to meet their rigorous demands, but finally I earned my degree. I found it a very stimulating influence on my whole ministry to go back to school. (Even after being a college president for six years, you're never too old to learn.) Many people have found a whole new stimulating vocational life open to them by paying the price to get some advanced training either in their chosen field or in another.

God has given you certain basic skills. You will never get more than he gave you, but through training, discipline, and practice you can improve and refine those skills. Personally, I don't believe God will do anything for us vocationally that we can do for ourselves.

6. Be faithful and watch for the open door.

Our Lord said, "These are the words of him who is holy and true, who holds the key of David. What he opens, no one can shut; and what he shuts, no one can open. I know your deeds. See, I have placed before you an open door that no one can shut" (Rev. 3:7 NIV).

I have found that our Lord is the master of the "open door." That is, he leads us to an open door of opportunity to serve him. The best advice I have ever heard is that we do not need a lifetime roadmap or master plan for our lives. We just need to stay in close fellowship with the Master, who does have a plan for our lives. So we should busy ourselves cleaning up the room we are now in and God will, in his own time, open another door for us. Once inside, we will find it too needs a lot of hard work, so we should busy ourselves cleaning up the second room. About the time we get that room cleaned up, there will be a third door open to us, then a fourth and so on. Finally we will look back and say, "Hasn't God been faithful to lead us into so many places of opportunity to serve him?" But in the meantime we need to be found "faithful," cleaning up the room we are in.

I shall never forget my first church. We were building a sign in front of the church, and I was in my study when the truck delivering bricks arrived. I signed for the delivery and the driver said, "Who do you have to unload these bricks?" I said, "We're paying you to deliver them." To which he replied, "I am a truck driver not a laborer. Unless you find someone to unload these bricks, I will return them to the plant!" So I jumped up in the truck and proceeded to unload the bricks. That was thirty years ago. I have never wanted for work. In fact, my only frustration is that I can't do all the things I would like to. I've often wondered how long that truck driver kept his job—with that attitude, probably not very long.

God doesn't ask us all to be successful or to hit a home run every time at bat. He does, however, ask that we be "faithful." That is something everyone should be. Right where we are. Don't let your interest in a new job keep you from being faithful where you are.

7. Anticipate the future with peace and confidence.

God holds the key to your future, so don't worry about it. Our Lord spoke about that many times in words like these:

Therefore I tell you, do not worry about your life, what you will eat or drink; or about your body, what you will wear. Is not life more important than food, and the body more important than clothes? Look at the birds of the air; they do not sow or reap or store away in barns, and yet your heavenly Father feeds them. Are you not much more valuable than they? Who of you by worrying can add a single hour to his life? And why do you worry about clothes? See how the lilies of the field grow. They do not labor or spin. Yet I tell you that not even Solomon in all his splendor was dressed like one of these. If that is how God clothes the grass of the field, which is here today and tomorrow is thrown into the fire, will he not much more clothe you, O you of little faith? So do not worry, saying, "What shall we eat?" or "What shall we drink?" or "What shall we wear?" For the pagans run after all these things, and your heavenly Father knows that you need them. But seek first his kingdom and his righteousness, and all these things will be given to you as well. Therefore do not worry about tomorrow, for tomorrow will worry about itself. Each day has enough trouble of its own. (Matt. 6:25-34 NIV)

It is one thing to be concerned about the future; it is quite another to worry about it. When you commit your way to God, you don't have to worry about the future. I have to remind myself of that fact every now and then. It helps to have many Bible verses hidden in your heart for instant recall. When you're in a ministry like mine, where you're dependent on the response to monthly mailings to carry on the Lord's work, you are very vulnerable to the erratic responses of people. Summer is a disaster, December is almost as bad, and January and February are slow starters. That leaves six good months out of the year. Recession, inflation, late mailings, foul-ups at the printers, the mailing house or some other vendor can even lose one of those months. Such ministries are well labeled "faith ministries"—you live week by week by faith. But then, who doesn't? Insurance companies and even banks can fail, and only God knows if Social Security will last. In the final analysis you're in good hands only when you trust the living God.

The one thing you have going for you is that your God is the God of the future. I have often comforted myself with this thought: "God has never failed anyone, Tim; so why should he make an exception of you? You're just not that important." God gets more glory for himself by being faithful.

He won't let you down! Remember Noah, Abraham, Moses, Job, David, Peter, John, Paul, and millions of others!

7

USES OF TEMPERAMENT IN THE WORKPLACE

As a student of psychology for over thirty years, I long ago made the observation that the business community had a much more effective model of human behavior than did the academic. The colleges seemed obsessed with humanistic psychology that started out on so many false premises we shouldn't be surprised that it changes every few years. We have seen Freudian psychology, once the shrine before which the university crowd gladly bowed, replaced by Rogerianism, behaviorism, Gestalt theory, reality therapy, transactional analysis, and much frustration—particularly by the patients whose only consistent observation was the exorbitant bill that came to their home each month.

What are the false premises of humanistic psychology? Very simply that: (1) man is an evolved animal; (2) man has no inherited conscience; (3) there is no creator God; (4) there is no absolute standard for behavior given by that God; (5) man, like the animals, has no soul—so when you're dead you're dead; and (6) man's ultimate end is self-actualization.

Given those basic assumptions, it is no wonder modern psychology has wrought such havoc in our society. We have more schizophrenic, mentally ill, depressed, suicidal, hostile, and upset people today than before we had psychologists. The reason is very simple. A basic axiom of all logic is: If you start out on a wrong premise, you will end up with a wrong conclusion. I've counseled enough psychologists and their wives to know that their solutions, without God, are impractical. They just don't work! Much of the advice given by secular humanist psychologists is not only wrong, but harmful.

Business is quite a different matter. Industrial psychology may not be given much shrift in the halls of academia, but it helps far more people than clinical psychology. And interestingly enough, it is based on the theory of the four temperaments.

For some reason, American psychologists have been heavily influenced by Sigmund Freud, although they have discounted many of his obsolete theories and developed a godless modern version of their own. But few American professors have embraced the scholarly works of Dr. H. J. Eysenck of England. He is highly respected in Europe and in the industrial, sales, and management fields of psychology in this country. In fact, most of the popular programs used in business management, sales, and personal development are based on his exhaustive research. And Dr. Eysenck is an advocate of the four temperament theory, which he ascribes to Hippocrates.

The Educational and Industrial Testing Service is a San Diego-based company that produces the E.P.I.—Eysenck Personality Inventory. The following diagram (Fig. 1) is an Eysenck trademark of

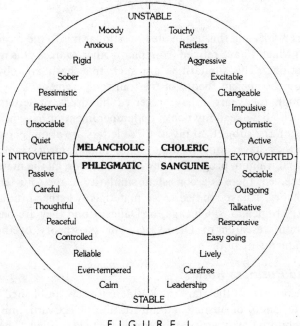

FIGURE I

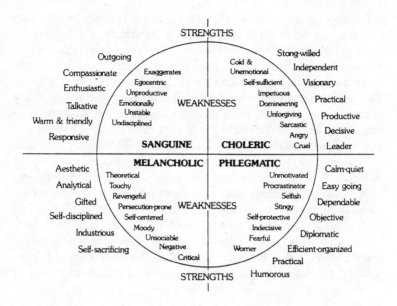

FIGURE 2

both his books and this test. Note how similar it is to the basic chart (Fig. 2) which I have refined from many other sources plus my own observations. The similarities are such that both are obviously based on the ancient theory of the four temperaments.

Through the years I have received hundreds of letters from people who have read my books on temperament or have heard my lectures on the subject. Many of those letters are about personality testing they have gone through, sales management training, or vocational training programs they have taken. In all the materials I have received, there is a consistent similarity to the four temperament theory. I have studied these materials, whether produced in Denver, Minneapolis, Chicago, or Dallas; I find they are based on the careful research of Dr. Eysenck or the theory of the four temperaments or both.

Harvard Business Review

For example, in the Harvard Business Review, published by the graduate school of business administration of Harvard University, Dr. Theodore Levitt wrote an interesting article entitled "The Managerial Merry-go-round," in which he points out: "People have different cognitive styles—that is, ways of gathering and evaluating information. Some are systematic thinkers, others intuitive thinkers, some are receptive thinkers and others perceptive thinkers. These styles seem to be inherent and are fairly fixed by the time people reach maturity. What is even more instructive is that the research found that these styles greatly affect the way people perform the jobs they choose, and can even determine the industries they enter" (*Fact and Fiction in Psychology*, Penguin Books, 1965, p. 55).

You will notice that this article is divergent from humanistic psychology's claim that all people are born neutral and that environment molds one's behavior. The business community recognizes that it is worthwhile to train management personnel at every level, but it also recognizes that there are inborn characteristics in people that are irreversible.

"Each of us marches to a different drummer; the secret of good teamwork is blending contrasting executive styles," argue Stuart Atkins and Allan Katcher, president and vice-president respectively of Atkins-Katcher Associates, Inc., management consultants in Beverly Hills, California. The following excerpts appeared in *Nation's Business* (March 1975):

> To get the best performance from your executive team, you have to orchestrate them, getting each to give his best and helping them to blend their strengths for peak performance as a group. To achieve this, you must analyze their different styles of operating. Everyone is a mixture of four basic behavior patterns, usually with one dominating. The others, less used, come into play when the situation calls for them. There are, however, no "good" or "bad" styles.
>
> A person whose dominant style is Supporting-Giving tends to be trusting, responsive, idealistic and loyal. He tries to do the very best he can whenever you assign him a task, and he sets high standards for himself and his people. Highly receptive to others' ideas, he cooperates and is helpful, a natural team player.

Personality profile testing

In recent years the business community has begun using a series of tests which they administer to screen employees for major industries. The individual takes a test consisting of 150 adjectives (mostly worked out by Dr. Eysenck). One firm sends a test to five of the prospect's friends to determine how the individual is seen by other people.

The test results do not use the terms sanguine, choleric, phlegmatic, melancholy; but anyone familiar with their meaning will recognize their parallel with "expressive," "driver" "analytical," and "amiable." Call it what you may, the final results are much the same.

One testing group calls them "four social styles" and points out that most people are a combination of at least two social styles. As you examine their instrument in Fig. 3, you will find a basic similarity to what we have studied as the four basic temperaments. The test results locate a person's primary and secondary social style.

A verbal description of each social style as pictured in Fig. 4 shows a marked similarity to our four temperament theory.

In the September 1979 issue of *Dallas* I found a very interesting article on the variety of Chief Executive Officers (CEO's) in the

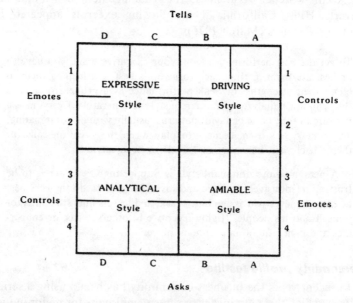

FIGURE 3

SHORTHAND DESCRIPTIONS
OF THE BASIC SOCIAL STYLES

	Asks / Controls		Asks / Emotes		
ANALYTICAL	Critical Indecisive Stuffy Picky Moralistic	Industrious Persistent Serious Exacting Orderly	Manipulative Excitable Undisciplined Reacting Egotistical	Ambitious Stimulating Enthusiastic Dramatic Friendly	**AMIABLE**
EXPRESSIVE	Conforming Unsure Ingratiating Dependent Awkward	Supportive Respectful Willing Dependable Agreeable	Pushy Severe Tough Dominating Harsh	Strong-willed Independent Practical Decisive Efficient	**DRIVING**
	Tells / Emotes		Tells / Controls		

F I G U R E   4

dynamic world of Metro Dallas. I've been to that city several times and even as I write this am standing in the Registry Hotel located in the heart of the boom growth of North Dallas.

Bill Sloan, author of *Life at the Top*, had noticed four styles of CEO's in the plush offices of the mirrored towers in Dallas. He called them "initiator, thinker, feeler, and sensor," titles used by many management consultants, but they are just different names for melancholy, phlegmatic, sanguine, and choleric. He used Mary Kay, the famous head of a gigantic cosmetic industry, as an example of a "feeler," which he describes as "sentimental, loyal and true blue," "thrives on personal relationships." He then explains she is heavily into the world of people and is an excellent motivator.

To him, Ross Perot, the genius who started out renting time on computers to sell to clients and today owns banks of computers and heads a multimillion dollar corporation in Dallas, is an example of an intuitor or melancholy whose creativity and penchant for innovation together with his workaholic drive have taken him to the top.

Not only did this personnel expert point out the four types of managers in parallel to the four temperament theory, but he confirms what I have long suspected. That all four types can make successful CEO's, but in different fields and with different styles. "Feelers" (or sanguines) make good sales managers, personnel directors, and goodwill ambassadors. "Intuitors" (melancholies) make excellent advertising executives, public relations directors, heads of research, or anything that demands creativity. "Thinkers" (phlegmatics) are best suited as finance directors, heads of engineering groups, executive vice-presidents, etc. The sensor (choleric) is in charge and can run any kind of corporation if given the right personnel.

Whether you call them "thinkers" or phlegmatics, "intuitors" or melancholies, they are the same. You are talking about inherited temperament that can be improved, educated, and refined, but does not change. Mary Kay was a "feeler" at four years of age, and as a supersuccessful sanguine she is still a "feeler," "toucher," or people-person. No doubt she has learned discipline, organization, and management, but she was a born motivator with charisma to burn.

We all inherited a temperament that produces our "style." No one style is better than another, but each fits different kinds of work better than others. Management would be advised to spend more time discovering an employee's temperament so he can train him for the work for which he is best fitted.

Four types—the dominant model

During the past fifty years many theories of behavior have been proposed. The most effective and long lasting are based to some degree at least on a model of four types or styles of behavior. People are different. They act differently, respond differently, and react differently.

One government training specialist pointed out that the November 1982 issue of *Training* magazine listed fifteen of the most common theories. Some of the most common are listed on the following pages. Admittedly, they are abbreviated drastically but notice how each fits under one of the four temperament theory categories. Although the authors may not wish to admit to such similarity to the world's most ancient theory of behavior which we have been studying, when put on this chart (Fig. 5) it would seem such similarities exist.

This chart (Fig. 5) could only have been produced by a thorough student of both the four temperaments and the modern attempts to explain or test man's behavior on Eysenck's research. I reproduce it here for students of both fields so they can see how the modern trends are taking us back to the days of Hippocrates and even to Agur in the Book of Proverbs.

The business community for the past twenty years has been increasingly aware of the practicality of the temperament theory. They may call him expressive instead of Sparky Sanguine, but they mean the same temperament. They may call him driver-analytical, but they still mean the choleric-melancholy temperament.

I predict that whatever they call it, the business community because of its commitment to practicality, cost effectiveness, and personnel development will lead us away from the unrealistic idealism of humanistic psychology to the more relevant four-temperament theory of behavior to explain why man acts the way he does and what he can do about it. The reason is very simple—it works.

The most obvious use of the four behavioral styles of business or the four-temperament theory comes in helping people to understand why they act the way they do and in helping them learn to modify their communication styles. The four-temperament theory of the ancients or the four-behavior styles of modern industry are an excellent way to present training programs. It is a handy aid in not only improving communication skills, but time management, leadership styles, performance appraisals, team building, conflict resolution, and improved productivity.

A while ago I sent the department heads of Family Life Seminars to a management conference conducted by Arthur F. Miller of People Management, Incorporated. This man, who has spent a lifetime in management training and consultation said that one out of two persons in the United States is in the wrong job. This increases job-related conflicts and stress in both the work place and in the employee's home or family life.

Now you see why I say our nation has ignored the four-temperament theory at its peril for many years. If the psychology departments of our major universities would once again return to the ancient theory of human temperament, update it, and use it on our 13 million college students and/or 20 million high school students, it would have a positive effect in both the workplace and family life.

Mr. Miller says that he is familiar with the inside personnel procedures of some of the companies in America, but unfortunately "no one has a plan to match an employee's job with his strengths and weaknesses." That would explain why so many people spend

THE FOUR-BEHAVIOR-STYLE THEORIES

	HIGH ASSERTIVENESS HIGH RESPONSIVENESS
1. BASIC SYSTEMS Stuart Atkins, LIFO® (Life Orientations)	Adapting-Dealing
William M. Marston, *"Emotions of Normal People"*	Inducement of Others
Medieval Four Temperaments	Sanguine
David W. Merrill– Roger H. Reid, *"Personal Styles and Effective Performance"*	Expressive
2. CONFLICT RESOLUTION Jay Hall Conflict Management Survey	Synergistic
Donald T. Simpson, *"Conflict Styles: Organizational Decision Making"*	Integration
Thomas-Kilmann Conflict Mode Instrument	Collaborating
3. PERFORMANCE APPRAISAL Robert E. Lefton et al., *"Effective Motivation Through Performance Appraisal"*	Dominant-Warm

HIGH ASSERTIVENESS LOW RESPONSIVENESS	LOW ASSERTIVENESS HIGH RESPONSIVENESS	LOW ASSERTIVENESS LOW RESPONSIVENESS
 Controlling-Taking	 Supporting-Giving	 Conserving-Holding
Dominance	Compliance	Steadiness
Choleric	Melancholy	Phlegmatic
Driver	Analytical	Amiable
Win-Lose	Yield-Lose	Lose-Leave
Power	Suppression	Denial
Competing	Accommodating	Avoiding
Dominant-Hostile	Submissive-Hostile	Submissive-Warm

FIGURE 5

their life doing a job they dislike and then go home to take out the frustrations on the people they love most, or ease their stress (temporarily) by drug or alcohol.

Hopefully the last decade of this century will find more emphasis on job fitness or helping people select the vocation in life for which they are best fitted. The temperament theory can really help this field.

As modern research continues to produce new and better ways of testing, training, and developing people's natural traits, work habits, and social styles, we will find a continuing use of the four-temperament theory. You, as a reader of this book, will be ahead of the pack because you understand the basic theory. And if you have experienced the powerful work of the Spirit of God as outlined earlier, you will already have a handle on overcoming your weaknesses and maximizing your potential.

8

OTHER WAYS TO USE
THE FOUR-TEMPERAMENT THEORY

The four-temperament theory is not a cure-all for everything, but it certainly is a good tool to use in helping us get along with other people. I have always presented it with two primary uses in mind: self-improvement, and improving your interpersonal relationships. But there are many other ways which you will find helpful. I shall suggest a dozen or so, then you can add some of your own.

I have found the temperament theory to be most helpful, and there is no end to the uses or applications you can make for it. However, the first and best use is on yourself. Once you have learned the theory and how to strengthen your own weaknesses, you will find it helpful in the following ways:

1. Counseling others. I mention counseling to begin with because that is one place I have personally used it in helping thousands of people. It is a wonderful tool for diagnosing people's problems. You cannot help anyone unless you know what their root problem is. Many times the things they say are not the real cause of their difficulties. To me, counseling is helping people apply biblical principles to their lives where they cannot apply them alone. Most counselees don't know why they are so miserable. Consequently, the first thing any counselor does is listen and try to diagnose the individual's major difficulty. If you understand the four temperaments, it streamlines the diagnostic process.

By watching the counselee carefully for giveaway signs through body language, speech, attitudes, and the general flow of their conversation, it is usually easy to diagnose an upset person's primary temperament. Once 1 have done this, I look for problems associated with their temperament. If he is a sanguine, I look for anger insecurity, lack of discipline, and sometimes immorality. If he is choleric, I look for anger bitterness, and other forms of hostility, self-justification, coldness, or eruptions and a tendency to run roughshod over others. If I am working with a melancholy person, I expect self-condemnation, depression, self-limitation, criticism, a negative and critical spirit, or ingratitude toward God and others. In a melancholy man I sometimes anticipate male impotence or in a woman the frustration of frigidity. Phlegmatics tend to clutter their lives with worry, fear, procrastination, and lack of motivation. I rarely have discovered immorality among phlegmatic men; but occasionally a phlegmatic woman, due to her tendency to "go along and keep the peace," may give in to the temptation.

All of these problems and others for the various temperaments need to be considered and addressed in the counseling room. Unless an individual is confronted with biblical standards of behavior, he will not be lastingly helped. Once you diagnose and confront the individual with the problem, she needs a spiritual prescription to build the cure on. But the administration of the prescription should be given with her temperament in view. Sanguines and phlegmatics need a midweek call just to check up on their faithfulness. They need that extra prod to get going. The choleric needs to be assured that the formula will work, and the melancholy needs to keep from making a three-hour production out of a twenty-minute a day assignment.

Counseling people can be an enjoyable experience if you see progress in most of them. Knowing and using the temperament theory is a tool for improving the counselor's success ratio.

2. *Using the temperament theory in selling.* The salesman who approaches people according to their temperaments will be more successful than the one who approaches everyone alike. People differ, and good salesmen know it and approach them accordingly.

Sanguines are impulse buyers and are notorious for having no sales resistance. They aren't interested in details, but enjoy success stories. They love being entertained, and usually they enact their biggest deals on the golf course or in the restaurant. Be sure to stress feelings, ego, and "everyone has one" and usually you will make a sale (80 percent of the time). Get a good down payment though, for he changes his mind easily.

Cholerics are tougher to sell. Being practical, they respond to need. Why do they need it? How will they use it? What real value does it have? How much will it be worth five years from now? Ask his opinion and listen as if to an expert. He loves bargains; so give him a discount. He is opinionated; so get the kind and color he wants. Don't try to con him, but be sure and show him how he can pay for it. If you have been convincing, he may buy. Don't clutter your presentation with too much detail. Give one or two success stories, but don't waste his "valuable time" talking too much. If he really wants what you have, he is a 70 percent sales prospect and not usually given to shopping around. Let him see it and handle it, then back off. He will sell himself.

Melancholies need facts, statistics, charts, and detail. Don't try to bluff them! If you don't know your product, don't even bother to call on them. They can ask more questions about your product than both the inventor and manufacturer ever thought of. When he asks a question, find the answer. But always tell the truth; he has a memory like an elephant. Leave a good brochure, go find the answer and then return. He has thousands of honest doubts and questions. Treat all his doubts and criticisms as requests for more information. He only buys the best he can afford; so convince him your product is the best on the market for the price. (If it isn't, go work for the best or don't try to sell him.) He doesn't want to hear a lot of success stories. He wants to know what your product will do for him, his home, or his company. Don't try to entertain him. He prides himself on the fact that he can't be bought. Send him something at Christmas time or after your first sale. Build a relationship of reliability and see that your firm services his account, and he will become a customer for years. Sales prospects are 50-50, but he gets terrible buyer's remorse the day after signing a contract. A follow-up call and enthusiastic report do wonders. And be sure to instruct him or his people on the use of your product. Remember, you're building a lifetime client. He has that potential.

Phlegmatics love to be "sold," but cannot be pressured. They like a combination of detail and success stories. They buy for many reasons, including prestige and practicality. Rarely do they buy the top of the line. Remember, they are not flamboyant. They prefer the stripped-down version. Give them plenty of latitude in choosing a price range ($20,000 or $50,000). Let them guide you to their needs. They beg to be entertained and love to be persuaded. Invite their wives along; it makes them feel important. They ask intelligent questions and must have all their fears assuaged or it's "no sale." Help them to see that your product will save money in the long run. Treat them with respect; don't fawn over them, but answer their questions and go back until they buy. The more attention you give them, the more obligated they feel. But after the sale, if you drop them like a hot potato they may never buy from you again. Like the melancholy, they can develop "buyer's remorse." They need assurance after the sale that they did the right thing—another success story or news about another company that just bought your product will do it. They usually use their old equipment one or two years longer than others.

I heard an interesting thing in a Chicago airport as I was writing the above. A businessman who identified himself as a "salesman for a major household product" and I began talking, and he asked what I was writing. When I described the four-temperament approach to selling, his eyes opened wide and I asked if he agreed. His response was interesting: "I can name people and describe examples of these four types. We deal with them every day."

3. *Using temperaments in managing people.* Good management involves selection, training, motivating, and controlling people as they work harmoniously toward a united goal. The first and most important thing in good management is to put the right people in the right place. We have already seen how understanding the four temperaments and applying this to people is helpful. But it is also a good tool for managers to use in getting the most out of people once they are on the payroll.

Sanguines are predictably unpredictable. Their natural lack of discipline makes them late and unprepared when they come to work each day. Either they must be trained to do detail work or provided with a secretary who can do it for them. Their greatest asset is production and sales. Don't expect them to conform to all company policy. The biggest task a manager has is guiding them to spend 90 percent of their time in their most productive area. If they cannot conform, they will become liabilities. I know a salesman who could not resist the temptation to throw in extra goodies to his customers and make extra promises that were not company policy in order to make sales. The company president told me, "He made so many sales his commissions were more than my salary. And when we fired him for giving away the company store, we discovered that his expenses, commissions, shipping charges, etc., cost us $800,000 more than our profits." Obviously, such individuals need close supervision, but they don't like it.

Cholerics are self-starters and quick-learners. Don't be afraid to delegate responsibility to them. But make sure they fully understand the guidelines, objectives, and limits. Expect confrontation. They will challenge your authority. Don't flunk their test. If you give them an inch, they will take three miles. And don't let them run roughshod over people. They need management training but are worth it because they can accomplish a ton of work. Just remember—he is after your job.

Melancholies are temperamental people. Make sure they are in the right field. They need constant encouragement that they have worth and are capable, and they usually are. Try not to give them too many things to do at the same time or they will explode, quit, or collapse. He is the one person who may foul up his homelife working too late or taking work home. Help him see that his brand of perfectionism is not necessary to the production of a top-quality product. With proper encouragement and reward he may be with you for life.

Phlegmatics are nuts-and-bolts, quiet people who can be depended on if you keep their eyes on the goals. But you must set their goals. By nature they would accept 55 percent of their capability. They work best under pressure but balk at high pressure; so keep it gentle, reasonable, and encouraging. They also need plenty of approval. Sometimes time-study training will be needed to help them make better use of their time. They may never defy you, but don't be surprised if they ignore you. They need constant reminders of productivity.

The thing all managers need to keep in mind is, don't expect other people to do things like you would. They are individuals. They have distinct talents and abilities. Help them function within those capabilities. I have found that most people, particularly Christians, will rise to a challenge if they are treated with love and respect.

4. *Use it in educating others.* The four-temperament theory is an invaluable tool in educating individuals. One of my criticisms of the monstrous business of education today is that they have ignored the temperaments of children in their teaching process. Educators have made a shambles out of our once great school system with their

untested theories that have set the learning process back instead of forward. The gifted melancholy student is a fast-learner who may not need rote learning. But to scrap the rote method for all students is to disregard their temperaments. The sanguine, choleric, or phlegmatic child needs rote learning and disciplined drills to become proficient. Gradually, as the basic principles of math, reading, or history begin to fall into place, he can become a self-starter thinker. Sanguines are restless, temperamental flitters; phlegmatics are daydreamers; and cholerics spin-off on their own tangents. A wise teacher will try to diagnose her pupils' tendencies and motivate them according to need. Sanguines and phlegmatics need prodding: cholerics need goals and knowledge as to why something is relevant; melancholies need exposure to the subject and encouragement. And as we have seen in a previous chapter, each temperament has subject strengths they enjoy and subject weaknesses. If you know his temperament, you can give him the encouragement he needs accordingly.

5. *Use the temperament theory to resolve personality conflicts.* Some people are so difficult, the Lord himself couldn't get along with them. During his day he clashed with the legalists who refused to believe in him and finally called them "whited sepulchres filled with dead men's bones." But most people with whom we clash are different temperaments; that's why we clash. For example, the melancholy perfectionist is orderly and precise. As such he is destined to clash with the free-spirited casual carelessness of the sanguine. They will irritate each other. The sanguine can get irritated by what he considers the fastidiousness of the melancholy. One great cause of conflict between the two is exactness of language. The sanguine guestimates on figures, mileage, and details, while the melancholy feels it his duty to "correct" the sanguine. No wonder they irritate each other, whether in marriage, business, or church. The melancholy destroys the sanguine's ego by such corrections, so the sanguine lashes out in retaliation with his best weapon—his tongue.

Cholerics have a similar problem. They walk faster, talk faster, and think faster than the laid-back phlegmatic. The relationship of the phlegmatic is both a source of irritation to the choleric and a challenge. The more the choleric tries to motivate the phlegmatic, the more the phlegmatic digs in his heels and stubbornly refuses to move. The hostility such interpersonal contacts can generate is incredible. However, sanguines can irritate cholerics also, but not for the same reasons that irritate the melancholy. But if you want to see an explosion, just watch a sanguine and choleric locked in personality conflict. The two temperaments that seem to have the least conflict are the sanguine and the phlegmatic.

There are two main reasons for personality clashes: (1) temperament conflicts—that is, two individuals that are so different they spontaneously act and react entirely opposite in almost every situation; or (2) we see our weaknesses in someone we love and tend to overreact. This often happens to a parent who clashes with a child who picks up the parent's weaknesses. The first is easier to resolve than the second.

Once you recognize that your conflict with another person is because your temperaments are so opposite, it is easier to accept that difference; you recognize it is not personal but natural. This is the old "equal but different" idea. You can respect the other person's right to be different from yourself without superiority or inferiority being involved. The problem is, many people tend to look down on another's differences.

That is where the Spirit-filled life is of great value. When we are filled with love, joy, peace, etc., including "meekness," we will find it easier to accept the erratic or different reactions of others. That is just one step to anticipating them. For example, I have a sanguine friend who used to drive me up the wall with his gross exaggerations. (He calls them embellishments.) I could never count on his facts, estimates, or schedules. Instead of getting irritated all the time, I just began dividing everything he said by four, and then I could realistically anticipate his cost estimates and projections. For my pessimistic friends, I just anticipate their gloom, doom, and despair mentality and work around it. For example, my dentist wanted to tear out my bridge and rework the whole thing. I challenged him to "patch it" and even suggested how. It took a lot of persuasion, but he finally did it against his better judgment saying, "It won't last!" I am now on my third year with that repair job, and he still can't believe it will hold. If you take no for an answer from some people, you will both be the losers for it.

The temperament theory won't solve all personality conflicts, but it can reduce them down to size and make them livable.

6. *Use the theory to understand the other members of your church boards and committees.* One of the proofs that the local

church is divinely inspired and empowered of God is that even democracy, demanded by most church leaders, still hasn't killed it. This is a day when everyone wants to be a part of the decision-making process. If the pastor is a dictator, the people complain that the church is dominated by one man. If it is a deacon-led church with seventy elders or deacons, there will be people who complain it entrusts too much power in the board. I have come to the conclusion that most people complain about any leader if he makes a decision they don't like.

I have worked with church boards for thirty-two years, and I can vouch for the fact that all four temperaments get on any board of seven or more people and usually react according to temperament. I'll never forget the time we were $56,000 in the red during a recession, and the melancholies on the eleven-member Board of Trustees wanted to cut salaries and lay off several staff members. It took all the optimistic persuasion I could muster to talk them into giving me more time, but they finally did—only to find that in seven months we had a small bank balance and had laid off no one. Before I heard about temperaments, I would have to fight harboring a bitter attitude toward such dooms-dayers. Once I recognized their natural tendency, I wrote it off as their temperament and refused to take it personally—or to give in without a fight.

Sanguine board members are talkers, not doers or listeners. They need to be given something to do and held accountable. Their talk at board meetings should be limited to their production.

Cholerics tend to take over if you give them a chance. But if you have a project of importance you want passed by a board you serve on, I suggest you talk to the cholerics in advance and get them on your team. When the meeting comes, they will carry the ball for you and will intimidate all the dooms-dayers into agreement.

Melancholies can be exasperating with their inexhaustible supply of questions. No matter what you bring up, they can think of objections, difficulties, and problems that will be encountered. It has always mystified me that they can always remember illustrations of those who failed trying to do what you suggest, but they can never remember those who succeeded.

Phlegmatics are easy to get along with on boards, particularly if you don't expect them to be anything. But if your proposal is going to cost them money, don't count on their support. Always present the cost of a project along with a reasonable plan for repayment, and your phlegmatic friends will go along with you.

Since no board or committee is made up of just one kind of temperament, but usually will have all four represented, you will find life as a leader, pastor, or chairman easier if you plan your presentation with all temperaments in mind. Preparation is the name of the game. But don't forget to pray. That's where the real power comes from.

7. *Use the temperament theory in parenting.* Every child is different not only in size, shape, looks, and intelligence, but in temperament blend. For that reason, you will find the temperament theory a helpful tool in parenting, particularly in the way you discipline. We have one child that I only gave two spankings during her entire childhood, and yet she is an unspoiled young woman today. The other three children? I won't estimate the times we went to the woodshed. What made the difference? Their temperaments.

Sanguine children are the easiest to love. They are born charmers, and if you aren't careful they will charm you out of obedience. Such children grow up to lie, cheat, and in some cases steal. Sanguines need love, but even more they need discipline. And don't let them sass you or they will learn to be disrespectful toward all adults.

Choleric children usually take more spankings to raise than any other type. And they can be willful! You must break their will, but be careful you don't break their spirit. How do you keep from breaking their spirit while you mold their will? By being loving and cultivating a close relationship while at the same time you demand obedience. They will test you—don't fail their test.

Melancholy children need love and security, while at the same time they need to learn self-sufficiency. They usually don't require a great deal of physical discipline, but will respond to a soft word of displeasure. One trait you must watch is criticism and a negative spirit, particularly if their secondary temperament is choleric. A MelChlor can be both negative and willful. Melancholy children need lots of parental reassurance that they do have worth and value—and that is what parents are for.

Phlegmatic children are easy to raise, particularly if you don't care if they never amount to anything in life. They don't cause trouble and rarely sass you back; they just live in their fantasy world of daydreams and function up to 60 percent of their potential—unless you prod them along. It is important to cultivate their curiosity level when they are very young. This is the one child that should rarely be kept in a playpen, for it is those early years, according to the experts, that ignite or stifle a child's curiosity, depending on whether he is free to inquire or confide. Like all children, they thrive on affection and do their best when gently but consistently pressured.

Child-training is almost a full-time vocation in the early years when a child needs what psychiatrist Harold Voth calls "mother constancy." That is why God gave children two parents—so one can be with them in those most formative years of life. Today's emphasis on working mothers (whether it is necessary or not) is destined to create a whole generation of rebellious or insecure young people. You don't have to be perfect or an expert parent to be a good parent, but parenting must be high on your priority list when your children are under ten. Ideally they will have one parent at home until they start working or playing sports after school.

For additional insight into good child-raising, see my wife's book *How to Develop Your Child's Temperament*.

The use and abuse of temperaments

Like any good concept, the temperament theory can be abused. It is not a cure-all for everything. And sometimes a person doesn't even fit into a temperament blend because his two temperaments are so evenly matched, or he may even have three temperaments. In addition, his childhood or lifetime experiences may have overemphasized or overdominated one temperament at the exclusion of the other. However, this theory is still the best tool for helping the largest number of people that has ever been devised.

Unfortunately, some people abuse this tool, which causes some to turn against it before giving it careful consideration. Here are the three most common ways of abusing the theory.

1. As a psyhological club to bludgeon their friends. One of the things that has turned more people against this theory than anything else is the thoughtless individuals who publicly humiliate their friends by analyzing them, with special emphasis on the negative characteristics. Parents can do this with devastating harm to their children.

I rarely tell a person what temperament I think he is even when he asks—and never do I tell him in public. Not that any temperament is a shame or should be, but no one likes to be stripped psychologically bare in public. Use it for self-help and understanding or to improve your relations with others, but never use it like a club. You may evoke laughter, but whether you know it or not, you will also evoke pain.

2. *As an excuse to indulge your weaknesses.* Improvement is what this book is all about—self-improvement, that is. But if you condone your temperament-induced weaknesses by saying, "It's because of my temperament," you're hopeless. It may be that your temperament makes you a twenty-four-hour-a-day nonstop talker. But you can improve—*if* you face that weakness and summon God's help to gain a quiet spirit. You may be a dominant compulsive, but don't say, "I'm a choleric melancholy and can't change." You're right—you can't because you *won't.* God can induce you though, with a hefty dose of compassion, much to the relief of your friends. But you must let him.

And don't think that because you're a melancholy, you have to go through life nitpicking everyone else, criticizing others, and making yourself depressed by indulging in self-pity. God can give you joy, peace, love, and a gracious spirit—if you want it.

Or if you happen to be a phlegmatic, don't sit around and let your life slip by because it takes too much effort to get out of your easychair: And don't excuse your passivity by saying, "That's the way I am." You have many positive traits; concentrate on those, and force yourself to be available to God to help other people. You will like the results better.

3. *To categorize everyone you meet.* While it is true, we all have a temperament combination, it is no service to you or other people to always think of them in the light of their temperament. In the first place, snap decisions can be wrong; and in the second place, you may forget the person while concentrating on his temperament. One thing we all need to develop is a sincere interest in and love for other people. Just as we learn to love and accept people regardless of their looks or physical characteristics, we need to learn to get acquainted with people regardless of their temperaments.

Our Lord looked into the *heart* of Nicodemus, Andrew, and others, not just their outer shell. While we do not have his divine ability to see the heart as it really is, we can learn to see the real person that is often shrouded by physical characteristics and temperament. The Bible speaks of "the hidden man of the heart." That is the real person—get to know him.

The proper use of the temperament theory

There are many good uses for the temperament theory that far outweigh any dangers or misuse the tool can be put to. We have already spent a whole chapter on these, but let me summarize this book by listing the three I think are the most important.

1. Self-acceptance. This theory helps you come to grips with who you are in the framework that exposes the fact that everyone has strengths and weaknesses.

2. Self-improvement. Once you have examined your weaknesses and understand why you act the way you do, you are better able to call upon God for his resources to improve your temperament by strengthening your weaknesses.

3. Understanding and accepting others. As long as you live, you will be confronted by people. When you understand why they do what they do, it is easier to accept and love them.

It is my sincere desire and prayer that reading this book is helping you in all three of the above uses of this theory. If it has, we will both be pleased.

In the event you are a teacher of these principles and would like to order a set of the overhead transparencies that go with it as a handy aid to communication, just write my office. Or if you have a specific question on temperament that is not answered in this book, please send it to me and I will include it in my next book on this subject.

In the meantime, I recommend taking the LaHaye Temperament Analysis as a very valuable help in further improving your temperament.

FOUR

TEMPERAMENT AND YOUR EMOTIONS

9

HOW TO DEAL WITH FEAR AND ANGER

"What you are emotionally is what you are!" may be too strong a statement to be true, but it's close. We are all such emotional creatures that our emotions can influence every area of our lives—for good or bad. I have noticed that whenever our emotions conflict for a length of time with any other area of our being, they eventually triumph.

Consider the power of emotion to influence the other three most important areas of life—mind, will, and body. No matter how intelligent a person is, when he gets emotionally upset he cannot think in an orderly fashion. Emotions can break his concentration and stifle his creativity. Some people's minds are totally dominated by their emotions. I well recall a professional scholar who had achieved world recognition at the age of twenty-seven. But his bad marriage kept him so distraught, fluctuating between anger and depression, that he squandered his potential and retired with less prestige and position than he had at twenty-seven.

Everyone has had the experience of letting their emotions impair their judgment. How often have you asked, "Why did I buy that car, house, dress, etc.?" You knew better, but you did it anyway. You made an emotional decision. I wish I had a dollar for all the people who asked, "Why did I marry him? We have nothing in common." Now you can see why I say all emotionally made decisions are bad decisions. The good life is one in which your mind controls your emotions, never vice versa.

The same, however, is true of your will. I don't care how strong-willed you are, if conflict between your will and your emotions lasts long enough, your emotions will win. That's why the Bible tells us to "flee youthful lusts" and sins. Our emotions are particularly powerful between the ages of fourteen and twenty-four. That is why the devil uses society, education, drugs, friends, and amusements on our young people during those years. He knows how vulnerable they are to making bad lifetime decisions when they are most emotionally combustible.

Physically it is the same. Doctors tell us that 65-80 percent of all illnesses are emotionally induced. What do they mean by that? Very simply, most people in our country ruin or break down their health long before necessary by indulging bad emotions for long periods of time. Good emotions seem to have a healthful effect on us; bad emotions destroy us. The Bible says, "A cheerful heart is good medicine, but a crushed spirit dries up the bones" (Prov. 17:22, NIV).

Two emotional culprits

All of us experience many emotions during our lifetime. But in my opinion they all stem from two basic roots—anger and fear. Fear was the first emotion to surface in the Bible after the fall. Adam said, "I was afraid" because he had disobeyed God. Since then billions have known guilt-induced fears, plus many other forms it takes. Anger caused the first family quarrel, which resulted in murder as you may recall, when Cain became "wroth" (a heart filled with anger) at his brother Abel and killed him.

Throughout the Bible there are literally hundreds of illustrations of the harmful effects of fear and anger. And there are hundreds of biblical admonitions to "fear not," "let not your heart be troubled," and "cease from anger." God knew that fear and anger feed on all mankind, working relentlessly toward our destruction or limiting our potential. Additionally, the Bible offers many antidotes to these two emotional cripplers.

These emotions and actions stem from the basic problem of fear. Some counselors spend too much time dealing with these symptoms rather than the basic cause. I am convinced that if we can help a person overcome his tendency to fear, he will automatically solve these other problems.

Perceptive questioners after my seminars have asked, "Why do you associate the emotions of anger and fear with your teachings on both the four temperaments and marriage and the family?" The answer is, anger and fear in their many forms are the most significant causes of limiting the strengths of a person's temperament and also are the principal causes of breakdown in marriage and the family.

In addition, I teach that the way to overcome your temperament weaknesses is to be filled with the Spirit. The Bible warns us against quenching the work of the Holy Spirit in our lives through "fear" (1 Thess. 5:16-19) and against "grieving the Spirit" through "anger" (Eph. 4:30-32). Anyone who doesn't quench the Spirit through fear or grieve the Spirit through anger walks in the Spirit as God commands us all to live (Gal. 5:16-18). For that reason we should examine carefully the relation between our inherited temperament and the emotional sin that so easily besets us.

The emotional predispositions of the temperaments

There is a sense in which all human beings experience fear and anger. But I have found that most people have a "besetting sin" tendency or what I call a temperament predisposition. That is, certain temperaments have a predisposition toward one emotional sin more than another. Its influence on their lives, of course, will depend on their second temperaments, their background, training, and of course their motivation. (To me, motivation means whether they do or do not have the Holy Spirit in their life to motivate them.)

As a pastor-counselor for many years, I specialized in helping fearful, angry and depressed people. It wasn't until later, when marital breakdown became so prevalent, even in that church, that I began to specialize in marriage counseling. Anyway, long before I learned anything about the four temperaments, I realized that the two cripplers of my counselees were fear and anger. It got so that before I opened my counseling room door and found a man or woman to be counseled, I knew in advance they were either fearful or angry. The only exceptions to that rule were those few people I met who had both problems.

When I read *Temperament and the Christian Faith* by the Norwegian theologian O. Hallesby, it fell open to me like an overripe melon. I saw that two of the temperaments had a predisposition for fear and two leaned toward anger. In the twenty years since then, I have researched everything I could find on the subject of temperament. I have tested over 6,000 people and studied thousands of counselees. And nothing has occurred to change that first impression. All melancholies and phlegmatics have a fear tendency, and all cholerics and sanguines have an anger tendency. Consider the chart on page 387 and the other emotional problems that stem from these basic emotions.

Fear is the paralyzing emotion that inhibits or restricts normal feelings of love, confidence, and well-being. It triggers negative thought patterns, breeding anxiety, worry, and the other emotions listed, which can multiply like a giant snowball and consume a person's entire life.

The chart on page 388 is used by permission of Dr. Jay Adams, from his excellent book *Competent to Counsel.* It shows the entire cycle of life activities. Now notice the next diagram which shows fear, worry, and anxiety at the core of a person's thinking. You can see how it reaches into every area of a person's life. Fear is not related only to one area of your life, like your vocation or profession. Fear is to your emotions what cancer of the blood is to your body; it invades the total person.

Everyone will face fear the first time he does anything dangerous in life; there is nothing new about that. Everyone is nervous or afraid when facing the trauma of driving a car, motorcycle, or airplane, or diving off a high diving platform, etc. That is normal fear. But those who let their fears inhibit them from attempting whatever they would like to do or should do have crossed the line from normal fears to destructive fears. The key as to which kind of fear it is seems to be whether we let our fears keep us from doing God's will.

Having acknowledged that everyone experiences fear, worry, and anxiety, it should be pointed out that some people have a greater problem with it than others. And the differences can be detected in early childhood. Watch the children in your next Sunday school program. That can be the most terrifying experience your child will have all year if he has a predisposition toward fear or if the prospect of getting up before a group terrifies him. If singing and giving a speech petrify him, that is fear. Some children, the sanguines and

Sanguine			Choleric	Melancholy			Phlegmatic

ANGER

Bitterness	Intolerance	Jealousy
Malice	Criticism	Attack
Clamor	Revenge	Gossip
Envy	Wrath	Sarcasm
Resentment	Hatred	Unforgiveness
	Seditions	

FEAR

Worry	Withdrawal	Suspicion
Anxiety	Loneliness	Depression
Timidity	Overaggression	Hesitancy
Indecision	Doubts	Haughtiness
Superstition	Inferiority	Shyness
	Cowardice	

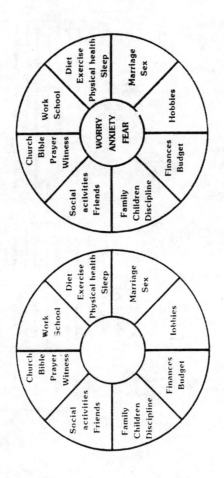

cholerics, love it or at least are not afraid of what others see them do or what others think of them. Not so with the melancholy and the phlegmatic. Those temperaments, since they are afraid to leave their mothers, as children they're afraid of getting hurt or being abandoned, and as teens they fear rejection by their peers much more acutely than do cholerics and sanguines.

I have pondered a great deal about the difference between the fears of the melancholy and those of the phlegmatic without coming to much of a conclusion. In many ways they are the same fears and have the same ill effects, except that the fears of the melancholy seem more intense and have a more inhibiting influence on him. Phlegmatics let fear inhibit their activities, but they don't get so upset over the incident. Melancholies who fear flying break out in a cold sweat, can't eat, and can't sleep even thinking about it. The phlegmatic just sets his stubborn jaw and says, "I don't want to go."

Vocationally, the phlegmatic is extremely security conscious. Whenever an opportunity comes up offering a choice between high pay and security, the phlegmatic will choose security. The melancholy can hardly make the choice. Both are driven by fear. Melancholies rarely change professions—it's too scary. Phlegmatics are easier to persuade to do something new than melancholies, but the new venture must offer more security than the present position. I suspect that one reason so many melancholies spend their lifetime in academic pursuits is because they feel secure there, having spent eighteen or so of their first twenty-three years of life there. (Admittedly, they are highly intelligent also.)

The fears of the melancholy that make him insecure about himself are also more intense than those of a phlegmatic. Somehow, even though the mild-mannered phlegmatic has a difficult time feeling capable enough to aggressively pursue something he wants or needs, his fear is not as intense as the melancholy who rejects himself and his abilities. Melancholies seem more self-centered than phlegmatics, so that compounds their fears. A self-centered person worries about everything, even his worry. One melancholy woman told me, "I suppose you noticed that I didn't take communion today. It was because I confessed all my sins, but I'm afraid there must be one or two sins I forgot." While we may admire her spiritual consciousness, we are appalled at her fears of displeasing God. No wonder these people are so sad. "An anxious heart weighs a man down" (Prov. 12:25, NIV).

Even the "fear of the Lord" becomes a pathetic fear—to such an extent that it can interfere with love for God. The Bible mentions hundreds of times that the righteous should "fear the Lord." That is not the same fear as worry, anxiety, and dread. You can't love someone you feel that way about. The word for "fear" as an attitude toward God means "revere, reverence, and special honor." The only people that should "fear" (dread) God are those who disobey him. If we love him, we obey him; and if we obey him, it is because we "revere" or "honor" him. These are not the same thing. Melancholies and some phlegmatics have a difficult time telling the difference, and it tends to cripple their spiritual lives.

The major difference that I can detect between the fears of the melancholy and those of the phlegmatic is that the melancholy's fears are more intense, last longer, occupy more of his thinking, and inhibit his life more. While the phlegmatic is a worrier and prone to limit himself by his fears, he has a relatively happy outlook on life and can forget his fears as soon as he returns to a more familiar place in life.

The results of fear

Fear is a cruel taskmaster which inhibits every area of one's life. To those in its grip, fear becomes the most powerful force in their life and it affects everything they do. The following are only part of the expensive toll it extracts.

1. *The emotional results of fear.* Every year countless thousands of individuals fall into mental and emotional collapse because of fear. Electric shock treatments and insulin shock treatments are becoming more and more common as forms of treatment to patients suffering from the tyrannical force of fear. Many a fearful person draws into a shell and lets life pass him by, never experiencing the rich things that God has in store for him, simply because he is afraid. The tragedy of it all is that most of the things he fears never happen. A young businessman addressing a sales company somehow came up with the figure that 92 percent of the things people fear will occur never take place. I cannot attest to the accuracy of his figure, but it is obvious in looking at anyone's life that the overwhelming majority of the things that cause our fear do not take place or are not nearly as severe as we thought they would be.

I counseled a woman who ten years before drove her husband from her because she was so emotionally upset due to fear. She became obsessed with the idea that another woman was going to take her husband away from her, and her emotionally upset mind caused such erratic and abnormal behavior in the home that she herself drove her husband away from her, though the "other woman" never existed.

The emotional cost of fear is very clearly seen in this statement by the late Christian physician Dr. S. I. McMillen: "About nine million Americans suffer from emotional and mental illness. As many hospital beds are filled by the mentally deranged as are occupied by all the medical and surgical patients combined. In fact, one out of every twenty Americans will have a psychotic disturbance severe enough to confine him in a hospital for the insane. Mental disease is indeed the nation's No. 1 health problem. What does it cost to take care of the patients in our mental hospitals? The annual cost is about one billion dollars. Besides, outside the asylums there are a vast number who do not need confinement but who are incapable of supporting themselves. They work little or not at all and constitute a great burden on the taxpayer." This cost does not include the heartache and confusion in the families from which these patients are admitted to sanitariums and asylums. Mothers and fathers are left to raise children singlehandedly, and children often go untrained or uncared for as a result of emotional illness of one parent or the other.

2. *The social results of fear.* The social results of fear are perhaps the easiest to bear, but it is difficult nonetheless. Fear-dominated individuals do not make enjoyable company. Their pessimistic and complaining spirit causes them to be shunned and avoided, thus further deepening their emotional disturbances. Many otherwise likeable and happy people are scratched off social lists and cause their companions to be equally limited simply because of ungrounded fears.

3. *The physical results of fear.* It is almost impossible to overestimate the harmful effects fear can have on one's physical body. In recent years doctors have called this dangerous cause for many of our physical maladies to our attention. The book that helped put this in perspective for me is *None of These Diseases* by S. I. McMillen. His thrust was essentially that Christians do not have

the same incidence of disease that non-Christians do because their emotions are better. I agree if we mean Spirit-controlled Christians. Obviously, a Christian whose emotions are love, joy, and peace is going to be much better off physically than one whose emotions battle fear, worry, and anxiety. The following diagram, reproduced from Dr. McMillen's book, shows the importance of the emotions to one's physical condition.

Notice how the emotion center (which the Bible calls "the heart") is neurologically tied in with all the vital organs of the body. Although the body can sustain an enormous amount of abuse, tension over a long period of time will eventually cause it to break down. Everyone seems to have his own tolerance level. In fact, some think every human being has his own point of least resistance—that is, a point which is most vulnerable to protracted stress. For some, an emotional upset will cause a breakdown in the kidneys, to others it might be their gallbladder, to others their colon or any of the fifty-one diseases listed by Dr. McMillen. Wherever it is, protracted stress caused by fear, worry, or anxiety will find it and the person will experience anything from high blood pressure to heart attacks, from gallstones to arthritis.

The sex drive is a good example of emotional effects on a person's physical body. Few things are more powerful than the sex drive; yet both men and women can be rendered inoperative sexually by fear. Fear of pregnancy, injury, or discovery can render a normal woman frigid. Fear of rejection or feared inability to perform can make a normal man impotent. Fear feeds on itself and causes physical maladies, which in turn increase one's fears. It is a vicious circle.

Other diseases mentioned by Dr. McMillen are high blood pressure, heart trouble, kidney disease, goiter, arthritis, headaches, strokes, and most of the same fifty-one illnesses which he listed as caused by anger. In illustrating the effect of fear upon the human heart, he quotes Dr. Roy R. Grinker, one of the medical directors of Michael Reese Hospital in Chicago: "This doctor states that anxiety places more stress on the heart than any other stimulus, including physical exercise and fatigue." Dr. McMillen points out that fear causes a chemical reaction to take place in the human body, as when the saliva seems to be drained from our mouth as we stand up in a speech class to speak. Such a reaction does not harm a person, because it is short-lived, but that type of experience indulged in

EMOTIONAL CONTROL
OF PHYSICAL ORGANS

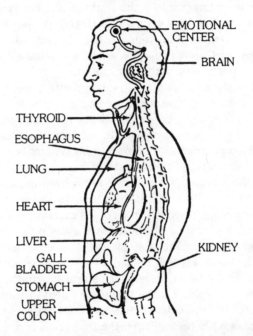

EMOTIONAL
CENTER

BRAIN

THYROID

ESOPHAGUS

LUNG

HEART

LIVER

GALL
BLADDER

STOMACH

UPPER
COLON

KIDNEY

ULCERS OF STOMACH AND INTESTINE
COLITIS
HIGH BLOOD PRESSURE
HEART TROUBLE
STROKES
ARTERIOSCLEROSIS

KIDNEY DISEASE
HEADACHES
MENTAL DISTURBANCES
GOITER
DIABETES
ARTHRITIS

hour after hour because of fear can cause physical damage to the body.

A doctor friend explained it to me in this way. We have an automatic alarm bell system that rings whenever we are confronted with an emergency. If the doorbell rings at 2:00 A.M., you are awakened suddenly and in complete control of your faculties, no matter how sound a sleeper you happen to be. This is God's natural gift to the human being. What has happened is that your adrenal gland has been triggered by the fright of the emergency and has secreted adrenaline into your bloodstream, causing you to be immediately in control of all your faculties. In fact, you will probably be stronger and more mentally alert than normally so that you might adequately cope with the problem.

When I pastored a country church in South Carolina, one of the men of the congregation was speeding his expectant wife to the hospital. As they came down the muddy mountain road, the front of the car slipped into the ditch. In the face of the emergency his adrenal gland pumped adrenaline into his system; he leaped around in front of the car and literally slid it back up onto the road, got back into the car, and drove his wife to the hospital. The next day in the parking lot of the hospital he tried to prove to incredulous friends that he had lifted the front of his car, but to his amazement he could not budge it one inch. He used every ounce of energy and strength at his command, but the car would not move. What he didn't understand was that he had possessed supernormal strength because of his God-given emergency alarm system the night before that was not available for the parking lot demonstration.

My doctor friend explained that this does not cause any damage to the human body because after the emergency is over the adrenal gland settles down to its normal function and the bloodstream throws off the excessive adrenaline chemical with no ill effects. That is not the case, however, for the man who sits down at one o'clock in the afternoon to pay his bills and suddenly is overcome with fear because he does not have enough money in his checking account to pay for everything he owes. Hour after hour, as long as he worries, his adrenal gland is pumping adrenaline into his bloodstream, a process which can ultimately create much physical damage. This is sometimes the cause of excessive calcium deposits and sometimes produces the pain-racked bodies of arthritis sufferers.

I know a lovely Christian lady who has been afflicted with arthritis and was finally restricted by the disease to a wheelchair. She had had every medical treatment known to science and was finally told by her third arthritis specialist, "I'm sorry, Mrs. _____, but we can find nothing organically wrong with you. The cause of your arthritis is emotional." When I heard that analysis, my mind went back to my childhood when she was in perfect health. Even though we enjoyed going to her house for the delicious cookies that she baked, we referred to her as "the professional worrier." She worried about everything. She fretted over her husband's employment, yet he worked years for the same company and never knew a day without pay. She was apprehensive about the future of a daughter who today has a lovely home and six children. She was anxious about her weak, sickly son who grew up to be a six foot, four inch, 225-pound tackle for a Big Ten football team. I can hardly think of anything she didn't worry about, and all to no avail.

No wonder the Lord Jesus said in his sermon on the Mount, "Take no thought for your life, what ye shall eat, or what ye shall drink; nor yet for your body, what ye shall put on . . ." (Matthew 6:25). Literally, he said, "Take no anxious thought." The Holy Spirit also tells us, "Be careful [anxious] for nothing" (Phil. 4:6). Anxiety and worry which stem from fear cause untold physical suffering, limitations, and premature death not only to non-Christians, but also to Christians who disobey the admonition to "commit thy way unto the Lord; trust also in him" (Ps. 37:5).

One day I called upon what I thought was an older woman who was bedridden. I was amazed to find that she was fifteen to twenty years younger than I had estimated. She made herself old before her time by being a professional worrier. As gently and yet as truthfully as I could, I tried to show her that she should learn to trust the Lord and not worry about everything. Her reaction was so typical it bears repeating. With fire in her eye and a flash of anger in her voice she asked, "Well, someone has to worry about things, don't they?"

"Not if you have a heavenly Father who loves you and is interested in every detail of your life," I replied. But that dear sister didn't get the point. I hope you do!

Thank God we are not orphans! We live in a society that accepts the concept that we are the products of a biological accident and a long unguided process of evolution. That popular theory, which is rapidly falling into scientific disrepute, is not only incorrect but is enslaving mankind in a prisonhouse of physical torture due to fear. If you are a Christian, memorize Philippians 4:6-7. Then, every time you find yourself worrying or becoming anxious, pray. Thank God that you have a heavenly Father who is interested in your problems, and turn them over to him. Your little shoulders are not broad enough to carry the weight of the world or even your own family problems, but the Lord Jesus "is able to do exceeding abundantly above all that we ask or think" (Eph. 3:20).

How thrilled I was recently when a little girl in our Beginners Department quoted her memory verse for me. She said, "I learned in Sunday school today what God wants me to do with my problems. For he said, 'Casting all your care upon him; for he careth for you.' 1 Peter 5:7." Much of the physical suffering and consequent heartache, including financial difficulties, that occur in the average Christian home would be avoided if believers really acted upon that verse.

4. *The results of fear.* As already mentioned, fear quenches or stifles the Holy Spirit, and so keeps us from being effective in this life and steals many of our rewards in the life to come. Fear keeps us from being joyful, happy, radiant Christians, and instead makes us thankless, complaining, defeated Christians who are unfaithful. A fearful person is not going to manifest the kind of life that encourages a sinner to come to him and say, "Sir, what must I do to be saved?" If Paul and Silas had let their fears predominate, the Philippian jailer would never have been converted and we would not have the great salvation verse, Acts 16:31.

Fear keeps the Christian from pleasing God. The Bible tells us, "Without faith it is impossible to please God" (Heb. 11:6) The eleventh chapter of Hebrews, called the "Faith Chapter," names men whose biographies are given in sufficient detail throughout the Scriptures to establish that they represent all four of the basic temperament types. The thing that made these men acceptable in the sight of God is that they were not overcome by their natural weakness of either fear or anger, but walked with God by faith. Consider these four men, representative of the four temperament types: Peter the Sanguine, Paul the Choleric, Moses the Melancholy, and Abraham the Phlegmatic. It is difficult to find more dynamic illustrations of the power of God working in the lives of men than these four. "God is no respecter of persons." What he did to strengthen their weaknesses, he will do through his Holy Spirit for you!

You may be surprised to know that God used more fear-prone people than anger-prone in Bible times to serve him. That may be because the undisciplined or willful Christian has a harder time overcoming his rebellion than fear-prone people have in overcoming their fear. But be sure of this—all of those he used had to overcome their fears before they were usable by him. What he did for them, he will do for you. Remember, God is no respecter of persons. But before we consider how to overcome fear, we should examine what causes it.

What causes fear?

Because fear is such a universal experience of man and because most of the readers of this book will be parents who can help their children avoid this tendency, I would like to answer this question simply in layman's terms. There are at least eight causes of fear.

Temperament predisposition. The most significant reason people have a problem with fear is because of their inherited temperament. By this time you know which temperaments have the greatest problem with it. In a sense, all people have a predisposition to fear, due to sin in the human race and its subsequent guilt, and also due to the individual's temperament combination. Depending on the combination, of course, you will have either a strong or weak predisposition toward it. We have seen that MelPhlegs or Phleg-Mels will have the greatest problem with it. However, even the choleric will have *some* tendency toward fear by virtue of his identification with the human race, and also his secondary temperament can introduce an element of fear into him. Obviously Chlor-Sans would not be as fear-prone as ChlorMels or ChlorPhlegs, but all temperaments are going to have a tendency toward fear. It's just that some people have it more than others.

Childhood experiences may induce fear. Psychologists and psychiatrists agree that the basic needs of man are love, understanding, and acceptance. The most significant human thing that parents can do for their children, short of leading them to a saving knowledge of Jesus Christ, is to give them the warmth and security of parental love. This does not exclude discipline or the teaching of submission to standards and principles. In fact, it is far better for a child to learn to adjust to rules and standards in the loving atmosphere of his home than in the cruel world outside. There are, however, two specific parental habits I suggest you diligently avoid:

(1) Overprotection. An overprotective parent makes a child self-centered and fearful of the very things happening to him that his parent is afraid will happen. Children quickly learn to read our emotions. Their bodies can far more easily absorb the falls, burns, and shocks of life than their emotions can absorb our becoming tense, upset, or hysterical over these minor experiences. The fearful mother who forbids her son to play football probably does far more harm to his emotional development by her repeated suggestions of fear than the damage done to Junior if his front teeth were knocked out or his leg broken. Legs heal and teeth can be replaced, but it takes a miracle of God to remove the scar tissues of fear from our emotions.

(2) Domination. Angry, explosive parents who dominate the lives of their children or who critically pounce upon every failure in their lives often create hesitancy, insecurity, and fear in them. Children need correction, but they need it done in the proper spirit. Whenever we have to point out our children's mistakes, we should also make it a practice to note their strengths and good points, or at least criticize them in such a way as to let them know that they are still every bit as much the object of our love as they were before.

The more I counsel with people, the more convinced I am that the most devastating blow one human being can inflict upon another is *disapproval.* The more a person loves us, the more important it is for us to seek some area in his life where we can show our approval. A six-foot, two-inch husband in the midst of marriage counseling said rather proudly, "Pastor, I have never laid a hand on my wife in anger!" As I looked at his timid, cowering, 110-pound wife, I knew by the look in her eye what she was thinking: "Well, I would a thousand times rather that you beat me physically than constantly run me down and club me with disapproval."

The Spirit-filled parent is inspired through his loving compassionate nature to build others up and to show approval whenever possible. Even in the times of correction he will convey his love. To do otherwise with our children is to leave lasting fear scars on their emotions.

A traumatic experience. Child assault or molesting leaves a lasting emotional scar that often carries into adulthood, causing fear concerning the act of marriage. Other tragic experiences in childhood frequently set fear patterns into motion that last throughout life.

During the past few years our family has enjoyed some wonderful occasions waterskiing. The only member of the family that has not tried it is my wife, and she is deathly afraid of the water. I have begged her, encouraged her, and done everything I could to entice her to get over this fear of the water, but to no avail. Finally one summer I gave up. She made a Herculean attempt to overcome this fear by donning a wetsuit that could sustain her body in water. She then put on a life jacket, which also by itself could sustain her in water, and very hesitantly lowered herself over the side of the boat. The moment her hand left the security of the boat and she was floating freely in the water, I noted a look of terror in her eyes. For the first time I really understood how frightened she was of the water. Upon questioning her, I found that it all went back to a childhood experience in Missouri when she came within an eyelash of drowning. These experiences leave hidden marks on a person's emotions that often follow him through life. However, the Holy Spirit is able to overcome the effects of such an experience, as I shall point out a little further on.

A negative thinking pattern. A negative thinking pattern or defeatist complex will cause a person to be fearful of attempting any new thing. The moment we start suggesting to ourselves "I can't, I can't, I can't," we are almost certain of failure. Our mental attitude makes even ordinary tasks difficult to perform when we approach them with a negative thought. Repeated failures or refusal to do what our contemporaries are able to accomplish often causes further breakdown in self-confidence and increases fear. A Christian need never be dominated by this negative habit. By memorizing Philippians 4:13 and seeking the Spirit's power in applying it, one can gain a positive attitude toward life.

Anger. Anger can produce fear. I have counseled with individuals who had indulged bitterness and anger until they erupted in such explosive tirades that they afterward admitted, "I'm afraid of what I might do to my own child."

Sin produces fear. "If our heart condemn us not, then have we confidence toward God" (1 John 3:21) is a principle that cannot be violated without producing fear. Every time we sin, our conscience reminds us of our relationship to God. This has often been misconstrued by psychiatrists who blame religion for creating guilt complexes in people which, they say, in turn produces fear. A few years ago our family doctor, who at that time was not a Christian, made the following statement to me: "You ministers, including my saintly old father, do irreparable damage to the emotional life of men by preaching the gospel." I questioned his reason for such a statement and he said, "I took my internship in a mental institution, and the overwhelming majority of those people had a religious background and were there because of fear induced by guilt complexes."

The next day I attended a ministers' meeting where Dr. Clyde Narramore, a Christian psychologist from Los Angeles, gave a lecture on pastoral counseling. During the question period I told him of the previous day's conversation and asked his opinion. Dr. Narramore instantly replied: "That is not true. People have guilt complexes because they are guilty!" The result of sin is a consciousness of guilt, and guilt causes fear in modern man just as it did to Adam and Eve in the Garden of Eden. A simple remedy for this is to walk in the way of the Lord.

Lack of faith. Lack of faith, even in a Christian's life, can produce fear. I have noticed in counseling that fear caused by lack of faith is basically confined to two common areas.

The first is fear concerning the sins of the past. Because the Christian does not know what the Bible teaches in relationship to confessed sin, he has not come to really believe that God has cleansed him from all sin (1 John 1:9). Some time ago I counseled with a lady who was in such a protracted period of fear that she had sunk into a deep depression. We found that one of her basic problems was that she was still haunted by a sin committed eleven years before. All during this time she had been a Christian, but had gone through a complete emotional collapse, haunted by the fear of that past sin.

When I asked if she had confessed that sin in the name of Jesus Christ, she replied, "Oh, yes, many times." I then gave her a spiritual prescription: to make a Bible study of all Scripture verses that deal with the forgiveness of sins. When she came back into my office two weeks later, she was not the same woman. For the first time in her life she really understood how God regarded her past sin, and when she began to agree with him that it was "remembered no more," she got over that fear.

A man I counseled who had a similar problem gave me a slightly different answer when I asked, "Have you confessed that sin to Christ?" "Over a thousand times," was his interesting reply. I told him that was 999 times too many. He should have confessed it once and thanked God 999 times that he had forgiven him for that awful sin. The Word of God is the cure for this problem, because "Faith cometh by hearing, and hearing by the word of God" (Rom. 10:17).

The second area in which people are prone to be fearful because of lack of faith concerns the future. If the devil can't get them to worry about their past sins, he will seek to get them to worry about God's provision in the future, and thus keep them from enjoying the riches of God's blessing today. The psalmist has said, "This is the day which the Lord hath made; we will rejoice and be glad in it" (Ps. 118:24). People who enjoy life are not dreading tomorrow or worrying about the past; they are living today.

Anyone who thinks about the potential problems and difficulties he might encounter tomorrow will naturally become fearful, unless he has a deep, abiding faith in God's ability to supply all his needs. My wife shared with me a very beautiful saying she heard which bears repeating: "Satan tries to crush our spirit by getting us to bear tomorrow's problems with only today's grace."

If you are worrying about tomorrow, you can't possibly enjoy today. The interesting thing is that you can't give God tomorrow; you can only give him what you have, and you have today. Dr. Cramer quoted a comment by Mr. John Watson in the *Houston Times* which read: "What does your anxiety do? It does not empty tomorrow of its sorrow, but it empties today of its strength. It does not make you escape the evil; it makes you unfit to cope with it if it comes."

Habit can intensify fear. Never underestimate the power of habit to intensify any negative force, particularly an emotion such as fear. Anything you do frequently becomes easier to do the next time. A fearful person creates a deeply ingrained habit of responding to every difficult or different circumstance in life with fear. It becomes what psychologists call "a conditioned response." Each time a certain condition occurs, he becomes fearful. Such conditioning can make people lifetime servants of fear unless the Lord is allowed to come into their lives and empower them so that fear does not rule them for life.

Once a link in this fear chain is broken, it is easier to break it again, and so on until the "conditioned response" is broken completely and a new habit is begun, the facing of that same condition with faith instead of fear. Victory over one fear increases one's faith to try overcoming others, and a new life cycle based on faith can begin. As we shall see, faith is built one step at a time.

Now I think you are about ready to face the primary cause of fear. The above eight causes of fear are only contributing factors. The basic cause of fear is . . .

Selfishness. As much as we don't like to face this ugly word, it is a fact nonetheless. We are fearful because we are selfish. Why am I afraid? Because I am interested in self. Why am I embarrassed when I stand before an audience? Because I don't wish to make a fool of myself. Why am I afraid I will lose my job? Because I am afraid of being a failure in the eyes of my family or not being able to provide my family and myself with the necessities of life. Excuse it if you will, but all fear can be traced basically to the sin of selfishness.

Don't be a turtle

A Christian woman went to a Christian psychologist and asked, "Why am I so fearful?" He asked several questions: "When you enter a room, do you feel that everyone is looking at you?" "Yes," she said. "Do you often have the feeling your slip is showing?" "Yes." When he discovered she played the piano he asked, "Do you hesitate to volunteer to play the piano at church for fear someone else can do so much better?" "How did you know?" was her reply. "Do you hesitate to entertain others in your home?" Again she said, "Yes." Then he proceeded to tell her kindly that she was a very selfish young woman. "You are like a turtle," he said. "You pull into your shell and peek out only as far as necessary. If anyone gets too close, you pop your head back inside your shell for protection. That shell is selfishness. Throw it away, and start thinking more about others and less about yourself."

The young lady went back to her room in tears. She never thought of herself as selfish, and it crushed her when she was confronted with the awful truth. Fortunately she went to God, and he has gradually cured her of that vicious sin. Today she is truly a "new creature." She entertains with abandon, has completely thrown off the old "shell," and consequently enjoys a rich and abundant life.

Who wants to be an oyster?

A similar statement is made by Dr. Maltz in his book *Psycho-Cybernetics*: "One final word about preventing and removing emotional hurts. To live creatively, we must be willing to be a little vulnerable. We must be willing to be hurt a little, if necessary, in creative living. A lot of people need a thicker and tougher emotional skin than they have. But they need only a tough emotional hide or epidermis, not a shell. To trust, to love, to open ourselves to emotional communication with other people is to run the risk of being hurt. If we are hurt once, we can do one of two things. We can build a thick protective shell, or scar tissue, to prevent being hurt again, live like an oyster, and not be hurt. Or we can 'turn the other cheek,' remain vulnerable and go on living creatively.

"An oyster is never 'hurt.' He has a thick shell which protects him from everything. He is isolated. An oyster is secure but not creative. He cannot 'go after' what he wants, he must wait for it to come to him. An oyster knows none of the 'hurts' of emotional communication with his environment, but neither can an oyster know the joys."

How to overcome fear

You can learn to live without fear, worry, and anxiety. The key is to learn to live by faith. We will now illustrate how replacing fear with faith will change your whole life and set you free. Instead of being uptight and negative when faced with a challenge, you can appraise all life situations with confidence. This is a blessing which God has offered all of his children. Unfortunately, many have not taken advantage of it.

Through the years as a counselor I have developed a simple but very workable step-by-step procedure for overcoming worry and fear. We know it's possible, for our Lord said, "Do not be anxious about anything" (Phil. 4:6, NIV; cf. Matt. 6). If you have a problem with fear, memorize these steps and follow them *daily.*

 Face your fear reactions as sin (Rom. 14:23). "Everything that does not come from faith is sin" (NIV). Remember, it is not unusual to feel fear or apprehension when you do a scary thing, particularly for the first time. But if your fear keeps you from doing what you should, or if the fear absorbs your thoughts for a period of time, it is wrong.

Don't justify fear! As one woman said, "If you had my background you would be afraid, too." To which I said, "You may be right, but all that would prove is that we are both wrong." Those who will not face fear as a sin but try to excuse or justify it are incurable. Instead, look objectively at your fear; admit it is sin and that God does not want you to be dominated by it.

Confess your fear as a sin (1 John 1:9). God is in the sin removal business. That is why he sent his Son to die on the cross for us, that his Son might "cleanse us from all sin" (1 John 1:7). After you have confessed it, thank him for his cleansing and go on your way rejoicing.

Ask God to take away the habit of fear (1 John 5:14-15). "This is the assurance we have in approaching God: that if we ask anything according to his will, he hears us. And if we know that he hears us—whatever we ask—we know that we have what we asked of him" (NIV).

We have already seen that fear is a habit that God does not want to rule over you. This verse promises not only victory over that sin, which is contrary to his will, but also promises to give you the "assurance." He will give victory.

Ask for the filling of the Holy Spirit (Luke 11:23). "He who is not with me is against me, and he who does not gather with me, scatters."

Some Bible scholars tell us that step four is not necessary. That the minute we confess our sins in Jesus' name we are refilled by his Spirit. And they may be right (though I have not seen any Scripture to justify that claim). But personally I like to make sure. God won't be upset at us if we ask unnecessarily. Since Jesus told his disciples to ask for the Holy Spirit, I see no problem asking for his filling even though he is already inside me. Frankly, I ask several times a day.

Thank him by faith for victory over fear (1 Thess. 5:18). "Give thanks in all circumstances, for this is God's will for you in Christ Jesus."

Thank God verbally as an act of faith which appropriates the experience and makes it real.

Repeat! Repeat! Repeat! Repeat that formula every time you become fearful and *gradually* it will no longer dominate you. One of the greatest misconceptions of the Spirit-controlled life is that it is an experience we have that lasts for life. That is neither biblical nor possible! If you are a fearful person, you may be excited to read the above formula for conquering fear. (I hope you are.) The problem is, you try it once and have deliverance for two or three hours and then get discouraged because your fears return.

Don't forget the habit factor. How old are you? That is how long you have had a temperament-induced tendency to be fearful and turn it into a lifetime habit. That habit won't vanish immediately; with God's help you can have victory, but it will come *gradually*. Each time you become fearful, face your sin, ask forgiveness, ask to be refilled, and thank him by faith that you are. You have broken one more strand of the rope of habit that has bound you in its grip. Gradually you will see your former fears lose their power over you.

A classic illustration

Fear was not my personal problem, as I will confess in a later chapter. Anger was my "thing." But typical of "opposites attract in marriage," the woman I love was a very fearful minister's wife until God filled her life by his Holy Spirit and she tried this formula. Since then, I have watched that sweet fearful lady, too afraid to speak to a handful of women in our church, blossom into a full-blown rose of personality that still amazes me. If you had told me she would learn to speak to large audiences, head the largest women's organization in America, take an aggressive stand against secular humanists, feminists, and liberals, I would not have believed it—but I've seen it. Her life in these past seventeen years is a testimony to the power of God to give a person victory over an emotional tyrant.

In her book *Spirit-Controlled Woman*, Bev has told her story. Here is how she said it. And remember, I saw it and testify that these things are true:

"Unlike many couples, my husband and I were filled with the Spirit in the same week and began the process of change. Previous to being filled with the Spirit, I had limited my ministry to working with children under the sixth grade. Gradually I began accepting speaking opportunities with women's groups and even mixed audiences in our Family Life Seminars. Today I am speaking to large women's groups all the time with my organization Concerned Women for America.

"After making so much progress in conquering this fear of speaking, the director of a mission board wrote to my husband to thank him for writing *Spirit-Controlled Temperament*, which he said was 'required reading for all our missionary trainees. There is just one problem with it. You tell how God delivered your wife from her fear of public speaking, but later admit she couldn't join you and the rest of the family in water skiing because she was afraid of the water. The problem is that our nonswimming missionary candidates readily identify with her and use her as an excuse for not learning to swim, which could prove fatal to some of them.' He went on to graciously ask, 'Isn't the fear of water just as much a sin as the fear of anything else?'

"Tim had to get me the Kleenex box after hearing that one. Finally I decided he was right and decided to take action. I lined up a heated swimming pool and a phlegmatic instructor. Then, dressed in Tim's rubber wetsuit I strapped on a lifebelt and armed myself with the New Testament. Going into the water I would quote: 'I will never leave you nor forsake you,' and other verses on assurance of God's provision. Eventually I was able to discard the unnecessary paraphernalia and learned to swim. I will never be a U.S. Olympic candidate, but with God's help I conquered my terrible fear of water."

What God has done for Bev, he will do for you. If you have a problem with fear, anxiety, or worry, then follow these six steps to a transformed life.

10

FACING PRESSURE

"Man is born to trouble [pressure] as surely as sparks fly upward."
(Job 5:7, NIV)

Pressure is a part of life; no one escapes it. We are more conscious of it in this day of jet travel, computers, and frenetic activity than those who lived in farming communities fifty years ago. But no matter where you live or what you do in life you will experience pressure; it is inescapable.

The thing you need to know about pressure is that it isn't all bad. In fact, in many cases it is good for you. Without it you couldn't sustain life. Take your blood pressure as an example. If it is too high, it can kill you. But if it is too low the same thing can happen. Life without pressure would be empty and brief. You need pressure to provide not only life itself but motivation, variety, and activity.

In 1982-83 I went through the greatest pressure period of my life. After successfully pastoring churches for thirty years, I felt led of God to resign and launch a national television ministry. Instantly I was in pressure unlike anything I have ever known. I was unfamiliar with the field, had no base from which to operate, and found that television gobbles money faster than the federal government. God marvelously met my needs in those days of incredible pressure and inspired me to write *How to Manage Pressure Before Pressure Manages You*. In the process I discovered that all temperaments do not face pressure the same way. So I thought it wise in this book on temperament to include the different responses of the temperaments to this universal problem of mankind.

Sparky Sanguine facing pressure

Sanguines rarely get ulcers; we have already seen that they usually give them to everyone else. Since people are a major cause of pressure and sanguines love to be around people, they are never far from pressure, which usually they helped to create.

These light-hearted people are often very disorganized, generally arrive late for meetings, and are rarely prepared for whatever they are supposed to do. I have watched sanguine song leaders select the songs for an evening service while walking down the aisle of the church. Despite their lack of preparation, they usually do a creditable job because they exude so much charisma. Sanguines are such good actors and people-responders that they often do a better job on the platform than other temperaments who prepare carefully. One can't help but wonder how effective sanguines could be if they would only learn to plan for whatever lies ahead. Unfortunately, each time they get by with improvising under pressure, they learn that advance planning is not really crucial for success.

This could be the reason why sanguines are often "short-termers." That is, they run out of material after a time and must move on to their next job. Sanguine preachers, for example, usually stay in a church for only two or three years. Pressure tends to drive them to the golf course rather than to the study.

Because they are prone to be late, undependable, undisciplined, and unprepared, sanguines are never far from pressure. Can you visualize the personable, people-oriented homemaker who welcomes the neighbor in for a "fifteen-minute coffee klatsch," only to talk too long and discover that the party has ended only minutes before her husband is due home? She furiously whips through the house, trying frantically to set things in order for his arrival. Dinner is late, the house is a mess, and she is not prepared for his sarcastic insults; she lashes out in self-defense about her "overworked schedule" or "the pressures of three small children." Such reactions do little for a loving relationship.

Sanguines are quick of speech and often use their vocal chords to defend themselves when pressed. More aggressive types learn that in verbally attacking other people they can often intimidate them into submission, so they cover their mistakes by pressuring others. I know one sanguine who reminds me of the Saint Bernard dog we once had who after knocking me down at the front gate and breaking my glasses, put both paws on my shoulders and licked my face. Even though you are right in a disagreement with a sanguine, he will attack you and bluster; and when you leave, you have failed to confront him with the problem. In fact, he has made you feel that it was all your fault for bringing up the matter in the first place.

Women sanguines are often screamers. That is, their frustration is never far from the surface, so they scream at their children, husband, neighbor, or whoever is near. Male sanguines tend to talk too loudly, making demands or speaking more dogmatically than their grasp of the facts would allow. If one gives a sanguine enough rope, he will usually hang himself verbally.

One of the most uncomplimentary tendencies of a sanguine under pressure is his difficulty in honestly taking the blame for his mistakes. Because he commands a giant ego, needs the love and admiration of others, and lacks discipline, it is easy for him to pass the buck, blame others for his mistakes, and in some cases lie to get out of a trap. This is why parents of sanguine children need to concentrate on teaching them self-discipline and truth-telling. Otherwise they will develop a flexible conscience.

Some sanguines resort to weepy repentance when confronted with the pressure caused by their unkempt ways. Such repentance is usually short-lived; the sanguine has learned little or nothing from the experience.

Sanguines are easily intimidated by more forceful, cruel personalities. I have seen many highly emotional wives, with tremendous capabilities to love and be loved, become distraught because their husband cold-bloodedly used their quest for self-acceptance to brow-beat them into taking the blame for anything that goes wrong. It always pains me to hear a woman cry, "I know it is all my fault," when that is rarely the case. One woman was intimidated into accepting her husband's infidelity because he convinced her she was inadequate in bed; actually he acted immorally because he was sinful.

Lying never solves anything. The Bible enjoins us, "Speak every man truth with his neighbor" (Eph. 4:25). It takes sanguines a long time to learn that it is much easier to face those unpleasant pressures of life squarely, take full responsibility for mistakes, and then do two things: (1) solve the present difficulty; and (2) learn from the experience.

Most sanguines cannot endure emotional pressure very long. They will start talking, tell an unrelated joke, or run away from the problem. An example of this occurred in the rental car of a nationally famous minister in January 1980. Twelve of us had breakfast with former President Carter and asked several questions: Why did he not oppose abortion? Why had he endorsed the Equal Rights Amendment in view of the harm it would do to the family? Why did he refuse to support a voluntary school prayer amendment for our public schools? Five of us drove out of the White House grounds in deep silence. I was very depressed by what I had heard, and so were the others. Suddenly the most sanguine of the group split the silence with an unrelated and rather bizarre joke. He was reacting naturally to the emotional pressures that he felt at the moment.

As we have noted, sanguines often give ulcers to others because they will not face their problems and do something constructive about them. A sanguine manager, administrator, or minister, for instance, has an interesting way of trying to solve personal problems. If he senses another's displeasure, he will tactfully take him out for coffee, lunch, or an evening of entertainment. He will rarely discuss the problem, preferring to use his charismatic charm to disarm his friend's hostility or displeasure. He leaves that encounter feeling that he has solved his problem, whereas in reality he has only delayed judgment-day for a while. As a husband he will bring home a "peace offering" or "take the family out to dinner" to solve a problem. But as you know, that only relieves the immediate pressure; it does not really change anything. If only he would face issues realistically and do something about them, he would reduce most of his life pressures.

Because sanguines cannot tolerate the discomfort of pressure, they always react in some way—an explosive outburst, tears, jokes, lies, change of subject, or "fellowship." They cannot suffer pressure in silence. Fortunately their happy disposition easily forgets unpleasant circumstances; the first moving object or person that catches their eye gains their attention, and they mentally or physically separate themselves from the cause of their pressure temporarily. If sanguines could learn to use pressure as motivation toward problem-solving, their lives would be greatly enriched, and I believe they would be 25 to 50 percent more successful in their chosen fields.

Cholerics under pressure

No one can create more pressure than a choleric. He thrives on it—until his body breaks down with ulcers, high blood pressure, heart attack, or other physical adversities.

Some of the choleric's high pressure quotient is occasioned by his "god complex." Perhaps it would be better to label it an "omnipotence complex." Cholerics are always overinvolved. They are willing to tackle anything that needs to be done. They never ask, "Why doesn't someone else do something about this?" To almost any need they respond, "Let's get organized and put the troops to work!" Then they start barking orders to others.

Cholerics rarely get depressed when a project fails because they have thirty other irons in the fire to keep their overly active minds occupied. Instead of wallowing in self-pity over an insult, failure, or rejection, they busy themselves with their next project.

However, this penchant for taking on more than anyone could possibly accomplish often proves to be the cause of greatest pressures. Cholerics are extremely goal-oriented, but unless their secondary temperament is melancholy, they will not be adept at planning, analyzing, and detailing. In fact, they usually don't like it. Cholerics are doers. Consequently they may rush into battle before establishing a plan of attack, thus creating a great deal of pressure.

Many of the frenetic activities of the choleric should be put on a back burner. He is successful in the business world, not because his ideas are so well designed, but because he launches them while others are still determining theirs. Some of his better notions die on the drawing board, for a choleric has usually implemented his ideas and projects before he realizes that a better way exists. However, dogged determination stands him in good stead, for he usually finishes what he starts.

The choleric typically responds to pressure by refusing to give up. When he encounters an impossible situation, he glibly retorts, "Nothing is impossible." A choleric I know contends, "I never take no for an answer unless I hear it eight or ten times." Even then he is apt to press doggedly onward. Pressure discourages some people, but not the choleric; it simply serves as grist for his mill. Thriving on opposition, in some cases he will clench his teeth and press on regardless. At other times his creative mind will envision a crafty device to achieve his ends. It may not be legal, honest, or fair, but that doesn't always deter him.

Because of their penchant for adopting excessive loads and their natural inability to delegate responsibility, cholerics tend to take their extra time away from the family. Their ten-hour days soon increase to twelve and fifteen hours, the day off becomes another working day, and vacation time never seems to arrive. Consequently the family suffers.

Interpersonal relationships are not a choleric's strength, and work pressures compound this. He tends to be impatient with those less motivated than himself, critical and demanding of others, even unappreciative of people when they do well. If he is an employer, he usually experiences a high turnover at his place of business. His family members tend to give him a wide berth. Cruel and unkind by nature, he can be very cutting and sarcastic under pressure. Unless he seeks the help of God and walks in the Spirit, he will be prone to leave many damaged psyches and wounded egos in his wake. One choleric supervisor was reported to be "very productive, but leaves a trail of weepy subordinates." Gentle spirits should think twice before getting involved with cholerics.

The choleric's principal weapon is his tongue. No one can use it with greater dexterity and brutality. Because he enjoys pressure, he delights in heaping it upon others. His motto: "We do better under pressure."

Cholerics need to understand that there is more to life than money, success, or even accomplishment. Jesus said, "Man's life consists not in the things which he possesses" and "What shall it profit a man if he gain the whole world and lose his own soul?" (see Luke 12:15; Matt. 16:26). Mr. and Ms. Pressure-building Choleric may successfully launch projects, develop businesses, and construct churches—all to the benefit of others—but if such endeavors succeed at the expense of their relationship with spouse, children, parents, and others, "What shall it profit?"

In short, a choleric must establish the best priorities for his life and concentrate on them. A man without priorities may become engrossed in activities that may better have been left alone. The choleric needs to set his priorities in this order:

1. God
2. Wife
3. Family
4. Vocation

Then he needs to establish clearly defined goals, rejecting creative ideas that do not contribute to the realization of these goals. He also must develop a love for people, learning to encourage others and become interested in them. His time spent on people will be returned to him multiplied, because others will extend themselves in appreciation, thus relieving him of many of his pressures.

Martin Melancholy under pressure

Like everyone else, melancholies face pressure in life. But because of their sensitive, creative, and perfectionistic ways, everything in life is intensified, especially pressure. Probably no temperament bears more pressure in his heart and mind than does the melancholy. This may be why his mortality rate is approximately seven years lower than that of other types.

We have already seen that one's mental attitude can increase or decrease realistic pressure. That is bad news for a melancholy. One of his biggest problems in life relates to his mental attitude. A perfectionist by nature, he is extremely negative, critical, and suspicious—as critical of himself as he is of others.

One of a melancholy's consistent pressures is his desire to do everything perfectly. While commendable to a point, this trait can become maddening to others, for he often spends an inordinate amount of time on trivia or nonessentials at the neglect of more important matters. Sometimes he will neglect one assignment altogether until finishing a lesser project at 110 percent perfection level. Some melancholies cause pressure on their employer because they are perfection-oriented rather than production-oriented; consequently they don't produce enough to pay for their perfectionist productivity level.

Melancholy housewives and mothers are easily the best housekeepers and cooks. Dinner is always on time. But they may lack gracious flexibility. Woe to the child who tracks mud all over the freshly scrubbed kitchen floor! Or woe to the salesman husband who gets home late for dinner because he had to finalize that "big sale" at quitting time!

The melancholy's penchant for advance planning can drive the rest of the family off a cliff. Everything should be faithfully worried about! He often creates so much pressure contemplating and designing a vacation that all spontaneity and fun is eliminated.

Melancholies can worry themselves into pressure even when none exists. Most of the things they fear never materialize, but the pressure they build through worry is real. Such unnecessary fears often keep them from venturing out into something new, and as a result they build pressure through boredom, performing the same tasks repeatedly.

Since a melancholy person is predominantly an introvert, he will rarely externalize his pressures by angrily kicking things, swearing, or screaming—at first. His style is to internalize his pressure, comply with what is immediately expected of him, and mull it over until he gets himself so worked up that he lashes out in a manner totally out of character for him—anything from tears to murder. Some of the most vicious crimes committed by people with no criminal records have been accomplished by melancholies under intense pressure. Fortunately, few melancholies react in violence. Most say things of a cutting, hurtful nature for which they are later very repentant. Others ponder the problem and lapse into sulking silence.

Melancholy/cholerics—people who are predominantly melancholy with a secondary temperament of choleric—are the epitome of workaholics. They react to pressure with intensified work. Their choleric suggests new projects, and their melancholy tries to do everything perfectly. Such individuals are often frustrated by "the pressure of not getting anything done." Others can frustrate them, because they never quite measure up to melancholy perfectionism.

Everyone needs to deal with people by showing concern for them. Melancholies are usually so interested in themselves and their persistent brand of perfectionism that they have little sympathy for and acceptance of other fallible human beings. They would certainly attract more friends if they had more sensitivity. People interested in others never lack for friends.

Everyone needs a diversion—"All work and no play makes Jack a dull boy!"—but melancholies can become so work-oriented that they eat, sleep, and think work. Vacations make them feel guilty. The pressure of unfinished work makes it impossible for them to enjoy a simple game of golf. They can turn a relaxing walk through the park into a pressure-filled afternoon.

This inability to relax and learn to cope with the everyday pressures of life will ultimately lead to a breakdown emotionally, mentally, or physically. The melancholy's natural inability to cope with these problems by himself may account for the number of melancholies I have seen come to Christ, dedicate their lives to him, and learn to walk in the Spirit. When they are truly filled with the Spirit, they experience incredible changes that are immediately apparent to all. However, when they regress spiritually, their friends quickly sense the change. I have great respect for the potential of the person with a predominantly melancholy temperament, but only when he avails himself of the power of God. When he doesn't, his powerlessness is all too evident.

Even Phlegmatics face pressure

Phlegmatics detest pressure. In fact, they will do almost anything to avoid it. As we have seen, they do not thrive on controversy, but are peacemakers by nature. Consequently they will always steer around a problem if possible. Unfortunately, ignoring a real problem doesn't make it disappear.

It is easy to diagnose a sanguine's reaction to pressure, for he explodes loudly enough for everyone to see. Phlegmatics are different; as very internal people, they do nothing to excess. For this reason you must observe their responses carefully.

Their compulsion to avoid pressure causes many phlegmatics to become gifted procrastinators. This eventually increases their pressures, because tasks must be completed sooner or later and final decisions have to be made. Some phlegmatics use the old dodge, "We need more information," as an excuse for delaying an unpleasant deed. "Remove the pressure, not the problem" often becomes the phlegmatic way of life.

How well I remember three phlegmatics on a deacon board who appealed for "more time to study the matter" before deciding to expel a leader in the church who had divorced his wife of many years and married another woman. Actually he had made the mistake of marrying the second wife before his divorce was final, and the chapel inadvertently sent his new wedding certificate—signatures, dates, and all—to his home, where Wife #1 opened it. The man was a bigamist! Yet the phlegmatics wanted to delay one more month. Why? They rotated off the board before the next meeting.

Problems seldom vanish with time. Rather, they tend to return more robust and intimidating than before. I have found that it is usually best to solve them when they are still small enough to handle.

The phlegmatic under pressure frequently exhibits one exasperating trait: he flees from the pressured situation. Fathers of rebellious teenagers are likely to sneak out to the garage and putter in their workshop rather than take on their hostile youth. This does nothing for the wife, who laments, "He always leaves the discipline of the children up to me." Phlegmatic wives and mothers often are weak disciplinarians, not because they fail to recognize their children's need for discipline, but because they personally dislike the friction generated by confrontation. Many a phlegmatic employee puts up with years of second-rate treatment at work because he does not relish a confrontation with his boss. But "peace at any price" is not really a solution to anything.

Those who have lived with phlegmatics will acknowledge that they are stubborn. This stubbornness invariably surfaces when someone tries to pressure them into doing something they are unwilling to do. Like a burro, they will dig their feet in, arch their back, and stall. If they fill a place of authority, they can be maddening. Experts on trivia themselves, they can think of more reasons why a building permit or license should not be granted than ever occurred to those who made the laws. Have you ever tried to get something approved by the security-conscious inspectors at city hall? It is nothing short of amazing that the free enterprise system has succeeded in the face of phlegmatic foot-dragging.

Married phlegmatics are quite interesting sexually. A sexuality survey of 3,404 people included a question about temperament. I found that male phlegmatics were less promiscuous before marriage, registered less frequency of sex after marriage, and experienced less satisfaction than their female counterparts. Reflecting on this finding for several years while counseling hundreds of couples, I have come to the following conclusions. Phlegmatics are perfectly normal regarding the place of sexual activity in marriage, and they can be as sexually expressive and loving as anyone else. They enjoy tenderness, love, and affection, as long as it is not displayed publicly. However, they do not like pressure, conflict, or rejection; consequently they tend to let their partners lead.

I was surprised to discover from my sex survey that a rather high percentage of phlegmatic wives had indicated promiscuity before marriage. Because by nature they like to please others, they would often succumb to the pressure of an aggressive lover's advances. Since opposites usually attract, we should note, phlegmatics often find themselves in the company of more aggressive temperaments. Many of these women indicated that their premarital activity had burdened them with years of guilt. (More will be said about temperament and its effect on sexual expression in a later chapter.)

Phlegmatics are apt to blame other people for their mistakes. Adam must have been phlegmatic, for he started it all by complaining to God, "The woman whom Thou gavest to be with me, she gave me from the tree, and I ate" (Gen. 3:12, NASB). This still seems to be the phlegmatic pattern. When phlegmatics are confronted with a mistake, a sin, or an error, they will try to cast the blame onto someone else. It's not that they want to be deceitful; they just don't like the pressure of taking the full responsibility for their behavior. Others find this maddening: parents whose children point the finger at other siblings in the family, or the boss whose otherwise loyal, dependable, and careful employee blames a coworker under pressure.

The disadvantage of this trait to the phlegmatic himself is that he seldom learns from his behavior. Because blaming others frees him from the immediate pressure, he goes his cheerful way, not admitting that he needs to improve in this regard. As a result, he tends to repeat his mistakes.

Phlegmatic children are great daydreamers. They escape the nasty now by drifting off into a fantasy land. Some have trouble reading, spelling, or learning math because of this. When they grow up, this mental habit will serve as an escape hatch from unpleasant circumstances. No doubt many unhappily married phlegmatics have endured to the end by letting their minds drift to the Land of Oz. But this is not what the Bible means when it says, "Be content with what you have" or "Learn to be content whatever the circumstances" (see Heb. 13:5; Phil. 4:11, NIV). True contentment comes from God to those who walk with him. Daydreaming can become a form of unproductive phlegmatic escapism.

Summary

Whatever your temperament, you will face pressure in life. You cannot change that, nor are you responsible for it. But you are responsible for the way you respond to pressure regardless of your temperament. For there is one thing more important than your temperament in relation to how you respond to pressure, and that is your mental attitude. With God's help you can control your mental attitude.

One of the most important truths I have discovered since becoming a Christian is the need to maintain a thankful attitude—about everything. There are only two kinds of people: gripers and thankers (some identify them as groaners and praisers). Gripers are never happy; thankers always are. You have the capacity to be either, but if you allow the Spirit of God to control your mind, you will be a thanker.

We have referred several times in this book to the biblical command to "be filled with the Spirit" (or controlled by the Spirit) (Eph. 5:18). It should be noted that the second result of his "filling" or "control" will be thanksgiving—"always giving thanks to God the Father for everything, in the name of our Lord Jesus Christ" (Eph. 5:20, NIV).

In Psalm 1:1 God warns us against sitting around with gripers. Throughout the Old Testament God denounces and condemns gripers (Israel in the wilderness, Moses, Elijah, Jeremiah, and others). By contrast, in both the Old and New Testaments we read hundreds of challenges to be thankful. First Thessalonians 5:18 makes it clear that anything less is to be out of the will of God: "Give thanks in all circumstances, for this is God's will for you in Christ Jesus" (NIV).

I am convinced that one cannot be lastingly happy or learn how to control pressure unless he develops the mental habit of thanksgiving. And that is not easy. Personally I have to work on it constantly. After all these years of teaching, writing, and trying to practice a thankful mental attitude, one would think it becomes automatic. Not so! I look on the development of a habitual mental attitude of thanksgiving as if it were a large boulder which I consciously push uphill everyday. If I unconsciously forget thanksgiving, the stone rolls back down the hill a few yards, and I must start pushing again. It gets easier only as I walk in the Spirit and try to be grateful by thanking God for his goodness in the things I understand, and by thanking him by faith for what he is going to do in the things I do not understand.

Thanksgiving is an imperative in God's Word. Most Christians consider it an option. Without it you will drift into griping, which will destoy your positive mental attitude and increase your pressures.

Thankful living is a matter of daily developing a mental attitude of thanksgiving. It is not only "the will of God" for your life, but the secret to developing a positive mental attitude, which in turn is the key to controlling pressure. Admittedly, thanksgiving is not an easy habit or way of life to develop, but it is absolutely essential.

Some temperaments find thanksgiving to be easier than others, but I do not read in Scripture that God commands only sanguines and phlegmatics, "In everything give thanks." This is a universal command to us all, and it must be obeyed. Otherwise our life's pressures will control us instead of our controlling them.

Anyone who desires to work seriously on developing such a mental attitude should do the following:

Do a daily Bible study on all the verses related to thanking. Write down your findings.

Memorize one thanksgiving verse per week, starting with 1 Thessalonians 5:18 and Philippians 4:6-7.

Read Philippians through daily for thirty days.

Make a list of ten characteristics about your spouse (if married) or closest relative or friend (if single), giving thanks for each one daily for three months.

Make a list of ten other items for which you are grateful, thanking for them daily.

Do not permit your mind to think negatively, critically, or ungratefully—and never repeat such thoughts verbally. If you do, repent as soon as you realize what you have done, confess it as sin, and replace the thought with something for which you are truly grateful. Then quote one of the thanksgiving verses you have been memorizing.

Without consciously practicing thanksgiving, you will never develop a lasting positive mental attitude.

Learn contentment

"But godliness with contentment is great gain" (1 Tim. 6:6, NIV). "Keep your lives free from the love of money and be content with what you have, because God has said, 'Never will I leave you; never will I forsake you'" (Heb. 13:5, NIV).

"I am not saying this because I am in need, for I have learned to be content whatever the circumstances. I know what it is to be in need, and I know what it is to have plenty. I have learned the secret of being content in any and every situation, whether well fed or hungry, whether living in plenty or in want. I can do everything through him who gives me strength" (Phil. 4:11-13, NIV).

The man who popularized contentment "whatever the circumstances" and "in every situation" was the church's most celebrated jailbird. Paul had been imprisoned many times for faithfully preaching the gospel. Instead of griping and groaning, he had "learned to be content." How? By practicing the art of praise in a situation that would naturally breed complaints. Our modern jails are luxurious palaces by comparison with the Mamertine prison in Rome where Paul was incarcerated. I have seen it—or one like it—and it was dreadful. Lacking doors, lights, or creature comforts, it was a cold, damp cave with one opening at the top through which the prisoner was lowered. After he was placed inside, only his sparse food supply passed through that opening. Yet Paul had *learned* to be content.

Your prison may be an overcrowded apartment with more children than bedrooms, an office without windows, a car that barely runs, or a job well beneath your ability and income needs. It may be an unhappy marriage or overly possessive parents. Whatever the privation or predicament, have you learned to be content? If not, you can never gain contentment by moving to a bigger apartment, getting a new job, or leaving your partner. Most people want to change their circumstances as a means to achieving peace. To the contrary, satisfaction is learned by developing a thankful attitude where you are. Your present circumstances may not be Shangri-la, but they are your training ground. Since God wants to teach you contentment, learn your lesson as quickly as possible so he can speed you on to where he wants you to be. I am inclined to believe that many Christians spend their lives in the prison of discontent because they refuse to learn the lesson of satisfaction where they are.

Remaining cheerfully serene in the face of unpleasant circumstances is possible only through developing the art of "thanksgiving living." Thanking God for your present address in life is the first giant step toward learning contentment.

Learning to be content where you are *and* learning to develop a godly mental attitude of thanksgiving will reduce life's pressure down to an enjoyable level—regardless of what temperament you are. Work on it—you'll be glad you did.

11

TEMPERAMENT AND DEPRESSION

When I wrote my book *How to Win over Depression* ten years ago, it was because depression had reached "near epidemic proportions," according to *Newsweek* magazine, "and suicide was its all too often result." During that time my travels took me through the Dallas Airport where I picked up a newspaper and read, "Depression—The Leading Cause of College Suicide." I remember thinking, what would cause a young person in the prime of life (18-23 years) to take his life? The article made it clear—depression.

During this past decade the problem has gotten worse, not better. Today the leading cause of death in junior high school is suicide, and depression is usually the cause. The self-preservation instinct is powerful in human beings, and a person has to be so depressed that he overpowers that instinct before he can take his own life.

You may well ask, "What would cause a fifteen-year-old at the prime of life to deliberately end his life?" The emotional aftermath of a broken home through divorce is one factor and certainly easy access to harmful drugs is another. It has been my observation, however, that some temperaments have a greater problem with depression than others.

THE SANGUINE AND DEPRESSION A sanguine is rarely depressed when in the company of others. He is such a response-oriented person that the sight of another individual usually lifts his spirits and brings a smile to his face. Whatever periods of depression he does experience

almost invariably commence when he is alone.

The most pleasant characteristic of a sanguine is his ability to enjoy the present. He does not look back on unhappy experiences in his past, and he never worries about the unknown future. A delightful sanguine friend of mine affords a classic example. While traveling across the country he commented on the many people who approached me for counseling due to depression. Spontaneously he exclaimed, "You now, I've never had much trouble with depression; I guess it's because God has been so good to me. Actually, I can't remember ever having any real problems or difficulties in life. "His statement really astonished me, for I knew the man well. I was forced to recall that he failed to finish high school until he was almost forty years of age because he ran away from home and joined the Merchant Marines. While in the service he married, and after two children were born, one of them died of a rather strange and rare disease. This caused some bitterness on the part of his wife, who after several unhappy years divorced him and remarried. At the time my friend made his statement, he had been single for six years. Only a sanguine could recollect that type of life and say, "I've never really had any problems in life." But there would be much less depression if all temperaments could think that way.

Many undisciplined sanguines experience depression during the fourth or fifth decade of life. Their lack of discipline and weakness of will has usually made them rather unproductive, much to their own chagrin and self-disappointment. They are also prone to obesity by this time because of their inability to refuse fattening desserts and other delicacies. This lowers their self-esteem and heightens their tendency toward depression. Although they usually go through the motions of responding happily to other people, their tendency toward mild depression will increase. One writer likened them to Peter Pan—they wish never to grow up. Although they are well-liked and attractive, they are often undependable and without real substance.

As these charming sanguines, who usually act like overgrown children, become aware of their own shallowness, their insecurities are heightened. They become defensive, sensitive to slights or criticism, almost obsessed with others' opinions of them. It is not uncommon for them to become depressed at this point by engaging in self-pity. They may even blame their parents for indulging them so much in childhood that they never developed self-discipline; but it is very difficult for them to blame themselves, confess their sin, and seek the filling of the Holy Spirit for the strength of character they so desperately need.

If they do not face their problem realistically and learn to walk in the Spirit, they will fluctuate up and down between depression and happiness for a time until, in some childlike way, they settle for the life of mediocrity which they have brought on themselves, and then go through life fixed in a playful position far beneath their level of potential.

The Spirit-filled sanguine is different! The Holy Spirit not only convicts him of his self-pitying thought-patterns as sin, but guides him to those areas of productivity that make it easier for him to accept and appreciate himself. When a sanguine is filled with the Spirit, like the Apostle Peter in the Book of Acts, he becomes a productive and effective person, untroubled by lasting depression.

THE CHOLERIC AND DEPRESSION

The hard-driving, steel-willed choleric rarely gets depressed. His active, goal-conscious mind keeps him so motivated that he projects fourteen different programs simultaneously. If one of them proves baffling or frustrating, his disappointment is short-lived and he quickly pursues a fresh challenge. Cholerics are happy when busy, and thus they have little time to be depressed. Their frustration in life is that there are not enough hours in the day to engage in their endless supply of goals and objectives.

The rejection or insults that often set other temperaments off into periods of depression never face a choleric. He is so thick-skinned, self-sufficient, and independent by nature that he rarely feels the need for other people. Instead of feeling sorry for himself when alone, he spends the time originating new plans.

Emotionally he is the most underdeveloped of all the temperaments. For that reason he usually experiences very slight mood changes. Although he quickly becomes angry, he rarely indulges in self-pity. Instead, he explodes all over everyone else. Because he is so insensitive to others' opinions of him, he is not vulnerable to depression occasioned by people. If a choleric ever battles depression, it will come as a result of frustration, retreat, or what he considers the incompetence of other people.

By the time a choleric has reached the fourth or fifth decade of life, his activity-prone brain can often create a mental activity syndrome that makes his thoughts cancel or short-circuit each other, much like an overloaded switchboard. As a Christian, the choleric must learn to rest in the Lord and commit his way to him. An indomitable will and a spirit of self-sufficiency often cause him to be a useless, unproductive Christian because he insists on doing everything in the flesh instead of the Spirit. If he does successfully promote Christian activities, his pride makes him spiritually myopic and he fails to discern his carnal motivation.

The peace of the Holy Spirit that passes all understanding will modulate his thinking pattern, causing him to concentrate on the Lord first and then on the task. He must learn that God's program does not depend on him; rather, he needs to depend on God. He must further recognize that fulfilling the work of God is not enough; he must do it in the power of the Spirit. As the Bible says, "Not by might, nor by power, but by my spirit, saith the Lord of hosts" (Zech. 4:6). The Apostle Paul, possibly the best illustration of a Spirit-filled choleric used of God, had learned this well, for he said, ". . . when I am weak, then am I strong" (2 Cor. 12:10).

The flesh-filled choleric Christian can become depressed until he realizes this principle, because he gets frustrated by the lack of spiritual results from his hard-driving, fleshly efforts. Instead of blaming himself for his carnal, self-willed spirit, he may swell up in self-pity and withdraw from his church activities. His carnal spirit is often easily discerned by others in the congregation, and thus he may be bypassed when officers are elected. "I don't understand," he complains. "Isn't my hard work sufficient proof of my devotion to Christ?" Happy is the choleric who learns with James to say, ". . . If the Lord will, we shall live, and do this, or that" (James 4:15). If he seeks the priorities of the will of God through the leading of the Holy Spirit in his life, he will not only be more productive but also more composed. When once he comprehends that walking in the Spirit is the secret to spiritual productivity, he will gain consistency in his Christian life.

Another period of life during which a choleric is vulnerable to depression is retirement. Though he usually does not retire until age seventy or later, he must program into his thinking some added form of productivity or give way to depression.

A former business executive was forced to retire at sixty-five. Within six months he went in to see his pastor in a state of depression. It did not take the minister long to perceive that the unproductive inactivity of retirement was the culprit. In addition, of course, the executive was indulging in the sin of self-pity that laments, "My life is over, the period of my productivity is past, I am no longer good for anything." The pastor was leading a very dynamic church much in need of a businessman to coordinate and direct the business affairs. He challenged this man to be a $1.00 a year Christian worker. Today that church rates among the most efficient in the nation, and the energetic choleric business manager is thoroughly enjoying his retirement.

The ability of the Holy Spirit to literally transform a choleric tendency toward depression is illustrated superbly in the life of the Apostle Paul. If ever a man was an illustration of choleric temperament, it was Saul of Tarsus before he became a Christian. After his conversion, his indomitable choleric will, now directed by the Holy Spirit, surged forward throughout the Book of Acts. His response to confinement offers a classic illustration of depressing circumstances overcome through the invasion of man's spiritual nature by the Holy Spirit. Confined to the cold, clammy Mamertine Prison in Rome for preaching the gospel, he manifested not one sign of self-pity. Instead, this dynamic Christian took advantage of the opportunity to share his faith personally with every new Roman soldier assigned to him as a guard. Many of these men were converted— "All the saints salute you, chiefly they that are of Caesar's household" (Phil. 4:22). In addition, from this prison he penned the prison epistles, including his epistle of joy, the letter to the Philippians, in which he stated, "I have learned, in whatsoever state I am, therewith to be content" (Phil. 4:11). Spirit-filled cholerics will never become depressed.

Contentment is not natural, particularly when you are confined to a prison. Contentment is a learned mental attitude that requires the supernatural power of the Holy Spirit, particularly difficult for a choleric; but it can be learned.

Your prison is doubtless not a cold clammy prison in Rome. It may be a job you detest. It may be an unhappy marriage or a host of other circumstances. But whether it becomes a cause for depression or contentment is up to you. The Bible commands, "Gird up the loins of your mind" (1 Pet. 1:13). In other words, don't let your mind float along thinking of those things it wants to think about. If you do, it will take your emotions downhill—by thinking of self-pity, or selfish or self-centered thought-patterns.

What causes depression? Many things really. If you have a problem in this area you should examine my book *How to Win over Depression*, where I give eleven of the most frequent causes. The most common, however, is the self-pity we indulge in after rejection by someone we love or admire, an insult, or an injury. The real culprit is self-pity. The greater your self-pity, the greater your depression. That's why Paul challenges all of us to *learn* contentment—even in the face of rejection, insult, or injury.

Everyone knows what contentment is, or at least they think they do. But few people realize that it is the emotional result of mental thanksgiving—regardless of the prison they're in. Cholerics are rarely content. But they can "learn," by learning to be a thanker and a praiser.

THE MELANCHOLY AND DEPRESSION

Melancholies often are easily depressed because they are perfectionists. Most people could profit by having more perfectionistic tendencies, but the true perfectionist is made miserable by them. In the first place, he measures himself by his own arbitrary standard of perfection and gets discouraged with himself when he falls short of that standard. The fact that his standard is usually so high that neither he nor anyone else could live by it rarely occurs to him. Instead, he insists that his criterion for perfection is "realistic."

In addition to perfectionism, he also is very conscientious and prides himself on being dependable and accurate. Naturally, all of his friends fall short of this standard, so it is not uncommon for him to become depressed about himself and his associates. Very rigid and inflexible, he finds it difficult to tolerate the slightest deviation from what he considers to be the measure of excellence.

Such perfectionist-prone melancholies can love their children dearly while at the same time becoming depressed by them. Children are notoriously disorganized and unpredictable; they follow their own schedules and insist on acting like children. A rigid melancholy parent finds it difficult to cope with such unpredictability, and consequently may experience depression. Sometimes a melancholy mother may become ambivalent toward her own children, loving them intensely while at the same time being filled with anger and bitterness at them. The carefree, happy-go-lucky little tyke who insists on trekking across the clean kitchen floor with his wet rubbers can be a source of irritation to any mother, particularly to a melancholy. Before she was married, she probably could not retire for the night until her shoes were lined properly and the bathroom was in perfect order. Children automatically change that, but perfectionists find it difficult to cope with such change; consequently, depression is their outlet. They become angered at the lack of perfection in others and indulge in self-pity because they are the only ones striving for lofty goals. Such thought patterns invariably produce depression.

In fairness to melancholy people, they are as critical of themselves as they are of others. As a result, they tend to develop an inadequate view of themselves. From early childhood they construct a disparaging self-image on the screen of their imagination. As they get older, unlike some of the other temperaments who learn to accept themselves, they tend to reject themselves even more. Consequently their periods of depression increase, If they were permitted to verbalize their criticisms in childhood, they are apt to be verbally critical in adulthood. Each time they indulge in oral criticism, they only embed the spirit of criticism more deeply in their minds; and critics are never happy people!

One day I had an opportunity to see this principle in action. As I submitted to an airport examination before boarding a plane, the security officer began to criticize the individuals who flew on that airline as "slovenly, inconsiderate, disorganized, and ungrateful people." I took it just about as long as I could, but finally, looking at him with a big smile (I find one can say almost anything if he smiles) I observed, "You must be an unhappy man!" He looked at me rather startled and replied, "Why do you say that?" "Because you're so critical. I've never met a happy person who is a critical person." After inspecting my baggage, he said, "Thank you, sir, I needed that." To my amazement he turned to the next customer and said, "Hello, how are you? So glad to have you on our airline." I don't know how long he will profit by that experience, but I am certain that he has the capability of making himself happy or miserable in direct proportion to the way in which he thinks and talks to people.

Not only are melancholy people rigid perfectionists and conscientious individuals, but they possess a low threshold of anxiety and tension. The American way of life is not conducive to happiness for such people. We live in a hyperactivity-prone, choleric society, as Dr. Paul Tournier verifies in a chapter on temperament in his book entitled *The Healing of Persons*. It seems that Western civilization, where the gospel of Christ has had its most profound influence, reflects a highly choleric population. This would be characteristic of the Teutonic or Nordic race, whose people tend to represent a high percentage of choleric temperament. Such individuals settled in Scandinavia, Germany, parts of France, Ireland and England, the very countries producing most of the American settlers. Although it would be difficult to prove, it would seem that the most courageous, hearty, and choleric members of Europe came over to settle this country. Consequently, their progeny would include a level of choleric, activity-prone citizens, which may account for our industrialized, fast-moving, high-pressure environment. Such an atmosphere is not the best for a melancholy, for he is not interested in achieving massive production, but perfection and quality. It is not uncommon to hear a melancholy professional man complain, "We just don't have time to be accurate anymore."

This may explain why so many of the hippy or "freak" people drop out of the mainstream of society today. Rejecting its mad pace and witnessing its lack of perfection through the eyes of idealism, they seek a more passive culture. This may be one reason some of them will speak favorably about a governmental system that has totally enslaved people into passivity in contrast to the free enterprise system, which they think has enslaved people to activity.

I have repeatedly observed that many of the young people who have "copped out" of our society are very sensitive, gifted, idealistic young people indulging in escape rather than making an honest attempt to alter society. Dr. Tournier notes that some of the Indian or Oriental cultures place a higher priority on the mystic or passive individual. Thus Mahatma Gandhi, whose fastings were symbolic of passive resistance, became a national hero. By contrast, in the Western world the dynamic, productive choleric is the hero. Whatever its cause, the frantic pace we live in today contributes heavily to the melancholy's tendency toward depression.

Two characteristics of the melancholy which mutually short-circuit each other are his natural desire to be *self-sacificing* and his *self-persecution* tendency. Unless he is careful, this conflict will likely make a martyr out of him. Ordinarily he chooses the most difficult and trying location to ply his vocation. When others seem to be more successful or gain more renown, instead of facing realistically the fact that he has chosen the path of self-sacrifice, he indulges in self-pity because his journey winds uphill and leads through arduous straits.

The determination of a melancholy to gripe and criticize merely compounds his negative thinking and ultimately brings him to despair. For that reason 1 Thessalonians 5:18 can come to his rescue! If he painstakingly and consistently follows its formula, he will never become depressed. "In every thing give thanks: for this is the will of God in Christ Jesus concerning you."

Although everyone is vulnerable to his own mental thinking pattern, none is more responsive than the melancholy. Among his other creative gifts, he harbors the great ability to suggest images to the screen of his imagination—probably in living color with stereophonic sound. Because melancholies are moody by nature, they may regard their moods as spontaneous, but it has been learned that moods result directly from thinking patterns. If a melancholy guards his thought processes and refuses to indulge in the mental sins of anger, resentment, self-persecution, and self-pity, he will not yield to his predisposition toward depression.

The powerful influence of the mind on our moods can easily be illustrated by an experience I had with my sons when they were growing up. One Sunday night as they were going to bed we reminded them, as millions of children are faithfully reminded by loving parents, "Don't forget—tomorrow you have to get up early and go to school." In unison they sang, "Do we have to go to school tomorrow?" Assuring them that this was a necessary part of their lives and accepting their grumbling with customary parental long-suffering, I sent them off to bed. Needless to say, Monday morning they woke up in a sour mood. I sincerely hated to foist them off on their schoolteacher that day.

The next week the same boys were lying in the same bed at night. As I tucked them in I admonished, "Don't forget—you've got to get up early tomorrow because we're heading for Disneyland!" You can imagine the happy chorus that greeted my announcement. The next morning both boys bolted out of bed excited and expectant, as they anticipated the thrilling trip ahead. As I sat at the breakfast table that morning, I contemplated the difference in moods within just one week. Their metabolism seemed to function better, their eyes were clearer, their faces shinier; the whole world looked better because they reflected an improved mental attitude. The melancholy who recognizes the power of the subconscious mind to influence his moods will seek the power of the Holy Spirit to orient his thinking patterns positively.

It is hard to select one period in life that a melancholy finds more depressing than another. Usually his depressions become apparent in early childhood; unless he is spiritually motivated by the power of God, they tend to follow him all his life. Because he is supersensitive and self-centered, he reads things into every activity, at times becoming almost obsessed with the idea that people don't like him or that they are laughing at him.

One day the business manager of Christian Heritage College, my wife (who was the registrar), and I were having lunch together in a restaurant. Suddenly a melancholy college-age man with a gaunt look on his face appeared at the edge of our table and asked, "Pardon me, but may I ask you folks if you were laughing at me?" Naturally we were shocked into silence. Finally I explained, "Young man, I don't think we've ever seen you before in our lives." With that he excused himself and walked away. Reflecting on the incident, we concluded that during our laughter and conversation we must have looked in his direction, which gave that troubled young man the impression that we were laughing at his expense. Equally as substantial are many of the depression-causing events in the life of the average melancholy.

Fortunately for the melancholy, he possesses an unusual *creative ability* to project all kinds of images on the screen of his imagination. Once he fully realizes that his feelings are the direct result of constructing wholesome mental images of himself and his circumstances, he is well on the road to recovery and prevention of future bouts of depression. Melancholy people risk depression primarily because of the continual misuse of their creative imagination. That is, on the imagination screen of their mind they project negativism, self-pity, helplessness, and despair. Once they realize that their creative suggestions can either work for or against them, they can carefully project only those images that are pleasing to God. Such thoughts will lift their spirits, stabilize their moods, and help them to avoid depression.

Through the years, more melancholy temperaments found their way into my counseling room than any other type. At first I thought it was because I have a magnetic attraction for depression-prone individuals. Later I realized that the creative melancholy has a greater difficulty getting his act together. His creative thought process can find just too many problems and imperfections or conjure up too many imagined rejections, insults, or injuries.

Even more than the choleric, he needs to concentrate on thanksgiving as a way of life. Griping, criticizing, and complaining always have a depressing effect on a person's mood. If you are going to "learn" contentment and inner peace, it will be through thanksgiving. And interestingly enough, that is the will of God for your life anyway (1 Thess. 5:18)!

THE PHLEGMATIC AND DEPRESSION

As a general rule, a phlegmatic person is not easily depressed. His unique sense of humor signals a happy outlook on life, and rarely does he reflect much mood fluctuation. It is possible to know a phlegmatic all his life and never see him truly angry, for no matter what the occasion, he tends to mentally excuse the person who has offended, injured, or rejected him. His ability to adjust to unpleasant circumstances is unbelievable to the other three temperaments, which find it easy to gripe or criticize mentally and verbally.

If a phlegmatic ever does experience depression, it is usually aimed at his own lack of aggressiveness. Many times his practical, capable mind devises a suitable plan of action for a given set of circumstances, but because of his passive inclination or his fear of being criticized by others, he keeps it to himself. Consequently, driven by family or other group pressure, he may find himself pursuing a plan inferior to his own. This can produce irritation which, when followed by self-pity, will make him depressed. Fortunately, his depression is short-lived most of the time, for in a brief time one of those amazingly interesting characters called human beings comes along to amuse and entertain him.

At one critical period in life the phlegmatic is most vulnerable to depression. During the fifth or sixth decade he often becomes aware that the other temperaments have passed him by vocationally, spiritually, and in every other way. While he was passively watching the game of life as a spectator, his more aggressive friends were stepping through the doors of opportunity. His security-mindedness has checked him from attending upon daring adventures in life, and thus his existence may seem rather stale to him during this period. If he indulges in self-pity, he will definitely become depressed.

Instead of blaming his fear or indolence, he finds it much easier to reproach "society" or "the breaks" or "my luck." Such a person should learn from the Lord Jesus early in life to attempt great things for God, for Christ said, "According to your faith be it unto you" (Matt. 9:29).

No one is in greater need of external motivation than a phlegmatic. But he often spends his life resisting pressure. Rarely does he take on more than he can do or become overinvolved. The only thing I have ever seen a phlegmatic become overinvolved in was keeping from getting overinvolved.

Frankly, he needs to get overinvolved. He is the *only temperament* I say that about. Sanguines take on everything and finish nothing. Cholerics take on everything and wear themselves out doing it. Melancholies take on the most difficult things that others won't do and ruin their health. Not phlegmatics. They live to a ripe old age protecting themselves. Someone has said, "A phlegmatic is the only type of person who can jam fifty years of living in a 100-year lifetime." And most of those years will be basically depression-free.

Summary

You can't help being the temperament you are. And there is no one temperament that is better than another. Each is unique with its own set of strengths and weaknesses, including the tendency to easy depression or a carefree way of life. But you can control your mental attitude or thinking process. If you inherited a choleric or melancholy temperament, it is wise to face it honestly and realize you will have to fight all your life against indulging in self-pity and criticism. If you are a combination of the ChlorMel or MelChlor temperaments, you will have to fight off those thought-patterns particularly hard. But it can be done! With God's help you can learn to be a thankful, content person, but you will have to work on it all your life.

Every time you find yourself griping in the spirit of your mind, confess it as sin and begin praying to God for who and what he is in the midst of your circumstances. Don't indulge your natural inclination to self-pity. You will be both out of the will of God and miserable. Make thanksgiving a way of life, and depression will lose its deadly influence on you. "Give thanks in all circumstances, for this is God's will for you in Christ Jesus" (1 Thess. 5:18, NIV).

12

HOW TO COPE WITH ANGER AND HOSTILITY

Fear may be the first emotional problem ever to face the family and it may even afflict more people than the second; but it is not the family's Number One enemy. That dishonor is reserved for anger, which sometimes takes the form of hostility and wrath.

More wives have been battered, and children abused and psychologically destroyed by the violent outbursts of anger than anyone knows. It is impossible to overexaggerate the damage this emotion does to the family, marriage, and all other interpersonal relationships.

A pastor friend in northern California called to ask if I would meet with a dedicated couple from his congregation who happened to be in San Diego, trying to work out their marriage problems. This ChlorSan husband and MelPhleg wife had been married seventeen years and acknowledged two problems. First, both admitted, "We cannot communicate." Second, the wife added, "He turns me off sexually. I am absolutely dead toward him." Sue's story was pathetic. Raised in a German immigrant family with five children, her father "ruled the roost with an iron hand." She lamented, "Mealtimes were always a terror for me, because if Father got upset, he would pound his fist so hard that the dishes and silverware would leap off the table. I always promised myself that I would never marry a man like my father." When Bill came along, he seemed so sweet and kind that she fell in love with him and they soon married. "Three weeks after our wedding, it happened," she continued. "Something set him off, and he pounded his fist on the table so hard that the dishes and silverware leaped into the air. As they clattered down onto the table, I thought, *I've married a man just like my father!"*

Anger and fear stifle communication

Sweethearts rarely have trouble communicating before marriage. In fact, they can talk on the phone by the hour. But to destroy that relationship it only takes the angry action of one to set up a fear reaction in the other. Oh, they usually make up and renew their tenderness and communication, but the damage is done. Each has seen the other in his true light. Consequently, the spirit of free communication will be inhibited. The anger of one builds a formidable block in the wall that obstructs communication. The self-protective reaction of fear keeps the other from expressing himself freely, and thus another block is added to the wall. Gradually such outbursts and reactions build an impenetrable wall until the former lovebirds are not really communicating at all, apprehensive that the anger of one will be ignited or the fear of the other will cause added pain. Tears, silence, and pent-up feelings all play their part, and before long they need counseling because "we can't communicate anymore." Lack of communication is not the problem. Anger and fear are the culprits! In this chapter we will examine its results and its remedy.

Pressure doesn't make your spirit

Bill defended his actions by saying, "She has no idea of the pressures I'm under, and she takes my outbursts too seriously because of her background. What she doesn't realize is that all men have to let off steam. I don't really mean the things I say, but she won't forgive me when I apologize." In other words, Bill doesn't want to change. He expects Sue to live with an angry man just as her mother did.

What Bill didn't recognize is that pressure does not make your spirit—it merely reveals it. What a man is under pressure is what he is! If you explode under pressure, you are admitting that underneath a carefully constructed facade you are an angry person. Some people have more tolerance and can take more pressure than others, of course, but if you are an angry individual, your weakness will show up sooner or later by the way you act, react, or think. And we all know that the home is potentially the world's greatest pressure cooker. That is why anger and its various forms of hostility are the family's Number One problem.

One hostile husband told me, "Well, I have to find someplace where I can be myself." Yes, he did, and that was his problem— himself. A person at home always reveals his true nature. We can put up a front outside the home, but under the pressures of family living the real individual manifests himself. I have found only one remedy. Let God change the real you so that your hours at home can be pleasant and those who love you most will not be threatened.

Anger and masculinity

Many men seem to have the strange idea that anger is a justifiable masculine trait. "Every man gets angry," they exclaim. Some would insist that a man who doesn't have an anger problem isn't a real man. Nothing could be further from the truth! Man's natural tendency toward anger has probably started more wars, created more conflict, and ruined more homes than any other universal trait.

Anger seems to be a man's way of expressing his frustrations, but it is a mistake to deem it a beneficial emotion. In fact, it inhibits sound judgment and thinking. A nineteen-year-old lad who had a fight with his girlfriend backed out of her driveway and "laid a hundred and five feet of scratch" in front of her house. In seven minutes he was dead. His anger robbed him of good judgment as he floorboarded the gas pedal at ninety-five miles an hour, failed to navigate a freeway curve, and sped straight into eternity. Anger struck again.

Newspapers have been carrying reports lately from hospital emergency wards and welfare agencies that child abuse is alarmingly on the increase. Over 10,000 children died last year due to such mistreatment. What could cause any adult to so abuse a helpless child? Frustration due to anger! Brokenhearted parents have wept as they related stories of their "abnormal behavior," registering amazement that they were capable of such action. They aren't basically "abnormal"; they just never learned to control their anger, and when a sufficient level of frustration was reached, they committed an act which they regretted for life. Such anger-laden behavior is not limited to the lower socioeconomic members of society, although their living conditions may accelerate frustrations. I have seen otherwise respectable people destroy their children through anger.

A minister asked me to counsel his wife for an unrepentant "affair" she was having. Expecting to see a siren walk into my office, I was surprised to find a gracious, soft-spoken woman of forty-five who told her story through her tears. Her husband was a dynamic minister very successful in his church and admired by everyone. But he had one sin she could not excuse. He was an angry, hostile man whom she considered "overstrict and physically abusive of our three children. He cannot control his anger and has on one occasion beaten our oldest son unconscious." When the boy reached nineteen, he ran away and joined a hippie group. Brokenheartedly she said, "From that day on I lost all feeling for my husband."

An extreme situation like that never occurs suddenly. It had been building up for years, primarily related to major disagreements over disciplining the children. She had learned to live with his other angry explosions but could not endure his manhandling of the children. Too fearful to voice her real feelings, she witnessed her husband's angry frustrations worked out on the heads, faces, and backsides of their children. Although she only interrupted on extreme occasions, she acknowledged "dying a little" each time he abused them. As it turned out, her "affair" was simply retaliation to spite her husband.

When the minister came in, he was obviously desperate. I was never sure if he sought help because he really loved his wife or if he was just trying to save his ministry. When confronted with his hostilities, he retorted, "If a man can't let down and be himself at home, where can he?" I was silent for a long time. As he sat there thinking he finally admitted, "That sounds pretty carnal, doesn't it?" Before leaving, he realized that his anger was as bad or worse than her adultery. Although this man was able to salvage his marriage, as far as I know he has never regained his son. In all probability, more sons have been alienated from their fathers because of Dad's anger than anything else. And the tragic part of it is that the son will probably treat his son the same way. Angry fathers produce angry children.

The devastating consequences of anger

Anger, hostility, or wrath—or, as the Bible calls it, "enmity of heart" or "malice"—is as old as man. Doubtless you recall the first family squabble in recorded history. "Cain was very wroth (angry) and . . . rose up against Abel his brother, and slew him" (see Gen. 4:5). Ever since that tragic day, millions have died prematurely, and countless marriages have broken up because of anger. The number of children subjected to emotional tension in the home due to the anger of adults staggers the mind. Any counselor will acknowledge that most of his emotionally scarred clients are the victims of someone's anger. It is a nearly universal emotional problem with devastating consequences, particularly in the home. Even as I write this chapter, our local newspaper carries the story of a pro-football player whose wife killed him in his sleep with an eight-inch kitchen knife. Only protracted anger which turned into the white heat of rage would make a person take another's life.

Temperament and anger

The only temperament that will not have an inherent problem with anger is the phlegmatic. But since no one is 100 percent a phlegmatic, even he will encounter the difficulty to one degree or another, depending on his secondary temperament. As we have seen, a PhlegMel will experience the least problem with it, depending of course on the percentages of his two temperaments. The two temperaments that have the greatest problem with it are the two extremes, as shown on the next chart. Sanguines, you will recall, are instantly eruptive and forgiving, cholerics eruptive and grudging. Melancholies take longer to explode, preferring to mull over self-persecuting thoughts and to harbor revengeful plans until they, too, are capable of unreasonable expressions of wrath.

The gravity of this problem cannot be overestimated! Of the 949 couples I have joyfully united as husband and wife during my years in the ministry, I am happy to say that only two dozen, to my knowledge, have divorced. Perhaps this is because I have asked each couple to make a sacred promise that "before you ever spend a single night separated by duress, you will come to see me." Except for a few couples whose problem in the early days pertained to sexual difficulties which were resolved in a short period of time, every other couple's problem was anger!

Anger not only destroys home life but ruins health. A book we mentioned previously, *None of These Diseases*, lists fifty-one illnesses that can be caused by tension produced by anger or fear—including high blood pressure, heart attack, colitis, arthritis, kidney stones, gallbladder troubles, and many others. For years I have quoted Dr. Henry Brandt, who says, "Approximately 97 percent of the cases of bleeding ulcers without organic origin I have dealt with are caused by anger." At a seminar in Columbus, Ohio, a medical doctor identified himself as an "ulcer specialist" and reported, "I would take issue with Dr. Brandt—it's more like a hundred percent!" At the same seminar a young doctor who identified himself as an internist informed me, "Yesterday afternoon I treated five patients with serious internal complications. As you were talking, I made a mental note that all five were angry people."

Doctors have warned us for years that emotionally induced illness accounts for 60-85 percent of all sicknesses today. What they mean is that tension causes illness. Anger, fear, and guilt are the primary causes of tension, and are clearly the major culprits of poor health.

Suppressed anger and bitterness can make a person emotionally upset until he is "not himself." In this state he often makes decisions that are harmful, wasteful, or embarrassing. We are intensely emotional creatures, designed so by God; but if we permit anger to dominate us, it will squelch the richer emotion of love. Many a man takes his office grudges and irritations home and unconsciously lets this anger curtail what could be a free-flowing expression of love for his wife and children. Instead of enjoying his family and being enjoyed by them, he allows his mind and emotions to mull over the vexations of the day. Life is too short and our moments at home too brief to pay such a price for anger.

Dr. S. I. McMillen makes these interesting statements:

"The moment I start hating a man, I become his slave. I can't enjoy my work any more because he even controls my thoughts. My resentments produce too many stress hormones in my body and I become fatigued after only a few hours' work. The work formerly enjoyed is now drudgery. Even vacations cease to give me pleasure . . . the man I hate hounds me wherever I go. I can't escape his tyrannical grasp on my mind. When the waiter serves me porterhouse steak with french fries, asparagus, crisp salad, and strawberry shortcake smothered with ice cream, it might as well be stale bread and water. My teeth chew the food and swallow it, but the man I hate will not permit me to enjoy it . . . the man I hate may be many miles from my bedroom, but more cruel than any slavedriver, he whips my thoughts into such a frenzy that my innerspring mattress becomes a rack of torture."

So many real-life situations come to mind as I write about the appalling effects of anger that I scarcely know where to begin. I have seen it produce impotence in a twenty-seven-year-old athlete, make normal women frigid, render a twenty-four-year-old physical education teacher incapable of expressing love to her husband, and, in short, annihilate normal love responses. I have visited hundreds of people in hospitals who could have avoided the entire problem had they been relaxed in the spirit instead of being angry. I have even buried many before their time because, like Moses before them, they indulged the secret sin of anger.

In my opinion, the physical damage caused by anger is only exceeded by the spiritual harm it fosters. Anger shortchanges more Christians and makes more spiritual pygmies than any other sin. It has caused more church strife and "turned off" more young converts than anything else. It grieves the Holy Spirit in the life of the believer (see Eph. 4:30-32) and almost destroyed my own health, and ministry.

Anger is sin, sin, sin

In two of my previous books (one written ten years ago) I deliberately identified anger as a sin and offered a scriptural remedy that not only changed my own life but has been used by thousands of others to resolve the problem. Since then several writers have taken issue with my premise and tried to justify anger, insisting: "It is natural," "Anger is universal," "All anger is not sin," or, as one indicated, "The person who never consciously feels any anger is emotionally ill." Some counselors get so agitated that they write lengthy epistles to correct my "misunderstanding of the universal problem of anger." One man was so irritated that he ended his letter by saying, "You're wrong! Wrong! Wrong!"

I agree that there is a place for short-term unselfish anger that is not injurious to others and does not involve sin. But such anger is objective, on behalf of others. I am convinced there are two reasons that self-induced anger is sin. (1) The Bible, my base of reference, is extremely clear in condemning anger—over fourteen times; (2) It is essential to accept the sinfulness of anger in order to effect a cure.

Consider these Bible verses carefully.

Cease from anger, and forsake wrath. (Ps. 37:8)

Be not hasty in thy spirit to be angry: for anger resteth in the bosom of fools. (Eccles. 7:9)

Better is a dinner of herbs where love is, than a stalled ox and hatred therewith. (Prov. 15:17)

Better is a dry morsel, and quietness therewith, than an house full of sacrifices with strife. (Prov. 17:1)

It is better to dwell in the wilderness, than with a contentious and an angry woman. (Prov. 21:19)

A wrathful man stirreth up strife: but he that is slow to anger appeaseth strife. (Prov. 15:18)

He that hath no rule over his own spirit is like a city that is broken down, and without walls. (Prov. 25:28)

Make no friendship with an angry man; and with a furious man thou shalt not let go: Lest thou learn his ways, and get a snare to thy soul. (Prov. 22:24-25)

He that is slow to anger is better than the mighty; and he that ruleth his spirit than he that taketh a city. (Prov. 16:32)

Hatred stirreth up strifes: but love covereth all sins. (Prov. 10:12)

But now also put off all these; anger, wrath, malice, blasphemy, filthy communication out of your mouth. (Col. 3:8)

Wherefore, my beloved brethren, let every man be swift to hear, slow to speak, slow to wrath: for the wrath of man worketh not the righteousness of God. (James 1:19-20)

Many other verses could further illustrate that God condemns anger in the human heart. In fact, the meaning is so clear and easily understood that I shall resist the temptation to comment on them and simply let the Word of God speak for itself.

The best verses to use if you wish to justify anger are Ephesians 4:26-27—

"In your anger do not sin": Do not let the sun go down while you are still angry, and do not give the devil a foothold. (NIV)

Since this is the only biblical text that seems to condone anger, we ought to examine it carefully. It carries two serious qualifications: to be angry (1) without sinning, and (2) without carrying it to the next day.

Qualification 1 forbids any sinful thought or sinful expression of anger. Frankly, people never visit my counseling room with emotional distress from that kind of anger, because "righteous indignation" (which is my label for anger without sin) does not create hangups. And qualification 2 obviously demands that this innocent anger not linger past sundown. Those who terminate their anger at sundown will not cultivate emotional problems either. Incidentally, verse 27 suggests that if innocent anger is permitted to burn past sundown, it "gives the devil a foothold."

The solution to the apparent conflict between the fourteen verses that condemn anger and Ephesians 4:26-27, which seem to condone it, is really quite simple. The Bible permits righteous indignation and condemns all selfishly induced anger. You experience righteous indignation when you see an injustice perpetrated on another. For example, when a bully picks on a child, you feel a surge of emotion (righteous indignation) and go to the aid of the child. You do not sin in this, nor is it difficult to forget such externally induced anger after dark. But when someone rejects, insults, or injures you, that is a different matter. Is your emotion without sin? And do you forget it after dark?

The Lord Jesus' earthly expressions of anger provide another example. When he drove the moneychangers from the temple, his action was impersonal—"You have made my Father's house a den of thieves" (see Matt. 21:13). His anger at the Pharisees later was kindled because they were spiritual wolves leading the sheep astray, not because they were hurting him. In fact, when his beard was plucked out, or when he was spat upon and nailed to a cross, he showed absolutely no anger. Instead we hear those familiar words, "Father, forgive them, for they know not what they do." Our Lord never showed selfishly induced anger! Why? Because as a human emotion it is always a sin.

Those who use Ephesians 4:26 to justify the human frailty of anger tend to overlook a very important fact. Just five verses further on in that same context we read:

> Let all bitterness, and wrath, and anger and clamour, and evil speak-ing, be put away from you, with all malice: And be ye kind one to another, tender-hearted, forgiving one another, even as God for Christ's sake hath forgiven you. (Eph. 4:31-32)

It is quite clear from all of this that righteous indignation is acceptable, but personally induced sin is wrong. What is the differ-ence? Selfishness! Selfishly induced anger, which is the kind most of us experience and that which causes so much personal and family havoc, is a terrible sin. That is why Scripture says, "Let all bitter-ness, [all] wrath, and [all] anger be put away from you." As we shall see, it is curable, but only after you face it as a sin.

The subtle problems of bitterness and resentment

A woman once commented, "I never get angry; I just become bitter." Many others would admit the same about resentment. Let's understand something very clearly—the Bible condemns all human bitterness, resentment, and indignation. They are just subtle forms of anger.

At a seminar many years ago, Bill Gothard made a statement to the effect that every couple he counseled for marital disharmony had either married without the approval of their parents or had developed a conflict with one or both parents that eventually created conflicts with the couple's relationship. When a person who had attended the conference shared that thought, I remember considering it a bit extreme. Since then, however, the Christian counselor on our church staff, Pastor Gene Huntsman, and I make this question concerning the couple's relationship to their parents a standard inquiry, and without exception we have found Mr. Gothard's formula to be correct. People who harbor bitterness and resentment toward a parent, brother, sister, or boss are bound to let it spill over and injure their relationship with others. Resentment and bitterness preserved in the recesses of the mind are like cancer; they grow until they consume the whole person. That is why people who cannot forget an unfortunate childhood, rejection, or injury are invariably miserable people.

One of my favorite secular writers, a plastic surgeon, counselor, and lecturer, has authored three self-help books that have benefited millions. In one of his best-selling books he tells about two counselees with "choking sensations." One, a middle-aged salesman who suffered from an inferiority complex, occasionally woke up dreaming of being choked to death by his mother. The other was a young father who loved his wife but on two occasions awakened from a dream with his hands clutching her throat with such a resolute grip that he was terrified. The good doctor accurately diagnosed both problems. The salesman hated his mother and even though he had not seen her in years, she filled his thoughts. The young husband hated his father and subconsciously transferred it to his wife. These cases may seem extreme to you, but they are not really unusual, for they demonstrate the natural result of harboring bitterness, resentment, and anger in your heart and mind. Remember this: bitterness and love cannot burn simultaneously in the same heart. Bitterness indulged for those you hate will destroy your love for those most precious to you.

One of my most pathetic cases concerned a young mother of two who tearfully confessed to feelings of such anger at her infant when he screamed that she sometimes entertained "thoughts of choking him." She then added, "I'm afraid I will do something harmful to my baby." "Upon questioning, we discovered that she had been rejected by her father and clung to bitter thoughts about that rejection. Her rancorous attitude was eating her up, in spite of the fact that her father had been dead for five years.

Seven steps for curing anger, bitterness, or resentment

Many years ago, after over thirty years of being an angry, hostile ChlorSan, I had a life-changing experience with God. Gradually my anger responses lessened from "most of the time" to "only occasionally." Today they are so infrequent that I enjoy an inner peace I wouldn't trade for that old hostile way of life, even for the youth it possessed. Since then I have shared the following remedy with thousands of people, many of whom will testify that it has changed their lives. It may not seem "scientific" to some, but I like it for two reasons: it is biblical, and it works.

1. *Face your anger as sin!* The giant step in overcoming anger is to face it squarely as sin. The minute you try to justify it, explain it, or blame someone else, you are incurable. I have never known anyone to have victory over a problem unless he was convinced it was wrong! That is particularly true of anger. If you have any question at this point, then just reread the Scriptures on pages 441-443 and consider the commands you find there.

2. *Confess every angry thought or deed as soon as it occurs.* This is a giant step too. First John 1:9 says, "If we confess our sins, he is faithful and just to forgive us our sins, and to cleanse us from all unrighteousness." Inwardly I groaned as I read the advice which the plastic surgeon prescribed for the two men who came to him with anger-induced emotional problems. Essentially, he urged them to replace their hateful thoughts by concentrating on some successful or happy experience in life. I remember asking, "But what does that do for guilt?" Absolutely nothing! The blood of Jesus Christ alone, which is adequate to cleanse us from all sin, is available to all who call upon him in faith.

3. *Ask God to take away this angry thought-pattern.* First John 5:14-15 assures us that if we ask anything according to the will of God, he not only hears us but also answers our requests. Since we

know it is not God's will that we be angry, we can be assured of victory if we ask him to take away the habit. Although secular man may remain a slave to habit, the Christian need not. We are admittedly victims of habit, but we need not become addicted to patterns of conformity when we have at our disposal the power of the Spirit of God.

4. *Forgive the person who has caused your anger.* Ephesians 4:32 instructs us to forgive "one another, even as God for Christ's sake hath forgiven you." If a parent, person, or "thing" in your life occupies much of your thinking, make a special point of formally uttering a prayer of forgiveness aloud to God. Each time the hostile thoughts return, follow the same procedure. Gradually your forgiveness will become a fact, and you will turn your thoughts to positive things.

A charming illustration of this came to me after a seminar for missionaries in South America. A lovely missionary had been plagued with anger problems that almost kept her from being accepted by her board. A Christian psychologist challenged her that she must forgive her father, but she replied, "I can't." He said, "You mean you won't! If you don't forgive him, your hatred will destroy you." So in his office she prayed, "Dear Heavenly Father, I do want to forgive my father. Please help me." She acknowledged having to pray that prayer several times, but finally victory came and with it the peace of God. She is a well-balanced and productive woman today because she forgave. You cannot carry a grudge toward anyone you forgive!

5. *Formally give thanks for anything that "bothers" you.* The will of God for all Christians is that "in every thing give thanks . . ." (1 Thess. 5:18). Thanksgiving is therapeutic and helpful, particularly in anger reduction. You will not be angry or depressed if in every insult, rejection, or injury you give thanks. Admittedly that may be difficult at times, but it is possible. God has promised never to burden you with anything you cannot bear (1 Cor. 10:13). Naturally, at times such thanksgiving will have to be done by faith, but God will even provide that necessary faith. Learn the art of praying with thanksgiving.

6. *Concentrate on thinking positive thoughts that include love for others—including the former object of your wrath.* The human mind cannot tolerate a vacuum; it always has to dwell on something. Make sure you concentrate on what the Scripture approves,

such as things that are ". . . true, honest, just, pure, lovely, of good report . . . virtue [and] praise" (Phil. 4:8). People with such positive thoughts are not plagued by anger, hostility, or wrath. It is essentially a matter of subjecting every thought to the obedience of Christ. Anger is a habit—a temperament-induced, sinful habit—ignited through the years by unpleasant distresses and circumstances that can control a person every bit as tenaciously as heroin or cocaine, making him react inwardly or outwardly in a selfish, sinful manner. Unless you let the power of God within you change your thinking patterns, your condition gradually ruin your health, mind, business, family, or spiritual maturity. In addition, it grieves the Holy Spirit (Eph. 4:30), robbing you of the abundant life which Jesus Christ wants to give you.

7. *Repeat the above formula each time you are angry.* Of the hundreds who claim that this simple formula has helped them, none has indicated that it happened overnight. In my case, I had over thirty years of practice at being angry. Fortunately, it didn't take that long to gain victory.

It really works

One reason God has given me the opportunity to minister to so many angry people is because I know where they are coming from. First Corinthians 1:3-4 tells us we can comfort others with the same comfort God has used in comforting us. Basically what that means is that we can minister to others in the same areas we have been ministered to. That doesn't mean we can't minister in areas we have never experienced, because when you help people with the Word of God you are using truth, and truth works no matter who uses it. But it seems God often uses us in a special way with those who have similar troubles as those in which he ministered to us.

Although I am not proud of it, I must confess that in the early years of my ministry, I was a dedicated, hard-driving choleric minister with an anger problem. God met me in a very personal way at a conference where my dear friend, Dr. Henry Brandt, was speaking on anger. That experience changed my life. The Holy Spirit brought in a new peace and joy that transformed my habit of anger, bitterness, and wrath. It didn't happen overnight. It started that day by facing anger as a sin and was followed by many applications of the formula. I have found that anger destroys peace; confessing the sin restores it. The first day I must have used the formula fifty times. The next day it was only forty-nine times. But gradually the habit pattern of anger began to diminish and I became a new man. Today some of the things that used to enrage me only serve to make me laugh. I can't say I never get angry; after all, I still have the same predisposition to anger I've always had. But the expressions are so less frequent I wouldn't go back to that old way of life for anything in this world. And very honestly, my wife agrees. We both know that the most enriching thing to happen to our marriage in over thirty years was when God's Spirit began a special new work on my natural anger. I would never trade love, joy, and peace for anger, bitterness and wrath. Anger never did anything positive to a marriage, but the Holy Spirit's love, joy, and peace really do.

It works for all ages

A seventy-year-old man came to me after a seminar in his church and said, "Dr. La Haye, I should have heard your message on anger over forty years ago. I have been an angry man all my life. Do you think a man seventy years old is too far gone or would your formula work for me?" As I looked into his eyes—I'll be honest—I really didn't know. I had only been teaching the formula about two years at that point and my church, counseling, and seminar ministry was mainly with under-fifty types. As I looked at him, I prayed silently, "Lord, what should I tell this man?" I have learned that when you pray that prayer he usually calls Scripture to mind, so I blurted out, "With man this is impossible, but with God nothing is impossible to you!" Then I heard myself say, "My God is able to supply all your needs." These verses encouraged him, and he walked away to try the formula for himself.

Two years later I was holding meetings in Phoenix, and he and his wife attended. Afterward he came up to give me a "progress report." He said, "I am a changed man. If you don't believe it— here, ask my wife." That is the acid test! For what we are at home is what we are. The smile on her face and the nod of her head made it clear—God the Holy Spirit had given her a new husband. You're never too old or too far gone to change. God is for you and will give you all the help you need. It's up to you.

FIVE

TEMPERAMENT IN
LOVE AND MARRIAGE

13

DO OPPOSITES REALLY ATTRACT?

Self-understanding is only one benefit gained from knowing the theory of the four basic temperaments. In addition, it helps you understand other people, particularly those closest to you. Many a matrimonial battleground is transformed into a neutrality zone when two individuals learn to appreciate their partner's temperament. When you realize that a person's actions result from temperament, rather than being a tactic designed to anger or offend you, this conduct is no longer a threat or an affront.

"We are so hopelessly mismatched that we have to get a divorce," lamented a couple one Tuesday evening in my office. To my question, "Where did you get that idea?" they replied, "We have been to a Christian counseling center which gave us a battery of psychological tests, and that's the conclusion our counselor came to." I spontaneously responded, "That is the worst advice I have ever heard given by a Christian. It is unbiblical in your situation and will only compound your problems." The husband groaned, "Do you mean God wants us to be this miserable the rest of our lives?"

"No," I replied, "there is a much better way! God is able to give you the grace to adjust to and accept each other's temperament." Since they knew nothing about temperament, I proceeded to show them my chart, and before long they could determine the true nature of their completely opposite temperaments. Upon my promise to counsel them, they agreed to cancel their scheduled appointment with an attorney the following Thursday and delay further talk of divorce.

This chapter contains the principles I shared with them. I am convinced that any couple—with God's help—can understand and accept each other's temperament, ultimately reaching a perfect adjustment, if they want to.

I proceeded to teach them the four-temperament theory which you have already studied in this book. It was obvious he was a strong choleric with sanguine traits, and she was about equally balanced between phlegmatic and melancholy. That is about as opposite as you can get.

They were quite amazed to find that they were not so different from other married couples and that most people marry opposites. Fascinated by the theory and concerned about their three teen-age children, they agreed to come in for counseling once a week. During that time they began to grow spiritually and rededicated their lives to Christ and today, seventeen years later, are happily married. So happily that when I was in their home socially a few months ago I was impressed that people meeting them today would not believe they had ever had marital problems.

Interestingly enough, they are still opposites, and they will be as long as they live; but they have learned, with God's help, how to accept and get along with their opposite partner. It hasn't always been easy, but neither is divorce! I've had to go through divorce with many couples, and without exception it has always been worse than they had expected. Even the most friendly divorce I know has produced emotional disturbances in the two children that neither couple anticipated. And in addition to the guilt they bear for the weight they have heaped upon their children, they have to live with the knowledge they disobeyed God's standard. Now that they are both remarried, they discover they have a new opposite partner with whom they must learn to adjust.

No matter who the couple is and no matter how much they love each other, every couple goes through an "adjustment stage" that experts say lasts about three years. Divorce is three times lower among those married longer than three years. Those first three years are crucial. They often make or break a marriage. And the reason? It is during that period we all discover two things about our partner, (1) they are not perfect, and (2) in the areas where we are opposites, we clash.

The notion that opposites attract each other did not originate with me; it has been around for a long time. World-famous psychologist Dr. Carl Jung believed that opposites not only attract each other, they hold a particular fascination for each other. An article published in *USA Today* (September 15, 1983) reported on a new theory that showed that "thinkers tend to attract feelers," and that both types need to understand that tendency in their mate. I find that very interesting because sanguines make judgments on feelings (intuitively) while mels and phlegs have to analyze everything before reaching a decision. And these are the groupings that usually attract each other.

Why opposites attract each other

What could be more opposite than male and female? Yet they still attract each other after thousands of years. In fact, the future of the race is dependent on such attraction. Unfortunately, they fail to realize that their physical differences are only symbolic of the many other differences in their natures, the most significant of which are their temperaments.

A negative is never attracted to another negative, and positives repel each other in any field—electricity, chemistry, and particularly temperament. Instead, negatives are attracted to positives and vice versa. I have found that almost universally true of temperaments.

Have you ever wondered what attracts you to other people? Usually it is the subconscious recognition of and appreciation for their strengths—strengths that complement your own weaknesses. Consciously or otherwise, we all wish we could eradicate our particular set of weaknesses, and we blissfully admire the strengths of others. If given enough association with the person who sparks our attraction, we experience one of two things. Either we discover weaknesses in them similar to our own and are understandably turned off by them, or we discover other strengths we are lacking, which translates admiration into love. If other factors are favorable, it is not uncommon for such couples to marry.

Like temperaments rarely cohere. For instance, a sanguine would seldom marry another sanguine, for both are such natural extroverts that they would be competing for the same stage in life, and no one would be sitting in the audience. Sanguines, you see, need an audience to turn them on. Cholerics, on the other hand, make such severe demands on other people that they not only wouldn't marry each other, they probably would never date—at least not more than

454   TRANSFORMING YOUR TEMPERAMENT

once. They would spend all their time arguing about everything and vying for control or authority in their relationship. Two melancholies might marry, but it is very unlikely. Their analytical traits find negative qualities in others, and thus neither would pursue the other. Two phlegmatics would rarely marry, for they would both die of old age before one got up enough steam to propose. Besides, they are so protective of their feelings that they could "go steady" with a person for years before saying or otherwise communicating, "I love you." One phlegmatic man had courted an exceedingly patient Christian lady for four years. Finally her patience snapped and she asked, "Have you ever thought about our getting married?" He replied, "A time or two." She countered, "Would you like to?" He then answered, "I think so." "When?" He responded, "Whenever you would like." Years later he acknowledged that he had wanted to marry her for two years but was afraid to ask. Can you imagine how long they would have waited if she, too, had been a phlegmatic?

In the Western world, where couples choose their own partners, you will find that generally opposite temperaments attract each other. For a previous book, I surveyed several hundred couples who understood the temperaments and fed their responses into a computer. Less than .4 percent indicated that they matched the temperament of their spouses. Ordinarily I found that sanguines were attracted to melancholies and cholerics to phlegmatics, although that is by no means universal.

Sanguines, who tend to be disorganized and undisciplined themselves, are apt to admire careful, consistent, and detail conscious melancholies. The latter, in turn, favor outgoing, uninhibited individuals who compensate for the introvert's rigidity and aloofness. The hard-driving choleric is often attracted to the peaceful, unexcited phlegmatic, who in turn admires Rocky's dynamic drive.

After the honeymoon, the problems from this kind of selection begin to surface. Sparky Sanguine is not just warm, friendly, and uninhibited, but forgetful, disorganized, and very undependable. Besides, he gets quite irate if his lady love, a melancholy, asks him to pick up his clothes, put away his tools, or come home on time. Somehow Rocky Choleric's before-marriage "dynamic personality" turns into anger, cruelty, sarcasm, and bullheadedness after marriage. Martin Melancholy's gentleness and well-structured life-style becomes nitpicky and impossible to please after marriage. Philip

Phlegmatic's cool, calm, and peaceful ways often seem lazy, unmotivated, and stubborn afterwards.

Learning to adapt to your partner's weaknesses while strengthening your own is known as "adjustment in marriage." Hopefully, it will comfort you to know that no matter who you marry or what temperament you select, you will have to endure this adjustment process to some degree. Additional encouragement will be found in the fact that God, by his Holy Spirit, has given you ample resources to make a salutary adjustment.

I am not suggesting that single people look for a person that is opposite for a mate. What's wrong with marrying for love, in the will of God, of course? Actually, I know several happily married couples that are very similar in their temperament. For example, one couple we know well are both introverts. She is a PhlegChlor and he is a MelPhleg. Because of his walk with God he is a happy, well-adjusted person. And most of their friends think they are alike, but they aren't. I also know a pair of extroverts who married. She is a ChlorMel, and he is a SanMel. Theirs was a stormy household for a time because both were volatile and clashed a great deal until they learned about temperament.

One of the reasons I favor long courtships is because they usually give a couple time to expose the weaknesses of their temperament to their proposed partner. Another reason is that it allows for explosions like those they will encounter in marriage to reveal themselves. However, the couples that come to me "hopelessly mismatched" are already married to a person who thinks differently, feels differently, and responds differently than themselves. Some of these differences are just the natural difference of the sexes. In spite of what the feminists say, men and women are different.

Personally, I don't believe there are any "hopeless" cases with God. You show me two people who are willing to trust God and obey his rules for interpersonal behavior and I will show you a couple that has learned to be happy in marriage. It isn't easy, but it certainly is an improvement over the disharmony experienced in many families today.

Through the years I have developed a series of steps these couples need to take to rekindle their love. If these steps are followed, any couple can have happiness.

God is the author of marriage. He intended that it be the happiest, most fulfilling experience in a person's life. And millions have found it so long before anyone had discovered temperament. Now that we have this theory to assist us, the adjustment to a happy marriage should be every couple's goal. And these steps to temperament adjustment will help.

1. *Slam the divorce door.* Easy divorce has done nothing to help the longevity of marriage. In the state of California I warned our leaders that if they reduced the waiting period for a divorce decree from one year to six months it would double the divorce rate in ten years. I was wrong; we doubled it in seven years.

I have found that as long as the divorce door remains open, it retards the adjustment to a happy marriage. And if you are a Christian, it is not a legitimate option for you. God has made it clear in his Word that you are wed for life. So acknowledge that and close that door. Never use it as a threat to your spouse, or even entertain it as an option in your mind, for if you do Satan will entice you with the idea every time you experience pressure and unhappiness. By slamming that door in your mind, you open yourself fully to the resources of God to bring the sparkle of love back into your relationship.

2. *Admit to yourself that you are not perfect.* Humility is the best possible base for establishing any relationship between two people. That is true particularly of marriage because the couple spends so much time together. True love for another person is built on humility.

A healthy look at your own temperament will enable you to recognize that you have not brought only strengths into your marriage and that God is not finished with you yet. He is strengthening your weaknesses and improving you all the time. In fact, you probably have a long way to go. Realistically facing the fact will help you accept step three.

3. *Accept the fact that your partner has weaknesses.* Repeatedly we have discerned through the study of temperament and temperament blends that all human beings reflect both strengths and weaknesses. It cannot be otherwise until the resurrection, when we will be made perfect in Christ. The sooner you face the fact that anyone you marry will have weaknesses to which you must adjust, the sooner you can get to the business of adjusting to your partner.

Resist all mental fantasies of "If only I had married _____!" or "If only I had married another temperament." That is not a live option, so why not accept your partner's weaknesses?

4. *Pray for the strengthening of your partner's weaknesses.* God is in the temperament-modification business. By his Holy Spirit and through his Word, he is able to provide the strengths your partner needs for the improvement of his or her temperament weaknesses. But it will never happen if you are on his or her back all the time. If a temperament weakness produces a consistent pattern of behavior such as tardiness, messiness, legalism, negativism, and so on, it may be advisable to talk lovingly to your partner about it once; but after that, just commit the matter to God. If you take the place of the Holy Spirit in your partner's conscience, he will never change; but if you remain silent on the issue and love your partner as he is, then the Holy Spirit can get through to him.

The Bible says, "The effectual fervent prayer of a righteous man availeth much" (James 5:16). As you pray, God will work on your partner.

5. *Apologize when you are wrong.* Everyone makes mistakes! Fortunately, you don't have to be perfect to be a good person or partner. A mature person is one who knows both his strengths and weaknesses and develops a planned program for overcoming his weaknesses. That presumes you will make mistakes. We must ask, then, Are you mature enough to take full responsibility for what you have done? If in anger you have offended your partner in word or in deed, you need to apologize. God in his grace has given us the example and the means for repairing mistakes and offenses. An apology reaches into another's heart and mind to remove the root of bitterness that otherwise would fester and grow until it choked your relationship. That is why the Bible exhorts, "Confess your faults one to another . . ." (James 5:16).

6. *Verbalize your love.* Everyone needs love and will profit from hearing it verbalized frequently. This is particularly true of women, whatever their temperament. I once counseled a brilliant engineer, a father of five, whose wife left him for another man whose salary was one-third her husband's. After a bit of probing, I learned that he had not expressed his love for ten years. Why? He didn't think it was necessary. Verbalizing love is not only a necessity for holding a couple together, but an enrichment of their relationship.

After five or ten years of marriage the man is responsible for 80 percent or more of his wife's self-acceptance. That is more important than most people realize, for if a person doesn't love and accept himself he will have a very difficult time loving and accepting others. And the best way for a man to help his wife gain self-acceptance is by verbally reassuring her of his acceptance and love. Instead of harping on her weaknesses and beating her down continually, he should comment positively on her strengths. It enriches her self-esteem and motivates her to try harder. Some ill-advised men are afraid of the procedure, thinking it will make her complacent. Just the opposite is true. Women thrive on approval, compliments, and love. Disapproval and humiliation destroy; approval enriches. The man who wants a wife who thinks well of herself can help her become that way.

This is not just psychologically sound advice. More important, it is a command. "Husbands, love your wives" occurs four times in Scripture. Once (Eph. 5:26-30) we are commanded to love her as Christ does the church. Such love illustrates the way our Lord reassures the church of his love—through his Word. You know yourself that occasionally you entertain doubts about God, his love, and perhaps his forgiveness. What reassures you? His Word. That is one reason I advise that we all read it daily. But that is the same way you can reassure your wife of your love—by verbalizing it. Giving her jewelry and gifts and providing other thoughtful and tangible expressions of your love is important. But she will never cross beyond the need to hear your "Honey, I love you!" or "Honey, I admire your ability to _____." (And wife, neither will he.)

Summary

We are not today what we once were, nor are we what we will be, particularly if we let God work in our lives. And that person you are married to is not in their final form. Trust God to gradually conform him or her to the image of his Son.

In the meantime learn to be friends, partners, and lovers. That is rarely easy, and for most of us it takes a long time, but with God's help it can be done. As God and time wear off some of the rough edges of your and your partner's natures, you will find more pleasure in your relationship than irritations—provided you are not selfish. Nothing destroys like selfishness.

Adjusting to another person, particularly one with a temperament opposite your own, is not easy and it is not done quickly. But like anything of real value, it is worth the investment. And someday you will realize you are married to your best friend. That is the ideal marriage.

14

TEMPERAMENT AND SEXUALITY

We are all sexual creatures. That is nothing to be ashamed of—we were made so by a holy and loving God. The idea that sex and sexual feelings are evil is a distortion of the devil. History reveals countless individuals who were shipwrecked by refusing to come to grips with their sex drive. Some try to pretend it isn't there, others abuse it to their own destruction. Like everything else in life, sex has its place and proper function.

The Bible makes it clear that the only place for sexual expression is marriage. History shows the untold human suffering that is caused when that standard is violated. Everything said about our sexuality in this chapter is said in the biblical context of one man and one woman as long as they both live. That is still God's plan, and it is still the best way for anyone to express his sex drive.

When my wife and I wrote *The Act of Marriage*, it was not popular for ministers to write explicit manuals on sex. But I had been a pastor and family counselor for so many years I knew that sexual inadequacy was one of the basic causes for adultery and divorce among Christians. I had counseled many Christians who had been married from one month to forty-one years who found sex "unpleasant, distasteful" or "the worst part of marriage." God never intended it to be so.

Think about it a moment. Would a loving God design two human beings to have an experience an average of 125 times a year for fifty years that was "unpleasant" or "ugly"? Hardly! And the Bible is not silent on the subject. Sex in marriage is not just for the propagation of the race; it is for love, communication, oneness, and just plain pleasure. If you do not find lovemaking pleasurable, you need to read *The Act of Marriage*. God has used it in the lives of many people to open up to them a lifetime of enjoyment.

We had two major purposes in mind in writing that book. One was to prepare innocent Christian young people who had kept themselves sexually pure to read one manual that would open the door to a lifetime of meaningful sexual enjoyment when they married. Today, with a million and a half copies in print, it is the one book most often recommended by pastors for the couples they marry to read before and during their honeymoon.

The second reason was to help Christians already married who were not getting all the benefit from this God-designed experience to read one book that could change their attitude, inform them on this delicate subject, and answer the many questions they might have on the subject from a Christian perspective.

I saw the "sexual revolution" coming. I knew that although it would never be approved by the Bible-believing church, it would have a great influence on many of the people in our churches. That has happened in our generation. The permissiveness, the overemphasis and near-obsession with sex in our society has destroyed far too many homes even in our churches. I believe the two best safeguards to help a couple keep their sacred wedding vows and maintain sexual purity all through their marriage are: (1) a strong spiritual life, and (2) a healthy, expressive sexual relationship.

Sexual dysfunction or disharmony was said by one researcher to be 90 percent of the cause of the breakdown between divorced couples. That seems high to me, but even if it is only 60 percent we can see how powerful an influence sex is to a marriage. And since we have already established the fact that temperament is the most powerful single factor in influencing all of human behavior, it follows that a person's temperament will have an extremely powerful influence on a man or woman's sexual behavior.

Everyone knows that men and women are different sexually— not only from a physical equipment standpoint, but mentally and emotionally. Their appetites are different, and so are their inhibitions. But their different temperaments also have a bearing on their different attitudes, appetites, and requirements. Many writers and sex researchers fail to take into account the influence on a couple's sexual functions or the drives of their different temperaments. That failure has led to a lot of inaccurate conclusions.

It is wrong to say that "women are sexually less aggressive than men." For example, sanguine women can be more aggressive than some phlegmatic men. However, much more research is necessary in this area to be definitive. For this chapter, I have made some observations about the differences in the sexual attitudes, appetites, and pleasures of each of the temperaments, both male and female, based on my counseling experiences. These observations will have to suffice until more complete research is done. But all married people will benefit if they understand the sexual needs and likely responses of their mate. I try to cover them in this chapter. If you are not married, it would probably be best that you skip reading the following.

Special considerations

Sexual expression is not just a physical experience. It involves emotions, mind, body, mental attitude, temperament, physical fitness, sex education, and other factors. Two identical people of the same sex and temperament can have entirely different sexual capabilities and demands. For example, a melancholy wife, raised by a loving, thoughtful father who welcomed her into his heart anytime she wanted to sit on his lap, is likely to be a warm, affectionate wife who thoroughly enjoys lovemaking. (Incidentally, the best preparation for sex in marriage for a young woman is to have enjoyed a healthy relationship with her father all through life.) If, however, that same young woman has been rejected by her father as a child, she is likely to be frigid. After the wave of libido that encouraged her to marry has subsided and after the novelty of marriage is over (three to nine months for a melancholy), her *amour* may decline and her frigidity take over. Her response may have nothing to do with her husband's behavior or personality, and it may have nothing to do with her true love for him. Such women need counseling, patient husbands, and the power of God to overcome such difficulties.

Traumatic experiences can also make a vast difference in the sexual expression of both men and women. Even sanguine men can be warped in their mind and feel insecure if they were molested by a homosexual as a child. Melancholies can be almost rendered impotent by the guilt, shame, and insecurity of such an experience. And we hear all too frequently today of the tragic psychological blocks to sex some women have, caused by child molesters. One choleric woman confessed that she was "totally dead sexually. When my husband makes love to me, I cannot feel a thing; it is as if I am sexually insensitive." At my probing it was revealed that she had been molested by a stepfather regularly from six years old until she was seventeen years of age and could not gain the maturity to put a stop to it. What caused her insensitivity? Blind rage! She hated that man so much, it killed her capacity to love anyone else. I am happy to say she is perfectly normal today, but it took time and much forgiveness.

Now you see why I say that sex is complex. Like a 125-piece orchestra, it works best when all the instruments are in tune and functioning in unison. If one instrument is out of tune, it won't have too much ill affect; but if a dozen instrumentalists don't play on cue, it may be terrible. Fortunately, there aren't that many components to good sexual harmony, but it still is best when all the factors contribute toward the same goal—mutually satisfying expressions of love. Like a great orchestra, great sex takes training and practice. The difference is that in God's plan sexual training in marriage must be conducted with another person who knows as little about it as you do. That is why the more you know about your partner's needs in advance, the easier it is to relate to them. It is also essential to maintain open lines of communication between each other; this hastens the training process.

Married couples will find the analysis of the sexual responses of the four temperaments as presented in this chapter very helpful. After you have read them all for both the male and female, you should go back and study the temperament presentation of your partner and your own.

Sparky Sanguine's sexual responses

Sparky Sanguine is so responsive that it doesn't take much to "turn him on," and since he is so obvious about everything he does, his wife is instantly aware of his mood. A natural charmer, he thinks he can turn the head of a female marble statue with his flattery. And he can—unless he is married to her. He usually has a great appetite for everything, including lovemaking.

Most sanguines have very few hang-ups about sex and usually make it clear they enjoy it. If it isn't the most important thing in life for them, it's a close second. The sanguine husband is usually reluctant to take no for an answer; in fact, he can easily be hurt or deflated if his partner does not respond to his gestures of love. He may outwardly project the idea that he is God's gift to women, but underneath he has a great need for affection. If he is not satisfied at home, Sparky, more than any other temperament, may seek affection elsewhere, for two reasons: (1) the conquest of another woman is necessary to satisfy his powerful ego, and he finds lonely, unfulfilled women easy prey to his charm; (2) he is weak-willed and emotionally excitable; consequently, he is vulnerable to the unscrupulous woman.

The supersex emphasis of our day is very hard on Sparky, for he is easily stimulated. He has four basic needs in this area:

(1) Moral principles deeply ingrained in his heart and mind from childhood that show God's plan of one man for one woman "so long as they both shall live."

(2) The concept of "walking in the Spirit," particularly in his thought-life. Romans 13:14 says, "Make not provision (forethought) for the flesh, to fulfill the lusts thereof." If a sanguine indulges in immoral "fantasies," he will soon fan his passions out of control and will commit the sin of adultery to the heartache of his wife and himself. Once the moral barrier is broken, it is easy for him to repeat his sin. Sparky particularly needs to avoid all use of pornographic material whether magazine, movie, or television. He is visually stimulated, and such material is like pouring gasoline on his fire. It artificially stimulates his sex drive.

(3) A loving, responsive, affectionate wife who freely lets her husband know how much she enjoys his love and who rarely refuses his desires for sex. Husbands treated like that rarely stray, regardless of their temperament.

(4) Sparky Sanguine needs to learn to control his sex drive. He is an instant gratifier in everything, including sex. Many a wife who dearly loves her sanguine husband complains, "He is too quick" or "He doesn't wait for me" or "He takes too many shortcuts." Sparky needs to understand women and make a study of lovemaking. Most sanguines assume they know all about it. Nothing could be further from the truth. Good lovemaking is an art that must be learned. And sanguines need to learn to control their sex drive and hold off its expression until the wife is properly prepared.

Sanguines can be romantic, and most women like to be romanced. Sparky needs to control himself to adapt his satisfaction to his wife's need. The sexually satisfied wife will naturally enjoy sex more and want to engage in it more frequently. All husbands should make a quest of learning the art of bringing their wife to orgasm. This is a safeguard to a long and happy marriage. Sanguines can learn to be good lovers in marriage, but it takes learning, practice, and self-control.

One thing Sparky can do that will enrich his bedroom life is stop his lifetime habit of flirting with other women. He doesn't mean anything by it (usually), but his melancholy wife is surprised to see him; and although it may turn other women on, be sure of this—it is a giant turnoff to his wife. Be friendly, but not flirtatious.

The sexual response of Mrs. Sarah Sanguine

Very few differences in sexual response distinguish a sanguine man from a sanguine woman. Sarah Sanguine is a cheerful, happy, affectionate cheerleader-type who has the gift of making men feel "comfortable" in her presence. Her charming personality makes her a "hit" with all types of men, and in her naivete she can turn them on without realizing it. She usually thinks she is "just being friendly."

As a wife, Sarah has a tremendous amount of love to impart to her husband and family. Lovemaking is very important to her and it doesn't usually take too much coaxing to get her into the mood. Even if hurt or angry, she rather easily can moderate her attitude. Sanguines rarely carry a grudge, a trait essential for any marriage. She is the most likely type to greet her husband at the door with a "kiss with a future." Of all the temperaments, she is the one most likely to jolt her husband, after reading *The Total Woman*, by meeting him at the door dressed in boots and an apron.

Sarah rarely has hang-ups about anything, so she usually maintains a good attitude toward sex, often in spite of disastrously distorted misconceptions handed down from her mother. Her natural ability to express herself overcomes her inhibitions, and she quickly finds that she heightens her lovemaking enjoyment by being aggressive. Unless unwisely stifled by her husband, she usually learns early that passivity in lovemaking is not for her. Her sanguine moodswings vary, bringing great delight to her partner.

These wives have a tremendous desire to please their partners. With a reasonable amount of encouragement and cooperation, they usually succeed in this area of marriage, provided their shortcomings in other areas do not become their partner's obsessions.

Fun-loving Sarah Sanguines start out in marriage expecting to enjoy sex. The following suggestions will help them to realize that potential:

(1) Cultivate a strong spiritual life by walking in the Spirit, regularly studying the Word of God, and obeying his standards of moral behavior.

(2) Recognize your ability to excite men other than your husband and avoid flirtations that would provoke his jealousy or confront you with unnecessary temptations.

(3) Soften your extroversion so you will not embarrass your husband. A loud, overbubbly wife may gain the attention of other men, but she is certain to earn the disapproval of her husband.

(4) Sarah needs to concentrate on tenderly loving her mate, who will assure her of his approval and acceptance and dispense tender words of encouragement, attention, and affection. If she receives these, she will give attention to proper grooming, fashion, manners, good housekeeping, and whatever else will make her pleasing to her husband.

Sexually satisfying lovemaking is important to Sarah. She can happily endure almost anything in life if she is not starved for love. And let's face it—sex is an expression of love. It is a wise husband who does *not* pander it out for good behavior, but adapts himself to his wife's needs.

Rocky Choleric as a husband

On the surface a choleric suitor appears to be a great lover. Candy and flowers in abundance, politeness, kindness, and dynamic leadership make him appear to be the embodiment of manliness. Somehow that tends to change shortly after marriage as he takes the romance out of their marriage. Cholerics are such goal-conscious creatures that they are willing to do almost anything to attain their desires. Since the "sweet young thing" is subconsciously a goal before marriage, the choleric is willing to pay any price to win her hand. Once married, however, the goal is changed; now he wants to support her properly. Consequently, he may work from twelve to twenty hours a day. The hardest thing for a choleric male to understand is that his partner did not marry him for what he could give her, but for himself. When confronted with his wife's complaint that he doesn't love her anymore, he responds, "Of course I love you; I work like a slave to give you what you want." The truth of the matter is, he enjoys work.

Emotionally, a choleric is an extremist; he is either hot or cold. He can get furiously angry and explode over trifles, and his bride becomes terrified when she first sees these outbursts. His impatience and inability to lavish affection on her may produce a difficult adjustment for her. Showing affection is just "not his thing." One woman married to a choleric said, "Kissing my husband is like kissing a marble statue in the cemetery on a winter day."

The choleric's impetuous traits likewise hinder his proper adjustment to marriage. Just as she is apt to set out on a trip before consulting a road map, he is prone to take his wife to the bedroom without the slightest sex education. Somehow he thinks it will all work out!

Fortunately, a choleric possesses one important trait that helps his love life—he is always practical. Once he realizes that lovemaking involves more than preparing for a 100-yard dash—that he must be tender, gentle, affectionate, thoughtful, and sensitive to his wife's needs—he learns quickly. In the learning process he finds that affection is exciting and that watching the woman he loves respond to his touch is extremely fulfilling.

The most underdeveloped part of a choleric is his emotional life. And since lovemaking at its best is motivated by emotion, he has many needs:

(1) To show love and compassion for others. Nothing short of the personal experience of receiving Christ as Lord and Savior and learning to "walk in the Spirit" will provide the choleric with this ability. Even after his conversion, it often takes some time before the "love of God" characterizes his life.

(2) To understand that many people are not as self-sufficient as he. Even though they may be as capable, they will not be as confident that they can perform well. Rocky must realize that other people may tend to harbor doubts much more easily than he. If he will patiently show kindness and encourage his partner, she will be a better performer.

(3) To develop tenderness and affection for his wife and children and to voice his approval and commendation of them. He must

learn to say "I love you" quite frequently to his wife and act proud of her. Because the choleric is a natural leader, others tend to look to him for approval, love, and acceptance. He can wither them with a disapproving look and condemning word, or he can lift their spirits by going out of his way to approve and commend them. Those who have been rejected by him may tend to build a shell around their egos in order to protect themselves and to ward off future injuries. When the choleric father and husband becomes sensitive to the emotional needs of his family, he can even spark emotions within himself that would otherwise remain dormant. To say, "I love you" is not easy for him; but when he forgets himself, recognizing the importance of these words to his loved one, and concentrates on her emotional well-being, Rocky will learn quickly—and will thoroughly enjoy the response it brings.

(4) Rocky also needs to eliminate sarcasm and disrespectful speech from his vocabulary. Unkind and resentful words never turn a wife on.

(5) To learn to overcome his inner hostilities and anger for two reasons: first, "grieving the Spirit" through anger (Eph. 4:30-32) will keep him a spiritual pygmy all of his Christian life; second, the threat of instant choleric explosion inhibits the emotional expressions of his wife. It is difficult for a choleric Christian to realize that his spiritual life will affect his bedroom life, but it does—one way or the other.

The Choleric wife's sexual responses

Clara Choleric is usually an exciting creature, particularly if one does not have to live with her. She is extremely active in every area of life—a dynamic, forceful individual with multiple goals in mind. At the same time, she may feature a spitfire personality and a razor-blade tongue, dominating and controlling every activity in which she is involved.

In my late teens there was such a girl in our youth group. Many guys dated her because she was fun to be with, but they kiddingly remarked behind her back, "Don't marry Evelyn unless you want to be President of the United States."

The necessity of having a positive mental attitude toward love-making in marriage comes into focus when dealing with the choleric wife. If she observed a warm love relationship between her parents while she was growing up, she will probably enter marriage expecting to enjoy lovemaking. Cholerics usually achieve what they set out to do, and she will probably not be disappointed—nor will her husband.

On the other hand, if she has been raised by unhappy, bickering parents, if she has been molested or has endured other traumatic experiences in childhood, or if she has been taught that "sex is dirty" for either religious or other ill conceived reasons, she may encounter serious difficulty in relating properly to her husband. Cholerics are so opinionated that once obsessed with the idea that "sex is not for nice girls," they might reject the angel Gabriel carrying a message on a stone tablet saying "marriage is honorable in all." But once convinced that God wants her to enjoy sex she can usually make a quick transition to a happy love life.

Choleric wives often acquire several potential hang-ups in this department. They are not usually given to open affection, and thus they often stifle their husbands' advances before their own motor rolls into action. In addition, if not Spirit-filled they tend to demasculinize a man by dominating and leading him in everything—including sex. It takes a Spirit-led, thoughtful choleric woman to recognize that she ignores her husband's ego at her own peril.

We have observed that opposites attract each other in marriage; consequently, a choleric woman will usually select a passive partner. If she isn't especially fond of lovemaking, they may go for long periods without it because he may be too passive to say or do anything about it. Whether or not he raises the issue, you can be sure he doesn't enjoy the abstinence! Ultimately an explosion occurs and almost always with serious consequences.

It is to the choleric wife's credit, however, that she will usually adjust and become a very enjoyable partner once she learns how important a good bedroom life is to her husband. She must realize that the success of her marriage may well depend upon her performance and willingness to let her husband maintain leadership in this intimate area of their life.

Like her male counterpart, Clara Choleric has many needs. These are some of the most important for her to consider:

(1) To "walk in the Spirit" in order to provide victory over her hot temper and sarcastic tongue, and to develop her emotional capability in showing love and affection. Being loving and affectionate is certainly easier for some temperaments than others, but God would never have commanded that we love one another if he

had not known it was possible for all. Cholerics may need to work at it a little harder than some, but the more they express it, the easier it comes.

(2) To learn forgiveness—especially for her father, if necessary. No woman can fully enjoy her husband if she hates her father. This is especially true of strong-minded, opinionated, willful cholerics. They will vent their frustrated wrath on their husbands, stifling their expressions of love. One reason a choleric woman may have this problem is that as a little girl she may have resisted her father's affections; and because he did not understand, he closed her out of his heart and had little to do with her—he simply did not know how to reach her. Not realizing why she was rejected by her daddy, she increasingly withdrew from showing any normal expressions of emotion toward him and fostered a growing resentment toward men.

(3) To avoid heaping sarcasm, criticism, and ridicule on her husband, particularly in the lovemaking area. Cholerics exude so much self-confidence that, even without saying anything, they cause others to feel inadequate. The choleric woman needs to let her husband know how much she values him as a man and a lover. No compliment is sweeter and cherished longer than one which appreciates the masculinity or femininity of one's partner.

(4) To take time to express love to her husband. Cholerics are often night people. Early-bird husbands may crawl into bed at ten or eleven o'clock, hoping for a little tenderness and love. But they fall asleep while their choleric wives finish a book, clean the house, or pursue countless other activities which their active minds suggest. Many choleric wives could improve their love lives just by going to bed earlier.

(5) To learn submission by biblical standards. A choleric likes to lead and usually makes a good leader, but by the grace of God and in obedience to his Word, such a wife needs to bring herself into submission to her husband. If she attempts to assume the husband's role and responsibilities in the home, she is courting disaster. A passive husband will give his wife more love, respect, and flexibility if she encourages him to take the responsibility and leadership of their home.

The Melancholy husband's sexual responses

Marvin Melancholy is a supreme idealist. He usually goes into marriage without any sex education because he idealistically believes that "everything will work out." If he is blessed with an amorous and exciting wife who has no hang-ups, everything usually does work out; but if he marries someone as naive as he, they may come home from their honeymoon in a depressed state. When the love life of a couple is deficient, it can create a shaky experience for a melancholic husband. His wife will especially be turned off by his depression, further complicating matters. It is usually quite difficult for him to seek counseling until his marriage enters a precarious phase.

The melancholy, more than any other temperament, has the capacity to express true love. He is a loyal and faithful partner unless he overindulges in impure thoughts and becomes involved in pornography. When Marvin Melancholy enjoys a good sex life with his wife, he will almost overextend himself in every other area of their marriage in thoughtfulness, kindness, and emotion.

Among the melancholy's greatest assets is his romanticism. He does the work of preparation beautifully: soft music, dim lights, perfume—those things that delight the romantic heart of a woman.

Because he is extremely analytical, Martin quickly learns what his wife finds pleasurable and enjoys bringing her fulfillment. If everything goes well for them, this couple can become great lovers.

Melancholies are such perfectionists that they almost refuse to accept anything less than perfection. Many a melancholy man can come home all "revved up" for his wife only to have his ardor cooled by dirty dishes in the sink or kids' toys in the middle of the floor. In fact, I know one melancholy husband who could be turned on by watching his wife get undressed for bed and turned off because she didn't hang up her clothes. At a time like that, a sanguine or choleric wouldn't even notice the clothes!

The sensitive traits of the melancholy that on most occasions make him aware of his wife's needs for tenderness and love may also work against him at times. He is prone to interpret his wife's lack of immediate response when he first initiates lovemaking as rejection. If his wife is in a coy mood, as women frequently are, and wants mild pursuit, he is apt to think she doesn't desire him and gives up before she can reveal her true feelings.

The melancholy individual has a tremendous amount of love to give to others if granted the slightest encouragement. These are some of his most obvious needs:

(1) Maintaining a vital, personal relationship with God, and a daily Spirit-filled experience that keeps him "others-oriented" instead of obsessed with himself. No selfish or self-centered person will be a good lover, no matter what his temperament. A real test of whether or not a melancholy is walking in the Spirit appears when he breaks that self-centered syndrome.

(2) Learning to give unconditional love, not rewarded love. A wife once told me that her husband was a natural-born nitpicker. "He has a long checklist for housekeeping, and if I don't rate an 'A' before we go to bed, he will not make love to me," she complained.

(3) Avoiding a critical and pessimistic attitude, the two biggest problems of a melancholy. Because of his perfectionism, he often has unrealistic standards of achievement for himself and others. This in turn causes him to become frequently disillusioned when things and people don't measure up.

(4) Maintaining a positive and wholesome thought life (Phil. 4:8). He should never indulge in revengeful thought patterns of self-pity, but always "in every thing give thanks" (1 Thess. 5:18).

(5) Being married to a woman who is not easily offended and can cheerfully encourage him when he is down, reassure him of his manhood when he is insecure, and take his criticism lightly. As long as she knows he is moody, she can patiently wait a little while for his mood to change.

(6) Concentrating on God and thanking him for his partner's strengths. He must regularly encourage her with verbal assurances of love and approval. I have seen many a sanguine wife go through a personality change under the constant criticism of a melancholic husband. Unfortunately, when he is finished even Martin Melancholy doesn't like his creation.

The Melancholy wife's sexual responses

Martha Melancholy is an unpredictable love partner, for she has the greatest of all mood swings. On some occasions she can be as exciting and stimulating as any sanguine. On others she has absolutely no interest in anything—including love. She may meet her husband at the door and sweep him off his feet right into the bedroom, or she may ignore his arrival completely.

Martha Melancholy is the supreme romantic, and her moods are as apparent as the noonday sun. When in the mood for love, she resorts to dinner by candlelight, soft music, and heavy perfume. (If she's married to a sanguine, that works quite well; but if her husband is a choleric, she may be in trouble, because he often detests perfume.)

Although she has the capability of enjoying ecstatic love at heights that would asphyxiate other temperaments, she rarely is interested in setting world records for frequency. To her, quality is always preferable to quantity. Of all the temperament types, she is the most apt to engage in bedroom roulette—that is, she dispenses love as a reward for good behavior. However, no man worthy of the title will put up with that!

A melancholy is often plagued with unreal prudishness, especially if her mother had a problem in this area. She may use trumped-up religious arguments to excuse her sexual abstinence; her real problem, however, probably stems from her premarital resolution that sex is undesirable, and she has never given herself the opportunity to learn otherwise. She is the type who saves lovemaking only for propagation—rarely for pleasure. A study of the Scriptures can teach her differently.

Little things can quickly be turned into mountainous problems for Martha Melancholy. Her husband's inability to balance the checkbook, his forgetting to run an errand, or his forgetting to bathe may thoroughly upset her and send her into frigid revenge. She feels he didn't keep his part of a bargain, so she need not keep hers—and thus she refrains from lovemaking. What she doesn't realize is that she is cheating herself out of both the enjoyment of lovemaking and the loving approval of her husband.

I counseled a melancholic wife who had not made love with her partner for several weeks. She was only interested at night, but by the time she was ready for bed, he had collapsed. She complained, "He goes to bed tired, and he never even takes time to bathe or brush his teeth. In the morning I am a zombie and he is charged up. But I can't stand his body smells and bad breath then!" I suggested that she learn to accept her husband and not try to change him. This was hard medicine for a wife to take, but before long she discovered that by cooperating with him, he was quite willing to modify his habits for her.

Another hang-up common to Martha Melancholy is jealousy. Not given to "insincere flirtation," she often marries a man who is outgoing and friendly to all. It is not uncommon for her to ride home in icy silence after a party because her husband "flirted with every woman there." Since her husband's male ego gets so little food at home, he unwisely seeks it at social gatherings. And he may often think, "Nothing I do ever satisfies that woman!"

Seated across from the beautiful wife of a wealthy and dynamic Christian businessman, I was startled to hear his wife ask me, "Would you explain why I am so jealous of my husband even when I know I have no reason for it?" It seems that he had dismissed three successive secretaries and finally hired the homeliest gal he could find just because of his wife's jealousy, but it still didn't solve her problem. I responded, "The problem is not with your husband; you just don't like yourself." Tears ran down her cheeks as she admitted to strong feelings of self-rejection. Later her husband commented concerning their love life, "When her groundless suspicions make her jealous, I can't touch her. But when she is sorry for her accusations, she can't get enough of me. I never know whether to expect feast or famine!"

Martha's biggest problem in life will be the tendency toward self-pity. A melancholy can follow the slightest insult or rejection with self-pitying thoughts that plunge her into a state of depression until she is not interested in love or anything else.

The emotional capability of a melancholy is so extensive that she has the potential of being an exciting and fulfilling love partner if her weaknesses don't overpower her strengths. Here are some of her specific needs:

(1) A vital and effective relationship with Jesus Christ, walking in his Spirit, so that she may enjoy the love, peace, and joy he gives to make her an effective person.

(2) A thankful attitude for all the blessings God has given her, never thinking or verbalizing criticism for the things that don't please her. She will discover that a positive mental attitude combined with thanksgiving can give her a happier outlook on life and make her a more pleasant person for others to enjoy. This attitude will also help her to accept herself as she is; self-condemnation will destroy her. It is very difficult for others to like her if she does not like herself.

(3) Acceptance of her husband as he is, permitting God to make any changes that are needed. Her submission to him should not be dependent on his behavior, but on her obedience to God.

(4) Encouragement and reassurances of love from her husband. A thoughtful and verbally expressive husband who proves his

love in many other areas of their marriage will be rewarded in this one.

(5) The request that God give her an unconditional love for her husband and the ability to love him to the point that she forgets about herself. She needs to realize that married love is beautiful because it is God's plan for married partners. Our Lord promises that a woman who gives herself without reservations to her husband will be loved. He said, "Give and it shall be given unto you," and "Whatsoever a man soweth, that shall he also reap." If a woman sows love, she will surely reap it in abundance.

(6) The lesson of forgiveness. Almost every durable marriage requires forgiveness along the way. Because an unforgiving attitude will always destroy a relationship, the partners must realize that their harmony requires it and God commands it (Matt. 18:35; Mark 11:25).

The Phlegmatic husband's sexual responses

Not much is known about the bedroom life of Phil Phlegmatic. He is without doubt the world's most closed-mouth individual, particularly concerning his personal life. What is known about this intimate area usually comes from an irate partner; consequently, the information could well be biased. In fairness to the phlegmatic male, therefore, any suggestions we make concerning his lovemaking responses have to be evaluated on the basis of deductive analysis and hearsay reporting. His secondary temperament will also have a powerful influence on his expression, as will his background and mental attitude.

Some assume that because a phlegmatic is easygoing and prone to be unmotivated, he may not be a very spirited lover; but that may not always be true. If a study of the habits of phlegmatics is indicative, we find that they usually accomplish more than they are given credit for. They just don't make noise and attract much attention to their achievements like other temperaments. Rather, they make good use of the effort expended. When they want to do something, they follow through effectively and promptly in their own quiet way. We suspect that is the way they make love.

One characteristic of phlegmatics should help their love life: their abundant kindness. Rarely, if ever, would Phil Phlegmatic embarrass or insult his wife; sarcasm is just not his way. Women usually respond to a man who is kind to them. On that basis he should have little trouble gaining love from his wife, if he desires it.

Another trait that is surely a great advantage is that a phlegmatic rarely gets angry and seldom creates irritation in others. If his fiery partner screams at him for some reason, his response usually extinguishes the fire because he is a master of the "soft answer." Consequently, the storm has usually passed by bedtime, and he can conveniently act as if it never happened.

Phlegmatic men often have a way of getting things to go their way by waiting for them. They are patience personified, apparently able to outwait others into action. Their love life is probably like that. As the intensity of their youthful sex drive cools down somewhat, they patiently teach their partner to originate lovemaking. And it may be that phlegmatics may get used to a less frequent than average lovemaking schedule as their drive cools. This could be habit. Sexual frequency in marriage is often related to habit. Those who perform three times a week develop a habit for that frequency level. The same person's life-style could change and sex could develop into a once-a-week habit. Phlegmatics are great for developing habits for everything.

One observation I have made about phlegmatic husbands is that their wives sometimes complain about lack of frequency. The only wives I have had decry this lack of loving have been married to phlegmatic husbands. Whether this lack of sex drive is induced physically, temporarily, or is the result of quiet resentment is difficult to determine. However, most of these men are not aware of how important it is to their wives' self-image and self-acceptance for them to make love to her frequently—particularly as she gets older.

Three areas may cause the phlegmatic man serious trouble. First, he tends to be reluctant to assert himself and take leadership unless it is thrust upon him. When he does lead, he performs his tasks admirably. However, when he fails to take the leadership in the home, his wife can become very disillusioned. The wife who expects such a husband to assume the initiative in the bedroom may soon feel unloved. Sometimes she loses respect for her phlegmatic husband because he doesn't seem to assert his manhood.

A second danger spot is phlegmatic selfishness, making him stingy, stubborn (in a polite way), and self-indulgent. Yielding to these weaknesses can produce resentment in a wife who complains, "He doesn't give me enough grocery money, and he never takes me out. All we ever do is what he wants to do." As we have already seen, resentment stifles love.

The third potential danger area to a phlegmatic is that be tends to crawl into a shell of silence when things fail to work out. Since he usually finds it difficult to talk about anything, he probably finds it hard to teach his partner what he finds exciting in lovemaking. Consequently, he may silently endure subpar relations for years and cheat both himself and his partner out of countless ecstatic experiences which God meant them to enjoy.

The kindhearted, soft-spoken, gentle phlegmatic may appear to outsiders as a man who has conquered his weaknesses, but those who live with him recognize his quiet needs. These are some of the most pertinent in the area of his love life:

(1) A dynamic relationship to Jesus Christ that motivates him to think of the needs of his wife and family rather than indulge in his own feelings and solitude.

(2) A more aggressive attitude in everything, especially in consideration of his wife's needs in lovemaking.

(3) Greater expression of his love and approval for his wife. He must learn to talk more freely about his own desires and needs, especially if the couple is confronting problems. This need to communicate requires his continual efforts.

(4) A wife who will understand and accept his seeming lack of motivation without resentment, one who will tactfully use her feminine wiles in arousing him at the appropriate time.

(5) A wife who will try to adapt her metabolic timetable to her partner's to maximize what vitality he has, one who appreciates his strong, silent tendencies and the depth of his nature, giving thanks for it rather than chafing at his inclination toward passivity. If she starts nagging, he will crawl into his shell and shut her out.

The Phlegmatic wife's sexual responses

As a general rule, the easiest person in the world to get along with is a phlegmatic, especially a woman. She loves to please people and usually gives in to her more forceful mate rather than create turmoil. She is easily satisfied and often turns her affection and attention on her children if trouble arises between her and her husband.

Her passive personality will usually characterize her bedroom life; she rarely initiates lovemaking, but because she wants to please her partner she almost never turns him down.

One of the most powerful influences in a phlegmatic's life, an influence which will strongly affect her lovemaking, may be fear and the anxiety which it causes. Such a woman may fear pregnancy (although she doesn't have a corner on that problem), disclosure, embarrassment, and a host of other real and imagined dilemmas. One of her fears is that her husband may lose respect for her if she appears eager or forward in lovemaking, though quite the opposite is the usual reaction.

In spite of her gracious, kind, and pleasant spirit, Polly Phlegmatic has several needs to become a better wife and love partner:

(1) To accept Jesus Christ as her Lord and Savior. Many phlegmatics have a hard time acknowledging that they are sinners (and they act so nice that others will likely agree, but self-righteousness has kept many out of the kingdom of God). As she learns to "walk in the Spirit" each day, the phlegmatic woman will gain motivation to overcome her passivity, love to overcome her selfishness, and faith to overcome her fears. When armed with such attributes from God, she can become an exciting partner.

(2) To create and maintain an interest in her appearance. Phlegmatic mothers often get so tired after their babies arrive that they become careless about their personal appearance—their hair, their attire, and often their weight. When a wife ceases to care how she looks to her man, she has clearly lost her self-esteem. Her husband's love and respect will also fade. A wife need not be a raving beauty to maintain the high regard of her husband, but her appearance night after night will indicate what she thinks of herself and of her husband. Any man should appreciate the fact that his wife is tired once in a while, but five nights a week is a cop-out.

Some Christian women have used 1 Peter 3:3 as an excuse to let their "outward appearance" run down—at the expense of their marriage. That passage says that a godly wife will spend more time cultivating her spiritual life than her physical, but by no means does it teach that she is to neglect either one. Remember, a woman is the most beautiful flower in a man's garden, and even roses need to be cultivated, pruned, and cared for.

(3) Polly needs to organize her daily life and sustain a regular schedule. A phlegmatic wife finds it easier to neglect her housekeeping chores than anyone else except a sanguine. She enjoys "coffee klatches," and before she realizes it hubby is due home. Since opposites attract each other, it is not uncommon for a phlegmatic

wife to create such resentment in her more fastidious partner that it spills over into their bedroom life. His uncharitable outburst may cause a stubborn phlegmatic to "refuse to clean up," producing further disharmony. Consequently, she needs to take pride in homemaking; her husband will respect and treat her better, and even more important, she will respect herself more.

(4) She needs to appreciate a thoughtful lover and strong, gentle husband. She requires a lover who learns how a woman functions best and takes time to arouse her to orgasm. Once she has learned that art, her desire for the experience will overpower her tendency to passivity, and she can learn to be an exciting partner. He needs to be a strong, gentle husband from whom she can draw courage to overcome her fears, one who will encourage and not browbeat her. A wise husband will verbally assure his wife of her worth and his love.

(5) She needs to learn to overcome her inability to speak the words she feels and communicate with her husband and family. Words do not come easily for her, especially about the intimacies of her love life. Phlegmatics need to push themselves in every area of life, and lovemaking is no exception. Polly Phlegmatic needs to remember the needs of her partner and forget her own; they will both be happier for it.

Other considerations

There are a number of other things that influence harmonious sexual relations during the length of a fifty-year marriage. I have noticed that young mothers with two or more children at home are not as interested in lovemaking as they were at twenty or as they will be at thirty-five and forty. Partly due to physical exhaustion and partly due to fear of pregnancy, their interest can wane. Men, on the other hand, react to pressure. Loss of employment can stifle even the most powerful male sex drive, as can financial pressures. Job advancement in his thirties can become a god to a man, making his sexual activity perfunctory or deficient. And sometimes nothing his wife does is able to change him.

One of my observations, shared by other counselors with whom I have discussed the matter, is that wives tend to get more interested in lovemaking as they get older while men tend to require it less frequently. That is particularly true after her children leave the nest and she feels unneeded by anyone but her husband. He then becomes the special object of her love in every way, including sex. Lovemaking at that point in time becomes a psychological need. And why shouldn't it? Everyone needs to be needed, and everyone needs love. In addition, the children are out of the home and the fears of discovery or interruption that bothered her in her twenties and thirties are now gone.

During her menopause a good wife may become sexually erratic. Hormonal changes going on in her body over which she has little or no control can cause her to be amorous one day and cold the next. Her usual supply of vaginal fluid may dry up or run out right in the middle of lovemaking. All women at this stage of life need much love and understanding. They also need to see their doctor. He can not only help shorten this period of her life, but he can recommend medication that will help control her emotions and body functions. Many women testify that heavy doses of Vitamin E during that period are also helpful.

Men, too, need patience as they mature. For some men, it is the retirement stage that turns them off. It is still true that a person's most important sex organ is his brain. Once he begins to realize his life is not over at sixty-five, he can be sexually active on into his nineties if his health permits.

Every couple goes through stages, changes, and adjustments in their sex life, just like everything else in their relationship. And although their temperament is not the only influence on their sexual responses, as we have seen, it is certainly one of the most powerful.

All four temperaments possess the capacity to become loving, satisfying marriage partners. As we have seen, each has its area of strength and weakness. Consequently, each is capable of overcompensating in an area of strength or developing a hang-up in an area of weakness. For that reason, it is helpful for every partner to know their mate's temperament so that they can approach each other in the most suitable fashion. Remember—love gives! When a partner administers love, he will in return receive all the love he needs.

One of the advantages of knowing the four temperaments is that it becomes easier to appreciate why your partner acts or reacts the way he does. That in turn helps you to accept his individual foibles and work with them, not against them.

We have a lovely sanguine friend named Molly who told me how God used the temperaments to resolve a pet peeve that was hindering her love life. Her husband, Pete, a melancholy/phlegmatic, regularly checked up on her. When he put his arm around her in bed as she snuggled close to him and warmed up to his mood, he would ask, "Molly, did you lock the back door and turn the heat down?" Though she answered, "Yes, Pete," he would jump out of bed, run through the dining room and kitchen, and check the back door and the thermostat. By the time he returned, her mood had turned to ice and she gave him the cold shoulder. This went on night after night—except when he became amorous enough to forget to ask the aggravating question.

One night Pete, an accountant by profession, brought home several income tax reports, spread them out on the dining room table, and began to work. Molly stood in the doorway, watching a strange charade: four times he added up a column of figures, put the answer on a slip of paper, and turned it over. When he finished the fourth one, he turned them all right side up and smiled to himself. They all agreed, so he wrote the answer on the tax form. Suddenly Molly realized that Pete didn't just check up on her; he even double-checked himself! She was proud of his reputation as an accurate accountant, and now she realized that the striving for perfection which made him successful in business was the same trait that caused him to check up on her.

That night she was ready for him! He put his arm around her, and she snuggled up close as usual. But when he asked, "Molly did you lock the back door and what about the heat?" she sweetly replied, "I sure did, honey, but if you want to check, it's okay by me." He got up and trotted through the dining room and kitchen; as usual, the door was locked and the thermostat turned down. But that night when he crawled back into bed, he didn't encounter a frosty iceberg!

Once you have diagnosed your partner's temperament you can lovingly cooperate with it instead of clash with it and will enjoy a long and enjoyable love relationship.

SIX

TEMPERAMENT AND YOUR SPIRITUAL LIFE

15

TEMPERAMENT AND SPIRITUAL GIFTS

During the past few years we have heard a great deal in the church about spiritual gifts. Much of it has been healthy in that it pointed out that God wants to use all of his children in some positive way in his kingdom. It also makes everyone realize he has real worth. Without God in their lives many people never feel they make any significant contribution to life. A Spirit-controlled Christian should not have that feeling.

Bible teachers are not in complete agreement on what spiritual gifts are and where they come from. I have been silent on the subject up until now, even though I have written several times on the Spirit-filled life. Basically the reason was because when I finally did put something in print I wanted to have my thoughts well in mind so that my ideas would be a positive help to people. The differences among Bible teachers on this subject indicate that no one has the last word on spiritual gifts. And after you have read this chapter you still will not have the final teaching. But it will be related to you and your temperament and hopefully will make you think and be helpful to you.

First of all, I don't think spiritual gifts are things you do not have any aptitude for before you become a Christian. I believe they are God's control of our naturally inherited temperament, directing its use in a manner that will glorify his Son Jesus Christ.

Most Bible teachers treat spiritual gifts as if they are additives, things we did not have before receiving Christ and had access to the power of the Holy Spirit to overcome our weaknesses. I do not agree. My father had a beautiful Irish tenor singing voice and an ear for music (neither of which I inherited). He could play a piano by ear and accompany himself. So when he accepted Christ, he kept right on singing—only different songs in different places and for a much different purpose. Gaining the power of God allowed him to use the talent he already had to communicate the gospel of Christ and glorify him. I believe that is the way spiritual gifts always work, except sometimes he uses gifts or talents we had before salvation that were unused and may have been unknown. For example, a person may have had the gift to teach before his salvation and never knew it. His vocation may not have provided an opportunity to express that gift, and he didn't even know he had it. But after salvation, the pastor or Sunday-school superintendent, under inspiration of the Holy Spirit, may have asked him to take a class, and before long he has a spiritual gift used to the glory of God. He didn't get a new gift, he was inspired by the Spirit of God to use his natural talents.

The same thing has happened to people who had never felt they were public speakers, or because of traumatic experiences when, as children, they were too afraid to speak. After their conversion God puts a burden in their heart to preach the gospel and they do a beautiful job. New gift? No; God unlocks the restrictions of fear that kept the natural talent silent prior to salvation.

There is a close kinship between talent and human temperament. We have seen in our study of the four temperaments that each of us has at least ten strengths which we inherited at birth. (Personally, I have found at least five more plus the secondary temperament's contribution, making a total of more than twenty-five talents or temperament strengths available to every person.) When a person is touched by the Spirit of God and has a corresponding strength through the Spirit available to him, he is now able to be used of God in the area of his naturally inherited temperament.

God is abundantly able to perform miracles and do with any of us as he sees fit. After all, he is the Sovereign God. If he chooses to give some an added talent they did not have before salvation, that is his divine right. Usually, however, he uses our existing talents—whether they were known previously to us or not. The following, however, is my definition of a spiritual gift.

A spiritual gift is the use God makes of an individual's natural talents when touched by his Holy Spirit. Such use will always glorify him. Rulers, for example, were rulers before salvation. They could have been rulers if they had never become Christians. Now, however, that they are born-again children of God, they no longer run roughshod over other people; they rule honestly, and their basic motive is no longer selfishness, greed, or pride. It is now one of love, gentleness, and long-suffering. The same is true of the car salesman whose natural spirit of charisma makes it possible for him to sell a car even with a bad paint job. Such a person, when filled with the Holy Spirit, may have the gift of evangelism and will, as he walks in the Spirit, lead many to the Savior. However, some who receive the gift of evangelism were so psychologically straitjacketed before salvation they did not realize they had that potential until filled with the Spirit.

In addition, the gift of evangelism is one gift every Christian has to one degree or another. I have seen the most introverted individuals lead many people to Christ. It is a matter of obedience, availability, persistence in sharing the Word of God through the power of the Holy Spirit. Anyone who has heard the gospel can receive Christ, if he so chooses. Faith comes by hearing "the word of Christ" (Rom. 10:17, NIV). That doesn't mean faith comes by hearing the Word from a person with the gift of evangelism, nor does it mean faith comes by hearing the Word from a sanguine. Faith can come by reading the Word of God without the presence of any human instrument—except to put that Bible in the motel room or print that gosel tract. In that sense, all Christians have the potential of the gift of evangelism either directly or indirectly. And I believe that is our primary purpose for being on this earth—to be used of God to evangelize. When Christians give their tithes and offerings to God through their church and other ministries, they are being used of God to evangelize. When they open their home for Bible studies, they are exercising the gift of evangelism. The reason I harp on this gift is twofold—first, to point out that we all have the potential to use this spiritual gift. Paul told timid Timothy, "Do the work of an evangelist," and he says it to each of us.

All Christians have all of the gifts

The other reason I used the gift of evangelism as an illustration was to point out that we all have all of the gifts to one degree or another, depending on our temperament. Cholerics have the gift of ruling much more than they have the gift of serving or giving, but they can serve. Those who have the gift of mercy are not usually endowed with a strong dose of the gift of ruling. But they can rule, and they can always rule better when controlled by the Holy Spirit.

I do not agree with the theory advanced by some Bible teachers that we all receive one spiritual gift and ought to find out what it is and exercise it. That is a nice theory, but there is no scriptural support for such an idea and it doesn't fit my observations of people in the real world. It is more accurate to recognize that we all have all of the gifts, but depending on our individual temperament combination they will be in differing priorities. To some, ruling will be first. To others, serving will be first. Knowing your temperament will help you determine your spiritual gifts. But before we get to pointing out the various priorities of gifts according to temperament, we should examine the definition of the gifts.

Spiritual gifts defined

There are thirteen different spiritual gifts that are operative today that are referred to in three passages of Scripture.These gifts should not be confused with the nine fruits of the Spirit (Gal. 5:22-23). The fruits of the Spirit are gifts given to us by the Spirit of God when he comes into our lives to strengthen, lead, and empower us. Our spiritual gifts are the natural traits or talents we received at birth which now the Holy Spirit will use to some degree in our lives if we make ourselves available to him.

The three basic passages that contain these thirteen spiritual gifts are Romans 12:3-9; 1 Corinthians 12:7-31; and Ephesians 4:11-13. Some are repeated in each section. Some, like apostles, were for first-century use only. The following thirteen are the spiritual gifts I believe are operative today, along with their definitions applied to you. Those with asterisks require a special calling from God to enable us to use them in the offices given in the church today. However, they may be used in some parallel manner. For example, you may not be called of God to be a "pastor" to shepherd a flock of Christians. Yet, you may be serving as a Sunday-school teacher, department superintendent, or youth leader and doing the work of pastor—shepherding a group. You may not be called as a missionary-evangelist, yet you may be evangelizing regularly. Look on these as ministry gifts, and don't limit them in your mind to an office of the church. Look on them as potential areas in which you may serve your Lord.

1. Mercy: The ability to cheerfully suffer the hurts of others, enabling you to minister to them in their time of need.

*2. Pastor shepherding: Guiding, feeding, and protecting the flock of God.

*3. Teaching: Communication of biblical truth; your greatest joy is in helping others to understand the truths of God.

4. Helps: The ability to thoughtfully anticipate the needs of others and joyfully assist them in fulfilling their calling and duty.

5. Wisdom: The ability to apply the principles of God's Word to the practical, everyday problems and choices of life in order to determine the will of God both for oneself and others.

*6. Evangelism: The ability to proclaim the gospel to individuals or groups for the purpose of winning them to Christ. In a sense, all Christians have this gift for direct or indirect use. The Christian that never uses this gift to some degree has an unfulfilled feeling.

*7. Prophesying: Spirit-empowered preaching that clearly sets forth the Word of God primarily to Christians, calling them to righteous living.

8. Exhorting: The capacity to encourage, motivate, and strengthen others in the faith, to confront them with their behavior, and to challenge or advise them in conforming to the will of God as it is revealed in his Word.

9. Knowledge: The ability to learn the facts of God's creative universe and relate them to his revealed Word.

10. Government: The ability to lead others in administering the work of God. Such a person is capable of enlisting others in serving the Lord.

11. Discernment: The capacity to distinguish between truth and error and the ability to make good decisions.

12. Giving: The ability to make money and joyfully give it
                 to the work of the Lord.

13. Faith: An unusual trust in God, enabling you to
                 launch divinely ordained projects that turn vi-
                 sion into fact.

As a person matures in his Christian life, he will naturally
increase in his effectiveness in expressing these gifts. The two
areas over which you have control of the expansion of these gifts
are the Word of God and faith. The more you know the Word
of God, the better each of these gifts will function in your life.
It's as though God gave them to you in infancy and you are to
develop them. You are to exercise these gifts by faith. If you don't
use a gift, it tends to atrophy, like the muscles of your body. If you
step out by faith and use it, it becomes stronger. God leads us from
"faith unto faith," from little steps of faith to larger. Teach a small
group and God will give you an opportunity to teach a larger
group. So it is with all our gifts; they need to be used or exercised
regularly.

Temperament and the priority of spiritual gifts

Temperament is one of the factors that makes us unique from
other human beings. Not only are there four basic temperaments and twelve blends of temperament, but there are differing
degrees of these temperaments (a 70 percent sanguine, 30 percent
phlegmatic might well be somewhat different than a 55 percent
sanguine and a 45 percent phlegmatic). In addition, you must
consider the differences of the sexes, IQ, education, and background.

As you can see, many things go together to make up the total
you. For that reason, it is impossible to predict what priority scale
every temperament combination will have. However, for vocational
purposes and to help Christians find the place in their local church
for which they are best equipped to serve their Lord, I have in "The
LaHaye Temperament Test" prioritized the spiritual gifts according
to the blends of at least two temperaments—one primary, the other
secondary. I arbitrarily established a 60 percent to 40 percent split.
That seems to be a common balance. The following are the priorities I have worked out.

SanChlor
Mercy
Evangelism
Pastoring
Teaching
Exhorting
Prophesying
Giving
Helps
Faith
Knowledge
Discernment
Wisdom
Government

SanMel
Mercy
Evangelism
Prophesying
Teaching
Exhorting
Pastoring
Giving
Wisdom
Knowledge
Discernment
Helps
Government
Faith

SanPhleg
Mercy
Evangelism
Pastoring
Teaching
Prophesying
Exhorting
Wisdom
Giving
Knowledge
Helps
Discernment
Government
Faith

ChlorSan
Teaching
Exhorting
Government
Prophesying
Knowledge
Discernment
Evangelism
Faith
Giving
Pastoring
Wisdom
Helps
Mercy

ChlorMel
Teaching
Exhorting
Prophesying
Government
Knowledge
Wisdom
Discernment
Evangelism
Giving
Pastoring
Faith
Mercy
Helps

ChlorPhleg
Teaching
Exhorting
Government
Prophesying
Knowledge
Wisdom
Discernment
Giving
Pastoring
Evangelism
Faith
Helps
Mercy

MelSan
Prophesying
Exhorting
Wisdom
Evangelism
Pastoring
Mercy
Teaching
Knowledge
Government
Giving
Helps
Discernment
Faith

MelChlor
Prophesying
Exhorting
Teaching
Wisdom
Government
Pastoring
Mercy
Knowledge
Discernment
Evangelism
Giving
Faith
Helps

MelPhleg
Wisdom
Prophesying
Teaching
Exhorting
Mercy
Pastoring
Knowledge
Government
Helps
Evangelism
Giving
Discernment
Faith

PHLEGSAN	**PHLEGCHLOR**	**PHLEGMEL**
Mercy	Pastoring	Pastoring
Pastoring	Mercy	Mercy
Teaching	Government	Wisdom
Helps	Wisdom	Helps
Wisdom	Helps	Prophesying
Evangelism	Teaching	Exhorting
Prophesying	Exhorting	Teaching
Exhorting	Evangelism	Government
Knowledge	Prophesying	Evangelism
Government	Discernment	Knowledge
Discernment	Knowledge	Discernment
Giving	Faith	Giving
Faith	Giving	Faith

These lists are not as complicated as they may seem, in that you only need to study one of the twelve—yours. Once you have diagnosed your temperament combination, you will just need to study that list that pertains to you to discover the priority list of your spiritual gifts. One indication would be to refer to the results of chapter 5, "Give Yourself a Temperament Test." However if you wish a more thorough analysis of your primary and secondary temperament and the appropriate list of twenty-four or more places you can serve your Lord in your own church and the fifty secondary vocations for which you are the most suited, you will want to order "The LaHaye Temperament Analysis."

Using your spiritual gifts

The above priority list indicates intensity of gifts in your life, the first gift being your most intense or the one that is your priority gift. Keep in mind, you have all of the thirteen gifts, but not in the same intensity. You will probably find that you feel more comfortable doing the first four gifts, reasonably comfortable doing the next five, but the last three or four may be difficult for you. Don't give up on these as the Lord directs your life. But I have found that we get our greatest satisfaction out of life in seeing our Lord in the top three to five priority gifts. This accords with the popular teaching today that the thing you do that gives you greatest pleasure in life is probably the exercise of your most significant spiritual gift.

It is my prayer that this chapter has helped you locate your primary spiritual gifts. Now dedicate them to God (Rom. 12:1-2; 6:11-13; 1 Cor. 6:19-20). By faith anticipate that he will use your life to glorify him. You may wonder why I repeatedly have said in this chapter to glorify the Lord Jesus Christ. It is because that is the test of the work of the Holy Spirit. Our Lord said of the Holy Spirit, "He will bring glory to me" (John 16:14, NIV). If you and I fulfill the will of God for our lives, it will be to glorify Jesus. And that is why he gave us his Holy Spirit, who will make your gifts holy and use them to glorify the Son of God.

16

TEMPERAMENT AND YOUR RELATIONSHIP WITH GOD

Any Christian, regardless of his temperament, can become a spiritual person. However, his temperament will influence both his spirituality and its expression. One thing we have learned so far in our study of human temperament is that we are not all cut out of the same mold. We are unique individuals. I have been studying temperament and people for many years and so far have never met two people with the same combination of temperaments. When people come to Christ, he meets them where they are and has the same plan for all to be conformed to his image (Rom. 8:29). That is true spirituality.

What is spirituality?

Before we can examine the influence of temperament on a Christian's spiritual life, we must first determine what spirituality is. It certainly is not an emotional feeling that transports us into a mystical relationship with God. It is a state of being that takes time for the Holy Spirit to develop in any temperament. You can be saved in an instant and raptured in a "twinkling of an eye," but it takes a long time to become a spiritual person.

I combine maturity and spirituality. A baby Christian may be spiritual momentarily, but only a mature Christian will be spiritual in the sense of true spirituality. Paul must have had that in mind when he told the Corinthians, "And I, brethren, could not speak to you as to spiritual people but as to carnal, as to babes in Christ" (1

Cor. 3:1, NKJV). These Corinthian Christians were babies because they were still carnal. They had not matured or grown up spiritually. They were saved, but they were factious, critical, contentious, and had other problems not associated with a truly spiritual person. Paul had spent a great deal of time in Corinth with these people, but they had not abandoned the influence of the Greek world around them. Consequently they were baby Christians—even long after they should have been mature.

We should be careful not to confuse true spirituality and seniority. As a pastor for over thirty years, I know all too well the problem the local church gets itself into when it elects people to its boards and committees on the basis of seniority rather than spiritual maturity. Just because a person is an active tithing man of a congregation does not make him qualified for service on the deacon board—or to be the pastor of the church. Seniority may qualify you for retirement, but it does not make you a spiritually mature person.

By contrast, you don't have to wait a decade to be a spiritually mature person. Most of the early Christian leaders were active leaders before they had been saved more than five to ten years. We see the same thing today. We have four- or five-year Christians who are far more spiritually mature than some who have spent fifty years as active church members.

A spiritually mature Christian is one who is controlled by the Holy Spirit (Eph. 5:18) and manifests the nine fruits of the Spirit (Gal. 5:22-23), who walks in holiness, who knows the Word of God and diligently seeks to do his will because he loves him (John 14:21). While that does take time, it does not take a lifetime. The Apostle Paul spent three years in Arabia after his conversion before Barnabas brought him up to Antioch to begin serving as an elder. By this time he was spiritually mature enough to take a position as a teacher of the Word. Several years later he became a leader in his own right. But this was a gradual process.

Although it is impossible to say when a person becomes spiritually mature, I think we can gain insight from 1 John 2:12-14 where we find three stages of growth compared to the spiritual life: "little children," "young men," and "fathers."

A spiritual child is one who is newly born again. While salvation is a free gift, spiritual growth is the result of growing in grace and the knowledge of our Lord through study of his Word and faith.

A newborn "babe," as Peter calls him, or a "little child" as John labels him, is not going to be a victorious Christian most of the time. He may experience an up-and-down life spiritually for a time until his commitment to the Word makes him an overcomer. At that point, he is a "young man" in Christ; that is, he overcomes the "wicked one" by "the word of God [which] abideth in you" more often than he is overcome. Note the gradual growth process. Finally, as this person continues studying the Word, walking in the Spirit and in obedience to the Word, he believes such a faith is based on knowing God and becomes a father of the faith. One thing about fathers—they spiritually reproduce themselves in other people. That will be the result of being conformed to our Lord's image. As he served the Father by seeking that which was lost, so will we, both directly and indirectly.

In this day of instant everything, we need to understand that there are no shortcuts to maturity—physical or spiritual. There is, however, one major difference between physical maturity and spiritual maturity—*you*. In the physical it is almost automatic. If you eat three meals a day and get a reasonable amount of exercise and rest, you will gradually mature into adulthood. Spiritually, it depends on *you*. God is for you, the Holy Spirit is available to you, and you have the Word to study (probably in five different translations). How fast you grow depends on how long it takes you to learn the principles, wisdom, and knowledge of God found in his Word and to incorporate this into your daily life.

Of one thing I am certain—there is no such thing as spiritual maturity without Bible study. It may come through hearing in church, TV, cassettes, Bible school, or through reading and studying the Word for yourself. But just as you can't grow physically without food, you can't grow spiritually without the spiritual food of the Word of God. That may be why the Bible refers to itself as milk, bread, and meat.

Personal Bible study and your temperament

The success of your spiritual life is dependent on the effectiveness of your personal Bible study, not your temperament. However your temperament will influence your Bible study habits just as surely as it influences your physical eating habits.

Sanguines are spontaneous, undisciplined people who really have to work at being consistent about anything. That certainly includes their personal study of the Word. They are as quick to see its importance as any temperament, but their problem is doing on a regular basis what they know to be valuable. They are so susceptible to external stimulation and so interested in everything that it is easy for them to get chased off in other pursuits. And of all people, television can be the slavemaster of the sanguine at the expense of his spiritual life. Mr. and Mrs. Sanguine of all the temperaments need to make the rule that can transform their spiritual life—"no Bible, no breakfast." That is, they should say, If I don't have time to read the Word on a given day, I won't take time to eat breakfast. If they keep that commitment, they will soon develop a consistent devotional life.

Cholerics are self-disciplined people as a rule, but their problem is that they seldom see the need for personal Bible study. Their attitude usually is, "I go to church to hear the Word, but the Bible is an old book and I have so many important things to think about that it isn't that vital for me." This may be why so many cholerics are shallow spiritually and why they do not experience spiritual growth. They can see how important it is to others, but think it's not necessary for them. And even when they do see the need to be consistent daily in the Word, they may find truths that apply to others and not to themselves. However, once convinced that without God their life is rather futile, they can learn to develop effective spiritual habits.

Of all the temperaments, the melancholy is most apt to be consistent in his daily Bible study, reading, and memorization. He is usually interested in anything that is good for him and once convinced, he will work tirelessly. However, he may get so technically involved, he does little to apply the Word to his own life. Or he may castigate himself for falling so far beneath what the Bible holds out as the word of encouragement and blessing. One thing I suggest to all temperaments is that they keep a spiritual diary of what God says to them on a daily basis. It is really a simple but practical way to be edified by the Word. In fact, I have developed a daily spiritual diary-chart that is extremely helpful in keeping such a record and in helping a person get maximum benefit from his study of the Word.

Phlegmatics, the nicest of the temperaments, have a problem with consistency. They procrastinate over everything, including their Bible study. It isn't that they don't believe it's important, but by the time they read the newspaper and talk to their friends on the phone or putter around, it is time to go to work or school or whatever. Naturally, they feel convicted when they go to church and make a vow to be different, but seldom do their Bible study habits change. They would never think of going to church without taking their Bible, but seldom use it between Sundays.

Phlegmatics need to realize that they should get involved with serving God, and that they won't have spiritual depth unless they discipline themselves and develop a regular devotional life. One thing I have noted—regular Bible study never just happens. Those whom I have found who are consistent in having a daily study in the Word set a specific time and usually a specific place and follow a specific formula. This may seem somewhat regimented to a phlegmatic, but he will never be consistent for God or develop a devotional life unless he does. And never will any other temperament.

Prayer life and your temperament

Prayer is as essential to a Christian's spiritual life as breathing is to his physical life. All Christians pray. How they pray, however, is almost as varied as people. There are essentially two things that have a pronounced influence on your personal prayer life: (1) your instruction, and (2) your temperament.

The Bible is filled with teachings, commands, and actions on prayer—from "pray without ceasing" to ". . . let your requests be made known to God." There are hundreds of promises regarding prayer. It seems to be God's means of blessing his children and supplying their needs. If you haven't done a Bible study on prayer you should, and you will find a wealth of material to work with.

But it isn't just formal instruction in the Word that gives you your instructions on prayer. Your pastor-teacher or the individual God sends you to instruct you in his ways will have a profound influence on your prayer life. For instance, prayer patterns will become a model for your own. When you observe the prayer life of a Christian you admire, you are often prone to consider his prayer life to be the secret to his spiritual life. And that is generally speaking not true. His prayer life is the result of his instruction, role model, spiritual life, and his temperament.

Remember, temperament influences everything you do. You should have that fact fully implanted in your mind by this point in our study. It isn't the only factor, but it is probably the most important. And certainly you will find that in the case of your prayer life temperament plays an important role.

Sanguines are quick, unpredictable, and spontaneous about everything—why not their prayer life? Sparky is the type who wakes up with the birds in a happy mood, so he probably praises the Lord in the morning. He may even do it during his morning shower. He usually isn't too much on prayer lists or records, but his favorite verse on prayer is, "Pray without ceasing." To him, that means he doesn't have to set aside a specific time for prayer, he just talks to God (and people) whenever he feels like it and about anything he thinks about. One sanguine told me, "I feel guilty when I promise to pray for someone and forget. So now I pray instantly in my heart as soon as they request a place in my prayers, 'Lord, bless this person!'" That's probably better than nothing, but not much. Sanguines, unless they are unusually challenged by God or some friend who has a great deal of influence on them, usually have a rather shallow prayer life. They are not much for solitude and contemplation; consequently, they would rather spend time with people than long periods of time with God.

Cholerics are activists personified. Like Martha, they would rather spend time serving their Lord than talking with him. Their spirit of self-sufficiency has a tendency to limit what they discuss with God. If they can figure out what to do in a given situation, they would rather do it than talk to their heavenly Father about it. They save "the big ticket" items—that is, the projects or subjects they can't figure out—as the ones to pray over.

Once a Christian learns by the school of hard knocks (and that is usually what it takes) that he must commit "all his ways" to the Lord, he develops the habit of praying while doing something else. Driving, jogging, yard work—anything that does not require concentration becomes an opportunity for him to pray. Paul must have prayed that way; as he walked from city to city en route to serve God he would "pray without ceasing." One of the enemies of a choleric's prayer life is his overactive mind. He no sooner begins his prayer time and he thinks of something that needs to be done. The best way I have found to solve that problem is to keep a notepad by your chair or place of prayer and write down every idea that comes to mind while praying so you can get right back to prayer. It is the best way to maintain your prayer concentration.

Mr. or Ms. Melancholy, however, usually have the most extensive prayer life. They seem to have a capacity for God and communion with him that is unequalled by any of the other temperaments. I find it instructive that all the prophets were melancholy to one degree or another. They are famous for their ability to commune with God. The melancholy with a high degree of choleric temperament will resort more to a life of prayer than any other. He enjoys solitude and serious contemplation. He is easily regimented to schedule and style. He will often make a prayer list and pray consistently. As a pastor for years, I found the saints with the most effective prayer ministry were usually melancholy. Not always— God can give any of us a burden to be a prayer warrior, but it seems melancholies have more consistent prayer habits.

One area Mr. Melancholy has to work on, however, is to avoid letting his moody disposition or his spirit of criticism lead to griping or complaining to God. This can ruin his prayer life. For him most of all, the advice of Paul is appropriate, "in every thing give thanks, for this is the will of God in Christ Jesus. . . ." Once Mr. Melancholy develops the habit of praying with thanksgiving, which is a lesson we all need to learn, he can develop a very effective prayer life.

The phlegmatic Christian can also become a man (or woman) of prayer *if* he will guard against drowsiness. He can enjoy worship and does love God, but any time he strikes a sedentary position, his enemy is sleep. For that reason I suggest the phlegmatic Christian learn to pray pacing the floor or in a standing position. He does well with a prayer list and is often moved with compassion for the needs of others.

One of the things that helps the phlegmatic Christian is that he likes routine. It is hard for him to work prayer in on a regular basis into his life, but once he does so and develops a routine, it is equally as hard to forget it. Of all the temperaments, he is as likely as any to become effective as a man of prayer.

Temperament and living by faith

Many years ago I came to an interesting observation in my Christian life, and today I have seen nothing that would cause me to change my mind. Very simply, it is this: faith is more important than intelligence or talent.

I came to this conclusion in answering the question, "Why does God seem to use some people more than others?" I think that it is a very legitimate question, as is the second that bears on it—"Why does God use some very ordinary people more than some of the more talented and intelligent?" Now that does not mean God does not use gifted people. The Apostle Paul was obviously a brilliant man with the best education available in his day, and God used him mightily. Yet he also used Peter, James, and John, who were ordinary and "unlearned men." I have seen the same thing in churches I have served. I have seen God use brilliant scholars and people with very average talent and low IQ. I have seen him seem to bypass some brilliant Christians as well as ordinary saints.

Then I discovered the common denominator. God is no respector of persons—he uses anyone, from Balaam's ass to the wisest man who ever lived or who ever will live. What is that common denomination? *Faith.* God himself said, "Without faith it is impossible to please God." The one thing that raises one Christian above another is not looks, brains, talent, or even opportunity; it is faith. Second Chronicles 16:9 tells us that "the eyes of the Lord run to and fro throughout the whole earth, to shew himself strong in the behalf of those whose heart is perfect toward him." In this context, the "perfect" that God has in mind is faith. God's eyes are continually running up and down the earth looking for men and women of faith. The New Testament tells us that the one thing God requires in stewards is *faithfulness.*

We have already seen that faith comes through the Word of God. It also comes through the Holy Spirit, for it is one of the nine fruits or results of the Spirit according to Galatians 5:22. But there is another way the gift of faith comes into our lives—from one step of faith to another step of faith (Rom. 1:17). That is, as we take one step of faith, it stretches our faith for the next step. People who never trust God for the first step of faith will never become strong in faith and God will not use them very much—regardless of how much natural ability they might have. Romans 14:23 says, "Whatsoever is not of faith is sin." Many Christians limit God's use of their lives by the sin of unbelief. Sometimes that follows the pattern of their temperament.

Sanguines are the quickest to step out by faith if they are spiritually motivated. But then they are quicker on the trigger in everything. Venturesome by nature, it is not hard for them, particularly in their youth, to launch new ventures or projects impetuously. And surprisingly enough, God meets their need and somehow blesses what seems to others a very impetuous move, if their heart is right. Not given to complex thinking, it is usually easy for them to take God at his Word and step out by faith.

When it comes to personal soul-winning, the sanguine has the easiest time. He likes people, is rarely intimidated by them, and if spiritually motivated will share his faith readily. Success in soul-winning encourages his faith, and he finds it easier to do it the next time, until someone asks a theological question he has not thought of. It is perhaps easier for sanguines to take God at his Word and act upon it than any other, at least on the short run. Consistency is not one of his gifts, however.

A choleric can also be a man or woman of faith. However, he is such a visionary, project-oriented person with a strong sense of self-confidence that it is sometimes difficult to tell whether his faith is in God or himself. If he comes to real faith in the living God and that he is indeed operative in our present day, it is not difficult for him to take God at his Word and claim the promises of God for himself. He is not usually troubled by theoretical doubts or self-condemnation. Consequently, he is willing to venture out on a new project and expect God to supply. Once he proves God by successfully achieving step one, he is ready for a second step of faith. And his steps tend to get bigger. There is no seeming limit to his vision if he continues in the Word and walks with God. Many of the Christian organizations, mission societies, and Christian education institutions were founded by cholerics or choleric sanguines who, like Paul, "believed God."

Melancholy saints can go either way when it comes to faith. They either limit God by unbelief and do nothing, or attempt great things for God and do them. It all depends on their mood at the time, and that is usually influenced by their spiritual life. Unfortunately for them, they have a difficult time taking God at his Word, for two reasons. One, they are naturally endowed with analytical skills and theoretical questions that if pressed too far always lead to doubt. And two, they often destroy their potential for faith by self-condemnation. Mr. Melancholy usually feels unworthy of the blessings of God—even though he may live a more godly personal life than the sanguine or choleric who ventures out in faith. The melancholy tends to feel unworthy and asks, "Why me?" The sanguine and choleric tend to say, "Why not me?"

The melancholy person with his uncanny ability to analyze things can foresee more negative problems (real or imagined) in any project than any of the other three temperaments; this does nothing for faith. He needs to keep his eyes on the Lord's sufficiency, not the anticipated problems. He is the one kind of builder who will not only plan on the high side of every anticipated cost, but will program in a 10 to 15 percent contingency factor to cover the unexpected. By that time, the cost estimate is so high he does not have the resources or faith to proceed.

One asset a melancholy does have is his vivid imagination. That can help him in two ways if he concentrates. First, he can visualize the stories of the men of faith in the Bible, and this can electrify his own faith. And second, if he forces himself to keep his eye on the goal he can see it more vividly than others, and this always results in a forward movement. He also has a good memory, so once he has taken a step of faith he can remember God's faithfulness, which encourages him to take another step of faith.

Living by faith is possible, of course, for the phlegmatic, but it isn't easy. You don't read where Matthew, Bartholomew, Andrew, or James made a mad rush to get out of the boat and walk on water. Who was it? Sanguine Simon Peter, of course. We have seen that fear, worry, and anxiety are a way of life to many phlegmatics. Obviously, these negative emotions do nothing for faith, but rather kill or intimidate it.

One of the things that contributes to the phlegmatic's doubts and unbelief is his passive way in the Word or his procrastination. If he would force himself to study his Bible, the Word would build faith in him; but although he believes in the necessity of a daily quiet time, it is not usually his habit. Consequently, when the door of opportunity opens to him, he lacks the faith to step inside. I have

known phlegmatic Christians to attend church faithfully for twenty
years and never do anything in the way of church service. It wasn't
that they didn't love God or that they did not live a godly life. Their
problem was lack of faith. They could always think of enough
"respectable" excuses to talk themselves out of the opportunity to
walk by faith. Lacking the illustration of God's faithfulness at that
first step of faith, it is likely phlegmatics will not take the second.
They are capable, intelligent people who limit themselves by unbelief unless they walk in the Spirit and begin trusting God. Once they
embark on the life of faith, they experience a whole new dimension
to life that becomes contagious. Even for them a step of faith leads
to another. Like the melancholy, they must develop the habit of
looking at God and his resources, not at circumstance or their
anticipation of consequences.

The Apostle Peter is often ridiculed by preachers and Bible
teachers for sinking as he walked on the water to Jesus. The truth is,
of all the disciples he was the only one with sufficient faith to walk
on water. To this day that feat has only been accomplished by our
Lord and Peter. What made the difference—bigger feet? More
intelligence? Of course not—faith made the difference. At a moment in time Peter had more faith than the other disciples, and he
walked on water.

Are there opportunities you have passed up due to lack of faith?
Probably! Most of us have. That's why you should develop your
faith through regular study of the Word and walk in the control of
the Spirit, being obedient to all you know God wants you to do.
Take that step of faith.

Be sure of this. No one takes giant steps of faith who has not
already taken baby steps. God leads us from faith to faith.

Temperament and personal holiness

This is an unholy age in which to live. And unfortunately we do
not hear much about the holiness God requires of Christians. That,
in my opinion, is why so much immorality, carnality, and world-
liness is creeping into our churches today. Be sure of this—no one
will be spiritually mature who does not practice mental holiness,
and today you will have to work at it. The best place to start is to
examine what the Word says on the subject. Consider the following:

Be ye holy; for I am holy. (1 Pet. 1:16)

Pursue peace with all men, and holiness, without which no man will see the Lord. (Heb. 12:14)

Seeing then that all these things shall be dissolved, what manner of persons ought ye to be in holy conversation and godliness . . . ? (2 Pet. 3:11)

Having therefore these promises, dearly beloved, let us cleanse ourselves from all filthiness of the flesh and spirit, perfecting holiness in the fear of God. (2 Cor. 7:1)

Holiness is not easy, but it is essential. And like faith, little steps lead to bigger steps—in either direction. And your temperament is no help! I have found that all temperaments have a problem with holy thinking, particularly men. Our Lord taught men not to look at women in lust. In so doing, he established the male Christian's principle source of temptation. Godly men, regardless of temperament, have learned to look at women without lusting. Jesus did not say a man could not look at women. It is looking and lusting that is sin. A godly man will learn to look on women admiringly, as he can legitimately look on any beautiful object with approval. But it takes mental discipline and spiritual determination to learn to recognize the line between looking and lusting and to refuse to cross it. And if he fails, he must quickly and silently face his sin, confess it, and look at something else.

Sanguines are so receptive and responsive to sight, they must be particularly careful what they see. It is wrong and dangerous for any Christian to watch suggestive movies or TV, and pornography should never have a place in any Christian's thought-life. All temperaments are vulnerable to sensual sins; that's why they are usually addressed first in a catalog of sins in Scripture (for example, Gal. 5:19-21), but sanguines particularly so.

Cholerics think they have an advantage in their thought-life. They see beyond the temptation to the consequences, which often has a cooling effect on them—unless, however, they care to justify immorality somehow, and then they are capable of anything. One experienced choleric Christian I know tried to excuse his infidelity by blaming his beautiful but frigid wife with the remark, "Living with her is like having a delicious dish of candy that you can't touch." A cholerically clever retort, but really undisguised unholiness!

Melancholies are less likely to indulge or justify unholy thoughts than all the temperaments. They are usually as critical of themselves as they are of others, so they tend to quickly label unholy thoughts as sin. In addition, once they taste the joy of unbroken fellowship and communion with God, they are unwilling to lose it to unholy thinking. However, their tendency to indulge self-pity can ruin their relationship to God and make them vulnerable to any kind of unholy thinking.

Phlegmatics seem so nice and clean, but they are human too. If they aren't careful, they too can be swept along the tempting road of impure thoughts. They tend to spend more time fantasizing than any other temperament. If unchecked, those fantasies can become impure, ruining their spiritual life.

The best scriptural challenge I know in this regard is 2 Corinthians 10:5; practice it throughout your entire life:

> Casting down imaginations, and every high thing that exalts itself against the knowledge of God, bringing into captivity every thought to the obedience of Christ.

How you face afflictions

Everyone has afflictions in life—even Spirit-controlled Christians. Our Lord, who was perfect and sinless and on whom "the Spirit rested without measure," was afflicted, grieved, sorrowed. As you know, he even wept! Job, one of the godliest men who ever lived, suffered the premature death of his children, loss of his cattle and goods, and even of his health as a testimony to man and Satan that God is able to supply the needs of the afflicted saint.

You, too, will suffer affliction, if you have not already. Sickness and death are a part of life. Insult, injury, and rejection are common to all men, and Christians are not exempt. And your first reaction will often be the result of your temperament. I say first, because if you are a Bible-taught Christian, you will follow your natural reaction with the kind the Bible requires, and that is extremely helpful.

Sanguines explode whenever anything goes wrong, so that is their first response to affliction. Tears, anger, or laughing are their usual repertoire of tools, and not always at the most opportune time. In fact, I'll make a confession. One of the things *some* sanguines do that most irritates me is laugh at the most inappropriate times and events. It's just a nervous relief valve that helps them live with the pressures by letting some steam escape. Then after a short time they rush off to something else. Have you heard the story of the sanguine golfer on the sixteenth hole who saw a funeral procession drive slowly by? He put his cap over his heart and stood momentarily at attention. When his companion asked, "Was that a friend?" he replied, "Yes. If she had lived five more days, we would have been married twenty-seven years!"

Escape from reality is a temptation for all temperaments. It can be overpowering to sanguines—much to the annoyance of friends and loved ones.

The choleric reaction to affliction can sometimes be as external as the sanguine, but he will invariably respond with, "What can I do about this?"—either expressed or implied. He may be aching inside, but hides his true feelings by activity. He is not too sympathetic, and since most afflictions are shared by other family members he may be a source of irritation and grief to them.

Melancholies are predictable in the face of unexpected adversities. Their response is, "Why me?" or "What have I done to deserve this?" And it is downhill from there, as they indulge the sinful thinking pattern of self-pity to the hilt. Finally depression sets in to complicate their life and get them completely out of fellowship with God. Being creative can be a disadvantage when you permit it to turn negative.

Phlegmatics seem unflappable, and they are almost. But they still hurt inside. Just because they don't scream, holler, or laugh hysterically doesn't mean they aren't concerned or are ignoring the real difficulties they face. It's just not their style to become external. They are prone to go off by themselves and grieve quietly. Their chief weapon is silence.

What is a person to do?

Since all the reactions above are wrong, what is a person to do? Heed the words of Scripture: "Count it all joy when you fall into grievous testings (afflictions)" (James 1:2). Instead of reacting in the flesh (temperament), react in the Spirit by learning to praise the Lord *in* the circumstances. Not *for* them, but *in* them. There is a difference! There are some circumstances in life for which we cannot give thanks or "count it all joy." But there are no circumstances in which we Christians cannot count it all joy or give thanks for God and what he is able to do in the midst of our affliction. The key, regardless of temperament, is the direction of our look. If we look only at the problem, which is normal, we will respond according to our temperament. If, however, we look to God, we will respond according to the scriptural power within us.

One thing to keep in mind in evaluating the effects of a person's temperament on his spiritual life is the fact that all people are a combination of two or more temperaments. Consequently, there will be a blending effect on their response to everything. Remember that the resources of God are more than sufficient for any combination of temperaments. If a Christian becomes unspiritual, he cannot blame it on his temperament combination, but on the fact that he refused to avail himself of God's adequate resources.

Your Achilles' heel

We have already dealt with the weakness of each temperament and how to apply the Spirit-controlled life to each in order to avail ourselves of the resources God has made available to us. However, there is one weakness that seems to follow a sex pattern rather than temperament, and this is probably the best place to discuss it.

Men are different, as we have seen, in regard to their temperament. Consequently, they will have temperament-induced weakness patterns. The same is true for women. But there is one area that men seem more vulnerable to than women and vice versa. I refer to finances and vocation for men, and children and family for women.

Finances and vocation

Nothing seems to test a man's faith more than financial pressures or economic loss or change. God has not only commanded man to be the principle breadwinner and protector of his family; he seems to have wired him psychologically so that anytime he is threatened in those two areas, it is a threat to his spiritual life. Worry, insecurity, anxiety, and frustration may grip him, causing his reactions to compound his problems.

Economical threats can actually strengthen a man if he turns immediately to God for his power and help. God will not leave or forsake us in those hours of adversity, and when we are forced to put him to the test his supply not only solves our problem but strengthens our faith.

Walt was not only a church member, he was a good friend. I had discipled him personally for several months, and he was growing very rapidly when it came time to go on a two-week vacation to Yosemite with his family. When he picked up his paycheck that Friday night, he unexpectedly picked up a pink slip saying his services were no longer required by the company and he was being terminated after twenty-two years of service.

When his wife said, "What are we going to do?" he said, "Go to Yosemite as we planned. We have been faithful in our walk with God; we have double-tithed this year during our Church Building Program. I am confident our faithful God will provide." So Walt and his family went on vacation, had a good time, and returned one day early to a ringing telephone. When he picked it up he heard his supervisor say, "Walt, where have you been? We've been trying to locate you for a week. We want you to report for work on Monday to Plant 2." What do you think that did for Walt's faith? It made a phlegmatic strong in faith, just the way God intended.

Family

Women, however, are not so troubled by money problems, and most don't seem to be as convinced as men about career, etc., depending of course on each family's circumstances. But children, marriage, and family? That's another matter! Women never come closer to sheer panic than when their children are in jeopardy— regardless of their temperament. I talked to a lovely mother of two teen-age girls who had just gone through a fire in her home. The second-story bedrooms were completely gutted, and the blaze almost took the life of one of the girls. The mother was so terrified that her daughter was still asleep in her bed, she fought through the smoke and flames to reach her and almost lost her life. Only the call of a neighbor telling her that the girl had jumped safely out the window made her turn back from certain death. That mother's life was not worth living at that moment if her daughter was lost.

Not only will the fear of fire do that, but any threat to her children. This divorced woman has all kinds of financial pressures, but first on her list is the well-being of her children. That's not unusual; it is part of the maternal instinct and true femininity. Such emergencies, however, are sometimes easier to bear than the long drawn-out threats a woman faces every day. Particularly is this true of single parents. Their understandable response of fear can strip them of their spiritual vitality. Or it can cause them to depend even more on their heavenly Father.

I am often accused of having a lot of faith. I attribute much of that to my widowed mother who turned her insecurities and problems over to God and developed an abiding faith in her heavenly Father that we kids found contagious.

Always bear in mind—God's resources are sufficient for any temperament and any sex. Claim them—they are yours for the taking.

The bottom line

Many Christians think they are spiritual but are not. Some don't understand what a spiritual Christian is, and some are just kidding themselves thinking they are spiritual because they go to church regularly, tithe, and are faithful marriage partners. A spiritual person will do all of these things and many more. One thing he will do is walk in the control of the Holy Spirit and thus fulfill the will of God (Eph. 5:17-18; Gal. 5:16-18). But there is more. In fact, this may be the final test of spirituality.

The *New International Version* of the Scripture gives us new insight on this subject by translating an old familiar verse of Scripture just a bit differently. One of the first verses any Christian memorizes is Romans 12:1-2. But the NIV translates the first verse more accurately by changing "your reasonable service" to "spiritual worship."

King James Version	*New International Version*
I beseech you therefore, brethren, by the mercies of God, that ye present your bodies a living sacrifice, holy, acceptable unto God, which is your reasonable service.	Therefore, I urge you, brothers, in view of God's mercy, to offer your bodies as living sacrifices, holy and pleasing to God—which is your spiritual worship. Do not conform any longer to the pattern of this world, but be transformed by the renewing of your mind. Then you will be able to test and approve what God's will is—his good, pleasing and perfect will.
And be not conformed to this world: but be ye transformed by the renewing of your mind, that ye may prove what is that good, and acceptable, and perfect will of God.	

The bottom line to spirituality will be, who uses your body? That's what this life is all about. Who uses your body—God or Satan? A truly spiritual person so dedicates his life to God for whatever use the Heavenly Father wishes to make of it that he will do whatever it takes to be a "living sacrifice" or living vessel of service. He will do all the things mentioned above, including living his life under the control of the Holy Spirit, obedient to whatever God tells him to do. He will not grieve or quench the Spirit (Eph. 4:30-32; 1 Thess. 5:19) by indulging his naturally inherited weaknesses, but will so seek the kingdom of God (Matt. 6:33) that his life will be available to do whatever the Lord commands. His mind will be so renewed by the Holy Spirit through the Word of God that he will not conform to the paths of this world. And be sure of this—he or she, Mr. or Ms. Sanguine, Choleric, Melancholy, or Phlegmatic, will *be holy*. *True* spirituality, regardless of the temperament package with which it is housed, will *always* come *clothed* in holiness. And though more difficult for some temperaments, it is possible for all.

How to get your personalized
LaHaye Temperament Analysis

The LaHaye Temperament Analysis is the result of over fifteen years' research and is the most unique test of its kind available today. Each analysis is personally prepared and presented in a thirteen- to seventeen-page letter from the author (depending on your temperament combination and other pastoral information). It will provide you with the following information in a keepsake leatherette binder which will be of interest to you for years to come.

1. Your primary and secondary temperaments: The 92 percent accuracy level is extremely high. The standard IQ test is only considered 80 percent accurate.
2. Your vocational aptitudes, including at least fifty different vocations you could do comfortably.
3. An analysis of your three major vocational weaknesses with appropriate suggestions.
4. Your thirteen spiritual gifts in order of their priority, with an explanation for each.
5. The thirty vocations in your local church to which you are best suited.

6. Your ten major weaknesses, with appropriate suggestions on bringing them into control.
7. Positive personal suggestions on how to overcome your weaknesses.
8. If you're married, some suggestions on how to treat your mate.
9. If single, how to best face life as a single with your temperament combination.
10. If you are a parent, some suggestions on parenting for your type of temperament.

Obviously this test is not for those only casually interested in being the maximum person God wants them to be. If, however, you are really interested in personal self-improvement, you will find this test to be one of the most helpful things you have ever done.

Currently it is not available in bookstores, but can be purchased from Family Life Seminars.